The Heresy of a Curious Mind
Exposing Religion to Reveal God

Joseph Lumpkin

Joseph Lumpkin

The Heresy of a Curious Mind
Exposing Religion to Reveal God

Joseph Lumpkin

Fifth Estate Publishers,
Blountsville, AL 35031.

First Printing, 2013

Cover Design by An Quigley

Printed on acid-free paper

Library of Congress Control No: 2001012345

ISBN: 9781936533381

Fifth Estate, 2013

Table of Contents

This book is dedicated to my children and grandchildren, and all those who have the courage to think independently and deeply.

Special thanks goes out to my editors, Karhma Novak and Suzy Lowry Geno, who laughed at my jokes and cried at my grammar.

Author's Preface

You may read this book and come away with the idea that I do not believe in God. You would be mistaken. I simply do not believe in the church or those who run it.

Before starting research in preparation for the writing of this book, I was happy and comfortable in my theological cave. Like most Christians, I accepted what was being preached and taught without question. After all, questions would take effort to answer and would disturb the status quo. Even in the years of attending a small Baptist college, doctrine was discussed, but never challenged. It was defended and explained in order to make us conformed, not to the will of God, but to the stance of the church. One does not go to seminary to be educated, but to be indoctrinated.

After a few weeks of research in the labyrinths of historical and scientific resources, examination of doctrines and history became more and more painful. It was difficult to set aside my preconceived ideas, since I was very heavily invested in the church's teaching, which I had accepted. Years of study and more than one degree would be nullified if my cherished beliefs were wrong. The fellowship of those good souls in the denomination to which I belonged would be strained under the weight of my heresy. But it was too late to stop the accumulating insight.

Slowly, information mounted and I was forced to ask myself "Was I really that gullible? How could I believe without asking the deeper questions?" Now, the reader may have to ask the same question and decide; "Am I really that blind, or gullible?" Or, maybe the reader will decide it is the author who is the fool. In either case, it is my hope the information presented will induce thoughtfulness and higher blood pressure.

For continuing hypertension, don't miss the vast amount of information contained in the appendices. The data may be of interest. I know it made me shake my head in wonderment.

Introduction and Theology

Doctrine is like glass. The truth can be seen through it, but through it the truth cannot be touched.

Theology – noun (pl. -gies)
(1) - The study of the nature of God.
(2) - The study of religious beliefs and theory when systematically developed.
Greek, from theos 'god' + -logia (see -logy – denoting a subject of study.)

Theology, in the first definition, may be the most arrogant pursuit of mankind. It is the pinnacle of presumption to think that man could study, understand, or explain God. The study of theologians and their doctrine is far easier to apprehend. The effect of theologians and kings on our present day doctrines and religious practices cannot be denied. Some can barely be tolerated. Thus, in this book we will focus primarily on the second definition and leave the first to each individual and their personal encounter with God.

To get to the reason and history behind the formation of certain doctrine we must attempt to view Christianity outside the restricted context of church tradition and Bible alone. Historical documents will be used to confirm and supplement the writings and thoughts of the early church fathers.

The extreme to which the church has gone in order to protect and justify its various decisions regarding points of faith is fascinating, but tends to obscure the truth. Revisionist history, coercion, and propaganda were the order of the day when the major items of doctrine were being decided. In fact, many of those truths that we hold so dear in our Christian faith were decided, if not invented, through or because of political means, and not by theological insight. Many doctrines went well beyond what the early church held as truth. To look behind the curtain of church history, information should be viewed with a political as well as scientific bias, and compared to other historical documents of the time.

The reader is invited to consider the history and virtue of the doctrines of his church based on this new insight and to make a more educated personal stand.

Most Christians have not taken time to fully examine their own personal beliefs. They have not fully researched the doctrines of their own church. Many people accept what they have been told, indoctrinated in, or raised to believe. The deeper structure of their faith has never been critiqued or challenged.

Although after confronting these issues the reader may end the journey believing exactly as he or she began. If a single question causes discomfort or reexamination, this work will have served its purpose, which is to escape tradition and examine the Christian faith afresh, with newer and wider eyes.

1 Corinthians 2 (New King James Version)
 1 And I, brethren, when I came to you, did not come with excellence of speech or of wisdom declaring to you the testimony of God. 2 For I determined not to know anything among you except Jesus Christ and Him crucified.

Framework Of Christianity

As we look at various major systematic theologies, we are likely to see contradictions. There are contradictions between systems, and even more disturbing, there are contradictions within systems. It is not pleasant, and can even be painful, to come face to face with major errors in logic and practice within our own system of beliefs. We are trained to trust what we are told. We are trained to accept ambiguity. We are programmed to file conflicting statements under the heading of "mystery." But mystery, mistake, and misdirection are difficult to separate at times.

Believing that one system is superior to another is like children attempting to jump to the moon. Coming an inch or two closer makes little difference. However, holding on to one way or another, believing that it is the only way, makes for comfortable feelings of superiority and separation from others of differing views. With enough people practicing the same arrogance, a denomination is born and exclusivity begins. Others assure those within the group of their "rightness" and the delusion deepens. Those on the outside see clearly the idolatry of it all. It is the ability to raise doctrine or bible verse to the status of idol that births denominations.

Spiritually immature religious systems pile law upon law and rule upon rule to the point of exaggerated exclusivity, conformity, and control. This is spiritual arrogance, which leads to control. At times the immaturity is a function of age and development of the religion. Age usually brings grace, compassion, and mercy to individuals as well as to religions.

It may be an over-simplification, but let us take two major religions as an example and calculate one hundred years in the lifetime of religions as a single year in the life of a person.

The Christian year, 2009 is the Islamic year, 1430. That would make the first person 20 years old and the other person 14 years of age.

Christianity is a young adult, in this scheme, whereas Islam is pubescent. Christianity is only beginning to escape its rebellious, hostile, and selfish behavior. Islam has not. The Christian crusades only ended in the thirteenth century. That is close to the same age as Islam is now. Christians went on to conquer and kill countless people in the name of God for hundreds of years. Islam continues its warlike and egocentric behavior, even now. The main difference is that when Christians were at the height of blood lust there were swords and spears. The killing season of Islam gives them access to nuclear and biological weapons. Add to that the pathological exclusivity of young religions such as Islam and you have jihad here, jihad there, and everywhere a jihad.

What is more difficult to recognize is that personal systems are the same. In Christianity, those denominations that are prone to legalism, exclusivity, or regulation are those where members pay more attention to doctrine than communion with God and their fellow man. They are divisive and exclusive and at times hateful and aggressive.

Jesus never questioned anyone about his or her theology or doctrine. He wanted to know if the person was in a relationship with him.

He never told anyone they would be rich or successful. He knew that suffering was the only tool to break our illusion of control and superiority and bring us closer to God.

In short, as we look into the history, doctrines, and views of various denominations, let us keep in mind that many times we seem very sure about things we could not possibly know or prove to be true.

Fundamentalism in any religion brings division, intolerance, and hate. The opposite state of religion is spirituality. Spiritual maturity may be measured, not in exclusivity, or in the rules we keep, or how certain we are in our doctrines, but in our inclusive, loving treatment of others and the openness of our hearts toward God.

The Bible

In the ancient religious world, Judaism stood apart in several ways. In the pantheon of gods and the vast number of religions, Judaism had a book on which its followers relied as a record of both history and a codified system of rules. It did not matter that most Jews could not read, what mattered was that there was a touchstone and compass to rely on, and there were those in synagogues who could read the holy words to the worshipers. Later Jews would institute an educational regime that demanded young men be able to read and recite the Torah as a rite of passage to adulthood.

Following in the footsteps of the Jews, the early Christians would also become "people of the book." Modern day Christianity has come to rely so much on the Bible that entire denominations rise and fall based solely on unique interpretations of one or two verses. But is this reliance on the Bible out of perspective or out of balance? There will be many such questions and investigations pursued in this book, but because Christianity has taken its cue from Judaism and its focus on a book, we will begin our quest by challenging what we have been taught regarding the Holy Bible.

The preliminary, if not the primary questions to be addressed before we can continue, are those which will affect all other biblical investigations from this point forward. The framing of these questions is more difficult than may appear.

The first question is slightly easier than the next, but is bound to elicit an emotional, if not visceral response. The first question to answer is, "Do we really need the Bible?" Is the Bible necessary for our salvation? Is it necessary for one's "walk with Christ?" To put it another way, can we know and commune with God if we have no Bible?

Consider this – For approximately 400 years there was no consensus of what books would make up the volume we call the Bible. Although it is true that the Jewish converts had the Torah to depend on, the pagan converts had nothing, only the words of the apostles describing Jesus, his purpose, his death, and his resurrection. Did the first 400 years of believers go to hell for not following every detail of the not-yet-available book?

For over a thousand years after the Bible canon was established only the rich, powerful, and clergy had access to a Bible. The clergy revealed only a small amount of information to the illiterate working class under their control. It was within this time that church doctrine was instituted bring the masses under further control by convincing them that the church and its priests stood between them and heaven, or hell. Many of the church's doctrines made the masses spiritual slaves to the clergy as they began to lord over them the rite of baptism to remove original sin or the rite of communion for salvation.

Rates of infant mortality ran very high. Some sources place death rates for mother or child in childbirth at one in four. The instituted belief in original sin placed the newborn child in a position dangling over the pit unless the child was baptized as soon as possible, based on the belief that baptism removes Original Sin. To save the adult from hell, only the priest had the power to transubstantiate the host into the body of Christ to forgive those pesky personal sins and save the souls of the common man.

The clergy held the power and the Bible, yet, through it all, the common folk held fast to the simple story of Jesus, the Christ, the anointed one of God, and how he was born of a virgin, taught love and forgiveness, died for the sins of the world, and was resurrected by the spirit of God.

Do we need the Bible to be saved? I hope not. There were over 1400 years between the beginning of Christianity and the mass availability of Bibles via the invention of the printing press.

The second question is, "What is the Bible?" The flippant or sophomoric response may come closest to the basic truth. The Bible is a volume containing a collection of books compiled over time by consent of clergy or ruling authority to uphold and re-enforce a set of historical or doctrinal viewpoints. This would mean many available books not upholding a predetermined view would be deemed unfit and were not included. It would also mean as the church split or diverged to a significant degree their beliefs and therefore their Bible would change. As proof of this statement, we can compare the major "arms" of the Christian church and their Bibles.

The King James Bible contained 73 books, including the Apocrypha until 1782, when an American printer first removed the Apocrypha and produced an "unauthorized" version of the King James Bible. Most printers did not clear inventories and change to the sixty-six book version we know today until the late 1800's when editions of the "Official King James Version" began to be printed without the Apocrypha in 1885. Thus, most Bibles printed before 1885 still had the Apocrypha, or at least most of the Apocrypha. As it turns out, various religions have differing versions of the Bible, made up of divergent lists of books. The Protestant church has its sixty-six books, the Catholics have kept the Apocrypha. The Eastern Orthodox Church claims three more books than the Catholics, and the Ethiopic Church has a total of eighty-one books in its Bible.

The etymology of the word "apocrypha" means "things that are hidden," but why they were hidden is not clear. Some have suggested that the books were "hidden" from common use because they contained esoteric knowledge, too profound to be communicated to any except the initiated (compare 2 Esd 14.45-46). Others have suggested that such books were hidden due to their spurious or heretical teaching.

According to traditional usage "Apocrypha" has been the designation applied to the fifteen books, or portions of books, listed below. (In many earlier editions of the Apocrypha, the Letter of Jeremiah is incorporated as the final chapter of the Book of Baruch; hence in these editions there are fourteen books.)

Tobit, Judith, The Additions to the Book of Esther (contained in the Greek version of Esther), The Wisdom of Solomon, Ecclesiasticus, The Wisdom of Jesus son of Sirach, Baruch, The Letter of Jeremiah, The Prayer of Azariah, The Song of the

Three Jews, "Susanna, Bel, and the Dragon," 1 Maccabees, 2 Maccabees, 1 Esdras, The Prayer of Manasseh, and 2 Esdras.

In addition, the present expanded edition includes the following three texts that are of special interest to Eastern Orthodox readers are 3 Maccabees, 4 Maccabees, and Psalm 151.

None of these books is included in the Hebrew canon of Holy Scripture. All of them, however, with the exception of 2 Esdras, are present in copies of the Greek version of the Old Testament known as the Septuagint. The Old Latin translations of the Old Testament, made from the Septuagint, also include them, along with 2 Esdras. The Eastern Orthodox Churches chose to include 1 Esdras, Psalm 151, the Prayer of Manasseh, 3 Maccabees, and 4 Maccabees, which is placed in an appendix as a historical work.

At the end of the fourth century, Pope Damasus commissioned Jerome to prepare a standard Latin version of the Scriptures called the Latin Vulgate. Jerome wrote a note or preface, designating a separate category for the apocryphal books. However, copyists failed to include Jerome's prefaces. Thus, during the medieval period the Western Church generally regarded these books as part of the Holy Scriptures. In 1546, the Council of Trent decreed that the canon of the Old Testament included the Apocrypha with the exception of the Prayer of Manasseh and 1 and 2 Esdras. Later, the church completed the decision by writing in its Roman Catholic Catechism, "Deuterocanonical does not mean Apocryphal, but simply later added to the canon."

The position of the Russian Orthodox Church as regards the Apocrypha appears to have changed during the centuries. The Holy Synod, ruling from St. Petersburg was in sympathy with the position of the Reformers and decided to exclude the Apocrypha and since similar influences were emanating from the universities of Kiev, Moscow, Petersburg, and Kazan, the Russian Church became united in its rejection of the Apocrypha.

A full explanation of how the church of today got from the hundreds of books examined for canon to the eighty-one books of Ethiopia and finally to the mere sixty-six books of the Protestant Bible, is a matter of wide ranging discussion and varied opinions, to be taken up at another time. For now, let us simply acknowledge that the Bible many hold to with such passion and steadfastness is not the same book throughout Christendom. Thus, when one declares with pious passion, "I believe in the Bible!" We must immediately ask, "Which one?"

Below, we can see the differences between the canon of the Protestant, Catholic, and Orthodox bibles, including that of the Ethiopic Orthodox church. We have also listed those books used by the Church of Jesus Christ of Latter day Saints (LDS).

Old Testament
(Protestant)
1. Genesis, Exodus, Leviticus, Numbers, Deuteronomy, Joshua, Judges, Ruth, 1Samuel, 2 Samuel, 1 Kings, 2 Kings, 1 Chronicles, 2 Chronicles, Ezra, Nehemiah, Esther, Job, Psalms, Proverbs, Ecclesiastes, Song of Solomon, Isaiah, Jeremiah, Lamentation, Ezekiel, Daniel, Hosea, Joel, Amos, Obadiah, Jonah, Micah, Nahum, Habakkuk, Zephaniah, Haggai, Zechariah, Malachi.

Old Testament
(Roman Catholic)
2. Genesis, Exodus, Leviticus, Numbers, Deuteronomy, Joshua, Judges, Ruth, 1 Samuel, 2 Samuel, 1 Kings, 2 Kings, 1 Chronicles, 2 Chronicles, Ezra, Nehemiah, Tobit, Judith, Esther (includes additions to Esther), 1 Maccabees, 2 Maccabees, Job, Psalms, Proverbs, Ecclesiastes, Song of, Songs (Song of Solomon), Wisdom of Solomon, Sirach (Ecclesiasticus), Isaiah, Jeremiah, Lamentations, Baruch(includes Letter of Jeremiah), Ezekiel, Daniel (includes Susanna & Bel and the Dragon), Hosea, Joel, Amos, Obadiah, Jonah, Micah, Nahum, Habakkuk, Zephaniah, Haggai, Zechariah, Malachi

Old Testament
(Ethiopic Narrower Canon)
Genesis, Exodus, Leviticus, Numbers, Deuteronomy, Enoch, Jubilees, Joshua, Judges, Ruth, 1 Samuel, 2 Samuel, 1 Kings, 2 Kings, 1 Chronicles, 2 Chronicles, Ezra, Nehemiah, 3rd Ezra, 4th Ezra, Tobit, Judith, Esther (includes additions to Esther), 1 Macabees, 2 Macabees, 3 Macabees, Job, Psalms (+ Psalm 151), Proverbs (Proverbs 1-24), Täagsas (Proverbs 25-31), Wisdom of Solomon, Ecclesiastes, Song of Solomon, Sirach (Ecclesiasticus), Isaiah, Jeremiah, Baruch (includes Letter of Jeremiah), Lamentations, Ezekiel, Daniel, Hosea, Amos, Micah, Joel, Obadiah, Jonah,, Nahum, Habakkuk, Zephaniah, Haggai, Zecariah, Malachi.

Protestants, Roman Catholics, and Greek Orthodox Christians agree on the same 27 books for the composition of the New Testament; however some smaller groups of Christians do not. The Nestorian, or Syrian Church, recognizes only 22 books, excluding 2 Peter, 2 and 3 John, Jude and Revelation.

But wait, there's more. The narrow canon of the Ethiopic church contains 81 books but the broader canon contains several more books. The Ethiopian Orthodox Church includes the same 27 books in its "narrower" canon but adds 8 books to its "broader" canon: "four sections of church order from a compilation called Sinodos, two sections from the Ethiopic Books of Covenant, Ethiopic Clement, and Ethiopic Didascalia." In addition to the Protestant Old and New Testaments, the LDS church uses "The Book of Mormon," "The Doctrine and Covenants," and "The Pearl of Great Price."

Which Bible do you believe in? Why do you think your Bible is the correct one? If you are a member of a typical Protestant church, your Bible is among the smallest of all and its configuration is among the newest. Do you think God had less to say as time went on? Have you ever considered that you may be missing something of significance? With the exception of the Church of Jesus Christ of Latter Day Saints, who have added books to their canon list, in general the Bible seems to be shrinking as one views it from the time line beginning with the list of books considered for canon at Counsel of Nicaea, those held by the Orthodox Church, those held by the Catholic Church, and finally those books left in the Protestant Bible.

What about the books that are mentioned in the Bible, even quoted in the Bible, but not contained in the Bible? Are they worth looking into? There are several books mentioned in the Bible, which are excluded from it. They are not spiritual canon, either because they were not available at the time the canon was originally adopted, or at the time they were not considered "inspired." In cases where inspiration was questioned, one could argue that any book quoted or mentioned by a prophet or an apostle should be considered as spiritual canon, unfortunately this position would prove too simplistic.

Books and writings can fall under various categories such as civil records and laws, historical documents, or spiritual writings. A city or state census is not inspired, but it could add insight into certain areas of life. Spiritual writings which are directly quoted in the Bible serve as insights into the beliefs of the writer or what was considered acceptable by society at the time. As with any new discovery, invention, or belief, the new is interpreted based upon the structure of what came before. This was the way in the first century Christian church as beliefs were based upon the old Jewish understanding. Although, one should realize pagan beliefs were also added to the church as non-Jewish populations were converted, bringing with them the foundations of their beliefs on which they interpreted Christianity. In the case of Jude, James, Paul, and others, the Jewish past was giving way to the Christian present but their understanding and doctrine were still being influenced by what they had learned and experienced previously. It becomes obvious that to understand the Bible one should endeavor to investigate the books and doctrines that most influenced the writers of the Bible.

The LDS Church also asserts that books mentioned but not found in the Bible are of spiritual value. That is not to say that they are on the same level of inspiration, but only that they

17

carry value in understanding the Bible by forming a more full and detailed picture of history, customs, and beliefs.

The Dead Sea Scrolls found in the caves of Qumran are of great interest in the venture of clarifying the history and doctrine in existence between biblical times and the fixing of canon. The scrolls were penned in the second century B.C. and were in use at least until the destruction of the second temple in 70 A.D. Similar scrolls to those found in the eleven caves of Qumran were also found at the Masada stronghold which fell in 73 A.D. Fragments of every book of the Old Testament except Esther were found in the caves of Qumran, but so were many other books. Some of these books are considered to have been of equal importance and influence to the people of Qumran and to the writers and scholars of the time. Some of those studying the scrolls found in Qumran were the writers of the New Testament.

Knowing this, one might ask which of the dozens of non-canonical books most influenced the writers of the New Testament. It is possible to ascertain the existence of certain influences within the Bible by using the Bible itself. The Bible can direct us to other works in three ways. The work can be mentioned by name, as is the Book of Jasher. The work can be quoted within the Bible text, as is the case with the Book of Enoch. The existence of the work can be alluded to, as in the case of the missing letter from the apostle Paul to the Corinthians.

In the case of those books mentioned in the Bible, one can set a list as the titles are named. The list is lengthier than one might first suspect. Most of these works have not been found. Some have been unearthed but their authenticity is questioned. Others have been found and the link between scripture and scroll is generally accepted. Following is a list of books mentioned in the Holy Bible.

The Book of Jasher: There are two references to the book in the Old Testament:

2 Samuel 1:18 - Behold, it is written in the Book of Jasher. "So the sun stood still, and the moon stopped, until the nations avenged themselves of their enemies."

Joshua 10:13 - Is it not written in the Book of Jasher? And the sun stopped in the middle of the sky and did not hasten to go down for about a whole day.

There are several books, which have come to us entitled, "Book of Jasher." One is an ethical treatise from the Middle Ages. It begins with a section on the Mystery of the Creation of the World: It is clearly unrelated to the Biblical Book of Jasher.

Another was published in 1829 supposedly translated by Flaccus Albinus Alcuinus. It opens with the Chapter 1 Verse 1 reading: "While it was the beginning, darkness overspread the face of nature." It is now considered a fake.

The third and most important Book of Jasher, first translated into English in 1840. It opens with Chapter 1 Verse 1 reading: "And God said, Let us make man in our image, after our likeness, and God created man in his own image." A comparison of Joshua 10:13 with Jasher 88:63-64 and 2Sam. 1:18 with Jasher 56:9 makes it clear that this Book of Jasher at least follows closely enough with the Bible to be the Book of Jasher mentioned in the Bible.

Other books mentioned by name in the Bible are:

1. The Book of Wars of the Lord: "Therefore it is said in the Book of the Wars of the Lord." Num. 21:14

2. The Annals of Jehu: "Now the rest of the acts of Jehoshaphat, first to last, behold, they are written in the annals of Jehu the son of Hanani, which is recorded in the Book of the Kings of Israel." 2 Chronicles 20:34

3. The treatise of the Book of the Kings: "As to his sons and the many oracles against him and the rebuilding of the house of God, behold, they are written in the treatise of the Book of the Kings. Then Amaziah his son became king in his place." 2 Chronicles 24:27

4. The Book of Records, Book of the Chronicles of Ahasuerus: "Now when the plot was investigated and found to be so, they

were both hanged on a gallows; and it was written in the Book of the Chronicles in the king's presence." ... "During that night the king could not sleep so he gave an order to bring the book of records, the chronicles, and they were read before the king." Esther 2:23; 6:1

5. The Acts of Solomon: "Now the rest of the acts of Solomon and whatever he did, and his wisdom, are they not written in the book of the Acts of Solomon?" 1 Kings 11:41

6. The Sayings of Hozai: "His prayer also and how God was entreated by him, and all his sin, his unfaithfulness, and the sites on which he built high places and erected the Asherim and the carved images, before he humbled himself, behold, they are written in the records of Hozai." 2 Chronicles 33:19

7. The Chronicles of David: "Joab the son of Zeruiah had begun to count them, but did not finish; and because of this, wrath came upon Israel, and the number was not included in the account of the Chronicles of King David." 1 Chronicles 27:24

8. The Chronicles of Samuel, Nathan, Gad: "Now the acts of King David, from first to last, are written in the Chronicles of Samuel the seer, in the Chronicles of Nathan the prophet and in the Chronicles of Gad the seer." 1 Chronicles 29:29

9. Samuel's book: "Then Samuel told the people the ordinances of the kingdom, and wrote them in the book and placed it before the Lord." 1 Samuel 10:25

10. The Records of Nathan the prophet: "Now the rest of the acts of Solomon, from first to last, are they not written in the Records of Nathan the prophet, and in the prophecy of Ahijah the Shilonite, and in the visions of Iddo the seer concerning Jeroboam the son of Nebat" 2 Chronicles 9:29

11. The Prophecy of Ahijah the Shilonite: "Now the rest of the acts of Solomon, from first to last, are they not written in the Records of Nathan the prophet, and in the prophecy of Ahijah the Shilonite, and in the visions of Iddo the seer concerning Jeroboam the son of Nebat" 2 Chronicles 9:29

12. The Treatise of the Prophet Iddo: "Now the rest of the acts of Abijah, and his ways and his words are written in the treatise of the prophet Iddo." 2 Chronicles 13:22

The existence of a book can be inferred as well, this is clearly seen with several missing epistles. Paul's letter to the church at Laodicea: "When this letter is read among you, have it also read in the church of the Laodiceans; and you, for your part read my letter that is coming from Laodicea." Colossians 4:16 (Since three earlier manuscripts do not contain the words "at Ephesus" in Eph 1:1, some have speculated that the letter coming from Laodicea was in fact the letter of Ephesians. Apostolic fathers also debated this possibility.)

In Paul's first letter to Corinth, he predated that letter by saying: "I wrote you in my letter not to associate with immoral people" (1 Corinthians 5:9) (This could be a reference to the present letter of 1 Corinthians, but likely refers to a missing text.)

These writings were important enough to quote or refer to in subsequent writings preserved now as scripture. Matthew 2:23 cites a now fulfilled prophecy from "the prophets" that Christ would be a Nazarene (someone from Nazareth), but this prophecy is not found anywhere in any existing Old Testament canon.

Matthew was citing scripture, which is missing now. Another example of missing scripture is the text containing the words of Christ that Paul quotes in Acts 20:35 "remember the words of the Lord Jesus, how he said, 'It is more blessed to give than to receive.'" This saying of Christ appears in none of the Gospels. Here Paul was writing to foreign converts who were not around to hear Christ preach, so how were they to "remember" those words? Paul obviously must have been citing it from a sacred writing that they had, which we are missing.

Without question, the Bible alone shows that there are sacred writings that early Christians and Jews respected as scripture but which we no longer have. I could also add that the many books such as the Shepherd of Hermas, were respected by many early Christians as scripture but are no longer included in modern canons.

21

According to the theory of continuing revelation or evolving truth, one freely accesses the truth as it is made available. Those books quoted or mentioned in the Bible, even if they are found after the Bible canon was established, are considered spiritually valuable and are sought after. Each of us must decide our own stance on this issue. If the missing books of Corinthians or Ephesians were found and verified as authentic, would you add them to your personal Bible? What about books mentioned or quoted in the Bible, such as Enoch, Jubilees, or others? (Jude 15 is a direct quote from Enoch 2.) What if you were to find out that these books were only lost to the Western Christians and the Eastern Christian Church had included them all along in their Bible as canon? Would you consider the fact that the younger Protestant Church may have missed something important, or would you dig in your heels and proclaim that the sixty-six books were the only truth?

Some of these books are out there now and can be obtained easily in their modern English translation.
(To see a list of available translations go to www.fifth-estate.net.) *This site is basically selling his books and books of others. Its not a PDF file for the free reads.*
Surely there will be some who would quote Revelation 22: 18 – 19

Rev. 22:18 I warn everyone who hears the words of the prophecy of this book: If anyone adds anything to them, God will add to him the plagues described in this book. 19 And if anyone takes words away from this book of prophecy, God will take away from him his share in the tree of life and in the holy city, which are described in this book.

To those, I can only point out that this was a common curse of the time and was the only method of copyright available to the masses. A curse of this sort is found in many books written in the same period. Also, let us keep in mind that the Book of Revelation is not the Bible. It was written as a single book. The author never suspected we would place it in a volume and then pronounce the volume to be canon. The curse applies to Revelation only, if one believes in such curses. Protestants, like myself, should all pray the curse is impotent, since we have taken away several entire books to end up with our scant sixty-six book volume.

The Canon of the Bible

The Question of Canon must come first.
In classical Greek the world "canon" signifies properly, "a straight rod," or "a carpenter's rule." In the early ages of the Christian religion it was used with considerable indefiniteness of meaning, though generally denoting a standard of opinion and practice. Later it came to be used as a testing rule in art, logic, grammar, and ethics. Still later the sacred writings received the name of the "Canon of the Scriptures." When, we use the term, we may mean one of two things, or, indeed, both:

1. The Canon of Truth--referring to the restriction of the number of books that compose the sacred volume. As such it was first used in the year A.D. 367.

2. The Rule of Faith and Life--referring to the application of the sacred Scriptures as a rule of our lives. In this sense it is used in Galatians 6:16; Philippians 3:16.

The sense in which we use the word in this chapter is that those books are canonical which Christians have regarded as authentic, genuine, and of divine authority and inspiration. These books are to be found in the Bible.

Why was a Canon of the Bible necessary?

Old Testament canon had already been set. It would form the root that grew the flower of the Christian faith. The Old Testament was honored by Jesus, who read from it in the synagogue, thus it was accepted without question by the first Christians, who were Jews. This would form half of Christian canon. New Testament canon was being developed in the form of writings of the Apostles and their disciples. So long as the living voices of prophets and apostles were heard, there was no pressing need for a canon of Scripture. They were the canon. But as soon as these men were dead it became necessary that their writings be gathered together to know what their messages were to the churches, and to preserve those writings from corruption. These are the Gospels and letters to the churches. But soon there were numerous books being written under the names of the deceased Apostles.

Hence the question arose as to which of these were authentic and really inspired.

Of course, this overlooks the idea that men outside the immediate twelve and their students could be inspired.

Leave it to the irony of fate to accelerate the decision of which books are canon.

Between 302 and 311 A.D. the Emperor Diocletia began his last, largest, and bloodiest official persecution of Christianity. It did not destroy the empire's Christian community; indeed, after 324 Christianity became the empire's preferred religion under its first "Christian" emperor, Constantine. However, Diocletia's blood lust forced the first real pressure from the outside of the church to define canon.

In A.D. 302 the Emperor Diocletia issued in an edict that all the "sacred" books should be destroyed by fire. The question arose as to which books rightly deserved the name of inspired or sacred. Pagans were left to decide this, but they did so, to some degree, according to which books were held in the highest esteem by the Christian community itself.

The persecutors demanded that the Scriptures should be given up. The Christians refused. The reaction of the believers informed the Emperor's men as to which books were held as inspired among the Christian community.

At this time there were many Gospels, Epistles, and apocalyptic books such as Revelation in circulations. Some were even written by real apostles other than Matthew, Mark, Luke, and John, such as Thomas, Barnabas, and others. Even though some of these books were being read and circulated within the community, none made it into canon for reasons we will cover soon. There were also dozens of false and spurious gospels and epistles. People read some of these books as entertainment but counted them as less than inspired. They simply made for a good story.

Canon started with the books accepted as inspired by the majority of Christians. This we will explore in more detail.

For now, let us examine the Gospels.

Why Do We Have Only Four Gospels?
Some temperaments are attracted by the idea of self-discovery and internal spiritual searches, others want to be led and need stability. The early Church could provide for both.

Though the Church had the advantage of resting on a basis of the inspiration from the ancient roots of Judaism, its development was not fettered by its past. Jesus proved the Old Testament was true but now completed and accomplished in him. To believers, the Old Testament was passé, to a large extent, having been fulfilled. This single fact allowed the church to be re-founded and re-formed. Now, a New Testament was beginning with new revelation, new writers, and new beliefs.

At this point the church was open and free to move in any direction but was intellectually in a weak position until and unless it could define, articulate, and support specific doctrines. The roots of the church would supply the starting point, since there are no greater authoritative and inspired books than the ancient Jewish Bible. This would continue to be canon and would become the Old Testament. But, although a canonized New Testament was necessary to establish a more defined direction, the need for it was only slowly realized.

A community can only invest letters, books, or words with canonical authority if they are seen as having intrinsic merit, popular approval, and are perceived to have a high degree of authority and repute. Officials canonization cannot create scripture; it can only recognize as inspired, books, which are already thought to be authentic and have the merit of following a selected doctrine. This latter issue may be the most important over time. For, as a power structure forms that has the weight and following to choose and enforce canon, so does the goal of the governing body to ensure its continuation and control.

The formation of an authoritative canon of the New Testament would have been natural. It is the order of things that some books would be discarded and others embraced, simply because some were written better than others, seemed wiser, and were more sensible or applicable. However, the time line was greatly accelerated owing to the growing prevalence of schools of divergent theology, grouped together under the name of Gnosticism.

It must be stressed again that what is divergent is judged by those in control. One reason that Gnosticism did not gain an upper hand was the number of systems led by various Gnostic leaders differed too greatly and could not agree enough to gain unity. But common to them all is the idea that matter is evil, and therefore the material universe could not have been the creation of the Supreme God. Because of this, it was believed an inferior or lesser god was the creator, but the Supreme God gave us Christ, who came to deliver man both from this world and its lesser gods.

Gospels, Acts, and other writings circulated widely, in which Christ was created as a spirit and had no real body of flesh and blood. This means He suffered only in semblance on the cross. Other schools taught that the Christ spirit came down upon the man Jesus at the baptism with the sign of the dove descending on Him, and the Spirit was taken up again to heaven at the Crucifixion but before His death.

A quote signifying this was in the Apocryphal Gospel of Peter claiming that at His death Jesus proclaimed:
"My Power, My Power, why hast thou forsaken Me?"
In order to stop the splintering, religious authorities were forced to draw a line between books, which were "permitted to be read," and were accepted as true doctrine and those not accepted.

Leaders of competing theologies emerged. Marcion came to Rome from Pontus on the Black Sea in A.D. 139, and lived there for about four years, attending the Church in an attempt to persuade them of his doctrine. He was unable to convert the Roman Church to his views, so he proceeded to found a new church. He reasoned that there was so much obvious difference in temperament and tactics between the God of the Old Testament and the God that Jesus preached that they must be two different beings.

The Old Testament God he rejected as being punitive and the inferior of the two deities. This inferior God was the Creator of this evil world. The Superior and Good God was the deliverer of mankind and was revealed in Christ. This means the Apostles had misunderstood Christ, His nature, and purpose. Christ's new revelation was therefore repeated to Paul. With this in mind, Marcion created his own Bible to reflect his theology by carefully removing all Jewish-Christian texts in conflict with his own.

Marcion was dedicated and fervent in his beliefs and convictions and within his lifetime he had founded a well-organized church extending throughout the Roman Empire. Its members, in the asceticism of their lives and their readiness for martyrdom, were claimed to exceed those of the Catholic Church. But Marcion was overtaken by a growing presence. The emerging power would come to be known as the Catholic Church. This, however, gives way to misunderstanding since this church was the body united before the great schism, which began in 191 and was completed in 1054 from which the Orthodox Churches broke away. Or one could better say the Catholics broke from the single and unified communion.

The most powerful leader of the Roman arm sent a letter of excommunication to the leader of the Eastern arm of the church. Why? Because he refused to come under complete control of the Bishop of Rome. But here I digress.
Many gospels and epistles were circulating in the early church. Dozens were thought to be authentic. By the year A.D. 180 the four gospels had attained general recognition in the major churches of Antioch, Ephesus, and Rome.

Jerome tells us that Theophilus, the bishop of the church at Antioch around 180 A.D., wrote a commentary on the four Gospels. Theophilus quotes the Fourth Gospel of John as "inspired scripture."

Still, there were many other gospels that could have been considered, so why did we end up with only four? The answer can be explained in three reasons. One was the fact that these four particular gospels fit together, harmonized, and did not contradict each other, as some others would have. Secondly, they upheld the theology of the authorities choosing the books. The third reason seems very arbitrary. There were other gospels that would have harmonized fairly well. Granted, the number would have been small, but we could have easily had five, six, or maybe more gospels in the Bible.

Adversus Haereses, a representative of the official view at Rome and Ephesus in 185 wrote:

It is impossible that the Gospels should be in number either more or fewer than these. For since there are four regions of the world wherein we are, and four principal winds, and the Church is as seed sown in the whole earth, and the Gospel is the Church's pillar and ground, and the breath of life: it is natural that it should have four pillars, from all quarters breathing incorruption, and kindling men into life. Whereby it is evident, that the Artificer of all things, the Word, who sitteth upon the Cherubim, and keepeth all together, when He was made manifest unto men, gave us His Gospel in four forms, kept together by one Spirit... For indeed the Cherubim had four faces, and their faces are images of the dispensation of the Son of God... For the Living Creatures are quadriform, and the Gospel also is quadriform. [Ibid. iii. 11. 8]

The reasoning seems fanciful and contrived, but it is supremely interesting for what it implies. These gospels were accepted and circulated prior to the decision. They were the most popular among the churches. Beyond this, we have four gospels because someone thought it was the right number simply because there are four cardinal directions and a Cherub was described as having four faces.

It should be noted that even after slimming the number to four, there were still many attacks by other sects due to discrepancies between the four gospels. The thought was if the small number of select gospels could not totally agree then there was room for their selected gospels and beliefs also.

Today, most theologians look at the Gospel of Mark as the proto-gospel, which was used by Matthew and Luke as a source to write their own gospels. The Gospel of John was likely written outside the influence of Mark. Thus, the harmony of the gospels can be explained by the common source material of Matthew, Mark, and Luke. The reason for the discrepancies will be touched on later, but for now let us simply say that the Gospels are only what they say they are. They are the good news. They never purport to be history or any such precise writings. They are simply the memoirs of four men telling what they remember about those days when the good news was delivered.

So, with the majority of the Gospels written from the same source, and thus fitting together or harmonizing well, and with the reason to have only four gospels established, (albeit with a superficial and superstitious excuse), the church settled gratefully on Matthew, Mark, Luke, and John as the four cornerstones to build the New Testament.

But wait – these books are not really New Testament books. The new covenant between God and His people could not start until the price of a blood sacrifice was paid and accepted. Remember, the sign of acceptance was to be the resurrection of the perfect sacrifice. The result was to be grace, mercy, forgiveness, and the Holy Spirit as a comforter to His people. This was completed in the book of Acts which is not commonly called a gospel but which is in actuality the beginning of the New Testament.

Inerrant Scripture

From the very beginning of the faith, when letters and books were being copied by hand and passed from one person to the next, there were glaring errors. As letters were collected and compared, it became obvious that there were major problems.

Origen (185 – 254) wrote in his thesis, Contra Celsum, "We must say that an attempt to substantiate almost any story as historical fact, even if it is true, and to produce complete certainty about it, is one of the most difficult tasks and in some cases is impossible." To Origen, there were obvious discrepancies, such as the difference in chronology and geography concerning the story of Jesus cleansing the temple. Yet, since the Scriptures are inspired by the Spirit, they cannot contain errors, and at three different times in his commentaries Origen explicitly states, "inspiration implies freedom from error."

But how can the Scriptures be free from error, even if inspired by the Holy Spirit, when they contain such obvious problems? For Origen, the apparent distortion of historical information is not necessarily the result of some scribal or other literary error, but purposefully put into the text by the Holy Spirit as a reminder that we must not depend on the purely historical reading. Origen writes:

"The differences among manuscripts have become great, either through the negligence of some copyists or through the perverse audacity of others; they either neglect to check over what they have transcribed, or, in the process of checking, they make additions or deletions as they please."

"The divine wisdom has arranged for certain stumbling-blocks and interruptions of the historical sense to be found therein, by inserting in the midst a number of impossibilities and incongruities, in order that the very interruption of the narrative might as it were, present a barrier to the reader and lead him to refuse to proceed along the pathway of the ordinary meaning: and so, by shutting us out and debarring us from that, might recall us to the beginning of another way, and might thereby bring us, through the entrance of a narrow footpath, to a higher and loftier road and lay open the immense breadth of the divine wisdom."

He continued by saying, what may appear as errors to us are intended by the Holy Spirit, to call the reader's attention to "the impossibility of the literal sense", and therefore signal the need for "an examination of the inner meaning."

Origen believed, in his own words, that scripture "...contains three levels of meaning, corresponding to the threefold Pauline (and Platonic) division of a person into body, soul and spirit. The bodily level of Scripture, the bare letter, is normally helpful as it stands to meet the needs of the more simple. The psychic level, corresponding to the soul, is for making progress in perfection.... The spiritual interpretation deals with 'unspeakable mysteries' so as to make humanity a "partaker of all the doctrines of the Spirit's counsel."

Origen actually believed that it was impossible for the scriptures to have errors so the errors found in scripture must have been placed there by God to provoke us to look at some deeper meaning.

A pagan opponent of Origen, named Celsus was not so kind when he wrote, "Some believers, as though from a bout of drinking, go so far as to oppose themselves and change the texts of the gospels three or four or several times over, as to change its character to enable them to deny difficulties in the face of criticism."

There were variations between books, and that was bad enough, but after manuscripts of various books were combined into the codices to make the Bible, the errors or differences between the various Bibles translated from them would become all too apparent. One might assume that the older versions would be less corrupt, but that would not necessarily be true. Look at copies in terms of genetics and lineage. If the original epistle was copied two times in 80 A.D. and the second copy had an error, we have only one copy left that was not a corrupt version. Now assume the flawed copy made it to a library and was preserved but the faithful version is copied and the copies were copied through ten generations of copies. If one of these copies of the faithful version lands in a church in 600 A.D. it would have a much longer lineage. It would be natural to assume the 80 A.D. version was less corrupt, but in fact if the 600 A.D. version did not pick up errors along the way it would be the one that is true to the original text.

Now assume that through time we collect fragments here and there and at times we are fortunate enough to find the occasional complete books. We can compare versions and maybe even track the lineage or "text family" of the fragments and books. If we compare fragments or books which have various "text families" we may see that books from pedigree "A, B, and C" say one thing but "D" says something different. If they started out with different copyists we can assume that one made a mistake. It becomes especially obvious if the word is one that looks or sounds like the rest but does not make as much sense.

These explanations are, to say the least, simplistic but they give a glimpse into the issues at hand. Those are which manuscripts are the least corrupt and which ones should be used to translate into some other tongue, such as English, in order to produce a Bible? It is not like we do not have several manuscripts to choose from. We have hundreds of fragments. Men have been searching through churches, archives, libraries, sand dunes, caves, and hardened soil for a thousand years to find traces of ancient Christian books.

To prove a point, here is a list of the first 20 out of over 100 as they are categorized.

The list contains:
Papyrus numbers and collection, dates, contents, text family, owner or place.

P1 -P.Oxy. 2 - 3rd cent. - Matt 1- Alexandrian

Philadelphia, Pennsylvania- Univ. of Penn. Museum

P2 - 6th cent.- John 12 - Mixed
Florence, Italy -Museo Archeologico

P3 -6th–7th cent. -Luke 7, 10 - Alexandrian
Vienna, Austria – Österreichische Nationalbibliothek

P4 -3rd cent. - Luke 1-6 - Alexandrian
Paris, France - Bibliothèque Nationale

P5 -P.Oxy. 208 - 3rd cent. - John 1, 16, 20
Western London, England - British Museum
Pap. 782 + Pap. 2484

P6 -4th cent. - John 10-11 agrees with B & Q
Strasbourg, France - Bibliothèque de la Université
Pap. copt. 351r, 335v, 379, 381, 383, 384

P7 - 5th cent. - Luke 4 (This item has been LOST. It was
formerly in Kiev, Ukraine: Library of the Ukranian Academy of
Sciences)
Petrov 553

P8 - 4th cent.- Acts 4-6 - mixed: Alexandrian & Western
(Item LOST, formerly in Berlin, Germany: Staatliche Museen_
P. 8683

P9 - P.Oxy. 402 - 3rd cent. - I John 4
Cambridge, Massachusetts -Harvard Semitic Mus.

P10 - P.Oxy. 209 - 4th cent. - Rom 1 - Alexandrian
Cambridge, Massachusetts - Harvard Semitic Mus.

P11 - 7th cent. -I Cor 1-7 - Alexandrian
Leningrad, Russia - State Public Library

P12 - P.Amh. 3b – late 3rd cent. - Heb 1
New York, New York - Pierpont Morgan Library

P13 - P.Oxy. 657 - 3rd–4th cent. - Heb 2-5, 10-12 - Alexandrian
London, England - British Museum

P14 - 5th cent. - I Cor 1-3 – Alexandrian
Mt. Sinai -St. Catherine's Monastery Library

P15- P.Oxy. 1008 - 3rd cent.- I Cor 7-8 - Alexandrian
Cairo, Egypt - Egyptian Museum

P16 - P.Oxy.1009 - 3rd–4th cent. - Phil3-4 -Alexandrian
Cairo, Egypt – Museum of Antiquities

P17 - P.Oxy.1078 - 4th cent. - Heb9 - mixed
Cambridge, England – University Library

P18 - P.Oxy.1079 - 3rd–4th cent. -Rev1 – agrees with: A, B, and C
London,England –British Museum

P19 - P.Oxy.1170 -4th–5th cent. - Matt10-11 - mixed
Oxford, England – Bodleian Library

P20 - P.Oxy.1171 - 3rd cent. - Jas2-3 - Alexandrian
Princeton, New Jersey – University Library

(These are but a few. There are over a hundred more.)

This brings us to the next pertinent problem, which is that of translation. We should question the source text or codices used. Some sources are better and more faithful than others. For example, if we know that the Vulgate was corrupted we should not use that source. We should go back to a Greek source. The source of the Latin Vulgate was the codex

Changes in
many changes

Vaticanus, named for the fact it was housed in the Vatican library.

But some Greek sources have errors also. An example within the Vaticanus codex is found in Hebrew 1:3. In his book, Misquoting Jesus, Bart Ehrman describes how scribes battle over words within this chapter and verse, as with the entire Bible. According to most manuscripts the word Pheron is used and the verse is translated, "Christ bears all things through the word of His power." But in the Vaticanus the word Phaneron is used and the verse is rendered, "Christ manifests all things through the word of His power." Then a second scribe read it and decided that "manifests" is an uncommon word so he changes it back to "bears." A century later a third scribe notices the alteration done by the second scribe and assumes the second scribe had exercised too much freedom, presuming to alter the original text. He changed the word back to "manifests" and added a note of indignation to the margin that read, "Fool and knave, leave the old reading. Don't change it." Sermons and entire theologies turn on a single word. In some manuscripts the word may not even be there.

Experts compare texts and render a version they believe is as close to the original uncorrupted text as possible. Out of this practice a manuscript is built that will be used to render an English translation. Some manuscripts will be better than others. Some will have the latest discoveries incorporated into the manuscripts. Thus, first we must question the sources used. Since we had been hand-copying manuscripts for fifteen hundred years, errors that occurred early, or errors occurring in manuscripts that were being copied and passed around more than others become entrenched. In fact, they become an accepted part of our bible.

One such example is the story of Jesus and the woman caught in adultery. This is a wonderful story. It shows the grace and kindness of Jesus. It is also absent certain details like, where was the man who was also caught? Was he also forgiven? Was the law of punishment simply forgotten by the priests as the story was told in the town? As it turns out, we do

hmmm

not have to speculate. The story is missing from the older manuscripts. A scribe, who had an apparent mind toward drama more than truth, added it.

The above example is used every Sunday to teach the mercy and forgiveness of Christ, but it is not likely that denominations were founded upon its existence. Not so with the next example.

In the closing verses on Mark, the story is building rapidly to a crescendo. Jesus has been resurrected. Mary has discovered his body is missing. She runs to tell the disciples. Jesus is on his way to them. They do not believe Mary, but then, there he is! Jesus appears! Then the disciples are told to go out into all the world, preach, make converts, and if you are a true believer there are signs that will follow you. You will be able to pick up snakes, drink poison, heal the sick, drive out demons, and speak in tongues.

The following section of Mark does not appear in the older or more reliable manuscripts.

Mark 16

9 When Jesus rose early on the first day of the week, he appeared first to Mary Magdalene, out of whom he had driven seven demons. 10 She went and told those who had been with him and who were mourning and weeping. 11 When they heard that Jesus was alive and that she had seen him, they did not believe it. 12 Afterward Jesus appeared in a different form to two of them while they were walking in the country. 13 These returned and reported it to the rest; but they did not believe them either. 14 Later Jesus appeared to the Eleven as they were eating; he rebuked them for their lack of faith and their stubborn refusal to believe those who had seen him after he had risen. 15 He said to them, "Go into all the world and preach the good news to all creation. 16 Whoever believes and is baptized will be saved, but whoever does not believe will be condemned. 17 And these signs will accompany those who believe: In my name they will drive out demons; they will speak in new tongues; 18 they will pick up snakes with their

hands; and when they drink deadly poison, it will not hurt them at all; they will place their hands on sick people, and they will get well." 19 After the Lord Jesus had spoken to them, he was taken up into heaven and he sat at the right hand of God. 20 Then the disciples went out and preached everywhere, and the Lord worked with them and confirmed his word by the signs that accompanied it.

Now, we have a problem, because entire denominations are based on the existence of this text.

At times the error is compounded.

Matthew 17:21 is a duplicate of Mark 9:29. It was apparently added by a copyist in order to harmonize the gospels, however, Mark 9:29 was not in the oldest manuscripts either.

At times there are even variations within the additions. In Mark 9:29 Jesus comments that a certain type of indwelling demon can only be exorcised through "prayer and fasting" (KJV). This is also found in the Rheims New Testament. But the word "fasting" did not appear in the oldest manuscripts. New English translations have dropped the word.

Slight alterations can have ripple effects that produce entire doctrines.

Luke 3:22 is a passage that describes Jesus' baptism by John the Baptist. According to Justin Martyr, the original version has God proclaiming, "You are my son, today have I begotten thee." Clement of Alexandria, Augustine, and other ancient Christian authorities agree on this version. The implication is that Jesus was first recognized by God as his son at the time of baptism. This would agree with certain Gnostic teachings. To distance the passage from the Gnostic viewpoint the words were altered to read, "You are my son, whom I love." This would come to be one of the passages on which the doctrine of the Trinity was based. Christian belief became set that Jesus was the son of God at his birth, (as described in Luke and Matthew) or before the beginning of creation (as in John), and not at his baptism.

Some additions are for theatrical effect and matter little to the overall message.

In John 5:3-4 "a great multitude" of disabled people waited by the water for an angel to come and "trouble the water," at which time it had healing properties for the first person who stepped in. A blind man was there. But the blind man could not see the water or the angel and those that were crippled stood little chance of being first. The passage seems out of place and makes little sense. Part of Verse 3 and all of Verse 4 are missing from the oldest manuscripts of John.

Scribes get carried away and begin writing instead of copying.

In John 21 the apostles are fishing and catching nothing. Jesus appears and tells them to throw the net on the other side of the boat. By doing so they haul in as many fish as the boat can hold. Jesus eats with them and then begins the famous dialogue with Peter about loving Jesus and feeding His sheep. There is general agreement among liberal and mainline Biblical scholars that the original version of the Gospel of John ended at the end of John 20. Scholars do not agree if John 21 was an afterthought or an addition, although most hold with the latter view.

Then, there are errors that reflect values and prejudices of the time.

1 Corinthians 14:34-35 appears to prohibit all talking by women during services. But it contradicts verse 11:5, in which St. Paul states that women can actively pray and prophesy during services. The question has been, "was this opinion for that one church or was this behavior to be held by all churches?"

It is obvious to some theologians that verses 14:33b to 36 are a later addition. Bible scholar, Hans Conzelmann, comments on these three and a half verses: "Moreover, there are peculiarities of linguistic usage, and of thought. [within them]." If they are removed, then Verse 33a merges well with Verse 37 in a seamless transition. If he is correct, many churches will have to re-think their sexist views.

In Revelation 1:11, the phrase "Saying, I am Alpha and Omega, the first and the last..." (KJV) which is found in the

39

King James Version was not in the original Greek texts. It is also found in the New King James Version (NKJV) and in the 21st Century King James Version (KJ21) The latter are basically re-writes of the original KJV. The Alpha Omega phrase is not found in virtually any ancient texts, nor is it mentioned, even as a footnote, in any modern translation or in Bruce Metzger's definitive 'A Textual Commentary' on the Greek New Testament, Second Edition.

Many sources, including United Bible Societies and Ontario Consultants on Religious Tolerance were used for the previous section and speak well to this issue.

Before we accept the version of the Bible we are reading we must be sure of its source. We must know if it was the most reliable source available. We must know how the manuscript was translated.

There are several ways to translate. The large number of translations are usually grouped into three main categories. A literal translation attempts to translate word for word and is a type of interlinear approach. They are usually the most accurate but also the most difficult to read. This is because English differs from Greek in the order of subject, verb, and predicate. The sentence structure becomes tangled and confusing. Then, there is that looming problem when words do not have an exact match and a phrase is used to render a word or two.

A dynamic translation attempts to keep the literal approach but restructures the sentences and grammar to make the Bible more readable. This opens the translation up to some degree of subjectivity and error.

Contemporary English translations are the easiest to read because they attempt to capture the meaning of the text and place the thought into modern English. The result is easy to read, but the text is highly subjective and should be approached with great care.

One should always question the purpose of a new translation. Was the translation commissioned for the purpose of expanding a particular denomination? In such cases it is quite possible that the wording and flavor of the text was bent to conform to the beliefs of the church body underwriting the translation. It would seem to be pure foolishness for a church to bend the scriptures to their will instead of re-examining and reforming their doctrine, but the former is done far too often.

One such obvious tact used in a modern church was that of the "New World Bible." The denomination using this version is adamantly opposed to the doctrine of the trinity. By altering their Bible by a single word, nay – a single letter, they manage to negate the existence of the trinity. They simply inserted the letter "a."

New World Translation of the Holy Scriptures
John 1:1
1 In [the] beginning the Word was, and the Word was with God, and the Word was a god.

Compare to the NIV, which echoes most other Bibles.

John 1:1 (New International Version)
1In the beginning was the Word, and the Word was with God, and the Word was God.

With such translations freely circulating, how can one claim the Bible is inerrant?
Most translations have the general error induced by starting with their own personal beliefs, and thus the subconscious prejudice of how the verse should be rendered.

Having covered the three main approaches to translations, it needs to be restated that every translation requires interpretation. At times this can be rather subjective. Why? Because languages do not translate word for word. Not every word has a unique word to match it in the other language. There are idioms, expressions, and metaphors that become meaningless in other tongues. Some languages even have different verb tenses and there is no direct single verb that fits the translation. Greek has verbs that indicate an action happening in the past with continuing effects back in time.

There are also verbs that indicate an event in the present with consequences continuing far into the future. English has no such equal. Some languages are richer in expression than English (such as Greek) or smaller in vocabulary (such as Hebrew). A translator must interpret the original meaning and find an equivalent wording. This is why at times a phrase will end up replacing a word or two. It is also why this makes the result subject to the biases of the translator. The translator must also attempt to put aside his personal beliefs so as not to bend a translation to mean something more or less than what it actually says.

This is a human process of choices and biases. Interpretations will differ and errors will occur.

To complicate things, all ancient manuscripts do not support a number of verses. Some verses only occur in latter versions, sometimes within only a set text family. Translators have to decide which verses to leave out of the text. Most translators will mark any verse left out of the majority of manuscripts with a note in the margin or a footnote with the omitted verse.

It is extremely ironic that one of the most well known and foundational sections of the Bible demonstrates both of the above points of translation and omission. It is the Lord's Prayer.

First, let us examine the The King James' version of The Lord's Prayer from Matthew 6:9-13: "After this manner therefore pray ye: 'Our Father which art in heaven, Hallowed be thy name. Thy kingdom come. Thy will be done in earth, as it is in heaven. Give us this day our daily bread. And forgive us our debts, as we forgive our debtors. And lead us not into temptation, but deliver us from evil: For thine is the kingdom, and the power, and the glory, for ever. Amen.'"

Now let us read the Lord's prayer in the NIV. Prayer from Matthew 6:9-13: "This, then, is how you should pray: 'Our Father in heaven, hallowed be your name, your kingdom come, your will be done on earth as it is in heaven. Give us today our daily bread. Forgive us our debts, as we also have forgiven our debtors. And lead us not into temptation, but deliver us from the evil one.'

Ignoring the difference between the Elizabethan English and modern English, there are two glaring differences in the last verse between the King James' Lord's prayer.

The KJV asks for deliverance from "evil" while the NIV asks to deliver us from "the evil one." There is a huge theological difference between the two. The Greek text actually uses an adjective with an article, making "the evil one" the only correct translation. We pray to be delivered from the evil one, not from any danger, disaster, or from the general ugliness of the world.

Look at the last line. "For thine is the kingdom, and the power, and the glory, for ever, Amen." This verse does not occur in older manuscripts. It only occurs as an addition to manuscripts of a certain "lineage" past a certain date. The doxology of the prayer is not contained in Luke's version. It is also missing from the earliest manuscripts of Matthew, representative of the Alexandrian text. It is present, however, in the manuscripts representative of the Byzantine text. To help date these two periods one should know that the Byzantine Empire began around 1557, and the Codex Alexandrinus is a 5th century Greek Bible, so we are talking about a period of almost one-thousand years.

Therefore the differences between the various English translations, such as the KJV and the NIV can come down to choices in interpretations as well as a choice of which ancient manuscripts to use as a source. Sometimes errors occur.

When errors do happen from the copyists' standpoint they can usually be attributed to a hand full of reasons. Errors in translations come from several directions. There are errors of the eye, where the copyist or scribe may read the text incorrectly, and transposing letters to make a new word and then write or interpret accordingly.

Errors of speech occur when a reader is dictating to a copyist and the scribe hears the word but confuses it with a word, which is pronounced in a similar manner but is incorrect.

Errors of the mind occur when the scribe reads a line and simply forgets the exact wording, producing an inexact copy, such as a substitute of the word "out" for "from" or the word "karpos (fruit) instead of "karphos" (speck). Other tricks the mind can play are to include explanatory notes found in the margins of many manuscripts within the main body of the text.

Intentional changes occur when a well-meaning scribe attempts to correct what he assumes to be an error in linguistics, which is not an error at all. Other intentional errors occur when attempting to align the Bible with biblical history, as it is understood at the time of copying.

A very obvious and specific error occurs when the scribe attempts to "harmonize" various passages in the Bible in order to make them less divergent or contradictory.

There are errors that can be introduced due to doctrine. These occur when one group decides to alter the manuscript to more closely reflect their own biases. Several of these may be found in the 16th century and include certain changes of an anti-Semitic view.

There are subtle changes that may occur in what is called "liturgical errors." These tend to be minor changes in word or flow to make the liturgy flow easier or make it easier to remember or follow.

In the more recent past, the errors of eye and mind were compounded when the printing press was invented. Errors usually assigned to one or two books could now be propagated through hundreds of Bibles at once.

King Charles I ordered 1,000 Bibles from an English printer named Robert Barker in 1631. It was an edition of the King James Bible. Only after the Bibles were delivered did anyone notice a serious mistake. In one of the Ten Commandments [Exodus 20:14], a very small word was forgotten by the printers. The word "not" was left out. This changed the 7th commandment to say "Thou shalt commit adultery!" Most of the copies were recalled immediately and destroyed on the orders of Charles I. But there are 11 copies still remaining. They are known as the "Wicked Bible." (The Bible museum in Branson - Missouri has one on display.) The printer was fined the equivalent of $400, a lifetime's wages at the time.

The word "not" was also left out in the 1653 edition. In 1 Corinthians 6 verse 9 it was printed: "Know ye not that the unrighteous shall inherit the kingdom of God" - instead of ""Know ye not that the unrighteous shall not inherit the kingdom of God." Again it was recalled immediately. It is known as the "Unrighteous Bible."

The Murderer's Bible - printed in 1801 - declared: "these are murderers" (instead of murmurers) and continued - "let the children first be killed" (instead of "filled.")

Perhaps the error in Psalm 119 verse 161 in a 1702 version summed it all up: instead of "princes" it read - "printers have persecuted me." It is known as the Printer's Bible.

These are but a few of the more noteworthy mistakes, but these mistakes must bring into question the doctrine of the inerrancy of the Bible. Most fundamental denominations hold to the fact that the Bible is complete and without error. It may be neither.

The history of the English Bible is a fascinating story. It serves to prove a point or two about how the church intentionally changed the Bible and then protected the alterations on penalty of death. Our starting point in this history is the production of Wycliff's hand-written English Bible, which was the result of the "Morning Star Reformation" led by John Wycliffe.

The first hand-written English language Bible manuscripts were produced in the 1380's A.D. by John Wycliffe, an Oxford professor. Wycliffe was a well-known theologian in Europe who stood in opposition to the teaching of the organized Church, which he believed to be contrary to the Bible. He enlisted his followers, called the Lollards, and his assistant Purvey, along with others to act as scribes to produce dozens of English manuscripts. They were translated out of the Latin

Vulgate, which was known to be somewhat corrupt, but was the only source text available to Wycliffe. The Pope was so infuriated by his rebellion, his actions, his teachings and his translation of the Bible into English, that 44 years after Wycliffe had died, the Pope ordered the bones of Wycliffe to be dug-up, crushed, and the dust of his bones were thrown in the wind to be carried out over the river.

John Hus was one of Wycliffe's followers. Hus actively campaigned for Wycliffe's work and ideas. Both men firmly believed that people should be permitted to read the Bible. They believed Bibles should be available in native tongues and all men should have the right to read it in their own language. Hus and Wycliffe openly opposed the tyranny of the Roman church. The edicts issued from the Pope threatened anyone possessing a non-Latin Bible with execution. The edict was carried out when Hus was burned at the stake in 1415, with Wycliffe's manuscript Bibles used as kindling for the fire. The last words of John Hus were that, "in 100 years, God will raise up a man whose calls for reform cannot be suppressed." Almost exactly 100 years later, in 1517, Martin Luther nailed his famous 95 Theses of Contention (a list of 95 issues of heretical theology and crimes of the Roman Catholic Church) to the church door at Wittenberg. The prophecy of Hus had come true.

Sometime in the 1450's Johann Gutenberg invented the movable type printing press. The result was amazing and immediate. Copies of books could now be mass-produced in a short time. Distribution for illegal books happened in an underground network. The first book to ever be printed was a Latin language Bible, printed in Mainz, Germany. This was essential to the success of the Reformation.

Thomas Linacre was a self-styled Greek scholar active in the 1490's. He was an Oxford professor, and the personal physician to Kings Henry the 7th and 8th. Thomas Linacre, a very bright man, decided to learn Greek in order to read the Bible for himself. After reading the Gospels and comparing the same texts to those in the Latin Vulgate, he wrote in his diary, "Either this is not the Gospel… or we are not Christians." The Latin had become so corrupt that it misrepresented and mangled the message of the Gospel. The church knew this but worked to keep a strangle hold on power instead of putting forth the effort to correct the Vulgate. Throughout all of this the Church threatened to kill anyone who read the scripture in any language other than Latin from any other source but the Vulgate. This was because many of the Vulgate's corruptions were intentionally placed to support church doctrine. Instead of building doctrine around the Bible, the church bent the Bible to support doctrine. This was not that difficult since Latin was not an original language of the scriptures and the conversion between Greek and Latin could be worded as the church wished.

John Colet, another Oxford professor was the son of the Mayor of London. In 1496 he began reading the New Testament in Greek. Soon after he decided to translate it into English for his students at Oxford. Later he provided texts for the public at Saint Paul's Cathedral in London. The people were so excited to actually read and understand the Bible, that within six months it was reported that each Sunday there were 20,000 people attempting to get into the church and an equal number surrounding the church to listen and possibly obtain a document. Fortunately for Colet, his political connections spared him from execution.

Erasmus was considered one of the greatest biblical scholars of all time. In 1516 he picked up the challenge of Linacre and Colet to correct the corrupt Latin Vulgate. He did this with the help of a printer named John Froben. Together, they published a Greek-Latin Parallel New Testament. He used the Greek, which he had managed to collate from a half-dozen partial old Greek New Testament manuscripts he had acquired. This produced the first non-Latin (Vulgate) text of the scripture to be produced in a millennium. The Greek-Latin Parallel New Testament focused attention on just how corrupt and inaccurate the Latin Vulgate used by the church was. Now people began to see how important it was to go back and use the original Greek and Hebrew texts. To translate the Bible into any native tongue more faithfully one must begin with the most accurate texts. Translations rendered from corrupt translations simply compounded error. The driving force keeping the act of translating illegal became obvious when Pope Leo X himself declared, "The fable of Christ has been quite profitable to me." The Pope feared loss of control and loss of revenue.

William Tyndale (1494-1536) holds the distinction of being the first man to ever print the New Testament in the English language. Tyndale was a true scholar and a genius. He was fluent in eight languages to the point that it was said one would think any one of them to be his native tongue. He is frequently referred to as the "Architect of the English Language", (even more so than William Shakespeare) as so many of the phrases Tyndale coined are still in our language today.

Tyndale was a Biblical translator and martyr; born most probably at North Nibley, about 15 miles south-west of Gloucester, England, in 1494. He died at Vilvoorden, about 6 miles north-east of Brussels, Belgium, Oct. 6, 1536. Tyndale was descended from an ancient Northumbrian family. He went to school at Oxford, and afterward to Magdalen Hall and Cambridge.

Tyndale translated the Bible into an early form of Modern English. He was the first person to take advantage of Gutenberg's movable-type press for the purpose of printing the scriptures in the English language. Tyndale held and published views considered heretical by the Catholic Church, and the Church of England established by Henry VIII. His Bible translation also included notes and commentary promoting these views. In the house of Walsh he disputed with Roman Catholic dignitaries, exciting much opposition, which led to his removal to London around Oct., 1523. A clergyman of the Roman Catholic Church once infuriated Tyndale by proudly proclaiming, "We are better to be without God's laws than the Pope's." Tyndale was enraged by what he viewed as the unreasonable and ungodly Roman Catholic heresies, to which he replied, "I defy the Pope and all his laws. If God spare my life ere many years, I will cause the boy that drives the plow to know more of the scriptures than you!"

Tyndale's translation was banned by the authorities, and His death would occur a few years thereafter.

Foxe's Book of Martyrs records that in that same year, 1517, seven people were burned at the stake by the Roman Catholic Church for the crime of teaching their children to say the Lord's Prayer in English rather than Latin.

In 1517 Martin Luther declared his intolerance for the Roman Church's corruption on Halloween in 1517, by nailing his 95 Theses of Contention to the Wittenberg Church door. Luther, who would be exiled in the months following the Diet of Worms Council in 1521 that was designed to martyr him, would translate the New Testament into German for the first time from the 1516 Greek-Latin New Testament of Erasmus, and publish it in September of 1522. Luther also published a German Pentateuch in 1523, and another edition of the German New Testament in 1529. In the 1530's he would go on to publish the entire Bible in German.

William Tyndale had wanted to use the same 1516 Erasmus text as a source to translate and print the New Testament in English for the first time in history. Tyndale showed up on Luther's doorstep in Germany in 1525, and by year's end had translated the New Testament into English. Tyndale had been forced to flee England, because of the wide-spread rumor of his project. Inquisitors and bounty hunters were constantly hounding Tyndale to arrest and kill him.

The authorities failed and Tyndale published his Bibles. They were burned as soon as the Bishop could confiscate them, but copies trickled through and actually ended up in the bedroom of King Henry VIII.

The public fascination continued to grow as well as the panic within the Roman Catholic Church. They attempted to counter the outcry by declaring the new translation contained thousands of errors. This became the excuse for burning hundreds of New Testaments. The fact was that they could find no errors in the texts. The church continued to enforce its edicts and anyone caught with a Tyndale Bible risked death by burning.

Having God's Word available to the public in the language of the common man, spelled disaster to the church. The church could not continue doing things that were so completely contrary to the Bible, such as selling indulgences (the forgiveness of sins one was planning to commit) or selling the release of loved ones from Purgatory.

Salvation through faith, not works or donations, was becoming the cry to battle. These were just a few things to come out of the Luther – Tyndale crusade.

Tyndale was betrayed by a fellow Englishman who was supposedly his friend. Tyndale was imprisoned for about 500 days before he was strangled and then burned at the stake in 1536. His last words were, "Oh Lord, open the King of England's eyes." This prayer would be answered in 1539, when King Henry VIII commanded the printing of an English Bible known as the "Great Bible."

Myles Coverdale and John Rogers were disciples of Tyndale. They continued the English Bible project after his death. Coverdale finished translating the Old Testament, and in 1535 he printed the first complete Bible in English. He made use of Luther's German text and the Latin as his sources. The first complete English Bible was printed on October 4, 1535, and is known as the Coverdale Bible.

John Rogers went on to print the second complete English Bible in 1537. It was, however, the first English Bible translated from the original Biblical languages of Hebrew & Greek. He printed it under the pseudonym "Thomas Matthew", a pen-name actually used by Tyndale at one time. He could have done this to honor the fact that a considerable part of this Bible was the translation of Tyndale before his murder at the hands of the church. The Bible was a composite made up of Tyndale's Pentateuch, his New Testament 1534-1535 edition, Coverdale's Bible, and some of Roger's own translation of the text. It remains known as the Matthew-Tyndale Bible. A second-edition printing was done in 1549.

In 1539, Thomas Cranmer, the Archbishop of Canterbury, hired Myles Coverdale at the command of King Henry VIII. His task was to publish the "Great Bible." It became the first English Bible authorized for public use. The Bible was distributed to Anglican Churches. One was chained to the pulpit, and a person to read the Bible was provided so that even the illiterate could hear the Word of God in plain English. William Tyndale's prayer had been granted three years after his martyrdom. Cranmer's Bible, published by Coverdale, was known as the Great Bible due to its great size: a large pulpit folio measuring over 14 inches tall. Seven editions of this version were printed between April of 1539 and December of 1541.

King Henry VIII had not actually changed his mind regarding publishing the Bible in English for the masses. He did it because he was angry with the Pope for refusing to grant his divorce. King Henry responded by marrying his mistress anyway, and having two of his many wives executed. Henry was the second son in the family and was destined to be a priest. Henry VIII had three siblings, two girls and one boy. His brother was called Arthur. Arthur was Prince of Wales. When Henry VII, his father, was still alive, Arthur died. Which made Henry VIII heir to the throne. Henry knew the church inside and out. In his anger he renounced Roman Catholicism, and removed England from Rome's religious control. Henry declared himself the new head of the Church. To this day the Kings of England are sworn to be "Defender of the Faith." His first act was to strike Rome in the heart of the church by funding the printing of the scriptures in English. This gave way to the first legal English Bible.

After King Henry VIII and then King Edward VI died, the reign of Queen "Bloody" Mary began. From 1540's through the 1550's she was possessed in her obsession to return England to the Roman Church. In 1555, she had John "Thomas Matthew" Rogers and Thomas Cranmer burned at the stake. Mary went on to burn hundreds for the "crime" of being a Protestant. This era was known as the Marian Exile. Religious refugees fled from England, but there was no truly safe place anywhere near except for Switzerland.

The Church at Geneva, Switzerland, was sympathetic to religious refugees and was one of only a few safe havens. Myles Coverdale and John Foxe, publisher of "Foxe's Book of Martyrs," along with Thomas Sampson and William Whittingham met there in the 1550's, with the protection of the great theologian John Calvin and John Knox, the reformer of the Scottish Church. They undertook to produce a Bible that would educate their families while they continued in exile. The New Testament was completed in 1557, and the complete Bible was first published in 1560. It became known as the Geneva Bible. Due to the use of the word "Breeches," which is an antiquated form of "Britches" (pants), some people referred to the Geneva Bible as the Breeches Bible. The Geneva Bible was the first Bible to add numbered verses to the chapters, so that referencing specific passages would be easier. Every chapter was also accompanied by extensive marginal notes and references so thorough and complete that the Geneva Bible is also considered the first English "Study Bible."

William Shakespeare quotes hundreds of times in his plays from the Geneva translation of the Bible. The Geneva Bible became the Bible of choice for over 100 years of English speaking Christians. Between 1560 and 1644 at least 144 editions of this Bible were published.

Examination of the 1611 King James Bible shows clearly that its translators were influenced much more by the Geneva Bible, than by any other source. The Geneva Bible itself retains over 90% of William Tyndale's original English translation. The Geneva in fact, remained more popular than the King James Version until decades after its original release in 1611. The Geneva holds the honor of being the first Bible taken to America, and the Bible of the Puritans and Pilgrims. It is truly the "Bible of the Protestant Reformation." The famous Geneva Bible has been out-of-print since 1644, so the only way to obtain one is to either purchase an original printing of the Geneva Bible, or a less costly facsimile reproduction of the original 1560 Geneva Bible.

In 1568, a revision of the Great Bible known as the Bishop's Bible was introduced. Despite 19 editions being printed between 1568 and 1606, this Bible, referred to as the "rough draft of the King James Version", never gained much of a foothold of popularity among the people. The Geneva may have simply been too much to compete with.

By the 1580's, the Roman Catholic Church saw that it had lost the battle to suppress the Bible and repress the people. In 1582, they ceased their fight for "Latin only" and began an official Roman Catholic English translation. In an attempt to continue control through the corrupt translation of the Latin Vulgate, it was decided that the English translation should use Vulgate as the only source text. Because it was translated at the Roman Catholic College in the city of Rheims, it was known as the Rheims New Testament. The Douay Old Testament was translated by the Church of Rome in 1609 at the College in the city of Douay. The combined product is commonly referred to as the "Doway/Rheims" or "Douay/Rheims" Version.

In 1589, Dr. William Fulke of Cambridge published the "Fulke's Refutation." Fulke printed in parallel columns the Bishops Version along side the Rheims Version, in an attempt to show the error and distortion of the Douay/Rheims.

With the death of Bloody Mary and then Queen Elizabeth I, Prince James VI of Scotland became King James I of England. The Protestant clergy, feeling less religious tyranny, approached the new King in 1604 with the desire for an updated and less confrontational Bible. The new translation was to replace the Bishop's Bible first printed in 1568. They wished to keep the scholarship and accuracy but do away with the rather acrid marginal notes proclaiming the Pope an Anti-Christ, and such. This suited the king, who many regarded as a closet Catholic. The leaders of the church desired a Bible with word clarification and cross-references, available to the masses.

In 1611 the first of the 16-inch tall pulpit addition was printed. It is known as "The 1611 King James Bible." A typographical error in Ruth 3:15 rendered a pronoun "He" instead of "She" in that verse in some printings. This caused some of the 1611 First Editions to be known by collectors as "He" Bibles, and others as "She" Bibles. Yes, I regret to say that even the sacred KJV had errors.

One year after the pulpit-size King James Bibles were printed and chained to every church pulpit in England, personal copies of the Bible became available.

One of the great ironies of history is that many Protestant Christian churches today declare the King James Bible as the only legitimate English language translation but it is not even a Protestant translation. Remember, the King of England is the "Defender of the Faith" for the Anglican Church, which is considered by most not to be a Protestant faith, but a Catholic sect.

After England broke from Roman Catholicism in the 1500's, the Church of England, also called "The Anglican Church," continued to persecute Protestants throughout the 1600's. One famous example of this is John Bunyan, who while in prison for the crime of preaching the Gospel, wrote one of Christian history's greatest books, Pilgrim's Progress. Throughout the 1600's, as the Puritans and the Pilgrims fled the religious persecution of England to cross the Atlantic and start a new free nation in America, they took with them their precious Geneva Bible, and rejected the King's Bible. America was founded upon the Geneva Bible, not the King James Bible. However, as time went on and the newer edition of the K.J.V. gained in popularity in America it eclipsed the Geneva Bible.

Until the appearance of the English Revised Version of 1881-1885 the King James Version was the Bible of choice for most. It is a little-known fact that for the past 200 years, all King James Bibles published in America are actually the 1769 Baskerville spelling and wording revision of the 1611. The original "1611" preface is deceivingly included by the publishers, and no mention of the fact that it is really the 1769 version is to be found, because that might hurt sales. The only way to obtain a true, unaltered, 1611 version is to either purchase an original pre-1769 printing of the King James Bible, or a less costly facsimile reproduction of the original 1611 King James Bible.

The differences between the two versions are easy to spot since there are no less than 24,000 differences in words, grammar, and punctuation between the four major revisions of the 1611 KJV between the 1613 and 1769 versions. (Here I must ask my Independent Baptist Brothers who defend the KJV as the only true Bible; "Which of these versions is the perfect word of God?")

In 1663 John Eliot published the first Bible printed in America. It was a translation in the native Algonquin Indian Language. The first English language Bible to be printed in America by Robert Aitken in 1782 was a King James Version. Robert Aitken's 1782 Bible was the only Bible ever authorized by the United States Congress. President George Washington commended him for providing Americans with Bibles during the embargo of imported English goods due to the Revolutionary War.

In the 1880's England planned a replacement for their King James Bible, known as the English Revised Version (E.R.V.). It would become the first English language Bible to gain popular acceptance after the King James Version. The widespread popularity of this modern-English translation was the first bible to eliminate the 14 Apocryphal books. Up until the late 1800's every Protestant Bible, as well as the Catholic Bibles had 80 books, not 66. The exception was the little known "Robert Aitken's Bible" of 1782. It was the King James Bible published without the apocrypha.

The inter-testament books written hundreds of years before Christ called "The Apocrypha" were part of virtually every printing of the Tyndale-Matthews Bible, the Great Bible, the Bishops Bible, the Protestant Geneva Bible, and the King James Bible until their removal from the K.J.V. around 1885. The original 1611 King James contained the Apocrypha, and King

James threatened anyone who dared to print the Bible without the Apocrypha with heavy fines and a year in jail. Only for the last 120 years has the Protestant Church rejected these books, and removed them from their Bibles. This has left most modern-day Christians believing the popular myth that there is something "Roman Catholic" about the Apocrypha. That was not true, and no consistent reason for the removal of the Apocrypha in the 1880's has ever been officially issued by mainline Protestant denominations. It is thought that since the Apocrypha had fallen into disuse and was thought of as a historical reference but not on the same spiritual level as the Old or New Testament, the removal made little spiritual difference and saved a little money.

Knowing all of the above... knowing how corrupt the Vulgate and all translations issuing from it are, I ask again, "Is the Bible inerrant?"

The Bible is a wonderful gift from God. It is a great road map to live by, but it is not God. The Bible has been passed through the hands of men. Scribes, copyists, translators, collectors, and printers have all made their marks. Men make mistakes. Nothing mankind has touched is without error. When we raise the Bible to the Status of God and begin worshiping the book instead of the Spirit who inspired it, we fall into legalism. Legalism breeds judgment, divisions, and hate. It is at this point that Christians begin hurting those of differing beliefs, including other Christians who may have another point of view. We fall into the same category as the extremists we so despise. Christian extremists have damaged more Christians than Islamists have ever hurt.

Sources: University of Texas at Dallas - on line library
williamtyndale.com
Regent University - on line library
American Bible Society

The Trinity

The Trinity, the doctrine that many hold so dear, is never mentioned in the Bible, and was not discussed nor considered by the early church. The doctrine was crafted in a political effort to unite the church in order that it might be more easily ruled and controlled.

Adolf von Harnack (May 7, 1851–June 10, 1930), a German theologian and prominent church historian, affirms that the early church view of Jesus was as Messiah, and after his resurrection he was 'raised to the right hand of God' but not considered as God. (See Mark 16:19). This was the baseline view by the church in the first century. From this point of view, an evolution of infiltration began that would culminate in the doctrine of the trinity.

Bernard Lonergan, a Roman Catholic priest and Bible scholar, explains that the educated Christians of the early centuries believed in a single, supreme God. This was the same basic view as held by the Jewish believers of the time.

As for the Holy Spirit, McGiffert tells us that early Christians considered the Holy Spirit "not as a separate entity, but simply as the divine power, working in the world and particularly in the church." It is the power or will of God working in the world.

Durant articulated the evolution of early Christianity when he said: "In Christ and Peter, Christianity was Jewish; in Paul it became half Greek; in Catholicism it became half Roman" (Caesar 579).

The Christian church has always been in turmoil. In the days of the Apostles the church was far from unified. Throughout his book "Orthodoxy and Heresy in Earliest Christianity", the German New Testament scholar, and early Church historian, Walter Bauer, explores the fact that Gnosticism influenced many early Christians forming heresies here and there throughout the budding Christendom.

In his work 'The Greek Fathers", James Marshall Campbell, a Greek professor, explains that the fear of Gnosticism was prevalent in the early church. Sects of Gnosticism varied in their Greek influence but the seeds were primarily of Greek origin and carried within it the mythos and theosophy of Plato and the Greeks that divided the universe into opposing realms of matter and spirit. In this world-view the body was a prison for the captive spirit like that of the "iron maiden" torture device of years to come.

The late Professor Arthur Cushman McGiffert interprets some of the early Christian fathers as believing Gnosticism to be "identical to" in all intents and purposes with Greek polytheism. Gnosticism had a mixed influence on the early Christian writers, sending them in various directions in their Christology. That these philosophies of the Greek, Romans, and Gnostics affected Christianity is a historical fact.

What did these philosophers teach about God? In Plato's Timeus, 'The Supreme Reality appears in the trinitarian form of the Good, the Intelligence, and the World-Soul'. Laing attributes elaborate trinitarian theories to the Neoplatonists, and considers Neoplatonic ideas as 'one of the operative factors in the development of Christian theology'. One of the questions posed in the book is simply, " What is real in Christianity." What would Christianity be if we were to find and eliminate most outside influences?

Durant ties in philosophy with Christianity when he states that the second century Alexandrian Church, from which both Clement and Origen came, 'wedded Christianity to Greek philosophy'; and finally, Durant writes of the famed pagan philosopher, Plotinus, that 'Christianity accepted nearly every line of him...'

As the apostles died, various writers undertook the task of defending Christianity against the persecutions of the pagans. The problem was that they were so tainted due to education and environment that some of the defenders did more harm than good.

The most famous of these Apologists was Justin Martyr (c.107-166). He was born a pagan, became a pagan philosopher, then a Christian. He believed that Christianity and Greek philosophy were related. As for the Trinity, McGiffert asserts, "Justin insisted that Christ came from God; he did not identify him with God." Justin's God was "a transcendent being, who could not possibly come into contact with the world of men and things." The Church was divided by Gnosticism, enticed by philosophy, and corrupted by paganism, but there were geographic divisions also, with East and West differing greatly.

As a reminder, sects of Gnosticism were differing combinations of Christianity and the Greek teachings, most centering around those of Plato. To the Gnostic Christians the material world and the spiritual world were very much at odds and could not coexist. Due to the increasing influence of Platoism and Gnosticism, the relationship between spirit and flesh as viewed by the church was shifting quickly. The body, once viewed as the vehicle and temple of the spirit and inseparable from it, was now viewed as a flesh prison for the spirit and opposed in nature to it. These views would turn the dancing and joyous Jewish celebration of life into repression and sorrow.

Changes would echo through time in various forms, ending in the stoicism of the sexual abstinence of priests and finally the self-flagellation of some monks. (Self-flagellation seems to have taken root in the dark ages during the plague when monks thought it would appease God if they punished themselves by beating themselves with whips.) In the early church the changes would be seen in the struggle to articulate the relationship between the various forms of the newly emerging Godhead. The Father was a spirit. The Holy Ghost was obviously a spirit, since it was the will of God who was pure spirit. It was the existence of Jesus and His position and state within the spiritual and material worlds that gives pause within the various sects of the early church.

The Eastern Church, centered in Alexandria, Egypt, and the Western Church, centered in Rome, Italy, grew in divergence.

The Eastern Church was inquisitive and had an environment of free thought as a reflection of the surrounding Greek culture. The theological development of the East is best represented in Clement and Origen.

Clement of Alexandria (c.150-220) was trained in the "Catechetical School of Alexandria," a place of training for Christian theologians and priests. Even though Clement was trained here, his views were influenced by Gnosticism. If one were to wish for a single focused statement explaining the Greek influence on the Christian Church, it would likely be the following by McGiffert; "Clement insists that philosophy came from God and was given to the Greeks as a schoolmaster to bring them to Christ as the law was a schoolmaster for the Hebrews." McGiffert further states that Clement considered "God the Father revealed in the Old Testament" separate and distinct from the "Son of God incarnate in Christ," with whom he identified the Logos.

Campbell continues this line of explanation when he says; "[with Clement the] philosophic spirit enters frankly into the service of Christian doctrine, and with it begins... the theological science of the future." However, it was his student, Origen, who "achieved the union of Greek philosophy and Christianity."

To sum up this bit of church history; Clement believed that just as the law was given to the Jews as a schoolmaster to bring them into the understanding that they needed a savior, philosophy was given to the Greeks to enable them to bring reason and a scientific approach to Christianity to establish its theology.

Campbell considered Origen (c.185-253) to be the founder of theology", the greatest scholar of the early church and the greatest theologian of the East. Durant adds that "with [Origen] Christianity ceased to be only a comforting faith; it became a full-fledged philosophy, buttressed with scripture but proudly resting on reason." However, the reason it rested on was directed and disciplined by the Greek style and content of thought. This is why in Origen the church experiences a changing view of God.

According to Pelikan"s Historical Theology, Origen was the "teacher of such orthodox stalwarts as the Cappadocian Father's, (Cappadocian was an area stretching from Mount Taurus to the Black Sea), but also the "teacher of Arius' and the "originator of many heresies."" Centuries after his death, he was condemned by councils at least five times; however, both Athanasius and Eusebius had great respect for him.

Origen turned his attention to the trinity, beginning with what he called the "incomprehensible God." He applied Stoic and Platonic philosophies in true Greek style. Origen believed the Father and Son were separate "in respect of hypostasis" (substance), but "one by harmony and concord and identity of will." If we stop at this point and poll members of most major denominations we are likely to find this to be the understanding of the majority, for how can a God who is pure spirit be of the same substance as Jesus, who is flesh and blood? Origen then went on to claim the Son was the image of God, probably drawing on the scripture where Christ proclaimed, "If you have seen me you have seen the father." In this he seems to contradict himself, anthropomorphizing to the point of endowing God with the limits of a human body made of a substance differing from that of which Jesus was made.

Keeping in mind that Gnosticism, as well as certain Greek philosophies, tend to divide the universe into realms of the spiritual and material, Origen, seeing those realms in opposition, maintained that there was a difference between "the God" and "God." He attempted to explained that "the God" [God himself] was a unity to himself and not associated with the world but, "Whatever else, other than him who is called is also God, is deified by participation, by sharing in his divinity, and is more properly to be called not "the God" but simply "God"" (Quotes are mine for clarification.) With such theological hair-splitting we enter into confusion and error.

As Origen and others introduced more and more Greek influences into the Eastern Church, it became more mystical, philosophical, and at times obtuse. This line of thought brought us from the Jewish proclamation of, Deuteronomy 6:4 "Hear, O Israel: The LORD our God, the LORD is one" and placed us into the first stage of the trinity by dividing God in twain. The simple and direct teaching of Christ to love God and treat others with dignity gave way to the complex, sophisticated, and often convoluted arguments as men found their self-importance in their ability to divide, and persuade.

It was Tertullian (c.160-230) who first coined the term trinitas from which we derive our English word "trinity." Tertullian writes, "...the unity makes a trinity, placing the three in order not of quality but of sequence, different not in substance but in aspect, not in power but in manifestation." Tertullian did not consider the Father and Son co-eternal. He considered God the creator of all. God must, therefore, pre-date everything that exists, even the first creative impulse, which would have created the pre-incarnate Christ. To clarify his belief Tertullian wrote, "There was a time when there was neither sin to make God a judge, nor a son to make God a Father." Tertullian also rejected the idea of God and Christ being co-equal. He reasoned that God was and contains everything, thus the Son cannot contain everything. He explains, "For the Father is the whole substance, whereas the Son is something derived from it." Another way to see his point is to say that all things are contained in or are part of God, thus Christ is in or part of God. The fullness of God could not be physically contained in Christ. (This statement flew in the face of Col. 2:9, which states that the fullness of the deity lives in Christ.) The idea of Trinitas is the beginning of the Trinitarian discussion in earnest, but it will take time to grow and develop into the full doctrine of the Trinity established under the political pressure of Constantine.

The world around the early Church was changing. The Roman Empire began to crumble and Constantine came to power. He wished to unify the Empire, and although he was a pagan, living in a society of polytheists, he chose Christianity, as a vehicle to work his will. What better way to unite a nation than through the growing monotheistic faith? But Christianity was far from unified; so to unify the empire the king had to unify the faith.

In 318 A.D., controversy over the matter of the Trinity had blown up again between Arius, a deacon, and Alexander, the bishop of the church in Alexandria, Egypt. Bishop Alexander of Alexandria and his deacon, Athanasius, believed there were three persons in one god.

This time Emperor Constantine involved himself. The emperor began to send letters encouraging them to put aside what the emperor called their "trivial" disputes regarding the nature of God and the "number" of God. As a polytheist, the emperor saw the argument over the semantics of whether one worshiped a single god, three gods or "three gods in one" as trivial and inconsequential. Arius, Presbyter in Alexandria, and Eusebius, Bishop of Nicomedia believed in only one indivisible god. According to the concept of homo-ousion, Christ the Son was consubstantial, that is to say the Son shares the same substance with the Father. Arius and Eusebius disagreed. Arius thought the Father, Son, and Holy Spirit were materially separate and different. He believed that the Father created the Son. Arius and his followers, the Arians, believed if the Son were equal to the Father, there would be more than one God. If one were to sum up the heart of the matter within the debate, it would be over the status of the Son as compared to the Father.

To exemplify the points of contention, an essay by Wright regarding Arius reports; "Arius was a senior presbyter in charge of Baucalis, one of the twelve "parishes" of Alexandria. He was a persuasive preacher, with a following of clergy and ascetics, and even circulated his teaching in popular verse and songs. Around 318 A.D., he clashed with Bishop Alexander. Arius claimed that Father alone was really God; the Son was essentially different from his father. He did not possess by nature or right any of the divine qualities of immortality, sovereignty, perfect wisdom, goodness, and purity. He did not exist before he was begotten by the father. The father produced him as a creature. Yet as the creator of the rest of creation, the son existed "apart from time before all things." Nevertheless, he did not share in the being of God the Father and did not know him perfectly. Wright concludes that before the 3rd century the "three were separate in Christian belief and each had his or it's own status."

The dispute became louder and more strident until it spilled over once again into the Christian community, causing division and controversy within the church body. The emperor's plan to unify the faith in order to unify the nation was being placed in jeopardy. In 325 A.D. the church faced two serious points of strife. The date of observance of the Passover on Easter Sunday had become an issue, and the concept of the Trinity was in full debate. Serious questions were being raised as to whether the church would remain intact. Letters from Constantine failed to settle the dispute, so the emperor called the "Council of Nicea."

Constantine chose leaders, which would represent each major division within the church and invited these bishops to join him in the seaside village of Nicea. There they formed a council, which Constantine hoped could unify the church. McGiffert tells us about the council. There were three main groups represented at this council: Eusebius of Nicomedia, who represented the Arian view of the Trinity, Alexander of Alexandria presenting the Athanasian version, and a very large party led by Eusebius of Cesarea. The Cesarea contingent was made up of those who wanted unity and peace. Their theological stance was not one so immovable and intractable that it would interfere with their desire for peace. It should be noted that Alexander of Alexandria was the bishop who was involved in the "discussion" with Arius, which began the final fray. He was so self-assured that he would not move on his idea of the Trinity. It is amazing that any man could be so self-assured about his knowledge of the mind and substance of God. It is presumption.

There is a general rule of negotiations. If you are sitting at the table with your enemies, the one who moves first loses. The moment a line is drawn or a position is articulated, it sets a limit on the discussion. If the 'negotiation is about price, the price stated would serve only as a limit from which to work. It was the mistake of Eusebius of Nicomedia to submit the Arian creed first. This served only to set a stage from which the other groups could spring. Their creed was summarily rejected. Then the more amicable of Eusebius of Cesarea submitted their creed, known as the Cesarean baptismal creed. Now the Alexandrian group knew where both parties stood. They would use this information to institute a brilliant political maneuver. Instead of submitting a creed of their own, the Alexandrian group modified the creed from Eusebius. The changes were not substantial enough to change the deeper intent of the creed. Eusebius was compelled to sign the creed. Now two of the three parties were united and the Arians were out of the negotiations. The majority of Eastern bishops sided with Arius in that they believed Christ was the Son of God 'neither consubstantial nor co-eternal' with his Father, but it no longer mattered.

Constantine saw well over two-thirds of the church in one accord, at least on paper. He now began to pressure all bishops to sign. Arians refusing to sign were exiled. Constantine exiled the excommunicated Arius to Illyria. Constantine's friend Eusebius, who eventually withdrew his objection, but still wouldn't sign the statement of faith, and a neighboring bishop, Theognis, were also exiled to Gaul. Constantine would reverse his opinion about the Arian heresy, and have both exiled bishops reinstated three years later, in 328 A.D. At the same time, Arius would also be recalled from exile; but for now, it was political blackmail.

The pressure from the emperor was so great and his reactions so feared that attendees justified their signatures thusly; Apuleius, wrote "I pass over in silence... those sublime and Platonic doctrines understood by very few of the pious, and absolutely unknown to every one of the profane." "the soul is nothing worse for a little ink."

Abu Al-Hassan Al-Nadwi reported that out of the 2030 attendees, only 318 readily accepted this creed ("Al-Seerah Al-Nabawiyya", p. 306). Only after returning home did other attendees such as Eusebius of Nicomedia, Maris of Chaledon and Theognis of Nicaea summon the courage to express to Constantine in writing how much they regretted having put their signatures to the Nicene formula, "We committed an impious act, O Prince," wrote Eusebius of Nicomedia, "by subscribing to a blasphemy from fear of you."

Thus Constantine had his unified Church, which was not very unified. McGiffert asserts that Eusebius of Cesarea was not altogether satisfied with the creed because it was too close to Sabellianism (Father, Son, and Holy Spirit are three aspects of one God). Lonergan shows just how much of the creed Eusebius took exception to as the words were explained. "Out of the Father's substance" was now interpreted to show that the Son is "out of the Father", but "not part of the Father's substance." "Born not made" because "made" refers to all other creatures "which come into being through the Son", and "consubstantial" really means that the Son comes out of the Father and is like him.

Lonergan goes on to explain that the language of debate on the consubstantiality of the Father and the Son has made many people think that the "Church at Nicea had abandoned the genuine Christian doctrine, which was religious through and through, in order to embrace some sort of hellenistic ontology." Nicene dogma marked the "transition from the prophetic Oracle of Yahweh... to Catholic dogma."

The evolution of the Trinity can be seen in the words of the Apostles' Creed, Nicene Creed, and the Athanasian Creed. As each of the creeds became more wordy and convoluted, the simple, pure faith of the Apostolic church became lost in a haze. Even more interesting is the fact that as the creeds became more specific (and less scriptural) the adherence to them became stricter, and the penalty for disbelief harsher.

In stark contrast, is the simple oneness of the Hebrew God. After the Council of Chalcedon in 451, debate was no longer tolerated and those opposing the Trinity were considered to commit blasphemy. Sentences ranged from mutilation to death.

Christians now turned on Christians, maiming and slaughtering thousands because of this difference of belief.

The reign of Constantine marks the time of the transformation of Christianity from a religion into a political system; and though, in one sense, that system was degraded, in another it had risen above the old Greek mythology. The maxim holds true in the social as well as in the mechanical world, that, when two bodies strike, the form of both is changed. Paganism was modified by Christianity; Christianity by Paganism. In the Trinitarian controversy, the chief point in discussion was to define the position of "the Son."

After the divisions regarding the Trinity had subsided, the church continued to narrow its tolerance and tighten its grip.

Creeds and, to a degree religions, are based on exclusivity. They seek to exclude all who do not conform to a certain set of beliefs. All others are excluded and usually punished, shunned, condemned, or killed. As people in power are inclined to do, the fist of control tightens over time. In following this pattern, creeds tend to get longer, more specific, and thus more exclusive. Points of little concern in one creed become of greater importance in the next creed, as we tend to increasingly choke on gnats.

What are the points of concern? What points should we sweat? To find out what the early church fathers thought, we could examine various Christian creeds. These are lists of basic and fundamental beliefs. Each creed was made up of statements of belief. These statements were considered points on which there must be agreement before someone could be accepted into the early church as a Christian. Departure from the basic points of faith was considered a heresy. Although the word "heresy" has taken on a tone we do not like to use today in our permissive society we should consider well the lines we should draw within our own lives beyond which beliefs or actions become unacceptable, lest we also slip into heresy.

The Nicene Creed

When the Council of Nicaea (A.D. 325) rejected the teaching of Arius, it expressed its position by adopting one of the current Eastern symbols and inserting into it some anti-Arian phrases, resulting in this creed. At the Council of Constantinople (A.D. 381) some minor changes were made, and it was reaffirmed at the Council of Chalcedon (A.D. 451). It is an essential part of the doctrine and liturgy of the Lutheran churches. Historically it has been used especially at Holy Communion on Sundays and major feasts (except when the Apostles' Creed is used as the Baptismal Creed).

We believe in one God,
the Father, the Almighty,
maker of heaven and earth,
of all that is, seen and unseen.
We believe in one Lord, Jesus Christ,
the only Son of God,
eternally begotten of the Father,
God from God, Light from Light,
true God from true God,
begotten, not made,
of one Being with the Father.
Through Him all things were made.
For us and for our salvation
He came down from heaven;
by the power of the Holy Spirit
He became incarnate from the Virgin Mary, and was made man.
For our sake He was crucified under Pontius Pilate;
He suffered death and was buried.
On the third day He rose again
in accordance with the Scriptures;
He ascended into heaven
and is seated at the right hand of the Father.

He will come again in glory to judge the living and the dead,
and His kingdom will have no end.
We believe in the Holy Spirit, the Lord, the giver of life,
who proceeds from the Father and the Son.
With the Father and the Son, He is worshiped and glorified.
He has spoken through the Prophets.
We believe in one holy catholic and apostolic Church.
We acknowledge one baptism for the forgiveness of sins.
We look for the resurrection of the dead,
and the life of the world to come. Amen.

The Old Roman Creed

AS QUOTED BY TERTULLIAN (c. 200)
With comparisons with De Virginibus Velandis,
Tertullian, and De Praescriptione
Below we compare versions of this creed.

The Old Roman Creed

AS QUOTED BY TERTULLIAN (c. 200)

De Virginibus Velandis	Tertullian	De Praescriptione
Believing in one God Almighty, maker of the world,	We believe in one only God,	I believe in one God, maker of the world,
and His Son, Jesus Christ,	and the son of God Jesus, Christ,	the Word, called His Son, Jesus Christ,
born of the Virgin Mary,	born of the Virgin,	by the Spirit and power of God the Father made flesh in Mary's womb, and born of her
crucified under Pontius Pilate,	He suffered died, and was buried,	fastened to a cross.
on the third day brought to life from the dead,	Brought back to life,	He rose the third day,
received in heaven,	taken again into heaven,	was caught up into heaven,

sitting now at the right hand of the Father,	sits at the right hand of the Father,	set at the right hand of the Father,
will come to judge the living and the dead	will come to judge the living and the dead,	will come with glory to take the good into life eternal, and condemn the wicked to perpetual fire,
	who has sent from the Father the Holy Ghost.	sent the vicarious power of His Holy Spirit,
		to govern believers, (In this passage articles 9 and 10 precede 8)
through resurrection of the flesh.		restoration of the flesh.

This comparison serves to show how incomplete the evidence provided is by mere quotations of the Creed, and how cautiously it must be dealt with. Had we possessed only the "De Virginibus Velandis", we might have said that the article concerning the Holy Ghost did not form part of Tertullian's Creed. Had the "De Virginibus Velandis" been destroyed, we should have declared that Tertullian knew nothing of the clause "suffered under Pontius Pilate." And so forth. While no explicit statement of this composition by the Apostles is forthcoming before the close of the fourth century, earlier Fathers such as Tertullian and St. Irenaeus insist that the "rule of faith" is part of the apostolic tradition. Tertullian in particular in his "De Praescriptione" insists that the rule was instituted by Christ and delivered to us by the apostles.

II. The Old Roman Creed

The Catechism of the Council of Trent apparently assumes the apostolic origin of our existing creed pointing to the old Roman form as a template. However if the old Roman form had been held to be the inspired utterance of the Apostles, it would not have been modified too easily at the pleasure of the local churches. In particular, it would never have been entirely supplanted by today's form. Printing them together best reveals the difference between the two:

Roman

(1) I believe in God the Father Almighty;
(1) I believe in God the Father Almighty Creator of Heaven and earth

(2) And in Jesus Christ, His only Son, our Lord;
(2) And in Jesus Christ, His only Son, our Lord;

(3) Who was born of (de) the Holy Ghost and of (ex) the Virgin Mary;
(3) Who was conceived by the Holy Ghost, born of the Virgin Mary,

(4) Crucified under Pontius Pilate and buried;
(4) Suffered under Pontius Pilate, was crucified, dead, and buried;

(5) The third day He rose again from the dead,
(5) He descended into hell; the third day He rose again from the dead;

(6) He ascended into Heaven,
(6) He ascended into Heaven, sitteth at the right hand of God the Father Almighty;

(7) Sitteth at the right hand of the Father,
(7) From thence He shall come to judge the living and the dead.

(8) Whence He shall come to judge the living and the dead.
(8) I believe in the Holy Ghost,

(9) And in the Holy Ghost,
(9) The Holy Catholic Church, the communion of saints,

(10) the Holy Church,
(10) the forgiveness of sins,

(11) the forgiveness of sins;
(11) the resurrection of the body, and

(12) the resurrection of the body.
(12) life everlasting.

Please note that the Roman form does not contain the clauses "Creator of heaven and earth", "descended into hell", "the communion of saints", "life everlasting", nor the words "conceived", "suffered", "died", and "Catholic." Many of these additions, but not quite all, were probably known to St. Jerome in Palestine (c. 380.--See Morin in Revue Benedictine, January, 1904) Further additions appear in the creeds of southern Gaul at the beginning of the next century, but Tertullian probably assumed its final shape in Rome itself some time before A.D. 700 (Burn, Introduction, 239; and Journal of Theology Studies, July, 1902). We are not certain as to the reasons leading to the changes, but it could be speculated that they were written as implicit defenses of heresies that were popular throughout the time of the alterations.

The Apostles' Creed

The Apostles' Creed, as we have it now, dates from the eighth century. However, it is a revision of the so-called Old Roman Creed, which was used in the West by the third century. Behind the Old Roman Creed, in turn, were variations, which had roots in the New Testament itself. While this creed does not come from the apostles, its roots are apostolic. It serves as a Baptismal symbol in that it describes the faith into which we are baptized and is used in the rites of Baptism and Affirmation of Baptism.

I believe in God, the Father almighty,
creator of heaven and earth.
I believe in Jesus Christ, His only Son, our Lord.
He was conceived by the power of the Holy Spirit
and born of the Virgin Mary.
He suffered under Pontius Pilate,
was crucified, died, and was buried.
He descended into hell.*
On the third day he rose again.
He ascended into heaven,
and is seated at the right hand of the Father.
He will come again to judge the living and the dead.
I believe in the Holy Spirit,
the holy catholic Church,
the communion of saints,
the forgiveness of sins,
the resurrection of the body,
and life everlasting. Amen.

*or "He descended to the dead."

Text prepared by the International Consultation on English
Texts (ICET) and the English Language Liturgical Consultation
(ELLC). Reproduced by permission.
This exposition of the creed was made at the request of
Laurentius, a Bishop whose See is unknown, but is conjectured
by Fontanini, in his life of Rufinus, to have been Concordia,
Rufinus' birthplace. Here is the English translation of the creed,
which Rufinus was asked to make commentary on. The date of
the writing was about 307 A.D.
I believe in God the Father Almighty, invisible and impassible.
And in Jesus Christ, His only Son, our Lord; Who was born
from the Holy Ghost, of the Virgin Mary; Was crucified under
Pontius Pilate, and buried; He descended to hell; on the third
day He rose again from the dead. He ascended to the heavens;
He sitteth at the right hand of the Father; Thence He is to come

to judge the quick and the dead. And in the Holy Ghost; The Holy Church. The remission of sins. The resurrection of this flesh.

The Chalcedonian Creed

The Chalcedonian Creed was adopted in the fifth century, at the Council of Chalcedon in 451, which is one of the seven Ecumenical councils accepted by Eastern Orthodox, Catholic, and many Protestant Christian churches.

We, then, following the holy Fathers, all with one consent, teach men to confess one and the same Son, our Lord Jesus Christ, the same perfect in Godhead and also perfect in manhood; truly God and truly man, of a reasonable [rational] soul and body; consubstantial [co-essential] with the Father according to the Godhead, and consubstantial with us according to the Manhood; in all things like unto us, without sin; begotten before all ages of the Father according to the Godhead, and in these latter days, for us and for our salvation, born of the Virgin Mary, the Mother of God, according to the Manhood; one and the same Christ, Son, Lord, only begotten, to be acknowledged in two natures, confusedly, unchangeably, indivisibly, inseparably; the distinction of natures being by no means taken away by the union, but rather the property of each nature being preserved, and concurring in one Person and one Subsistence, not parted or divided into two persons, but one and the same Son, and only begotten, God the Word, the Lord Jesus Christ; as the prophets from the beginning [have declared] concerning Him, and the Lord Jesus Christ Himself has taught us, and the Creed of the holy Fathers has handed down to us.

The Athanasian Creed

This creed is of uncertain origin. It was supposedly prepared in the time of Athanasius, the great theologian of the fourth century, although it seems more likely that it dates from the fifth or sixth centuries and is Western in character. It assists the Church in combating two errors that undermined Bible teaching: the denial that God's Son and the Holy Spirit are of one being with the Father; the other a denial that Jesus Christ is true God and true man in one person. It declares that whoever rejects the doctrine of the Trinity and the doctrine of Christ is without the saving faith. Traditionally it is considered the "Trinitarian Creed" and read aloud in corporate worship on Trinity Sunday.

Whoever wants to be saved should above all cling to the catholic faith.
Whoever does not guard it whole and inviolable will doubtless perish eternally.
Now this is the catholic faith: We worship one God in Trinity and the Trinity in unity, neither confusing the persons nor dividing the divine being.
For the Father is one person, the Son is another, and the Spirit is still another.
But the deity of the Father, Son, and Holy Spirit is one, equal in glory, co-eternal in majesty.

What the Father is, the Son is, and so is the Holy Spirit.
Uncreated is the Father; uncreated is the Son; uncreated is the Spirit.
The Father is infinite; the Son is infinite; the Holy Spirit is infinite.
Eternal is the Father; eternal is the Son; eternal is the Spirit:
And yet there are not three eternal beings, but one who is eternal;
as there are not three uncreated and unlimited beings, but one who is uncreated and unlimited.

Almighty is the Father; almighty is the Son; almighty is the Spirit:

And yet there are not three almighty beings, but one who is almighty.

Thus the Father is God; the Son is God; the Holy Spirit is God: And yet there are not three gods, but one God.

Thus the Father is Lord; the Son is Lord; the Holy Spirit is Lord: And yet there are not three lords, but one Lord.

As Christian truth compels us to acknowledge each distinct person as God and Lord, so catholic religion forbids us to say that there are three gods or lords.

The Father was neither made nor created nor begotten; the Son was neither made nor created, but was alone begotten of the Father; the Spirit was neither made nor created, but is proceeding from the Father and the Son.

Thus there is one Father, not three fathers; one Son, not three sons; one Holy Spirit, not three spirits.

And in this Trinity, no one is before or after, greater or less than the other; but all three persons are in themselves, co-eternal and co-equal; and so we must worship the Trinity in unity and the one God in three persons.

Whoever wants to be saved should think thus about the Trinity.

It is necessary for eternal salvation that one also faithfully believes that our Lord Jesus Christ became flesh.

For this is the true faith that we believe and confess: That our Lord Jesus Christ, God's Son, is both God and man.

He is God, begotten before all worlds from the being of the Father, and He is man, born in the world from the being of his mother -- existing fully as God, and fully as man with a rational soul and a human body; equal to the Father in divinity, subordinate to the Father in humanity.

Although He is God and man, He is not divided, but is one Christ.
He is united because God has taken humanity into himself; He does not transform deity into humanity. He is completely one in the unity of his person, without confusing his natures. For as the rational soul and body are one person, so the one Christ is God and man.

He suffered death for our salvation.
He descended into hell and rose again from the dead.
He ascended into heaven and is seated at the right hand of the Father.
He will come again to judge the living and the dead.
At his coming all people shall rise bodily to give an account of their own deeds.
Those who have done good will enter eternal life,
those who have done evil will enter eternal fire.
This is the catholic faith.

One cannot be saved without believing this firmly and faithfully.

Text prepared by the International Consultation on English Texts (ICET) and the English Language Liturgical Consultation (ELLC). Reproduced by permission.

As seen in the examination of these creeds or statements of faith, there is a tendency to expand and change creeds to defend against and virtually close the doors to all things viewed as heresies that rear their heads throughout the existence of the creeds. Thus, just as doctrines spring into existence as an argument and defense against errors in the faith, so creeds change for the same purpose. This sprawl tends to be destructive for several reasons, not the least of which is expanding creeds take expanded time to understand and defend each area of belief. Man's ability to corrupt is endless and man's heresies are endless, man's ability to tolerate

individual thought is miniscule. We are charged to work out
our own salvation with fear and trembling. Our ability to do
this is dependent on the church to allow free thought. The
heresy of free thought is seldom allowed.

When it comes to doctrine, to those that believe, no explanation
is necessary, but for those who do not believe, no explanation
will suffice.

To keep our eyes on the ball, the major questions need to be
asked again. For what purpose was the Bible written? How
should we interpret the Bible? Should the Bible be read as the
literal word of God? Is the Bible inerrant, or is it a group of
books written by men? How should we approach the Bible in
order to glean insight and not overreach the original intent of
the writers?

Virgin Birth

HUMAN PATHENOGENESIS

Christians celebrate the birth of a human baby to his mother, a young virgin named Mary. Is this scientifically possible? We know that wasps, fish, birds, and lizards can produce healthy offspring asexually, but what about people? Are virgin births possible without medical intervention?

Yes, but the chances are over a billion to one. I would call that a miracle.

Spontaneous asexual reproduction, which can occur to a human virgin, is called parthenogenesis. In cases of parthenogenesis (virgin birth), an ovum, or egg, starts to divide by itself without fertilization, producing an embryo.

Because there is no source of paternal chromosomes, duplication of maternal ones would be the only way to fill the needed number of chromosomes for the embryo. This asexual reproductive method is common among invertebrates but as we go up the evolutionary scale this ability declines. It becomes very rare among warm-blooded vertebrates. Certain conditions such as illness, pathogens, and external stimuli can produce pathological parthenogenesis, which has been observed in higher animals, such as the frog, fowl, and certain mammals, but this type of parthenogenesis usually gives rise to female offspring or sometimes an abnormal male.

In 1900 Jacques Loeb accomplished the first clear case of artificial parthenogenesis when he pricked unfertilized frog eggs with a needle and found that in some cases normal embryonic development ensued. In 1936 Gregory Pincus induced parthenogenesis in a rabbit's ovum by changing temperature and adding chemical agents. Artificial parthenogenesis has been achieved by mechanical, chemical, and electrical means. Several types of animal eggs have been used in experiments but the experiments usually result in incomplete and abnormal development.

The first cloned human embryo was produced in October 2001. Eggs had their own genetic material removed and were injected with the nucleus of a donor cell. This is not the same as parthenogenesis, which uses the intact nucleus and genetic materials. Attempts at artificial parthenogenesis in humans have not yet been successful. In one experiment human eggs were incubated under special conditions to prompt them to divide and grow. One embryo grew to six cells before it stopped dividing. In fact several types of experiments were devised but efforts met with only limited success. In spite of the failed experiments, there is still some evidence that parthenogenesis does occasionally occur in humans without outside intervention.

There are many instances in which impregnation has allegedly taken place in women without there being any possibility of the semen entering the female genital passage. In some cases it was found either in the course of pregnancy or at the time of childbirth that the female passages were obstructed. However, it must be stated here that some of these women were having sexual intercourse but studies at that time indicated that the path between vagina and ovaries were missing or occluded.

In 1956 the medical journal Lancet published a report concerning 19 alleged cases of virgin birth among women in England, who were studied by members of the British Medical Association. The six-month study convinced the investigators that human parthenogenesis was physiologically possible and had actually occurred in some of the women studied. Dealing with known methods, tests, and instrumentation of the 1950s may add a seed of doubt to the science and the conclusions of the experiments, but scientists of the time believed virgin birth was possible.

It is possible that some cases of human parthenogenesis involve self-fertilization rather than true virgin birth, as there are cases of sperm being produced in women by vestigial male reproductive glands. These are unused, and at times undiscovered glands, which are left over from embryonic development, that can achieve some low level of function under certain conditions, usually in cases of arousal or excitement.

Could a virgin conceive and give birth? Yes, but a number of rare events would have to occur in close succession, and the chances of these all happening in real life are virtually zero.

In normal fertilization the function of the sperm is two-fold. Its chemical makeup causes the egg to begin to divide. The genetic material of the sperm supplies half of the chromosomes needed to make the complete blueprint of the offspring. Fertilization and hereditary transmission are distinct operations and functions.

If the fertilizing enzyme (occytase) is isolated from the sperm and added to the egg, the egg would start to divide, but there would be no parental genetic material. If the egg could continue to segment and produce an offspring it would carry only maternal chromosomes. This experiment was attempted on sea-urchin eggs and caused them to develop. This enzyme (occytase) seems to be present in mammalian blood, since the addition of ox's blood to unfertilized eggs produced the same effects. This proved that chemical substances could replace one of the functions of the sperm – to trigger the segmentation of the ovum - while the other function of conveying genetic material can be dispensed with, in which case the offspring have purely maternal characteristics.

Eggs can show at least a beginning of segmentation under normal conditions, but sperm, which are highly alkaline, appear to accelerate the process by compensating for the excessive acidity of the medium surrounding the egg rather than a chemical deficiency in the egg itself. An acid condition of the blood prevents the parthenogenetic development of ova in the ovaries, while increased alkalinity appears to favor parthenogenetic development.

For a virgin to get pregnant, one of her eggs would have to produce, on its own, the biochemical changes indicative of fertilization. An egg will only start dividing when a spike in cellular calcium occurs. This normally occurs as a result of a sperm's entry during fertilization. But if the egg happens to experience a spontaneous calcium spike, it will start reacting as if it's been fertilized.

These events occur in the eggs or egg precursor cells of one out of every few thousand women. But what about the problem of the missing chromosomes? The egg would then have to divide abnormally to compensate for the lack of sperm DNA.

If an egg completes the final stage of a cell division known as meiosis II, it loses half of its genetic material to make room for the sperm's DNA. But if there's no sperm, each half of the divided egg cell will end up short, and both will die. In order for our virgin birth to proceed, the egg must, therefore, not complete meiosis.

Assuming both the calcium spike and the error in mitosis occur, the egg cell may then begin the process of parthenogenesis. When this happens to an egg-precursor cell, it can give rise to a tumor made up of many different types of tissue — liver, teeth, eye, and hair, for example, this is because unfertilized eggs lack specific instructions about gene expression from the sperm. Because of this, parthenogenesis in humans never produces viable embryos.

Fertilized eggs are working with two sets of genes, one set from the mother and one from the father. Some genes use only one copy, while the other remains dormant. Some of the signals for which copies should be turned off come from the sperm cell. So, if there's no sperm, certain genes will be over-expressed, and the "embryo" will die when it is only about five days old.

By eliminating a pair of maternal genes this problem can be avoided. A Japanese team was able to create, via parthenogenesis, a viable baby mouse that was seemingly unaffected by its lack of paternal imprinting. Although the scientists engineered these changes in the lab, there's at least a theoretical possibility that this could happen spontaneously via random gene deletions.

So, while it's possible for a human baby to be born of a virgin mother, it's very, very unlikely: These two genetic deletions might each have a one in one-billion chance of occurring, and that's not counting the calcium spike and division problem required to initiate parthenogenesis in the first place.

Is it possible for a virgin to have a child? Yes – but it would be a miracle, and would likely take an outside source of manipulation to begin the process and re-order the chromosome count.

Luke 1 (New International Version)
26In the sixth month, God sent the angel Gabriel to Nazareth, a town in Galilee, 27to a virgin pledged to be married to a man named Joseph, a descendant of David. The virgin's name was Mary. 28The angel went to her and said, "Greetings, you who are highly favored! The Lord is with you."
29Mary was greatly troubled at his words and wondered what kind of greeting this might be. 30But the angel said to her, "Do not be afraid, Mary, you have found favor with God. 31You will be with child and give birth to a son, and you are to give him the name Jesus. 32He will be great and will be called the Son of the Most High. The Lord God will give him the throne of his father David, 33and he will reign over the house of Jacob forever; his kingdom will never end."
34"How will this be," Mary asked the angel, "since I am a virgin?"
35The angel answered, "The Holy Spirit will come upon you, and the power of the Most High will overshadow you. So the holy one to be born will be called the Son of God.

References

J.B. Cibelli, R.P. Lanza and M.D. West, with C. Ezzell, 'The first human cloned embryo', Scientific American, Jan. 2002, http://sciam.com/explorations/2001/112401ezzell/index.html.

Raymond Bernard, The Mysteries of Human Reproduction, Mokelumne Hill, CA: Health Research, n.d., pp. 47-50, 56-63.

Ibid., pp. 3-10.

Ibid., pp. 11-28, 89-93.

Ibid., pp. 51-5, 117; F.H. Buzzacott and M.I. Wymore, Bi-sexual Man or Evolution of the Sexes, Health Research, 1966 (1912), pp. 32-4; Hilton Hotema, Secret of Regeneration, Health Research, 1963, ch. 204-205, 211.

Secret of Regeneration, ch. 208-210, 234; Gray's Anatomy, http://www.bartleby.com/107.

Peter Tompkins and Christopher Bird, The Secret Life of Plants, New York: Harper & Row, 1973, pp. 54-5, 197-9; R. VanWijk, 'Bio-photons and bio-communication', Journal of Scientific Exploration, vol. 15, pp. 183-97, 2001.

The Mysteries of Human Reproduction, pp. 42, 109.

Ibid., pp. 118-9.

Polygamy

One of the most difficult distinctions to make is the one between social and religious pressures. This became quiet apparent during a trip to Argentina. The plan was to go in with a team and build a church for a certain Pentecostal denomination. I had listened to church teaching and dogma for a couple of years. Some things seemed reasonable. Many did not, but at least the rules were applied across the board with equal rigidity to all. At least that is what I assumed before the aircraft landed.

After driving to the outskirts of Buenos Aires and into the countryside we arrived at the church. Services were being held in a large tent. There we met the church leaders.

In the U.S. version of the church, we were taught that no divorced person could hold a high church office. Certainly no remarried person could ascend to the throne of the pulpit. Now we were building a church so that a large congregation and several pastors could hold services in a brick building. Upon getting to know the pastors it became obvious that they were working under a different set of rules from their North American counterparts. Most of the congregation and all of the pastors were married but none were living with their wives. All were living with a mistress. Most had been with a paramour many years and had children within the second relationship.

For more than a half century Argentina had been under control of very conservative Catholic leaders. Many rules of the church had become law. Divorce was illegal in Argentina at that time. Social pressures had compelled the people to marry young and have children. If the couples separated they had no recourse but to continue their lives alone or in adultery.

Under these circumstances the church would have few people to man and expand the denomination in that country. So, does the church stand firm on its convictions or look the other way? In the end, denominations are organizations built on money and numbers. If you are in the U.S. and are a divorced person who is being discriminated against by a church, you should know that if you were the same person in the same denomination in another country you would be treated differently. The view is driven by social conventions.

The other side of the coin is equally amusing. During a trip to Trinidad and Tobago I was teaching a class in religious studies. Afterward a student approached to ask a few questions. He inquired into my church membership and education. When I mentioned the word "Baptist" he recoiled as if being shot.

Later I spoke to our host about the reaction. What I was told made me chuckle, but also heightened my concern about interactions between churches and cultures.

The Spiritual Baptist faith is based in Trinidad and Tobago. It has African influences but Spiritual Baptists consider themselves to be Christians. The Baptist faith was brought to Trinidad by the Merikins, former American slaves who were recruited by the British to fight for them during the Revolutionary War of 1812. Ex-slaves were settled in remote areas of Trinidad.

Whereas Voodoo is in Haiti and is a mixture of Catholicism and African pagan religions, in Trinidad and Tobago, the Spiritual Baptist faith is a mixture of Christian Protestantism and African Paganism and, even though they consider themselves to be Christian, they are related to Voodoo.

What does this have to do with polygamy? Hopefully, these little anecdotes will help us remember that when it comes to what is considered normal, we are dealing with two influences, which can be difficult to separate. The rules of society and those of religion collide and combine. If we wish to have a theological or religious debate we must seek to rightly divide the entangled cords of religion and culture.

While visiting India, missionaries met a man who had two wives. He had married a woman whom he loved and cared for. She was from a family of four and had a younger sister. Her parents died, leaving her younger sister to live on the streets.

The young woman would have been reduced to being a prostitute in order to survive. The older sister approached her husband, asking him if he would love and care for her younger sister, marry her, and save her from the nightmare awaiting her on the streets of Deli. The husband agreed and took the younger sister as his second wife. The two sisters live in harmony and safety for years, until the missionaries arrived.

After they managed to convert the husband the missionaries informed him it would be necessary to divorce one of his wives or go to hell for adultery. Thus, the Christian preachers assigned a helpless, loving, and innocent young woman to a life of hell as a street prostitute. She was found dead, having been raped, beaten, and stabbed.

The story is true and illustrates the damage and pain unlearned and narrow religious minds can produce. What sense could it possibly make to demand the divorce and destruction of a loving family in exchange for a particular brand of Christianity? Polygamy is not a theological problem. It is a cultural one. Some Eastern cultures permit this state of marriage today. Most Western cultures do not openly embrace polygamy, however, there are several churches practicing it and many groups or subcultures live in households where polygamy is practiced between consenting adults. Church members protect themselves from prosecution by taking one wife as a legal spouse and the other women as spiritual wives, joined by a pastor but not in a civil union.

In mainstream America, we have our own issues. Many churches, such as the Church of Christ and other denominations will not allow any person to hold office if they have been remarried. However, in my little area of the conservative South, the majority of members have lived with someone before marring another. The vast majority had intercourse at least once before getting married to some other person.

The wake-up call is that in Bible times there was no certain or distinct ceremony that marked the official beginning of a marriage. Pagans had various rites, and Jews had theirs, but the actual marriage was marked with sexual intercourse. If you slept with someone, you were married. (But then C.O.C. people should know this since they claim their church is not a religion or a denomination because it has supposedly been the same since the beginning. Right – I think that church was founded in 1923.) Even today marriages may be annulled if intercourse has not taken place. Further, in the Catholic faith there are times when a marriage may be annulled if children are not born and certainly may be annulled if consummation has not taken place.

The point is that we overlook mountains of cultural norms, which violate biblical norms, and then exclude and embarrass good people who have done little if anything wrong. So we allow the man who had sex with a dozen women, but did not marry until he was fifty, to lead the church because he has been married only once by cultural standards, but we rip a pastor out of the pulpit because his wife left him and he chooses not to die alone. Brilliant!

Judaism and Christianity are Eastern religions. Both were born in the Middle East. We in the west have managed to paint Jesus as a blue-eyed, brown-haired, thin man, when it is far more likely Jesus was a short, stocky, black-haired, brown-eyed individual. We placed our cultural imprint on how Jesus looked. We have done the same with marriage, stripping away what the Bible says and replacing it with our own societal norms. This is not the greater sin. The real error is to read and interpret the scriptures in this prejudiced light and then to force the error on all others under our authority.

That God Himself has more than one wife, in a symbol or type, comes as a shock to most Bible believing western Christians.

In Ezekiel 23 the Lord speaks of the divided kingdom of Israel as two wives who had committed adultery.

Ezekiel 23 (NIV)
Two Adulterous Sisters

1 The word of the LORD came to me: 2 "Son of man, there were two women, daughters of the same mother. 3 They became prostitutes in Egypt, engaging in prostitution from their youth. In that land their breasts were fondled and their virgin bosoms caressed. 4 The older was named Oholah, and her sister was Oholibah. They were mine and gave birth to sons and daughters. Oholah is Samaria, and Oholibah is Jerusalem.

5 "Oholah engaged in prostitution while she was still mine; and she lusted after her lovers, the Assyrians-warriors 6 clothed in blue, governors and commanders, all of them handsome young men, and mounted horsemen. 7 She gave herself as a prostitute to all the elite of the Assyrians and defiled herself with all the idols of everyone she lusted after. 8 She did not give up the prostitution she began in Egypt, when during her youth men slept with her, caressed her virgin bosom and poured out their lust upon her."

9 "Therefore I handed her over to her lovers, the Assyrians, for whom she lusted. 10 They stripped her naked, took away her sons and daughters and killed her with the sword. She became a byword among women, and punishment was inflicted on her.

11 "Her sister Oholibah saw this, yet in her lust and prostitution she was more depraved than her sister. 12 She too lusted after the Assyrians—governors and commanders, warriors in full dress, mounted horsemen, all handsome young men. 13 I saw that she too defiled herself; both of them went the same way." 14 "But she carried her prostitution still further. She saw men portrayed on a wall, figures of Chaldeans portrayed in red, 15 with belts around their waists and flowing turbans on their heads; all of them looked like Babylonian chariot officers, natives of Chaldea. 16 As soon as she saw them, she lusted after them and sent messengers to them in Chaldea. 17 Then the Babylonians came to her, to the bed of love, and in their lust they defiled her. After she had been defiled by them, she turned away from them in disgust. 18 When she carried on her prostitution openly and exposed her nakedness, I turned away from her in disgust, just as I had turned away from her sister. 19 Yet she became more and more

promiscuous as she recalled the days of her youth, when she was a prostitute in Egypt. 20 There she lusted after her lovers, whose genitals were like those of donkeys and whose emission was like that of horses. 21 So you longed for the lewdness of your youth, when in Egypt your bosom was caressed and your young breasts fondled. 22 "Therefore, Oholibah, this is what the Sovereign LORD says: I will stir up your lovers against you, those you turned away from in disgust, and I will bring them against you from every side- 23 the Babylonians and all the Chaldeans, the men of Pekod and Shoa and Koa, and all the Assyrians with them, handsome young men, all of them governors and commanders, chariot officers and men of high rank, all mounted on horses. 24 They will come against you with weapons, chariots and wagons and with a throng of people; they will take up positions against you on every side with large and small shields and with helmets. I will turn you over to them for punishment, and they will punish you according to their standards. 25 I will direct my jealous anger against you, and they will deal with you in fury. They will cut off your noses and your ears, and those of you who are left will fall by the sword. They will take away your sons and daughters, and those of you who are left will be consumed by fire. 26 They will also strip you of your clothes and take your fine jewelry. 27 So I will put a stop to the lewdness and prostitution you began in Egypt. You will not look on these things with longing or remember Egypt anymore.

28 "For this is what the Sovereign LORD says: I am about to hand you over to those you hate, to those you turned away from in disgust. 29 They will deal with you in hatred and take away everything you have worked for. They will leave you naked and bare, and the shame of your prostitution will be exposed. Your lewdness and promiscuity 30 have brought this upon you, because you lusted after the nations and defiled yourself with their idols. 31 You have gone the way of your sister; so I will put her cup into your hand. 32 "This is what the Sovereign LORD says: "You will drink your sister's cup, a cup large and deep; it will bring scorn and derision, for it holds so

much. 33 You will be filled with drunkenness and sorrow, the cup of ruin and desolation, the cup of your sister Samaria. 34 You will drink it and drain it dry; you will dash it to pieces and tear your breasts. I have spoken, declares the Sovereign LORD. 35 "Therefore this is what the Sovereign LORD says: Since you have forgotten me and thrust me behind your back, you must bear the consequences of your lewdness and prostitution." 36 The LORD said to me: "Son of man, will you judge Oholah and Oholibah? Then confront them with their detestable practices, 37 for they have committed adultery and blood is on their hands. They committed adultery with their idols; they even sacrificed their children, whom they bore to me, as food for them. 38 They have also done this to me: At that same time they defiled my sanctuary and desecrated my Sabbaths. 39 On the very day they sacrificed their children to their idols, they entered my sanctuary and desecrated it. That is what they did in my house. 40 "They even sent messengers for men who came from far away, and when they arrived you bathed yourself for them, painted your eyes and put on your jewelry. 41 You sat on an elegant couch, with a table spread before it on which you had placed the incense and oil that belonged to me. 42 "The noise of a carefree crowd was around her; Sabeans were brought from the desert along with men from the rabble, and they put bracelets on the arms of the woman and her sister and beautiful crowns on their heads. 43 Then I said about the one worn out by adultery, 'Now let them use her as a prostitute, for that is all she is.' 44 And they slept with her. As men sleep with a prostitute, so they slept with those lewd women, Oholah and Oholibah. 45 But righteous men will sentence them to the punishment of women who commit adultery and shed blood, because they are adulterous and blood is on their hands. 46 "This is what the Sovereign LORD says: Bring a mob against them and give them over to terror and plunder. 47 The mob will stone them and cut them down with their swords; they will kill their sons and daughters and burn down their houses. 48 "So I will put an end to lewdness in the land, that all women may take warning and not imitate you. 49 You will suffer the penalty for your lewdness and bear the consequences of your sins of idolatry. Then you will know that I am the Sovereign LORD."

Jeremiah 2
Israel Forsakes God
1 The word of the LORD came to me: 2 "Go and proclaim in the hearing of Jerusalem: " 'I remember the devotion of your youth, how as a bride you loved me and followed me through the desert, through a land not sown.
3 Israel was holy to the LORD, the firstfruits of his harvest; all who devoured her were held guilty, and disaster overtook them,' declares the LORD.
4 Hear the word of the LORD, O house of Jacob, all you clans of the house of Israel. 5 This is what the LORD says: "What fault did your fathers find in me, that they strayed so far from me? They followed worthless idols and became worthless themselves. "

Jeremiah 3
1 "If a man divorces his wife and she leaves him and marries another man, should he return to her again? Would not the land be completely defiled? But you have lived as a prostitute with many lovers — would you now return to me?" declares the LORD. 6 During the reign of King Josiah, the LORD said to me, "Have you seen what faithless Israel has done? She has gone up on every high hill and under every spreading tree and has committed adultery there. 7 I thought that after she had done all this she would return to me but she did not, and her unfaithful sister Judah saw it. 8 I gave faithless Israel her certificate of divorce and sent her away because of all her adulteries. Yet I saw that her unfaithful sister Judah had no fear; she also went out and committed adultery. 9 Because Israel's immorality mattered so little to her, she defiled the land and committed adultery with stone and wood. 10 In spite of all this, her unfaithful sister Judah did not return to me with all

her heart, but only in pretense," declares the LORD. 11 The LORD said to me, "Faithless Israel is more righteous than unfaithful Judah. 12 Go, proclaim this message toward the north: " 'Return, faithless Israel,' declares the LORD, 'I will frown on you no longer, for I am merciful,' declares the LORD, 'I will not be angry forever. 13 Only acknowledge your guilt — you have rebelled against the LORD your God, you have scattered your favors to foreign gods under every spreading tree, and have not obeyed me,' " declares the LORD. 14 "Return, faithless people," declares the LORD, "for I am your husband. I will choose you — one from a town and two from a clan — and bring you to Zion. 15 Then I will give you shepherds after my own heart, who will lead you with knowledge and understanding. 16 In those days, when your numbers have increased greatly in the land," declares the LORD, "men will no longer say, 'The ark of the covenant of the LORD.' It will never enter their minds or be remembered; it will not be missed, nor will another one be made. 17 At that time they will call Jerusalem The Throne of the LORD, and all nations will gather in Jerusalem to honor the name of the LORD. No longer will they follow the stubbornness of their evil hearts. 18 In those days the house of Judah will join the house of Israel, and together they will come from a northern land to the land I gave your forefathers as an inheritance.

Jer 31: 31 "The time is coming," declares the LORD, "when I will make a new covenant with the house of Israel and with the house of Judah. 32 It will not be like the covenant I made with their forefathers when I took them by the hand to lead them out of Egypt, because they broke my covenant, though I was a husband to them," declares the LORD.

Do we really believe God actually married these two whoring sisters? The two nations were His spiritual wives in type and shadow and in the metaphor of religious language. The metaphor was chosen because people of the time could relate to it easily. No one will dispute that in Old Testament times most leaders, kings, and men who could financially afford it had more than one wife.

According to the Torah or Old Testament, the law compelled Polygamy among God's people. It is interesting that in scripture there is a compulsion to have more than one wife. The command was not a specific command to have plural wives but polygamy had to occur as a consequence of obedience to another command, that a man was to raise up an heir for a dead relative. Keep in mind that this is God's command, through his prophet Moses, the proper name for the Law being "the Law of God, given to Moses." (Ezra 7:6, Nehemiah 10:29 & 2nd Chronicles 34:14) The law is described in Deuteronomy 25:5 (NASB) and says, when brothers live together and one of them dies and has no son, the wife of the deceased shall not be married outside the family to a strange man. Her husband's brother shall go in to her and take her to himself as wife and perform the duty of a husband's brother to her. It shall be that the firstborn whom she bears shall assume the name of his dead brother, so that his name will not be blotted out from Israel.

Deuteronomy 25:7 - 10 "But if the man does not desire to take his brother's wife, then his brother's wife shall go up to the gate to the elders and say, 'My husband's brother refuses to establish a name for his brother in Israel; he is not willing to perform the duty of a husband's brother to me.' Then the elders of his city shall summon him and speak to him. And if he persists and says, 'I do not desire to take her'."

1 Samuel 25:39 Then David sent word to Abigail, asking her to become his wife. 40 His servants went to Carmel and said to Abigail, "David has sent us to you to take you to become his wife." 41 She bowed down with her face to the ground and said, "Here is your maidservant, ready to serve you and wash the feet of my master's servants." 42 Abigail quickly got on a donkey and, attended by her five maids, went with David's messengers and became his wife. 43 David had also married

Ahinoam of Jezreel, and they both were his wives. 44 But Saul had given his daughter Michal, David's wife, to Paltiel son of Laish, who was from Gallim.

1 Chronicles 4:5 Ashhur the father of Tekoa had two wives, Helah and Naarah.

2 Chronicles 11:22 Rehoboam appointed Abijah son of Maacah to be the chief prince among his brothers, in order to make him king. 23 He acted wisely, dispersing some of his sons throughout the districts of Judah and Benjamin, and to all the fortified cities. He gave them abundant provisions and took many wives for them.

Here we will resist going further, for to list all of the times multiple wives were recorded in the Old Testament would take up too much of this book.

Now we know that the Old Testament permitted polygamy and under certain circumstances, compels a man to take his brother's wife, if he should die, in order to continue his inheritance. Where most casual Bible readers balk is in connecting polygamy to the New Testament. This is actually very simple and direct. Look at the NIV translation of the following verses.

1 Timothy 3

1 Here is a trustworthy saying: If anyone sets his heart on being an overseer, he desires a noble task. 2 Now the overseer must be above reproach, the husband of but one wife, temperate, self-controlled, respectable, hospitable, able to teach, 3 not given to drunkenness, not violent but gentle, not quarrelsome, not a lover of money. 4 He must manage his own family well and see that his children obey him with proper respect. 5 (If anyone does not know how to manage his own family, how can he take care of God's church?) 6 He must not be a recent convert, or he may become conceited and fall under the same judgment as the devil. 7 He must also have a good reputation with outsiders, so that he will not fall into disgrace and into the devil's trap. 8 Deacons, likewise, are to be men worthy of respect, sincere, not indulging in much wine, and not

pursuing dishonest gain. 9 They must keep hold of the deep truths of the faith with a clear conscience. 10 They must first be tested; and then if there is nothing against them, let them serve as deacons. 11 In the same way, their wives are to be women worthy of respect, not malicious talkers but temperate and trustworthy in everything.

12 A deacon must be the husband of but one wife and must manage his children and his household well. 13 Those who have served well gain an excellent standing and great assurance in their faith in Christ Jesus.

For centuries, through the vague wording of the KJV Bible, this passage was used by some denominations to exclude all divorced men and every woman from the clergy. It is true that the phrase can be interpreted, "A bishop must be a one-woman man." Some view the verse as a test for fidelity, pointing out that polygamy was not the norm in the Greco-Roman world. This is true but there was a great mixing of cultures and increasing pagan and foreign influences being transmitted from various sources. The Greco-Roman world was not the universe. There were other cultures to consider. Those in the Middle East, where Christ was born and was crucified, had their own customs.

First Timothy was written after the apostle Paul had been imprisoned in Rome for the first time. After he was released, he wrote this letter to Timothy, who by this time had served as a son in the gospel with the apostle for several years. He was probably in his late twenties or early thirties, and the apostle had sent him to Ephesus, the great commercial and pleasure resort on the shores of the Mediterranean in Asia Minor. In this great crossroad and cultural melting pot all cultures would be encountered and addressed.

Paul, being well educated and well traveled, would have known the farther East one traveled the more polygamy would be encountered. Many Bedouins, Arab tribes, and nomadic people practice polygamy still today. The meaning is made clear in the NIV Bible. In the verses above we see the admonition to limit one's household to a single wife if you wish to serve the church. It is not that having more than one wife was a sin.

Nowhere are we told that polygamy is now wrong. We are only told that having more than one wife is not the optimum condition if one is to serve the church. The reason seems axiomatic. One cannot take the time and energy needed to keep up more than one household well and also serve the widows and orphans along with the church community. Jesus, living in a society permitting polygamy, never addressed it as a problem. Why do we? It is not because of our religion, but how we chose to interpret it through the blinders of our society.

Polygamy in Judaism

Polygamy existed among the Israelites before the time of Moses, who continued the institution without imposing any limit on the number of marriages a Hebrew husband could enter into.

The Jewish Encyclopedia states, "While there is no evidence of a polyandrous state in primitive Jewish society, polygamy seems to have been a well-established institution, dating from ancient times and extending to comparatively modern days."

In later times, the Talmud, the body of Jewish civil and ceremonial law and legend comprising the Mishnah and the Gemara, restricted the number by the ability of the husband to maintain the wives properly. Some rabbis, however, counseled that a man should not take more than four wives. Polygamy was prohibited in Judaism by the rabbis, not God. Rabbi Gershom ben Judah is credited by forbidding polygamy in the 11th century outlawing it for a 1,000 years, a time frame that ended in 1987. His proclamation was directed to the Eastern European Jews, the Ashkanazi. The Mediterranean or Sephardic Jews continued to practice polygamy, believing the Rabbi did not have the authority to change divine order.

Will Durant, the author of "The Story of Civilization" states; "polygamy was practiced by rich Jews in Islamic lands, but was rare among the Jews of Christendom." According to Joseph Ginat, professor of social and culture anthropology at the University of Haifa, polygamy is common and growing among the 180,000 Bedouin of Israel. Polygamy is becoming more common among Mediterranean Jews living in Yemen, where rabbis permit Jews to marry up to four wives. In modern Israel, where a wife cannot bear children or is mentally ill, the rabbis give a husband the right to marry a second woman without divorcing his first wife. This is in accordance with Jewish custom and provides the husband with needed support while he takes care of the first wife. They did not make provisions for polyandry if the husband were ill or unfit.

While it could be argued, in a purely esoteric view, that God made one man and one women as the perfect model of marriage, before man was ejected from the Garden of Eden, either literally or metaphorically, he began killing his fellow man. In a land of war and death the number of men decreased to the point of societal collapse. Thus, two separate systems emerged. Polygamy and a religious welfare system served to provide for the widows and orphans.

The arrangement for widows and orphans functioned, as ours does today, mostly for the lower economic class. Jewish women could and did inherit land, property, and money. An eldest female or only child could stand to inherit the estate of a parent. Middle and upper class Jewish women were powerful and independent forces in families and communities. Wealthy women were the ones funding the ministry of Jesus. Women could be upwardly mobile, but for those women and children left, bereft and penniless, with no resources or hope of resources, the system did not supply any way to escape living in subsistence, again, much like our dole of today.

People desire a home and hearth of their own. No one wishes to live, not knowing where they will sleep or raise their child. Marriage was the only way for women to obtain consistent food, shelter, clothing, and a chance for their children to inherit position or land. Polygamy, under the social conditions of class and poverty, was the better path for women.

The church father Justin Martyr mentions that in his time Jewish men were permitted to have four or five wives.

History records the story of Babatha, who was a Jewish woman and a second wife. The record is interesting since it reveals much about the status of middle and upper class women of the time.

In 1960, archeologist Yigael Yadin discovered a leather pouch containing personal documents of a woman in a cave, which came to be known as the Cave of Letters, located near the Dead Sea. The documents found include legal contracts concerning marriage, property transfers, and guardianship, ranging in dates from 96 to 134 AD. The documents depicted a vivid picture of life for a middle class to upper class Jewish woman during that time.

Babatha was born in approximately 104 CE in Maoza. She lived in the port town of Maoza in what is now modern day Jordan at beginning of the 2nd century CE. She was likely the only child or eldest daughter since she inherited her father's date palm orchard upon her parents' deaths.

By 124 CE, she had been married and widowed with a young son, Jesus. The name, Jesus, was a very common name and more than one with that name was crucified. There was even more than one claiming to be the anointed one. Her son was not one of those. As far as we know he was an average child. By 125 CE Babatha was remarried to Judah, owner of three date palm orchards in the town of Ein Gedi (an oasis and town situated west of the Dead Sea). Judah already had a wife. Judah's other wife had a teenage daughter. It is uncertain whether Babatha lived in the same home as the first wife or if Judah traveled between two separate households, as polygamy was still allowed in the Jewish community.

The documents found in leather pouch offer information and insight concerning this marriage and her status in the relationship. In their marriage contract, Judah's debts become part of her liability, indicating a financial equality. In other words, Babatha was responsible for paying off her husband's debts if he were to die, become injured, or for some other reason could not pay.

In 128 CE, a legal document shows that Judah took a loan without interest from Babatha, showing that she had control of her own money despite the union. Now Judah was financially indebted to Babatha. Upon Judah's death in 130 CE, she seized his estates in Ein Gedi as a guarantee for payment against his debts, which she had covered through her loan to him, as stated in the marriage contract.

Another document of importance concerned the guardianship of Babatha's son. In 125 CE, Babatha brought a lawsuit to court against the appointed guardians of her orphaned son, citing their insufficient disbursement of funds. The document contains Babatha's petition that full guardianship responsibility of her son and his property be transferred to her control.

This is amazing insight into the range and depth of the place of Jewish women within polygamist marriages in the Jewish community at the time of the second century. We can assume it reflects marriage in general in that socio-economic class. But Jewish polygamy began to clash with Roman monogamy at the time of the early church and was eventually pushed out by way of newly established civil laws and social pressure.

When the Christian Church came into being, polygamy was still practiced by the Jews. We find few direct references to it in the New Testament. From this some have inferred that occurrences must have decreased, and that the Jewish people had become monogamous, but the conclusion appears to be unwarranted and skewed by incorrect interpretation. Josephus, in two places in his writings, speaks of polygamy as a recognized institution. Justin Martyr makes it a matter of reproach to Trypho that the Jewish teachers permitted a man to have several wives. Indeed when in 212 A.D. the "lex Antoniana de civitate" gave the rights of Roman Citizenship to great numbers of Jews, it was found necessary to tolerate polygamy among them, even though it was against Roman law for a citizen to have more than one wife. In 285 A.D. a constitution of Diocletian and Maximian forbade polygamy to all subjects of the empire without exception. But with the Jews, at least, the enactment failed and in 393 A.D. a special law was issued by Theodosius to compel the Jews to relinquish this national custom, but they did not conform.

Polygamy was not banned in the Jewish community until about 1000CE by Rabbi Gershom, a leading rabbi born in France. This, it was said, was to avoid persecution of the Jews arising from their variance from the social and legal norms in Europe at the time. Anti-Semitism was running unchecked and the good Rabbi was trying to protect his people by forcing them to fit in to the society and become less identifiable as "different" or "Jewish."

Modern practice
In the modern day, Rabbinic Judaism has essentially outlawed polygamy. Ashkenazi Jews have followed Rabbenu Gershom's ban since the 11th century. Some Sephardi and Mizrahi Jews (particularly those from Yemen and Iran)

continue the practice of polygamy in those countries where it is legal.

Israel has made new polygamist marriages illegal. Provisions were instituted to allow for existing polygamous families emigrating from countries where the practice was legal. Furthermore, former chief rabbi Ovadia Yosef and Israeli columnist Greer Fay Cashman have come out in favor of legalizing polygamy and the practice of pilegesh (concubine).

Among Karaite Jews, who do not adhere to Rabbinic interpretations of the Torah, polygamy is almost non-existent today. Like other Jews, Karaites interpret Leviticus 18:18 to mean that a man can only take a second wife if his first wife gives her consent (Keter Torah on Leviticus, pp. 96–97) and Karaites interpret Exodus 21:10 to mean that a man can only take a second wife if he is capable of maintaining the same level of marital duties due to his first wife. The marital duties are food, clothing, and sexual gratification. Because of these biblical limitations and because most countries outlaw it, polygamy is considered highly impractical, and there are only a few known cases of it among Karaite Jews today.

Christianity
The New Testament does not specifically address the morality of polygamy. 1 Timothy, however, states that certain Church leaders should have but one wife: "A bishop then must be blameless, the husband of one wife, vigilant, sober, of good behavior, given to hospitality, apt to teach" (chapter 3, verse 2; see also verse 12 regarding deacons having only one wife). Similar counsel is repeated in the first chapter of Titus. The admonition to have one wife is not, as some would have us believe, an edict against divorce, but an observation that a man married to multiple wives would not have time or resources to minister to members of a church and his extended family.

In modern times a minority of Roman Catholic theologians have argued that polygamy, though not ideal, can be a legitimate form of Christian marriage in certain regions, in particular Africa.

Periodically, Christian reform movements that have aimed at rebuilding Christian doctrine based on the Bible alone (sola scriptura) have at least temporarily accepted polygamy as a Biblical practice. For example, during the Protestant Reformation, in a document referred to simply as "Der Beichtrat" (or "The Confessional Advice"), Martin Luther granted the Landgrave Philip of Hesse, who, for many years, had been living "constantly in a state of adultery and fornication," a dispensation to take a second wife. The double marriage was to be done in secret however, to avoid public scandal. Some fifteen years earlier, in a letter to the Saxon Chancellor Gregor Bruck, Luther stated that he could not "forbid a person to marry several wives, for it does not contradict Scripture." ("Ego sane fateor, me non posse prohibere, si quis plures velit uxores ducere, nec repugnat sacris literis.")

"On February 14, 1650, the parliament at Nürnberg decreed that, because so many men were killed during the Thirty Years' War, the churches for the following ten years could not admit any man under the age of 60 into a monastery. Priests and ministers not bound by any monastery were allowed to marry. Lastly, the decree stated that every man was allowed to marry up to ten women. The men were admonished to behave honorably, provide for their wives properly, and prevent animosity among them."

In Sub-Saharan Africa, there has often been a tension between the Christian churches' insistence on monogamy and traditional polygamy. In recent times there have been moves for accommodation; in other instances, churches have resisted such moves strongly. African Independent Churches have sometimes referred to those parts of the Old Testament, which describe polygamy in defending the practice.

Latter Day Saint movement

The history of Mormon polygamy began with Joseph Smith, Jr. receiving a revelation on July 17, 1831 that some Mormon men who were specifically commanded to do so would practice "plural marriage." This was later published in the Doctrine and Covenants of the LDS Church).

Despite Smith's revelation, the 1835 edition of the 101st Section of the Doctrine and Covenants, written after the doctrine of plural marriage began to be practiced, publicly condemned polygamy. In 1850 this scripture was used by John Taylor to quiet rumors in Liverpool, England of Mormon polygamy.

Polygamy was made illegal in the state of Illinois during the 1839–44 Nauvoo era when several top Mormon leaders, including Smith, Brigham Young and Heber C. Kimball, took plural wives. Mormon elders who publicly taught that all men were commanded to enter plural marriage were subject to harsh discipline. On June 7, 1844 the Nauvoo Expositor criticized Smith for plural marriage. After Joseph Smith's murder by a mob on June 27, 1844, the main body of Mormons left Nauvoo and followed Brigham Young to Utah where the practice of plural marriage continued.

The waffling of the church on the subject of polygamy, or as they term it, plural marriage, seems to be centered around the political and social pressures against polygamy in conservative America. The explanation of the modern LDS church regarding the purpose of polygamy is to point to the persecution of male members and thus the decline of the number of men in the newly formed LDS Church. The writings of Joseph Smith do not seem to bear this out. The first or primary reason for the doctrine was based on the effort to re-establish pure and historical biblical doctrine, seeing as how polygamy was never spoken against in the New Testament. However, it did not decrease Smith's urgency to establish the doctrine. Some argue this was a divine unction while others are skeptical since he had been caught in affairs several times.

In 1852 Brigham Young, the second president of the LDS Church publicly acknowledged the practice of plural marriage through a sermon he gave. Additional sermons by top Mormon leaders on the virtues of polygamy followed. Controversy followed when polygamy became a social cause, writers began to publish works condemning polygamy. The key plank of the 1856 Republican Party platform was "to prohibit in the territories those twin relics of barbarism, polygamy and slavery". In 1862, Congress issued the Morill Anti-Bigamy act, which clarified that the practice of polygamy was illegal in all US territories. The LDS Church believed that their religiously-based practice of plural marriage (polygamy/polygyny) was protected by the United States Constitution. However, the 1878 Supreme Court voted in unison in the case of Reynolds v. United States and declared that polygamy was not protected by the Constitution. This was based on the longstanding legal principle that "laws are made for the government of actions, and while they cannot interfere with mere religious belief and opinions, they may with practices."

Anti-polygamy legislation in the U.S. led some Mormons to immigrate to Canada and Mexico. In 1890, LDS Church president Wilford Woodruff issued a public declaration announcing that the LDS Church had discontinued new plural marriages. The banning of an action by the authorities does not mean the populace will follow. The Smoot Hearing in 1904, documented that the LDS Church members continued practicing polygamy. The uprising from Congress and non-Mormons spurred the LDS Church to issue another Manifesto claiming that it had ceased performing new plural marriages.

In an act of self-preservation in 1910 the LDS Church began excommunicating those who entered into, or performed, new plural marriages. Even so, many plural husbands and wives continued to cohabit until their deaths. The last documented mainstream LDS polygamous marriage was the grandfather of current LDS apostle, Edward Eyring, and two distant cousins of Mitt Romney.

Fundamentalist Mormonism

Enforcement of the 1890 Manifesto caused various groups to leave the LDS Church. These groups believed polygamy was biblical and religiously correct and they were determined to continue the institution. Polygamy among these groups persists today in Utah and neighboring states as well as in Canada.

Polygamist churches of Mormon origin are often referred to as "Mormon fundamentalist" or Fundamentalist Latter Day Saints (FLDS). These churches are offshoots of the mainline Mormon church, though the LDS Church has disowned them.

The schism occurred because the revelation of Joseph Smith regarding plural marriage, or polygamy was rescinded by the church in order to become compliant with U.S. laws and allow Utah to become a state. At that time the group within the church broke away, maintaining that the law of God, as spoken through Smith, should be maintained over that of any government.

The religious basis of plural marriage came through a revelation to Joseph Smith that was written down in 1843, but it was apparently received by Smith and discussed with the church leaders prior to becoming doctrine. The commandment was the recreation of the marital order of the patriarchs of the Old Testament. Smith realized plural marriage, or polygyny, had never been stopped or changed in the Old or New

Testaments. Thus they viewed plural marriage as sacred, giving it the title of "celestial marriage."

Fundamentalists cite the revelation of Joseph Smith on polygamy as a foundation but they also cite the 1886 revelation to John Taylor, the third president of the LDS Church, as the basis for their authority to continue the practice of plural marriage.

The revelation of John Taylor was written on Monday, 27 September 1886. It reads:

September 27, 1886

My son John: You have asked me concerning the New and Everlasting Covenant and how far it is binding upon my people.

Thus saith the Lord All commandments that I give must be obeyed by those calling themselves by my name unless they are revoked by me or by my authority and how can I revoke an everlasting covenant.

For I the Lord am everlasting and my covenants cannot be abrogated nor done away with; but they stand forever.

Have I not given my word in great plainness on this subject?

Yet have not great numbers of my people been negligent in the observance of my law and the keeping of my commandment, and yet have I borne with them these many years and this because of their weakness because of the perilous times. And furthermore it is more pleasing to me that men should use their free agency in regard to these matters.

Nevertheless I the Lord do not change and my word and my covenants and my law do not.

And as I have heretofore said by my servant Joseph all those who would enter into my glory must and shall obey my law.

And have I not commanded men that if they were Abraham's seed and would enter into my glory they must do the works of Abraham.

I have not revoked this law nor will I for it is everlasting and those who will enter into my glory must obey the conditions thereof, even so Amen.

A fundamentalist author summed up the FLDS position: "In the revelation to John Taylor, dated September 27, 1886, the Lord said that he had not, could not and would not revoke the Law of Abraham which is Plural Marriage."

Celibacy

1 Timothy 4 (New International Version)
1 The Spirit clearly says that in later times some will abandon the faith and follow deceiving spirits and things taught by demons. 2 Such teachings come through hypocritical liars, whose consciences have been seared as with a hot iron. 3 They forbid people to marry and order them to abstain from certain foods, which God created to be received with thanksgiving by those who believe and who know the truth. 4 For everything God created is good, and nothing is to be rejected if it is received with thanksgiving, 5 because it is consecrated by the word of God and prayer.

Matthew 8 (New International Version)
14 When Jesus came into Peter's house, he saw Peter's mother-in-law lying in bed with a fever. 15 He touched her hand and the fever left her, and she got up and began to wait on him.

So, if the Catholic Church is correct and Jesus did tap Peter for the job of running the church or carrying forth the faith after He was killed, then Jesus designated Peter, a married man, to be the first pope. We will forgo the discussion of who was actually running the show after the death of Jesus. It was, by the way, James who was the heir apparent, and not Peter. But we will leave that for another day.

Priests had married in Judaism. The priesthood itself was usually a hereditary profession, and it would seem that Christ accepted this part of the tradition in his choice of Peter.

To be fair, in that day and time, Paul believed that due to the need of travel and the likelihood of martyrdom it was best if those spreading the Gospel didn't have a family. Paul did go on to mandate that bishops, elders and deacons be only "the husband of one wife." This was because polygamy among all ranks of the clergy persisted. Supporting a large family did not leave time or energy for the ministry. By the third century bishops were required to be monogamous.

There were certain pressures within the early church. Some were political and driven out of greed. Some were religious in nature.

Of the religious pressures were the teachings of the Gnostic Christians, which caused great focus on the evils of the flesh. Spirit and the material world were at odds in their theology. Thus, the idea was that what starved the flesh of its natural desires must also feed the spirit. Neoplatonism was alive and well, and a major influence in the life and beliefs of Augustine.

Neoplatonism was the dominant philosophy of the ancient pagan world from the time of Plotinus in the mid-third century A.D., to the closing of the schools of philosophy at Athens by the Christian emperor Justinian in A.D. 529. It incorporated the best of Aristotle, Pythagoras, Plato, and the Stoics, so as to make a synthesis of the collected wisdom of the ancient world. Neoplatonism was not only a philosophy; it also met a religious need by showing how the individual soul might reach God. Thus it presented with traditional Greek rationalism a scheme of salvation comparable with those schemes offered by Christianity and the Mystery religions. It also began to influence Christian thinkers, notably Augustine.

Before receiving the final push from Augustine, the change in the church's views on marriage began with the Council of Elvira in Spain in about 306 A.D., which prohibited bishops, deacons and priests from marrying.

Already in 305 A.D., before the Church's liberation under Constantine, the Council of Elvira in Spain passed the following decree: "That bishops, priests and deacons, and in general all the clergy, who are specially employed in the service of the altar, abstain from conjugal intercourse. Let those who persist be degraded from the ranks of the clergy" (Can. 33). And by the end of the fourth century, the Second Council of Carthage in Africa declared, "What the apostles taught in the early Church preserved, let us too observe." Celibacy, I insist, is not a post factum afterthought of the Church. It is an anti factum, reality, practiced by the Church and wanted by those who wanted to be Christ's priests."

But this was influenced only partially by pagan philosophies. A political storm of greed was building.

Shortly after The Council of Elvira, the early church fathers began to stigmatize sex as sinful in their writings. St. Ambrose (340-397 A.D.) wrote, "The ministerial office must be kept pure and unspoiled and must not be defiled by coitus," and the former libertine, and some would argue – former sex addict, St. Augustine (354-430 A.D.) even went so far as to consider an erect penis a sign of man's insubordination.

Let us remember, Augustine was fighting his own demons in this arena. Certainly there will be times, if one is an addict, that total abstinence is easier than moderation, but for those who have normal drives, the suppression of normal human drives usually gives way to corruption and re-direction of those drives. It may be from this simple statement that pedophilia and homosexuality within the priesthood arises.

Augustine thought, "spontaneous sexual desire is…the clearest evidence of the effects of original sin."

Augustine concluded that human government, (and this certainly included the church,) were an indispensable defense against the forces of sin. This, we assume, was because government of any sort sets limitations, rules, and punishments for actions it deems unsuitable. But this is nothing more than replacing the Old Testament law with man's law. The latter will work no better than the first. It is a change of heart that is needed, not a change of taskmasters.

In every instance Augustine talks about sex, he implies that it was wrong or at least the reasons for having sex were wrong. However, it seems that he takes this belief a little too far. Maybe this stemmed from his studying with the Manichees and their belief that the body was the cause of evil. Maybe it stemmed from his interpretation of Catholicism and the Bible. Truly, Augustine is the first writer to show a change from a liberal view of sex to an extremely conservative view of sex and to argue the benefits that he believed it brought him. Even though his book is clearly Catholic propaganda, he shows himself as a lost sheep found, a reformed sinner; and that is a powerful message for many people. Like any good fundamental preacher of any faith, he knew that if something were good for his addictive personality it must be good for and forced upon all people. In short, Augustine believed the devil was not in the details, but lived in his pants. The equation of sin with sex is evident throughout Augustine's writing.

"I intend to remind myself of my past foulnesses and carnal corruptions, not because I love them but so that I may love you, my God" (Augustine, 24).

From his birth in a North African town, Augustine knew the religious differences overwhelming the Roman Empire: his father was a pagan who honored the old Punic gods; his mother was a zealous Christian. But the adolescent Augustine was consumed with sex and high living, and not with God.

At age 17, Augustine set off to school in Carthage in North Africa. There the underachiever became enraptured with his studies and started to make a name for himself. He immersed himself in the writings of Cicero and Manichaean philosophers and rejected his mother's religion.

His studies completed, Augustine returned to his home town of Thagaste to teach rhetoric Manichaeism. The philosophy was based on the teachings of the Persian, Mani, and was a dualist corruption of Christianity. It taught that the world of light and the world of darkness constantly war with each other, catching most of humanity in the struggle. Along with the religion of Zoroastrianism, these two religions influenced the dualistic outlook of Christianity the most. Augustine tried to hide his views from his mother, Monica, but when she found out, she threw him out of the house.

Augustine moved to Rome and there he began attending the cathedral to hear preaching of Ambrose the bishop. He kept attending because of Ambrose's preaching. He soon dropped his Manichaeism in favor of Neoplatonism, the philosophy of both Roman pagans and Milanese Christians.

His mother finally caught up with him and decided to find her son a proper wife. Augustine had a concubine he deeply loved, who had given him a son, but he would not marry her because it would have ruined him socially and politically.

Some believe that the conjunction of the emotional strain of grief in abandoning his lover along with the shift in philosophies left Augustine in a mode of self-loathing, which centered on his sexuality, which he saw as the blame for his pain. He attempted to renounce sex. For years he had sought to overcome his fleshly passions and nothing seemed to help. Becoming hypersensitive regarding the least of transgressions, he would reflect even on prepubescent tricks. Writing about the pear stealing of his youth, he reflected, "Our real pleasure consisted in doing something that was forbidden. The evil in me was foul, but I loved it." The self-loathing reformed sex addict over-compensated and became unstable, yet, the writings of Augustine would shape the church in time to come.

With the advent of the Dark Ages around 500, the upheavals in society saw a decline in clerical discipline and with it, a return to marriage and even the keeping of concubines by priests. During this time, the wealth of the church was also increasing, a development not lost on Rome. Many priests were leaving church lands to their heirs, and others handed down land of their own through primogeniture.

Now, this may not have been such a big deal if it weren't for the fact that priests were becoming wealthy. A priest or bishop would inform someone with land and means that they might burn in hell for their actions (or inactions). But perhaps they could be absolved if they left their lands to the Church. The duke or earl or baron would sign over a portion of his land or funds to the cleric in return for Salvation.

The bishops were leaving these acquisitions to their heirs. So the families of the bishops were becoming wealthy and powerful, the heads of State were losing revenues from taxes and the church was losing an opportunity to become the richest nation on Earth.

In 1018 A.D., Pope Benedict began to get serious about the matter when he decreed that descendants of priests could not inherit property.

The Second Lateran Council finally made celibacy a law of the Church in 1139 A.D. Pope Gregory VII, who had assumed vast power by declaring himself the supreme authority over all souls, went even further by forbidding married priests from saying mass; he also forbade parishioners from attending masses said by them. Scholars believe that the first written law forbidding the clergy to marry was finally handed down at the Second Lateran Council in 1139 A.D.

The matter was brought up again in the 16th century, when dissenters tried to return to original Church doctrine, but the Council of Trent finalized the doctrine of celibacy in 1563 and the law finally became official doctrine at the Council of Trent in 1563.

In spite of all evidence showing the suppression of normal drives causes corruption and re-direction of such drives, Rome's position on the issue has remained unchanged. Money and land trump pedophilia and sexual abuse every time.

Just as a matter of curiosity, would it not be interesting to know if the popes that were so "motivated" to make celibacy for clergy mandatory actually followed their own orders? After all, if this command really was a holy order from on high the pope should also obey. But if it were a grab for power and riches then usually the head thief is above the law.

According to Wikipedia and other sources, there have been 265 popes. Many of them were sexually active within their papacy. Some were gay. There are various classifications for those who were sexually active at some time during their life. Periods in parentheses refer to the years of their papacies.

Married before receiving Holy Orders -

It was within canon law, and still is, for priests to have once been married before receiving Holy Orders. In the Eastern Rite branches of the Catholic Church, it is within canon law to be a priest and married (but one may not marry after ordination).

Their example of this is Saint Peter (Simon Peter), whose mother-in-law is mentioned in the Bible as having been miraculously healed (Matthew 8:14-15, Luke 4:38, Mark 1:29-31). According to Clement of Alexandria (Stromata, III, vi, ed. Dindorf, II, 276), Peter was married and had children and his wife suffered martyrdom. In some legends dating from at least the 6th century, Peter's daughter is called Petronilla.

Pope Clement I wrote, "For Peter and Philip begat children; [..] When the blessed Peter saw his own wife led out to die, he rejoiced because of her summons and her return home, and called to her very encouragingly and comfortingly, addressing her by name, and saying, 'Remember the Lord.' Such was the marriage of the blessed, and their perfect disposition toward those dearest to them."

Pope St. Hormisdas (514–523) was married and widowed before ordination. He was the father of Pope St. Silverius.

Pope Adrian II (867–872) was married, before taking orders, and had a daughter.

Pope John XVII (1003) was married before his election to the papacy and had three sons, who all became priests.

Pope Clement IV (1265–1268) was married, before taking Holy Orders, and had two daughters.

Pope Honorius IV (1285–1287) was married before he took the Holy Orders and had at least two sons. He entered the clergy after his wife died, the last pope to have been married.

Sexually active only before receiving Holy Orders -

Pope Pius II (1458–1464) had at least two illegitimate children (one in Strasbourg and another one in Scotland), born before he entered the clergy.

Pope Innocent VIII (1484–1492) (got to love that name) had at least two illegitimate children, born before he entered the clergy. According to the 1911 Encyclopedia Britannica, he "openly practised nepotism in favor of his children." Girolamo Savonarola chastised him for his worldly ambitions.

Pope Clement VII (1523–1534) had one illegitimate son before he took holy orders. Some sources identify him with Alessandro de' Medici, Duke of Florence but this identification has not been confirmed.

Pope Gregory XIII (1572–1585) had an illegitimate son before he took holy orders.

Sexually active after receiving Holy Orders -
Pope Julius II (1503–1513) had at least one illegitimate daughter, Felice della Rovere (born in 1483, twenty years before his election). Some sources indicate that he had two additional illegitimate daughters, who died in their childhood.[16] Besides, some contemporary (possibly libellous) reports accused him of sodomy. According to the schismatic Council of Pisa in 1511, he was a "sodomite covered with shameful ulcers."

Pope Paul III (1534–1549) held off ordination in order to continue his promiscuous lifestyle, fathering four illegitimate children (three sons and one daughter) by his mistress Silvia Ruffini. He broke his relations with her ca. 1513. There is no evidence of sexual activity during his papacy. He made his illegitimate son Pier Luigi Farnese the first Duke of Parma.

Pope Pius IV (1559–1565) had three illegitimate children before his election to the papacy.

Sexually active during their pontificate -

Along with other complaints, the activities of the popes between 1458 and 1565, helped encourage the Protestant Revolt.

Pope Sergius III (904–911) was supposedly the father of Pope John XI by Marozia, according to Liutprand of Cremona in his Antapodosis, as well as the Liber Pontificalis.However it must be noted that this is disputed by another early source, the annalist Flodoard (c. 894-966), John XI was brother of Alberic II, the latter being the offspring of Marozia and her husband Alberic I. Hence, John too may have been the son of Marozia and Alberic I. Bertrand Fauvarque underlines that the contemporary sources backing up this parenthood are dubious, Liutprand being "prone to exaggeration" while other mentions of this fatherhood appear in satires written by supporters of the late Pope Formosus.

Pope John X (914–928) had romantic affairs with both Theodora and her daughter Marozia, according to Liutprand of Cremona in his Antapodosis: "The first of the popes to be created by a woman and now destroyed by her daughter." (See also pornocracy)

Pope John XII (955–963) (deposed by Conclave) was said to have turned the Basilica di San Giovanni in Laterano into a brothel and was accused of adultery, fornication, and incest (Source: Patrologia Latina). The monk chronicler Benedict of Soracte noted in his volume XXXVII that he "liked to have a collection of women." According to Liutprand of Cremona in his Antapodosis, "they testified about his adultery, which they did not see with their own eyes, but nonetheless knew with certainty; he had fornicated with the widow of Rainier, with Stephana his father's concubine, with the widow Anna, and with his own niece, and he made the sacred palace into a whorehouse." According to The Oxford Dictionary of Popes, John XII was "a Christian Caligula whose crimes were rendered particularly horrific by the office he held." He was killed by a jealous husband while in the act of committing adultery with the man's wife. (See also pornocracy)

Pope Benedict IX (1032-1044, again in 1045 and finally 1047-1048) was said to have conducted a very dissolute life during his papacy. He was accused by Bishop Benno of Placenta of "many vile adulteries and murders."

Pope Victor III referred in his third book of Dialogues to "his rapes, murders and other unspeakable acts. His life as a Pope so vile, so foul, so execrable, that I shudder to think of it." It prompted St. Peter Damian to write an extended treatise against sex in general, and homosexuality in particular. In his Liber Gomorrhianus, St. Peter Damian recorded that Benedict "feasted on immorality" and that he was "a demon from hell in the disguise of a priest", accusing Benedict IX of routine sodomy and bestiality and was said to have sponsored orgies. In May 1045, Benedict IX resigned his office to pursue marriage, selling his office for 1,500 pounds of gold to his godfather, the pious priest John Gratian, who named himself Gregory VI.

Pope Alexander VI (1492-1503) had a notably long affair with Vannozza dei Cattanei before his papacy, by whom he had his famous illegitimate children Cesare and Lucrezia. A later mistress, Giulia Farnese, was the sister of Alessandro Farnese, who later became Pope Paul III. He fathered a total of at least seven, and possibly as many as ten illegitimate children.[40] (See also Banquet of Chestnuts)

Suspected to have been sexually active with male lovers -
Pope Paul II (1464-1471) was alleged to have died of a heart attack while in a sexual act with a page boy.

Pope Sixtus IV (1471-1484) was alleged to have awarded gifts and benefices to court favorites in return for sexual favors.

Giovanni Sclafenato was created a cardinal by Sixtus IV for "ingenuousness, loyalty,...and his other gifts of soul and body",according to the papal epitaph on his tomb. According to Stefano Infessura, in his Diarium urbis Romae, he had a predilection for young boys.

Pope Leo X (1513–1521) was alleged to have had a particular infatuation for Marc-Antonio Flaminio.

Pope Julius III (1550–1555) was alleged to have had a long affair with Innocenzo Ciocchi del Monte. The Venetian ambassador at that time reported that Innocenzo shared the pope's bedroom and bed. According to the The Oxford Dictionary of Popes, he was "naturally indolent, he devoted himself to pleasurable pursuits with occasional bouts of more serious activity."

Continuing with our fun facts, according to "futurechurch.org" here is a list of popes who were the sons of the supposedly asexual clergy.

Popes who were the sons of other popes or other clergy –

Name of Pope – Papacy

Son of St. Damascus I 366-348

St. Lorenzo, priest - St. Innocent I 401-417

Anastasius I Boniface 418-422 son of a priest

St. Felix 483-492 son of a priest

Anastasius II 496-498 son of a priest

St. Agapitus I 535-536 Gordiaous, priest

St. Silverus 536-537 St. Homidas, pope

Deusdedit 882-884 son of a priest

Boniface VI 896-896 Hadrian, bishop

John XI 931-935 Pope Sergius III

John XV 989-996 Leo, priest

The same source supplied the following list of popes who had children out of wedlock AFTER the celibacy decree was in force.

Popes who had illegitimate children after 1139
Innocent VIII 1484-1492 - several children

Alexander VI 1492-1503 - several children

Julius 1503-1513 - 3 daughters

Paul III 1534-1549 - 3 sons, 1 daughter

Pius IV 1559-1565 - 3 sons

Gregory XIII 1572-1585 - 1 son

History sources: Oxford Dictionary of Popes; H.C. Lea
History of Sacerdotal Celibacy in the Christian Church 1957; E. Schillebeeckx
The Church with a Human Face 1985; J. McSorley
Outline History of the Church by Centuries 1957; F.A.Foy (Ed.) 1990
Catholic Almanac 1989; D.L. Carmody
The Double Cross - Ordination, Abortion and Catholic Feminism 1986; P.K. Jewtt
The Ordination of Women 1980; A.F. Ide

God's Girls - Ordination of Women in the Early Christian &
Gnostic Churches 1986; E. Schüssler Fiorenza
In Memory of Her 1984; P. DeRosa Vicars of Christ 1988.

Transubstantiation

Transubstantiation comes from the Latin word, "Tansubsubstaniato", meaning "change of substance." This term was not incorporated into a creed until the Forth Lateran Council in A.D. 1215.

According to Catholic authorities, the word was first used by Hildebert of Tours (about 1079). His example was soon followed by Stephen of Autun (1139), Gaufred (1188), and Peter of Blois (about 1200). Several ecumenical councils also adopted the term, such as the Fourth Lateran Council in A.D. 1215, and the Council of Lyons (1274).

The Roman Catholic Church defined and explained Transubstantiation in the Council of Trent (1564) as follows, "By the consecration of the bread and wine, a conversion is made of the whole substance of the bread into the substance of the body of Christ our Lord, and of the whole substance of the wine into the substance of His blood; which conversion is, by the holy Catholic Church, suitably and properly called Transubstantiation."

"In this sacrament are contained not only the true body of Christ, and all the constituents of a true body, such as bones and sinews, but also Christ whole and entire."

"Christ whole and entire, is contained, not only under either species, but also in each particle of the same species." (Species here refers to bread and wine.)

The above information indicates that the Church of Rome teaches that when the priest blesses the bread, it becomes Jesus Christ himself and similarly the wine is Jesus Christ himself, but where did this doctrine come from and when did it start?

If we look at the scriptures and compare the actions of the early fathers we may see what they believed the bread and wine to be.

Acts 2:42 They devoted themselves to the apostles' teaching and to the fellowship, to the breaking of bread and to prayer.

1 Corinthians 10:14 Therefore, my dear friends, flee from idolatry. 15 I speak to sensible people; judge for yourselves what I say. 16 Is not the cup of thanksgiving for which we give thanks a participation in the blood of Christ? And is not the bread that we break a participation in the body of Christ? 17 Because there is one loaf, we, who are many, are one body, for we all partake of the one loaf.

What we know as communion today was called in scripture, "breaking of bread."

The term the "Lord's Supper" was found in notes taken from the Council of Carthage in A.D. 418.

Irenaeus used the term Oblation to agree with the description in 1 Corinthians 11:20 When you come together, it is not the Lord's Supper you eat, 21 for as you eat, each of you goes ahead without waiting for anybody else. One remains hungry, another gets drunk. 22 Don't you have homes to eat and drink in? Or do you despise the church of God and humiliate those who have nothing? What shall I say to you? Shall I praise you for this? Certainly not!

23 For I received from the Lord what I also passed on to you: The Lord Jesus, on the night He was betrayed, took bread, 24 and when He had given thanks, He broke it and said, "This is My body, which is for you; do this in remembrance of Me." 25 In the same way, after supper He took the cup, saying, "This cup is the new covenant in My blood; do this, whenever you drink it, in remembrance of Me." 26 For whenever you eat this bread and drink this cup, you proclaim the Lord's death until He comes.

Eucharist, meaning a thanksgiving, was used by Ignatius, Irenaeus, Origen and others. Justin Martyr, Origen, Eusebius and Chrysostom also call the communion "Memorial" because in it we remember the death of the Lord.

"Mass" was used by Eusebius as a term for the church service. It was not until Ambrose (374-397), that the term Mass was used to denote communion.

Up to this point the term Transubstantiation was never used, and there was no mention of any assumption of bread or wine being anything but symbols.

Documents written by the early church fathers indicates that the Didache, or Teaching of the Twelve Apostles (a document with a questionable dating of 50 A.D. – 200 A.D.) and Justin Martyr (died c. 165 A.D.) never assert the doctrine of the Real Presence of Christ in the sacrament.

Ignatius (died about 107 A.D.) comes the closest to hinting at Transubstantiation of anyone at the time when he rails against Gnostic antagonists when he says, "They do not admit that the Eucharist is the flesh of our Savior Jesus Christ, the flesh which suffered for our sins and which the Father, in His graciousness, raised from the dead." However, this does not mean he is protesting their disbelief in Transubstantiation. Many Gnostics of the time denied Jesus ever came in the flesh, believing him to be only a phantasm. His body, they claimed, was an illusion produced by His spirit.

However, by 200 A.D., we begin to find statements that the bread and wine are strictly Christ's body and blood. One statement occurs in an argument against the Docetists about the reality of Christ's earthly body. One wonders if this was an over-reaction to the Gnostic heresy. Tertullian (c. 160-220 A.D.) and Cyprian (c. 258 A.D.) indicate they believed in the symbolic aspect of the bread and wine representing the body and blood. The men accepted the representation of the elements as the body and blood. Tertullian stated "Christ, having taken the bread and given it to His disciples, made it His body by saying, "This is my body, that is, the figure of my body." Even Orgien, acknowledges "that they (bread and wine) are figures which are written in the sacred volumes; therefore as spiritual not as carnal, examine and understand what is said. For if as carnal you receive them, they hurt, not nourish you."

Serapion (c. 211 A.D.) refers to the elements as "a likeness." Eusebius of Caesarea (c. 339 A.D.) states, "We are continually fed with the Savior's body, we continually participate in the lamb's blood," but follows it up, "with the symbols of his body and saving blood." He states that Jesus instructed his disciples to make "the image of his own body," and employ bread as its symbol.

Both Cyril of Jerusalem (315 – 386 A.D.) and Eusebius of Caesarea denied Transubstantiation. Cyril stated, "Under the type of bread, His body given unto thee, and under the type of wine, His blood given unto thee." Eusebius qualifies communion as "Christ Himself gave the symbols of the Divine ceremony to His own disciples that the image of His own body should be made. He appointed to use bread as a symbol of His own body."

The Apostolical Constitutions (c. 380 A.D.) use words such as "anti-types" and "symbols" to describe the elements, though they speak of communion as the body of Christ and the blood of Christ.

The first move toward Transubstantiation seems to have been introduced by a friar named Anastatius, around A.D. 637. The friar decided to interpret the Lord's Supper in a very literal sense as no one had done before. This introduced the doctrine called, "Real Presence."

John Damascene (676 A.D. – 787 A.D.) is most famous as one who defended and favored the veneration of sacred images, holy pictures, statues and icons. His writings in the Eastern Church are what the Summa of St. Thomas Aquinas are to the West.

In A.D. 754, at the Council of Constantinople, John Damascene states, "The bread and wine are supernaturally changed by the invocation and coming of the Holy Ghost into the body and blood of Jesus Christ, and are not two, but one and the same... The bread and wine are not the type or the figure of the body and blood of Jesus Christ - ah, God forbid! - but the body itself of our Lord deified."

Opposition from within the Roman Catholic Church came in part from Pashus Radbert, who wrote "that there are many that in these mystical things are of another opinion." Others were also against this doctrine within the Roman Catholic Church. Aefric, Abbot of Malmesbury (A.D.905) and Berengarius (A. D. 1029), and St. Bede in the 8th Century joined in the chorus of dissenters over the years.

The Abbot of Corbie advanced the doctrine in A.D. 818 when he wrote a treatise stating, "What was received in the Sacrament is the same flesh as that which was born of the Virgin Mary, and which suffered death for us; and though the figure of bread and wine doth remain, yet you must absolutely believe that, after consecration, it is nothing but the flesh and blood of Jesus Christ." This doctrine was further developed and finally made a dogma by Pope Innocent III (1161-1216).

Now, we are over one-thousand years out from the earliest church leaders. We can see the doctrine of Transubstantiation has taken root, grown, and is now being written into church law. However, the Apostles never addressed this or even thought about this doctrine. They never acknowledged any change in the elements or believed in any corporal presence.

Later, as the epistles were being read and discussed some took to reading the words and interpreting their meaning as purely literal. At that time, most of those in leadership positions warned about this approach.

Even men who were supporters of the Roman Church and the papacy suggested that "there was nothing in the Gospels that may enforce us to understand Christ's words properly, yea, nothing in the text ('This is My body') hinders but those words may as well be taken in a metaphysical sense, as the words of the Apostle, 'the Rock was Christ'... That part, which the Gospel hath not expressed, viz., the conversion of the bread in the body and blood of Christ, we have received expressly from the Church." Bellarmine, (1542 – 1621A.D.) another Roman scholar admitted "there is no express place of Scripture to prove Transubstantiation without the declaration of the Church."

The scholars proclaimed, "Therefore, as we have been given a sound mind and are instructed to search the scriptures to see what is true and then to hold fast to what is true, we find the doctrine of Transubstantiation illogical! The Lord Jesus at the Last Supper handed the broken bread to the apostles and stated, "This is my body." However He was in his earthly body, 100 percent human. Yet this doctrine would destroy human nature by having the ability to be in multiple places at one time. Rome teaches that Christ is corporally on the altar but without any "accidents." Yet again, we are to deny all logic and sensibility to believe that Christ is present upon the altar! (Accidents, in this case means that it has no affect on any senses and cannot be discerned.)

How time and constant political pressure changes things. From the denials of the doctrine by church leaders in the first and second centuries, the pendulum swings slowly, over a thousand years, to the other side. St. Alphonsus de Liguori (1698 – 1787) was the author of the book, "The Glories of Mary." He was a Catholic Priest and theologian. Liguori wrote in his book, The Dignity and Duties of the Priest or Selva; "But our wonder should be far greater when we find that in obedience to the words of his priests - HOC EST CORPUS MEUM (This Is My Body) - God himself descends on the altar, that he comes wherever they call him and as often as they call him, and places himself in their hands, even though they should be his enemies. "

From these words, HOC EST CORPUS MEUM comes our words Hocus Pocus, said by those who thought the doctrine of transubstantiation was simply too much to believe. Pagans and non-papists alike not only condemned the doctrine, but ridiculed it as well. So wide spread was the disbelief that it made its way into our modern vernacular and came to mean anything seemingly magical but fraudulent, as expressed in the phrase, "That is just so much hocus pocus."

These alleged changes of the bread and wine into God Himself are not evident in any outward physical change.

Scientific tests have been performed to seek for any amount of blood in the Eucharist during and after the priest's blessing but none were ever found.

Protestants are very proud of their stance on Transubstantiation, but most have not escaped the cloying Catholic doctrine at all. It may be true that most Protestants do not believe the bread or wine becomes the body of Christ, but some churches insist on the bread and wine being blessed only by their own ordained ministers before being passed to the church members. The Methodist Church is one of these, according to their manual called, "The Book of Discipline."

Why do we need a priest to bless the bread and wine? Is the priest representing Christ to us? Are we not equal in the sight of God, or do we believe a four year degree at a religious college brings one some extra especial spiritual power? It is difficult to shake our roots. From Catholic to Episcopal to Methodist, traditions cling and cloud the truth. What is the truth? We are all the same in the eyes of God. Every believer is a priest. The bread is just bread. The wine is just wine… or if you are Baptist or Pentecostal, it is grape juice because we cannot drink like Jesus did.

Grape juice kept in animal skins and urns in the Israeli heat that did not become fermented… now that would be hocus-pocus.

Rapture

The word "Rapture" is not found in the English Bible. The word comes from the Latin verb rapere, which means "to carry off, abduct, seize or take forcefully." To see the flavor of the word, compare the words "rape" or "raptor", which is a type of bird of prey such as a hawk. The word rapere was used in the Latin Vulgate of 405 A.D. to translate the phrase from Thessalonians 4:17, which is the primary biblical reference. The word, "rapiemur" "we shall be caught up" translating the Greek word harpagÄ, which is the passive mood, future tense of harpazÅ.

Although the doctrine of the resurrection of the dead was taught by Jesus in the Gospels and was an accepted belief common to all Christians, there was no thought, nor discussion in the area of eschatology about the 'Rapture' until the Reformation. Although Christians from the very beginning accepted, as scriptures clearly state, that, at some point the faithful would be "caught up" with Christ, it was always assumed this was a resurrection message. In modern eschatology the same scriptures are interpreted as the doctrine of the 'Rapture'. The Christian denominations that actually put eschatological emphasis on it are mostly those that appeared after the Reformation.

The first known occurrence of a "rapture-like" theology or reference, which could be construed as a rapture doctrine, was that of Ephraem of Nisibis, in 373 A.D., who preached a sermon saying; "For all the saints and Elect of God are gathered, prior to the tribulation that is to come, and are taken to the Lord lest they see the confusion that is to overwhelm the world because of our sins."

The sermon was met with a thousand years of silence and the idea was rejected and ignored. The doctrine did not catch on enough to be repeated or even referenced as a consideration until it was re-visited in the Protestant Reformation and the rise of Dispensationalism.

Then in 1788 a precursor to the doctrine of the rapture appeared as an allusion. The story was written in a book penned in 1788 by a Catholic priest named Emmanuel Lacunza and published in Spain in 1812. The book spread, as did the intrigue of its storyline.

By combining verses and ideas from several books of the Bible, John Darby, a Brethren preacher, developed and taught the Rapture doctrine in 1827. Yes, the idea of the rapture, as set forth in most Protestant churches, has only been around since the early 1800's. This should give pause. It should cause us to ask if this is some new insight and revelation from God, or simply an idea derived from a combination of unrelated texts from various books of the Bible.

When relating texts from different books of the Bible we must always remember that we are reading separate books written at different times to various churches in differing areas for divergent purposes.

The evangelist, William Blackstone worked the idea into his book and popularized Rapture doctrine in his best seller, "Jesus is Coming." This was the "Left Behind" novel of its day. The idea of the rapture is a great read and makes for a heart stopping storyline. Popularity drove the idea from the novel into the pulpit.

In theological terms, the teaching of the rapture is a new doctrine. Its inception can be traced to an event in 1831 when Margaret McDonald, who claimed that God had shown it to her, first taught it, in Scotland. Chances are, she read it in the 1793 Blackstone novel, who probably heard of Derby's doctrine, who likely encountered the idea from Lacunza's audience.

The idea of the Rapture was slow to gain acceptance until it was promoted by John Nelson Darby, the founder of the Christian (Plymouth) Brethren movement. With the development of Fundamentalist Christianity around the turn of the 20th century, it was Cyrus Ignatius Scofield who became the champion of this new Rapture doctrine. The Rapture doctrine entered mainstream Christianity with its inclusion in the Scofield Reference Bible. There is no real history to the Rapture doctrine until the 1800's.

Since Christianity began, the texts used to justify the rapture theology were always regarded as 'resurrection' texts. Thus the earliest Creeds stated that Christ's return was the time when the Resurrection and Judgment Day would occur. The Nicene Creed reads; "He is seated at the right hand of God from whence He shall come to judge the quick and the dead."

The understanding of these texts is especially the case for 1Thessalonians 4:17 where the context is concern for the fate of those Christians who have already died. The text assures its readers that "the dead in Christ shall rise first" (1Thess. 4:16). "Rising" refers to rising from the dead and thus "resurrection" and not "rapture.

Other texts are as tenuous and weak at best especially when examined in the light of their context. For example, the expression "one shall be taken" in the Olivet Discourse of Matthew 24:40 references a flood first, signifying a disaster had occurred, and thus pointing to another disaster killing many people. For this reason as well as the historical timing of the verse, it has long been regarded by scholars as referring to the first century Roman catapult barrage of Jerusalem during the 42 month siege from A.D. 66 to A.D. 70 in which many people were randomly killed. This occurred after the time frame that Jesus would have given the speech, but during the time Matthew would have written the Gospel.

The verses used to define the rapture are vague in their timing and sequence, especially when added to those of the Book of Revelation. The indeterminate timeframe gave way to four distinct viewpoints. These are called, "pre-tribulation," mid-tribulation," "post-tribulation," and pre-wrath." (Also called pre-trib, mid-trib, post-trib.) Most would equate the category of mid-trib with that of pre-wrath, simply because the common belief is that the Anti-Christ will achieve world dominance and reveal himself only after he is half way into his seven year reign. It is in the latter half of this period that world chaos breaks out.

Here are some of the main scriptures used to form the rapture teaching.

Matthew 24:37-42

37 But as the days of Noe [were], so shall also the coming of the Son of man be. 38 For as in the days that were before the flood they were eating and drinking, marrying and giving in marriage, until the day that Noe entered into the ark, 39 And knew not until the flood came, and took them all away; so shall also the coming of the Son of man be. 40 Then shall two be in the field; the one shall be taken, and the other left. 41 Two [women shall be] grinding at the mill; the one shall be taken, and the other left. 42 Watch therefore: for ye know not what hour your Lord doth come.

I Thessalonians 4:13-18 But we do not want you to be uninformed, brethren, about those who are asleep, so that you will not grieve as do the rest who have no hope. For if we believe that Jesus died and rose again, even so God will bring with him those who have fallen asleep in Jesus. For this we say to you by the word of the Lord, that we who are alive and remain until the coming of the Lord, will not precede those who have fallen asleep. For the Lord himself will descend from heaven with a shout, with the voice of the archangel and with the trumpet of God, and the dead in Christ will rise first. Then we who are alive and remain will be caught up together with them in the clouds to meet the Lord in the air, and so we shall always be with the Lord. Therefore comfort one another with these words.

2 Peter 3:9-12

9 The Lord is not slow in keeping his promise, as some understand slowness. He is patient with you, not wanting anyone to perish, but everyone to come to repentance.10 But the day of the Lord will come like a thief. The heavens will

disappear with a roar; the elements will be destroyed by fire, and the earth and everything in it will be laid bare. 11 Since everything will be destroyed in this way, what kind of people ought you to be? You ought to live holy and godly lives.12 as you look forward to the day of God and speed its coming. That day will bring about the destruction of the heavens by fire, and the elements will melt in the heat.

1 Corinthians 15:52
"In a moment, in the twinkling of an eye, at the last trump: for the trumpet shall sound, and the dead shall be raised incorruptible, and we shall be changed."

Phillipians 3:21 "(Christ) shall change our vile body, that it may be fashioned like unto his glorious body, according to the working whereby he is able even to subdue all things unto himself."

Matthew 24:27-31
27 For as the lightning cometh out of the east, and shineth even unto the west; so shall also the coming of the Son of man be. 28 For wheresoever the carcass is, there will the eagles be gathered together. 29 Immediately after the tribulation of those days shall the sun be darkened, and the moon shall not give her light, and the stars shall fall from heaven, and the powers of the heavens shall be shaken: 30 And then shall appear the sign of the Son of man in heaven: and then shall all the tribes of the earth mourn, and they shall see the Son of man coming in the clouds of heaven with power and great glory. 31 And he shall send his angels with a great sound of a trumpet, and they shall gather together his elect from the four winds, from one end of heaven to the other.

Looking at these verses through the eyes of Christians from 33 A.D. to 1800 A.D. one can easily see how all of the verses were assumed to refer to the Resurrection of the Dead.

Men, bishops, scholars, and theologians, including those

who knew the apostles or their disciples or the students of the disciples, as well as all of Christianity making up the first 1800 years never thought these verses were anything but resurrection texts. Then, a book of fiction was written and a new doctrine emerged. But is it really Biblical or is it myth pressed into the populace by a good book?

The answer may come into a clearer light if one keeps in mind that scriptures quoted are from at least four separate books, written to different people or groups for various reasons and were not meant to be chained into the story of a rapture.

Eighteen hundred years after Jesus, someone writes a good book and a preacher decides to use the idea to fire up his crowd. A man puts a reference to the new idea in his bible notes. People read it and swallow the idea whole without question. The rapture makes for a great story and wonderful drama. It can bring a congregation to its feet or to the altar, but is it real, or are we just being manipulated by a good drama?

Apocalypse and the End of Days

The doctrine of the rapture was not needed to fire the imagination and produce predictions of the end of time. Apocalyptic proclamations are not directly related to the rapture. Indeed, the teachers of the rapture simply incorporated the doctrine of the rapture into a general apocalyptic view.

Even today there are differing views as to when the rapture will occur within the time of the apocalypse. These differences are called, "pre-trib," mid-trib," and "post-trib," and signify the three main schools of thought regarding the timing of the rapture to the apocalypse. The question is, "Will the church be taken to heaven before, during, or after the chaos, war, death, and destruction foretold in the Bible?"

However, the idea of the Apocalypse itself is based on a literal reading of the Book of Revelation and the assumption that all things written in the book point toward future events.

The Book of Revelation was written sometime around 96 A.D. in Asia Minor. The author was a Christian from Ephesus known as "John the Elder," or "John the Revelator." According to the Book, John was on the island of Patmos, which is not far from the coast of Asia Minor. The reason for his exile was, "because of the word of God and the testimony of Jesus" (Rev. 1.10).

Ephesus was both the capital of the Roman province of Asia and one of the earliest centers of Christianity. The book mentions seven Christian churches in the seven leading cities of Asia Minor -- Ephesus (2.1-7, Smyrna (2.9-11), Pergamon (2.12-17), Thyatira (2.18-29). Sardis (3.1-6), Philadelphia (3.7-13). and Laodicea (3.14-22). These were the centers of the Christian faith in the region at the time. Romans were persecuting Christians and this was what the author was dealing with personally also. The Roman administration was viewed as agents of the devil.

Thus, we have the perfect mixture for the writing of apocalyptic literature.

The Book of Revelation uses intricate and unusual symbolic language, allusions, and metaphor. It is difficult for modern readers to follow since many of the symbolic references are now lost. This would not have been the case for people in the ancient world. Not only were they more accustomed to complex apocalyptic literature; they were living within the symbols used within the book. Thus, it could be said that apocalyptic literature was good reading for "insiders." That is to say, it was written for people who already knew the situation and the meanings of the symbols that were used to portray it.

There were several reasons to write in this fashion. The primary one was to save your head from the chopping block. When writing about the emperor it is best to hide the meaning so the audience understands but the meaning could still be denied or ignored if needed.

Another problem for the modern reader is the time-line within the book. It is not linear. For example, events in chapter 12 do not follow in time after the events in chapter 11. Events in chapters 12-13 are meant to explain how those circumstances in chapters 5-11 came about. So the time-line of the story moves in circles, bringing the reader back to the "present situation" as it stood for the ancient readers of Revelation. But what was the situation?

It is now thought that a situation arose in Ephesus after the year 89 A.D. when Domitian instituted a new imperial cult sanctuary dedicated to his family, the Flavian dynasty. It had included his father, Vespasian, who as Roman general led the war against the Jews from 66-69 A.D. When the Emperor Nero was killed, Vespasian was summoned from Judea to Rome to become the new Emperor. Vespasian then appointed his elder son, Titus, as the commander of the legions in Judea. It was Titus who led the siege and destruction of Jerusalem in 70 A.D. When Vespasian died in 79 A.D., Titus became the next Emperor. Titus, however, died just two years later in 81 A.D., and this left the empire to Vespasian's younger son, Domitian. Domitian was known as a strong-willed emperor who tolerated no disagreement with his policies.

Since we are not able to take the time and hundreds of pages needed to discuss in depth the Book of Revelation and its symbols, we will simply give a couple of examples.

Look at the "beast from the sea" in Rev. 17. We can see it is the Emperor himself. This is made clear in a passage where the symbolism of the seven heads is spelled out.

Rev. 17:9 "This calls for a mind that has wisdom: the seven heads are seven mountains on which the woman is seated; also, they are seven kings, 10 of whom five have fallen, one is living, and the other has not yet come; and when he comes, he must remain only a little while. 11 As for the beast that was and is not, it is an eighth but it belongs to the seven, and it goes to destruction. 12 And the ten horns that you saw are ten kings who have not yet received a kingdom, but they are to receive authority as kings for one hour, together with the beast. 13 These are united in yielding their power and authority to the beast; 14 they will make war on the Lamb, and the Lamb will conquer them...

The "five fallen" refer to the five emperors who have died: Augustus (29 BC - 14 A.D.), Tiberius (14-37 A.D.), Gaius (37-41 A.D.), Claudius (41-54 A.D.) and Nero (54-68 A.D.). "One has a wound" refers to the emperor Nero, who died in 68 A.D. Nero was so horribly evil that contemporary legend had it that he would return from the dead to continue persecuting the Christians.

The angst and trauma Nero left in the Christian world is noted in an unusual bit of symbolism – the number 666.

An ancient type of numerology, called Gematria, was used to "encode" names into numbers.

In Hebrew Gematria, every letter has a corresponding number. Summing these numbers gives a numeric value to a word or name. In Hebrew, "Nero Caesar" is pronounced

"Neron Qe[i]sar." Adding the corresponding values yields 666, as shown:

נ = 50   ר = 200   ו = 6   נ = 50   ק = 100   ס = 60   ר = 200

thus:

נְרוֹן קְסָר = 666

Resh
Samekh
Qoph
Nun
Vav
Resh
Nun
200
60
100
50
6
200
50
 Resh = 200
Samekh = 60
Qoph = 100
Nun = 50
Vav = 6
Resh = 200
Nun = 50
Total = 666

But the really suggestive hint is that the oldest manuscripts don't agree on the number and some have 616 instead. It's much harder to concoct an explanation that fits both numbers, and only one of the proposed interpretations of the Number of the Beast accounts for both, and that is Nero.

Remember it was NeRON QeiSaR in Hebrew. But the final N of NeRON is optional. Removing the terminal "Nun" makes the name "Nero" rather than "Neron." Subtracting the letter N [Nun] and its value of 50 makes the numeric value 616, which may explain that particular variation found in some older manuscripts.

The hypothesis that 666 is a code for a Roman emperor seems to have historical support. The emperors were noted for their oppression of both Jews and Christians. Both communities were known to use numerology or gematria, as well as codes and symbols when living under Roman rule to avoid persecution.

The German Protestant theologian Ethelbert Stauffer, argued that gematria had been the most popular form of numerology among Jews but also in the rest of the Graeco-Roman world.

By portraying the Emperor and his provincial authorities as "beasts" and henchmen of the dragon, Satan, the author of Revelation was calling on Christians to refuse to take part in the imperial cult, even at the risk of martyrdom.

Based on an enormous amount of data, it seems clear that The Book of Revelation is not some oracle into the future, but a scathing indictment of the Roman Empire in that period and a call to arms for Christians of the time.

However, this does not stop those who read the Bible with an apocalyptic eye from applying the symbolism in some personal formula to predict the end of days. Indeed, man has been seeing the end of time coming almost from the beginning of time. Every year there are those predicting the end of days. There is a list of doomsday and Rapture prophecies, which begin in 2800 B.C. and end in 2012 A.D. in Appendix "A."

The list was harvested from several web sites and books. The number of false prophets and prophecies was so overwhelming that the list had to be trimmed down and limited to a stop date of 2012 A.D. The list clearly demonstrates the amazing amount of arrogance contained in certain churches, sects, and denominations as their leaders predict and predict and predict and fail. One must ask, "If a leader is so far off of the spiritual mark so many times in this area, should he or she be trusted in any spiritual area at all?"

However, let us not leave the discussion quite yet. There is still one more major view to examine.

Mankind is notorious for repeating errors. In fact, social, political, and economic errors tend to cycle. If we get passed the insanity of attempting to place dates on the end of time and we focus on the lessons within the book of Revelation, or any other books in the Bible, we will gain immense insight and preparedness for things to come. From the Roman oppression of the church, to the Chinese oppression at Tiananmen Square, to the revitalization of the emperor worship cult in North Korea, the evils of man never fail to repeat.

The call to the spirit within the Book of Revelation to be strong, to endure, and to resist bowing the knee to the evil forces in the world hold true from 70 A.D. to the end of time. We may not know when that will be, but we do know what it will take to endure to the end.

Revelation 3:12 (King James Version)
12Him that overcometh will I make a pillar in the temple of my God, and he shall go no more out: and I will write upon him the name of my God, and the name of the city of my God, which is new Jerusalem, which cometh down out of heaven from my God: and I will write upon him my new name.

Be sure to check out Appendix "A" for a good laugh.

Sabbath versus Sunday

The conversion of worship from Saturday (Sabbath) to Sunday was a slow process, taking several hundred years and the convergence of ideas from both governing and religious authorities.

It is interesting to note that the division of time into a seven day week is not a constant or global rule, nor has it always been that the world enjoyed this common measurement of time. The standard explanation is that the seven-day week was established as imperial calendar in the late Roman Empire, but it existed long before. The seven-day week was perpetuated by the Christian church for historical reasons. The British Empire used the seven-day week and spread it worldwide.

The first pages of the Bible explain how God created the world in six days and rested on the seventh. This seventh day became the Jewish day of rest, the Sabbath, Saturday.

Historians tell us that the birthplace of the 7-day week was likely in the area of Babylon or Persia. The week was brought westward and became known in Rome before the advent of Christianity.

Days of the week were once named after the seven planets known at the time. These were Saturn, Jupiter, Mars, the Sun, Venus, Mercury, and the Moon. Each had an hour of the day assigned to them, and the planet ruling or visibly brightest during the first hour of any day of the week gave its name to that day.

During the first century, the week of seven days was introduced into Rome from Egypt, and the Roman names of the planets were given to each successive day. Sunday was the first day of the week according to the Jews. Jewish tradition and religious law dictated that they worship on the Sabbath, or seventh day of the week. Since the Jewish people had come out of that area of the world that gave birth to the seven-day week, they simply aligned their worship to the new calendar with new names for days and worshiped on Saturday. But, knowing that Jesus and the apostles worshiped Saturday, how did the church begin to abandon the Sabbath for Sunday worship?

Historical records show that the weekly cycle has remained unchanged from Christ's time so that the Saturday and Sunday of those early centuries are still the Saturday and Sunday of today. This means that the simple explanation of a switched week or calendar is incorrect. The change from Saturday to Sunday was no mistake.

Let us trace the day of worship, beginning with Christ's time. According to Luke 4:16, it was Christ's "custom" to go to the synagogue on the Sabbath day. We are also told that the women who had followed Him from Galilee "rested the Sabbath day according to the commandment" (Luke 23:56). The book of Luke was written around 60 A.D. There were obviously no significant changes to the day of worship until then since Luke tells the story without any explanation about which day was the Sabbath.

Acts 13:14 tells us that Paul and the Apostles worshiped on the Sabbath. Acts also explains that this was the practice in all major cities, as Paul and the others traveled and preached in the synagogues on the Sabbath. Since the Book of Acts was written around 64 A.D., we can attest that there was no change in worship at that point in time.

The first mention of Sunday observance by Christians comes in the second century from both the cities of Alexandria and Rome. About A.D. 130 Barnabas of Alexandria refers to the seventh-day Sabbath as representing the seventh millennium of earth's history. He goes on to say that the present Sabbaths were unacceptable to God, who would make a beginning of another world (the eighth millennium). Therefore we are to keep the eighth day with joyfulness, the day on which Jesus rose again from the dead.

The above reference seems very odd and convoluted. Yet, it shows that the church of the time was working to lessen the importance of the Sabbath.

Justin Martyr in Rome provides a clear reference to Sunday observance around A.D. 150 stating, "And on the day called Sunday, all who live in cities or in the country gather together to one place, and the memoirs of the apostles (this is what he called the Gospels) or the writings of the prophets are read, as long as time permits; then, when the reader has ceased, the president verbally instructs, and exhorts all to the imitation of these good things." (At this time the church met on both Sabbath and Sunday.)

The church historian of the fifth century A.D., Socrates Scholasticus, wrote, "For although almost all churches throughout the world celebrate the sacred mysteries [the Lord's Supper] on the Sabbath of every week, yet the Christians of Alexandria and at Rome, on account of some ancient tradition, have ceased to do this." And Sozomen, a contemporary of Socrates, wrote, "The people of Constantinople, and almost everywhere, assemble together on the Sabbath, as well as on the first day of the week, which custom is never observed at Rome or at Alexandria." This means that from the time of Justin Martyr in 150 A.D., until the fifth century the church was going through a gradual change. First, the church worshipped on Saturday. Then they began to worship on both Saturday and Sunday.

The fourth century document, The Apostolic Constitutions, says to, "Keep the Sabbath, and the Lord's day festival; because the former is the memorial of the creation, and the latter of the resurrection." "Let the slaves work five days; but on the Sabbath-day and the Lord's day let them have leisure to go to church for instruction in piety."

It appears that Emperor Constantine, wishing to establish a single national holy day, was the author of the final decree that caused Christianity to eventually abandon the Sabbath.

In the early fourth century, Constantine, by his civil legislation, made Sunday a rest day. His "Sunday law" of March 7, 321 A.D., reads: "On the venerable Day of the Sun let the magistrates and people residing in cities rest, and let all workshops be closed. In the country, however, persons engaged in agriculture may freely and lawfully continue their pursuits; because it often happens that another day is not so suitable for grain-sowing or for vine-planting; lest by neglecting the proper moment for such operations the bounty of heaven should be lost."

This began the laws regulating Sunday observance, which we continue in our society under the name, "Blue Laws." It is obvious that this first Sunday law was not particularly Christian in orientation since the Emperor called the day the "venerable Day of the Sun." Constantine sought to merge pagan and Christian holy days to more easily govern the kingdom. He saw the path of least resistance in the change of Christian worship since at that time the church was meeting on the Sabbath to worship and on Sunday to celebrate the resurrection.

A friend of the Emperor and noted theologian, Eusebius, wrote in his commentary on Psalm 92, that Christians would fulfill on the Lord's day all that in this psalm was prescribed for the Sabbath, including worship of God early in the morning. Through the new covenant the Sabbath celebration was transferred to the first day of light (Sunday). By throwing his weight behind the Emperor's decree he assured special treatment for himself and Sunday as the day of worship for Christians.

But Christianity did not lose out completely. We got a few things from the forced amalgam with the sun worshipers. The iconology of the halo was brought into our paintings of Jesus and the saints.

The word "halo" originated from a Greek word that simply meant the sun, or the sun's disk. The pre-Christian Romans named their sun-god Helios and eventually began using the halo in their art, including portraits of their "divine" emperors. When the Romans created emperor worship, they borrowed the image of the halo as a symbol of power and divinity of the emperor. When Constantine brought Christianity into companionship within his state, Christians were exposed to halos from all quarters. The halo was carried into Christian imagery and used to symbolize purity or divinity.

But none of this makes it right. Now we know that the church was led into Sunday worship by a pagan ruler in his attempt to unite his people under certain customs. This meant taking the worship day of the Sun and combining it with the day to worship the Son. So what now? Let's see what bible scholar Jim Lindsey has to say.

The Sabbath
By James Lindsey

Introduction

The Sabbath is a term like any other that at first you think, yeah I know what that is, but then when pressed to define it for someone it seems unclear. Is the Sabbath a day, a shadow, is it ceremonial or moral, when did it begin and who was it for?

There are many today, if asked, "do you observe the Sabbath?" would say yes every Sunday or every Saturday. There would still be others who simply dismiss it as religious bantering with a "who really cares anyway" attitude.

The purpose of this chapter is to answer some of these questions surrounding the Sabbath from the perspective of a man who was reared believing if you don't observe the Sabbath, you are going to burn-up in hell with all those who worship the Sun on Sunday.

So what is the Sabbath?

I believe the answer depends on when you are asking the question. Do you mean during the Old Testament or New Testament period? The first use of the word in a traditional protestant bible is found in Exodus 16:23 relating to the Manna miracle in the wilderness. A careful reading of this verse in

145

context shows that the Sabbath was a part of the commandments (vs.28) of the LORD. The Sabbath was a test. You can see this in Deuteronomy 8:3. So what do we know so far?

* There is no mention of the Sabbath day until Exodus 16:23.
* The Sabbath was a part of the Lord's commandments.
* It was a test of faith.

Please note that some belief systems would argue against the first bullet point. I will address this shortly.

The next major reference to the Sabbath is found in the Ten Commandments in Exodus 20: 8-11 (KJV).
(Exo 20:8) Remember the sabbath day, to keep it holy. (Exo 20:9) Six days shalt thou labour, and do all thy work: (Exo 20:10) But the seventh day is the sabbath of the LORD thy God: in it thou shalt not do any work, thou, nor thy son, nor thy daughter, thy manservant, nor thy maidservant, nor thy cattle, nor thy stranger that is within thy gates: (Exo 20:11) For in six days the LORD made heaven and earth, the sea, and all that in them is, and rested the seventh day: wherefore the LORD blessed the sabbath day, and hallowed it.

There are instructions to: Remember – Keep it Holy – Labor six days – Seventh day is the Sabbath of the Lord thy God – Not do any work – Lord blessed the Sabbath day and hallowed it.

But to whom were these commandments given? I was reared by a sweet mother to believe that they were given to me. Yet when I look back a few verses to verse 2 it reads, "I am the LORD thy God, which have brought thee out of the land of Egypt..." Like most of you I have never visited Egypt and I was never brought out by the LORD from Egypt. So, to whom were these commandments given? Well to the slave nation of Israel, of course, whom the LORD took out of Egypt, through the Red Sea, and into the wilderness.

At this point I want to talk to people who believe that these 10 were a restatement of God commandments to their fore-fathers and therefore have always been. PLEASE look at

Deuteronomy 5: 2-4 for proof positive that this covenant was made with the nation of Israel exclusively at Horeb!
Deu 5:2 The LORD our God made a covenant with us in Horeb.
Deu 5:3 The LORD made not this covenant with our fathers, but with us, even us, who are all of us here alive this day. Deu 5:4 The LORD talked with you face to face in the mount out of the midst of the fire... (Bolding is mine for emphasis).

Can any reasonably intelligent human being really believe that God somehow forgot that he had made this same covenant with Abraham, Isaac and Jacob in the past? It is mind boggling to me, but there are some for doctrinal and false prophet protection will argue against this crystal clear statement!

So recapping as not to forget and to emphasize what we have seen so far from the scriptures:
* There is no mention of the Sabbath day until Exodus 16:23.
* The Sabbath was a part of Lord's commandments.
* It was a test of faith.
* It was a part of the Ten Commandments given exclusively to Israel upon deliverance from Egypt.

Yet some will ask, saying I agree with everything written above, but aren't these moral laws? And if moral laws, aren't we to abide by them even today? To you I say, no. Before you get flustered and angry and begin spouting proof texts to support your belief, let me explain. Just because something has value to a society, doesn't necessarily make it a moral law that must be followed as law.

Resting is a great benefit to humankind. Fatigue related depressions are a plague in modernized societies. Workaholism is separating families and leading to illnesses. Yet rest rejuvenates the mind, body, and spirit. So rest is good and has value to society. On another line of thought there is value to separating diseased people from healthy. It is called quarantining. It is used to protect both the ill and healthy from one another. Yet how many would support the lonely and humiliating practice of "leprosy" colonies today and requiring that people cry out "unclean." to prevent against unknown contact. To use the principles of resting and disease control is both wise and gracious. Yet to enforce old convenant laws today is unnecessary and ungracious.

So what does the Lord Jesus have to say about the Old Covenant that He Himself instituted with the people of Israel. After all it doesn't matter what I say, it's what Jesus teaches and requires that matters, right?

Galatians 4:21-31 is another crystal clear set of instructions for Christians today.

(Gal 4:21) Tell me, you who desire to be under the law, do you not listen to the law? (Gal 4:22) For it is written that Abraham had two sons, one by a slave woman and one by a free woman. (Gal 4:23) But the son of the slave was born according to the flesh, while the son of the free woman was born through promise. (Gal 4:24) Now this may be interpreted allegorically: these women are two covenants. One is from Mount Sinai, bearing children for slavery; she is Hagar. (Gal 4:25) Now Hagar is Mount Sinai in Arabia; she corresponds to the present Jerusalem, for she is in slavery with her children. (Gal 4:26) But the Jerusalem above is free, and she is our mother. (ESV)

Now that you have died to self and been rejuvenated by the Holy Spirit of Jesus Christ, why would you want to be under the bond woman of the law? It is simply crazy to be holding on to that which was sent away. So for every New Covenant Christian reading this book, most of you know this, however many do not. Christ died for everyone... yes everyone! And with his blood he instituted a new covenant. He died and we symbolically die with him too. At death we are freed from our covenant commitments, such as marriage. If you have died in Christ then you are a part of the New and better Covenant. You are the bride of Christ now. So let me ask you this, why are you holding on to the Old and the New together? It is like having an affair against your true husband or wife. So remember to be children of the correct parent.

(Gal 4:28) Now you, brothers, like Isaac, are children of promise. (Gal 4:29) But just as at that time he who was born according to the flesh persecuted him who was born according to the Spirit, so also it is now. (Gal 4:30) But what does the Scripture say? "Cast out the slave woman and her son, for the son of the slave woman shall not inherit with the son of the free woman." (Gal 4:31) So, brothers, we are not children of the slave but of the free woman. (ESV)

Let's pause again for a summary of what we have learned up to now:
* There is no mention of the Sabbath day until Exodus 16:23.
* The Sabbath was a part of Lord's commandments.
* It was a test of faith.
* It was a part of the Ten Commandments given exclusively to Israel upon deliverance from Egypt.
* The New Covenant equates Sinai with Hagar the bond woman of the flesh and better covenant with those who are free and true sons of God.

What has become known as the Jerusalem Council decision adds further insights. I recommend reading the entire account as I will pick out salient parts for my writing. Acts 15:5 tells us the point of discussion. The new believers in Christ at times were confused and didn't yet understand, in my humble opinion, exactly what the crucifixion provided. Praise God that he knew this would be the case and put leaders in place. In Acts 15: 5 we see

"But some of the believers from the party of the Pharisees stood up and said, "It is necessary to circumcise them and to command them to keep the law of Moses! " (HCSB)

Why was cutting the skin from a penis so important to these people. My guess is what it signified. Circumcision was the sign of the Old Covenant. If men still had to be circumcised then they still had to obey the Old Covenant commandments and laws in flesh. A lot was riding on this decision. Must Christians obey the Old Covenant and the entrance sign or is this simply unnecessary?

Act 15:19 Therefore, in my judgment, we should not cause difficulties for those who turn to God from among the Gentiles, Act 15:20 but instead we should write to them to abstain from things polluted by idols, from sexual immorality, from eating anything that has been strangled, and from blood. (HCSB)

I'm very gratified by the decision made at the Jerusalem Council all those many years ago. It seems to me that if the Ten Commandments were so important, the edict would have been; keep them and not just a few social expectable actions. For those who say that Christians today must obey the Old Covenant I simply say, no way! If that were the standard, we'd all be in hell and the Kingdom of God would be a deserted place when it came to human occupants.

I can also remember the argument as a young man, that the Ten Commandments were eternal and not a part of the Old Covenant because God spoke them and wrote them on a table of stone. This sounded pretty good on the surface, but then I realized years later that God spoke all the Old Covenant. Some parts were spoken directly to the people of Israel and as requested by the terrified people, some to Moses. But again what does the bible tell us on this matter? Lets look at Deuteronomy 4:12-14.

Deu 4:12 Then the LORD spoke to you from the fire. You kept hearing the sound of the words, but didn't see a form; there was only a voice. Deu 4:13 He declared His covenant to you. He commanded you to follow the Ten Commandments, which He wrote on two stone tablets.

Deu 4:14 At that time the LORD commanded me to teach you statutes and ordinances for you to follow in the land you are about to cross into and possess (HCSB).

Once again I ask, could it be said any simpler that the Ten Commandments are a part of the Old Covenant?

The scope of this writing is not large enough to go into all the Old Covenant aspect. I would encourage the reader to study the book of Leviticus and observe all the symbolic imaginary and shadows. The Sabbath Rest being Christ, the sacrifices all fulfilled in Christ, the Sanctuary on earth that was a poor representation of the one in heaven (read the book of Hebrews too) etcetera. Why is this reading important? It will help you to know without doubt how wonderfully our Lord and Savior Jesus Christ fulfilled the law and prophets completely and that to look back is to grasp at shadows. The shadow leads you only to the solid image and that is Jesus Christ. So Be Well and Live Saved!

This ends the contribution by Jim Lindsey.

To end this discussion, I would like to represent Romans 14 (KJV) in its entirety, for the sake of context.

Romans 14:1 Him that is weak in the faith receive ye, but not to doubtful disputations. 2 For one believeth that he may eat all things: another, who is weak, eateth herbs. 3 Let not him that eateth despise him that eateth not; and let not him which eateth not judge him that eateth: for God hath received him. 4 Who art thou that judgest another man's servant? to his own master he standeth or falleth. Yea, he shall be holden up: for God is able to make him stand. 5 One man esteemeth one day above another: another esteemeth every day alike. Let every man be fully persuaded in his own mind. 6 He that regardeth the day, regardeth it unto the Lord; and he that regardeth not the day, to the Lord he doth not regard it. He that eateth, eateth to the Lord, for he giveth God thanks; and he that eateth not, to the Lord he eateth not, and giveth God thanks. 7 For none of us liveth to himself, and no man dieth to himself. 8 For whether we live, we live unto the Lord; and whether we die, we die unto the Lord: whether we live therefore, or die, we are the Lord's. 9 For to this end Christ both died, and rose, and revived, that he might be Lord both of the dead and living. 10 But why dost thou judge thy brother? or why dost thou set at nought thy brother? for we shall all stand before the judgment seat of Christ. 11 For it is written, As I live, saith the Lord, every knee shall bow to me, and every tongue shall confess to

God. 12 So then every one of us shall give account of himself to God. 13 Let us not therefore judge one another any more: but judge this rather, that no man put a stumblingblock or an occasion to fall in his brother's way.

14 I know, and am persuaded by the Lord Jesus, that there is nothing unclean of itself: but to him that esteemeth any thing to be unclean, to him it is unclean. 15But if thy brother be grieved with thy meat, now walkest thou not charitably. Destroy not him with thy meat, for whom Christ died. 16 Let not then your good be evil spoken of:

17 For the kingdom of God is not meat and drink; but righteousness, and peace, and joy in the Holy Ghost. 18 For he that in these things serveth Christ is acceptable to God, and approved of men.

19 Let us therefore follow after the things which make for peace, and things wherewith one may edify another. 20 For meat destroy not the work of God. All things indeed are pure; but it is evil for that man who eateth with offence. 21 It is good neither to eat flesh, nor to drink wine, nor any thing whereby thy brother stumbleth, or is offended, or is made weak. 22 Hast thou faith? have it to thyself before God. Happy is he that condemneth not himself in that thing which he alloweth. 23 And he that doubteth is damned if he eat, because he eateth not of faith: for whatsoever is not of faith is sin.

This being said, the question remains, shouldn't we seek to do the better thing? The Sabbath was never abolished.
Knowing all of this, what will you do now?

Tithes and Offerings

In the 1970's I sat in front of my black and white TV watching the great Reverend Ike. He was a raucous black TV evangelist with a bright white suite and teeth to match. Ike would stir his audience by alternately showing his wealth and chastising his viewers for being poor. "If you believe money is the root of all evil, send me your evil." "Money is not the root of all evil. Lack of money is the root of all evil."

Reverend Ike had worked out all the angles. You could send in a donation and he would pray that you would receive money. If you felt like God had blessed you, he would take your praise offering. If you felt like your money was somehow impeding your spiritual growth, Ike was there to lessen your burden by taking your evil money or selling you lessons in how to create and handle wealth.

Reverend Ike, whose real name was Frederick Eikerenkoetter, once told his followers "the best thing you can do for the poor is not to be one of them." (Ike died in 2009)

According to Tvparty.com, a website about vintage TV shows, a newspaper ad from the 70's touting Reverend Ike is quoted:

"If you want 'pie-in-the-sky when you die' then Rev. Ike is not your man. If you want your pie now, with ice cream on top, then see and hear Rev. Ike on TV."

Millions of mostly poor people tuned in each week to hear sermons from the flamboyant Reverend Ike, who drove flashy Cadillacs and stood at the pulpit dripping in gold chains and diamond rings. When criticized for his lifestyle, Ike would defend himself by saying, "There is nothing wrong with a prosperous man of God;" referring back to his catch phrase, "The LACK of money is the root of all evil."

No, this wasn't a sitcom, farce, or satire. Ike's show was a Sunday morning religious must-see for countless poor people wishing and hoping for a way out of poverty and despair.

Ike was not the only televangelist, but he was one of the first to preach a prosperity message, the aim of which was to enable the preacher to prosper. By flaunting his riches and promising viewers they too can be rich, countless prosperity teachers turned the table on the poor, making them poorer. Throughout the early Seventies and even until today, it is the poor, desperate, and hopeless who keep the televangelists in their opulent lifestyle.

Reverend Ike was one of the first television evangelists who shamelessly pandered for cash and was openly proud of what he spent it on – gold, diamonds, new cars and beautiful women. Now the women are kept behind the scenes but little more has changed. Sleazy preachers with wives dressed like Bo Peep wearing a pink Dolly Parton wig waft across our TVs with little or no complaints from us. We snicker at the antics of preachers who hire hookers and then, sounding like our ex-presidents, claim they never had sex with that woman.

After other preachers saw what could be done to fleece the flocks through TV and radio, televangelists came out in droves to test their skills. Swaggart, Bakker, Crouch, Copeland, Capps, Bishop Eddie Long, and many more built empires on the backs of the poor. Begging for money, crying on cue, and promising God would bless the giver and curse those who did not obey. If the listener was not blessed the preacher would simply claim the giver did not have enough faith, did not give enough money, or had some unnamed sin in his or her life.

Our donations put thousand dollar suits on the backs of these charlatans. Our money put hookers in their beds, bought painfully horrid wigs and non-waterproof makeup for their wives, so that we could see their tears run like mud, down their cheeks as they pleaded for one more dollar. One would think this must truly be the Dark Age of Christianity, but it just gets worse.

Evangelist Oral Roberts attempted and accomplished the emotional blackmail of his followers by threatening to die on cue. He proclaimed; "God will take me home" unless the public donates $8 million over the next two months. If he truly

believed that heaven was a better place; one must ask w
did not keep his mouth shut and take the ride.

Bishop Bernard Jordan claims he is a "Master" Prophet. We
assume all that came before him must have been regular
prophets? But, if Jesus or Samuel had enough money, they too
could become a prophet, but only a regular prophet. Not a
master prophet. That would cost extra. According to his web
site, you too could become a prophet for a gift of $3000. Jordan
will gladly teach you the tricks of the trade.

This is a far cry from 1Tim6:8-10,20.
6But godliness with contentment is great gain. 7For we brought
nothing into the world, and we can take nothing out of it. 8But
if we have food and clothing, we will be content with that.
9People who want to get rich fall into temptation and a trap
and into many foolish and harmful desires that plunge men
into ruin and destruction. 10For the love of money is a root of
all kinds of evil. Some people, eager for money, have wandered
from the faith and pierced themselves with many griefs.

20Timothy, guard what has been entrusted to your care. Turn
away from godless chatter and the opposing ideas of what is
falsely called knowledge, 21which some have professed and in
so doing have wandered from the faith.
Grace be with you.

Is this really how tithing is supposed to work? Are we really
supposed to give out of our lack to men who are rich, in hope
that God will reward our faith? If we give away our child's
milk money is it God's responsibility to reward us?
What are tithes and offerings? Are we still supposed to tithe?

The dictionary defines the tithe as : one tenth of annual
produce or earnings, formerly taken as a tax for the support of
the church and clergy.
• (in certain religious denominations) a tenth of an individual's
income pledged to the church.

• [in sing.] (archaic) a tenth of a specified thing : he hadn't said a tithe of the prayers he knew.
verb [trans.] pay or give as a tithe : he tithes 10 percent of his income to the church.

In a brief historical search, one immediately finds that the idea and practice of the tithe is not a new one, nor is it confined to Judeo-Christian peoples. It was common among most warrior nations, of which ancient Israel was one.

"Tithes, a form of taxation, secular and ecclesiastical, usually, as the name implies, consisting of one-tenth of a man's property or produce. The tax probably originated in a tribute levied by a conqueror or ruler upon his subjects, and perhaps the custom of dedicating a tenth of the spoils of war to the gods led to the religious extension of the term, the original offerings to deity being "first fruits."

"Through the spoils of war, Edward was able to refill the bankrupt treasury. Heavily ransomed prisoners, brought fortunes in gold coin to their noble captors--who, in turn, paid a handsome tithe to the King." (Edward III: King of Illusions)

"It was traditional to give the Byzantine Government a set percentage of the spoils of war." (Chapter III: Eastern Expansion, emphasis added)

The Greeks and Romans practiced tithing.
"In the same manner the Greeks too, the Carthaginians, and the Romans devoted a tenth portion of the spoils of war to their deities." (On the Acquisition of Territory and Property by Right of Conquest)

"The Greek League against Persia, founded in 481 vows a tenth of the spoils of war to the shrine, and this happens, after Salamis and Plataea." (Herodotus on Greek Religion)

"During the twelfth century, evidence points to the growing significance of warfare between cities in Portugal, Leon, Castile and Aragon. Precise indications are demonstrated in the increasing concern of the makers of the municipal charters in three areas closely related to booty. The first is the royal demand to collect the one-fifth tax on the spoils of war, a tax the Christian rulers inherited from the Muslim practice of laying aside a portion of the gains of the jihad for Allah." (Spoils and Compensations) This practice continues today as the Taliban demands payment from the poppy growers and sellers of opium in Afghanistan to pay for their war against Christian nations.

"For his courageous role in helping to conquer the Volscian town of Corioli, Caius Marcius was offered a tithe. For declining to accept one-tenth of the spoils, he was named Coriolanus" (after the city he conquered.) (Roman Expansion to 133 BC)

"In the days of Abu Bakr much wealth came to the state on account of the spoils of war. The movable property won as booty on the battlefield was known as "Ghanimah." Four-fifths of the spoils of war were immediately distributed among the soldiers who had taken part in the battle. The remaining one-fifth went to the State. The State's one-fifth share was further divided into three parts. One part went to the family of the Holy Prophet, one part went to the Caliph, and one part was spent for welfare purposes." (Political, Social, Economic and Military Organization)

The tithe served a purpose. It could make a government rich, and allow them to wage war. Of these, the Catholic Church did both, and the Vatican became the wealthiest nation on Earth. A tithe to the church was a tax paid to the Vatican.

But, if we strip away the desire for wealth and war, and examine the tithe in a purely religious light, before the formation of the Vatican city-state, we may be able to see what it is and what it means in the New Testament age of grace.

The earliest Christian assemblies patterned themselves after the Jewish synagogues, which were led by rabbis who, like Paul, refused to profit from teaching God's Word. These men all had occupations. Paul, for example, was a tent maker. None took money from the church.

The Jewish rabbis had a saying: "Whoever does not teach his son a trade is as if he brought him up to be a robber." Accordingly, when Paul was on his second missionary journey and came to Corinth, the first thing he did was seek work to sustain his needs. Paul made tents during the week, or perhaps at night, but on the Sabbath he went to the Jewish synagogue to preach about Jesus to the Jews.

From Christ's death until Christianity became a legally recognized religion almost 300 years later, the majority of great church leaders took Jesus' words to the rich young ruler in Luke 18:22 literally "sell all that you have, give it to the poor, and follow me." Historians agree that for the first 200 years of Christianity, leaders and preachers took vows of poverty and worked for a living so that they were self-supporting.

1 Peter 5 (Holman Christian Standard Bible)
1 Therefore, as a fellow elder and witness to the sufferings of the Messiah, and also a participant in the glory about to be revealed, I exhort the elders among you: 2 shepherd God's flock among you, not overseeing out of compulsion but freely, according to God's [will]; not for the money but eagerly; 3 not lording it over those entrusted to you, but being examples to the flock. 4 And when the chief Shepherd appears, you will receive the unfading crown of glory.

There were times when one church supported missions to poorer churches. They donated funds to assist missionary trips to other Christians.

"I robbed other churches, taking wages of them that I might minister unto you; and when I was present with you and was in want, I was not a burden on any man; for the brethren, when they came from Macedonia, supplied the measure of my want . . ." (2 Cor. 11:8-9).

1 Thessalonians 2 (Holman Christian Standard Bible)
5 For we never used flattering speech, as you know, or had greedy motives —God is our witness — 6 and we didn't seek glory from people, either from you or from others. 7 Although we could have been a burden as Christ's apostles, instead we were gentle among you, as a nursing mother nurtures her own children. 8 We cared so much for you that we were pleased to

share with you not only the gospel of God but also our own lives, because you had become dear to us. 9 For you remember our labor and hardship, brothers. Working night and day so that we would not burden any of you, we preached God's gospel to you. 10 You are witnesses, and so is God, of how devoutly, righteously, and blamelessly we conducted ourselves with you believers. 11 As you know, like a father with his own children, 12 we encouraged, comforted, and implored each one of you to walk worthy of God, who calls you into His own kingdom and glory.

Having seen what greed and preaching for money had done to the Gospel, Paul sent a letter to Timothy warning him to keep watch for those who wished to make money off of the death of the Lord.

1 Timothy 6 (The Message)

2-5These are the things I want you to teach and preach. If you have leaders there who teach otherwise, who refuse the solid words of our Master Jesus and this godly instruction, tag them for what they are: ignorant windbags who infect the air with germs of envy, controversy, bad-mouthing, suspicious rumors. Eventually there's an epidemic of backstabbing, and truth is but a distant memory. They think religion is a way to make a fast buck.

In an attempt to keep in line with the apostles, early church fathers opposed tithing, but supported the free will donations of believers.

Clement of Rome (c95), Justin Martyr (c150), Irenaeus (c150-200) and Tertullian (c150-220) all opposed tithing as a strictly Jewish tradition. The Didache, a book of conduct and rules that was said to have come from the Apostles but was written around 150-200 A.D., condemns traveling preachers who stay longer than three days and ask for money. And travelers who decided to remain with the established leaders or churches were required to learn a trade.

ɔ hundred and fifty years after the death of Jesus and the ıshment of Christianity there was no tithe. What ha‚pened to change all of this? It is quite simple. The church morphed from a spiritual seat of power into a political power base. Like any political structure bent on its own growth and survival, it needed money.

Cyprian (200-258) was a great teacher and orator in Carthage. He was raised a pagan. Cyprian tried unsuccessfully to impose tithing on a governmental level in Carthage, North Africa, around A. D. 250. However at his conversion to Christianity, Cyprian gave away great personal wealth to the poor and lived under a vow of poverty. His idea of tithing included equal re-distribution to the poor. His ideas were not adopted.

Still, at that time there were those fighting to keep spirituality in the church. Many of the greatest spiritual leaders took vows of poverty and preferred to live in monasteries, but their numbers were too few.

Slowly, the need for money grew as the church grew. Most church historians agree that tithing did not become an accepted doctrine in the church for over 700 years after the death of Jesus. According to the best sources, in the year 585, the local church Council of Macon in France, tried unsuccessfully to enforce tithing on its members. This is the last known descent. The church was becoming much too strong. Soon it would have its way.

By the time Christianity became legal in the fourth century the church had acquired a solid structure and hierarchy. It was reborn as a political force whose organization needed money to pay its administrators and overseers. Its purpose turned from the spreading of the Gospel to self-perpetuation and the accumulation of wealth and power.

It is very important to understand the changing structure of the church and its growing demand for funds. Until the establishment of a centralized power, the church was a horizontally structured, grassroots movement. Believers "seeded" the word in others and small groups grew that gathered in homes throughout the area. Pastors or Bishops were overseers for groups in cities, which were spread out like clumps of grass in a desert. Letters were sent between them to keep in touch and encourage each other to persevere and conduct themselves correctly. Donations were kept within the area to supply the needs of the widows, orphans, and infirm. If needed, a wealthier church might send money to a less prosperous group. No money went to the church at Rome.

When a power base coalesced the structure was turned on its side. Now the Bishop of Rome gained control of Christendom. He appointed men to run the church, do his bidding, and report to him. This is the hierarchy of the modern church and almost every denomination. To sustain his office he needed money. To expand his empire he needed lots of money.

The Bishop of Rome, now known as the pope, a word meaning "father", appointed Cardinals, to rule regions, and bishops to rule cities and areas, and priests to rule the people. Now, we have a vertical political structure, whose job is to gather money and send it up the chain to the top. The Vatican became a city-state, ruling the world, waging wars, and through its wealth it changed the face of the world. The pope persuaded King Charlemagne and in the year 777 the king legally allowed the church to collect tithes. This was tantamount to taxation by the church. (See "The history of tithing", found in the Encyclopedia Britannica, Encyclopedia Americana and the Roman Catholic Encyclopedia.")

This was never the purpose of the tithe.

This is the secular history, but what does the Bible say?

The first mention of tithing was in Genesis 14:20 where Abraham 'gave tithes of all' to Melchizedek. Notice how Abraham did this freely. It was not a commandment from God. Abraham was a pagan and he gave the spoils of his conquests and wars freely. Then the next mention of tithing is in Leviticus 27.

Leviticus 27 (New International Version)

1 The LORD said to Moses, 2 "Speak to the Israelites and say to them: 'If anyone makes a special vow to dedicate persons to the LORD by giving equivalent values, 3 set the value of a male between the ages of twenty and sixty at fifty shekels of silver, according to the sanctuary shekel; 4 and if it is a female, set her value at thirty shekels. 5 If it is a person between the ages of five and twenty, set the value of a male at twenty shekels and of a female at ten shekels. 6 If it is a person between one month and five years, set the value of a male at five shekels of silver and that of a female at three shekels of silver. 7 If it is a person sixty years old or more, set the value of a male at fifteen shekels and of a female at ten shekels. 8 If anyone making the vow is too poor to pay the specified amount, he is to present the person to the priest, who will set the value for him according to what the man making the vow can afford.
9 " 'If what he vowed is an animal that is acceptable as an offering to the LORD, such an animal given to the LORD becomes holy. 10 He must not exchange it or substitute a good one for a bad one, or a bad one for a good one; if he should substitute one animal for another, both it and the substitute become holy. 11 If what he vowed is a ceremonially unclean animal — one that is not acceptable as an offering to the LORD - the animal must be presented to the priest, 12 who will judge its quality as good or bad. Whatever value the priest then sets, that is what it will be. 13 If the owner wishes to redeem the animal, he must add a fifth to its value.
14 " 'If a man dedicates his house as something holy to the LORD, the priest will judge its quality as good or bad. Whatever value the priest then sets, so it will remain. 15 If the man who dedicates his house redeems it, he must add a fifth to its value, and the house will again become his.
16 " 'If a man dedicates to the LORD part of his family land, its value is to be set according to the amount of seed required for it — fifty shekels of silver to a homer [i] of barley seed. 17 If he dedicates his field during the Year of Jubilee, the value that has been set remains. 18 But if he dedicates his field after the Jubilee, the priest will determine the value according to the

number of years that remain until the next Year of Jubilee, and its set value will be reduced. 19 If the man who dedicates the field wishes to redeem it, he must add a fifth to its value, and the field will again become his. 20 If, however, he does not redeem the field, or if he has sold it to someone else, it can never be redeemed. 21 When the field is released in the Jubilee, it will become holy, like a field devoted to the LORD; it will become the property of the priests. [j]

22 " 'If a man dedicates to the LORD a field he has bought, which is not part of his family land, 23 the priest will determine its value up to the Year of Jubilee, and the man must pay its value on that day as something holy to the LORD. 24 In the Year of Jubilee the field will revert to the person from whom he bought it, the one whose land it was. 25 Every value is to be set according to the sanctuary shekel, twenty gerahs to the shekel.

26 " 'No one, however, may dedicate the firstborn of an animal, since the firstborn already belongs to the LORD; whether an ox [k] or a sheep, it is the LORD's. 27 If it is one of the unclean animals, he may buy it back at its set value, adding a fifth of the value to it. If he does not redeem it, it is to be sold at its set value.

28 " 'But nothing that a man owns and devotes [l] to the LORD -whether man or animal or family land—may be sold or redeemed; everything so devoted is most holy to the LORD.

29 " 'No person devoted to destruction [m] may be ransomed; he must be put to death.

30 " 'A tithe of everything from the land, whether grain from the soil or fruit from the trees, belongs to the LORD; it is holy to the LORD. 31 If a man redeems any of his tithe, he must add a fifth of the value to it. 32 The entire tithe of the herd and flock—every tenth animal that passes under the shepherd's rod—will be holy to the LORD. 33 He must not pick out the good from the bad or make any substitution. If he does make a substitution, both the animal and its substitute become holy and cannot be redeemed.' "

34 These are the commands the LORD gave Moses on Mount Sinai for the Israelites.

Footnotes:
3. Leviticus 27:3 That is, about 1 1/4 pounds (about 0.6 kilogram also in verse 16
4. Leviticus 27:3 That is, about 2/5 ounce (about 11.5 grams also in verse 25
5. Leviticus 27:4 That is, about 12 ounces (about 0.3 kilogram)
6. Leviticus 27:5 That is, about 8 ounces (about 0.2 kilogram)
7. Leviticus 27:5 That is, about 4 ounces (about 110 grams also in verse
8. Leviticus 27:6 That is, about 2 ounces (about 55 grams)
9. Leviticus 27:6 That is, about 1 1/4 ounces (about 35 grams)
10. Leviticus 27:7 That is, about 6 ounces (about 170 grams)
11. Leviticus 27:16 That is, probably about 6 bushels (about 220 liters)
12. Leviticus 27:21 Or priest
13. Leviticus 27:26 The Hebrew word can include both male and female.
14. Leviticus 27:28 The Hebrew term refers to the irrevocable giving over of things or persons to the LORD.
Leviticus 27:29 The Hebrew term refers to the irrevocable giving over of things or persons to the LORD, often by totally destroying them.
(Quoted from biblegateway.com)

The "first tithe" described in the Torah actually goes not to the poor, but to the tribe of the Levites.

Torah presents the tribe of Levi as a class of itinerant scholars who collect taxes from free citizens. They do this because Levites do not own land and have no place to grow their food. Instead, they are fed by the people through a tax of one tenth of the food.

"Don't abandon the Levite in your gates, for he has no portion and inheritance among you"
(Deuteronomy 14:27).

More precisely, their inheritance is spiritual, not material: "Therefore, Levi has no portion and inheritance with his brothers; the Lord is his inheritance, as the Lord your God spoke to him" (Deuteronomy 10:9).

The first tithe, which is given to the tribe of Levi, is meant to compensate them for devotion to God's work: "And to the children of Levi I have given the tithe in Israel as a portion, in return for the service they serve, the service of the Tent of Meeting" (Numbers 18:21).

The second tithe also was not devoted solely to the poor. The agricultural cycle in the land of Israel is seven years in duration. In the seventh, or Sabbatical year, all produce is freely available to all. In the third and sixth years, there is a second tithe given to the poor. In the remaining four years, the farmer himself takes the second tithe, or its value, and consumes it in Jerusalem together with his family, taking due care to share it also with the less fortunate.
"And the Levite, who has no portion and inheritance with you, will come; and the stranger, and the orphan and the widow in your gates; and they will eat and be satisfied, so that the Lord your God will bless you in everything you do" (Deuteronomy 14:29).
Some think food was used because money was not available. This does not seem to be the case. Money was an essential everyday item. For example Abraham was very rich in silver and gold (Gen 13:2); money in the form of silver shekels paid for slaves (Gen 17:12); Abimelech gave Abraham 1000 pieces of silver (Gen 20:16); Abraham paid 400 pieces of silver for land (Gen 23:9-16); Joseph was sold for silver pieces (Gen 37:28); slaves bought freedom (Ex 23:11); court fines (Ex 21 all; 22 all); sanctuary dues (Ex 30:12); vows (Lev 27:3-7); poll taxes (Num 3:47+), alcoholic drinks (Deu 14:26) and marriage dowries (Deu 22:29).
Joseph gave Benjamin 300 pieces of silver (Gen 45:22). According to Genesis 47:15-17, food was used for barter only

after money had been spent. Banking and usury laws exist in Leviticus even before tithing. Yet the tithe contents from Leviticus to Matthew never include money from non-food products and trades.

The Biblical tithing obligation applies only to agricultural produce in the land of Israel. But for hundreds of years it has been customary to donate a portion of our income to charity, and the most accepted amount is one tenth of after-tax income. The Shulchan Aruch (authoritative Code of Jewish law) states that the average person should give one-tenth of his income to charity. However, this is only a custom. This custom retains the spirit of the original agricultural tithe. The personal element is maintained, as this tithe is distributed according to individual discretion.

Although money existed before tithing, the source of God's "tithe" over 1500 years was never money. It was the "tithe of food." Old Testament biblical tithes were always only food from the farms and herds of only Israelites who only lived inside God's Holy Land, the national boundary of Israel. No tithes were accepted from defiled pagan lands. The "increase" was gathered from what God miraculously produced and not from man's craft or ability.

There are 16 verses from 11 chapters and 8 books from Leviticus 27 to Luke 11 which describe the contents of the tithe. And the contents never (again), never included money, silver, gold or anything other than food from inside Israel! (See Lev. 27:30, 32; Num. 18:27-28; Deut. 12:17; 14:22-23; 26:12; 2 Chron. 31:5-6; Neh. 10:37; 13:5; Mal. 3:10-11; Matt. 23:23; Luke 11: 42).

Only those Israelites who earned a livelihood from farming and herding inside Israel were required to tithe under the Mosaic Law. Their increase came from God's hand. Those whose increase came from their own crafts and skills were not required to tithe products and money. The poor and needy did not tithe but received from the tithe freewill offerings.

The "whole" tithe, the first tithe, did not go to the priests at all. It was not even the "best" tenth (Lev 27:30-34). According to Numbers 18:21-24 and Nehemiah 10:37b, it went to the servants of the priests, the Levites. And according to Numbers 18:25-28 and Nehemiah 10:38, the Levites gave the "best tenth of this tithe" (1%) which they received to the priests who ministered the sin sacrifices and served inside the holy places. Priests did not tithe.

Revelation 1:6 (King James Version)
6And hath made us kings and priests unto God and his Father; to him be glory and dominion for ever and ever. Amen.

First-fruits and first-born offerings went directly to the Temple and were required to be totally consumed by ministering priests only inside the Temple (Neh. 10:35-37a; Ex. 23:19; 34:26; Deut. 18:4). The first-fruit was small enough to fit into a hand-held basket (Deut. 26:1-10; Lev. 23:17; Num. 18:13-17; Neh. 12:44; 2 Chron 31:5a). (Note: Levitical cities were not owned by the Levites. They were simply set apart for them, as the cities of sanctuary were set apart.)

The whole Levitical tithe went first to the Levitical cities and portions went to the Temple to feed both Levites and priests who were ministering there in rotation (Neh. 10:37b-39; 12:27-29, 44-47; Num. 18:21-28; 2 Chron 31:5b). While the Levites ate only the tithe, the priests could also eat from the first-fruits, first-born offerings and other offerings.

Jesus was a carpenter; Paul was a tent maker and Peter was a fisherman. None of these occupations qualified as tithe-payers because they did not farm or herd animals for a living. It is, therefore, incorrect to teach that everybody paid a required minimum of a tithe and, therefore, that New Covenant Christians should be required to at least begin at the same minimum as Old Covenant Israelites. This common false assumption is very often repeated and completely ignores the very plain definition of tithe as food gathered from farm increase or herd increase.

The widow's mite is an example of free-will giving and is not an example of tithing. According to Edersheim none of the

Temple's chests were for tithes. The poor received money from those chests before leaving the temple.

It is also wrong to teach that the poor in Israel were required to pay tithes. In fact, they actually received tithes! Much of the second festival tithe and all of a special third-year tithe went to the poor! Many laws protected the poor from abuse and expensive sacrifices which they could not afford (Lev. 14:21; 25:6, 25-28, 35, 36; 27:8; Deu. 12:1-19; 14:23, 28, 29; 15:7, 8, 11; 24:12, 14, 15, 19, 20; 26:11-13; Mal. 3:5; Matt. 12:1, 2; Mark 2:23, 24; Luke 2:22-24; 6:1, 2; 2 Cor. 8:12-14; 1 Tim. 5:8; Jas. 1:27).

In the Hebrew economy, the tithe was used in a totally different manner than it is preached and applied today. Once again, those Levites who received the whole tithe were not ministers or priests -- they were only servants to the priests.

Numbers chapter 3 describes the Levites as carpenters, metal workers, leather-craftsmen and artists who maintained the small sanctuary. And, according to First Chronicles, chapters 23-26, during the time of King David and King Solomon the Levites were still skilled craftsmen who inspected and approved all work in the Temple: 24, 000 worked in the Temple as builders and supervisors; 6,000 were officials and judges; 4,000 were guards and 4,000 were musicians. As political representatives of the king, Levites used their tithe income to serve as officials, judges, tax collectors, treasurers, temple guards, musicians, bakers, singers and professional soldiers (1 Chron. 12:23, 26; 23:2-5; 26:29-32; 27:5). It is obvious why these examples of using biblical tithe-income are never used as examples in the church today.

We see that the original tithing obligation of the Torah, and its modern-day equivalent, are far more than a simple "poor tax"; they served as a social security or food bank system. No priest ever got rich off of the tithe.

So what about the New Testament? Is tithing mentioned? We can see Jesus apparently endorsing tithes in Matthew 23:23 and Luke 11:42.

Woe to you, scribes and Pharisees, hypocrites! For you pay tithe of mint and anise and cummin, and have neglected the weightier matters of the law: justice and mercy and faith. These you ought to have done, without leaving the others undone. (Matthew 23:23)

These scriptures are the ones that people use as proof that Jesus commanded that we tithe today, but while Jesus was alive he was still operating under the Old Testament laws and the New Testament had not fully been ratified.

Hebrews 9:15-17 makes it clear that a new testament can only come in place after the death of the testator.

15 And for this reason He is the Mediator of the new covenant, by means of death, for the redemption of the transgressions under the first covenant, that those who are called may receive the promise of the eternal inheritance.

16 For where there is a testament, there must also of necessity be the death of the testator. 17 For a testament is in force after men are dead, since it has no power at all while the testator lives.

New Testament tithing is a gift or donation, not a tithe. This is defined clearly in Second Corinthians, which gives us the principles for giving today.

"So let each one give as he purposes in his heart, not grudgingly or of necessity; for God loves a cheerful giver." (2 Cor 9:7)

2 Cor 8:11 but now you also must complete the doing of it; that as there was a readiness to desire it, so there also may be a completion out of what you have. 12 For if there is first a willing mind, it is accepted according to what one has, and not according to what he does not have. 13 For I do not mean that others should be eased and you burdened; 14 but by an equality, that now at this time your abundance may supply their lack, that their abundance also may supply your lack—that there may be equality. (2 Cor 8:11-14)

Yes, Christians can be socialists.)

An Essay by Russell Earl Kelly, Ph. D. entitled, "TITHING IS NOT A CHRISTIAN DOCTRINE," sums it up this way:

"Christians are commanded to give freely, sacrificially, generously, regularly, joyfully and with the motivation of love for God and man. The following New Covenant free-will principles are found in Second Corinthians, chapters 8 and 9:

(1) Giving is a "grace." These chapters use the Greek word for "grace" eight times in reference to helping poor saints.

(2) Give yourself to God first (8:5).

(3) Give yourself to knowing God's will (8:5).

(4) Give in response to Christ's gift (8:9; 9:15).

(5) Give out of a sincere desire (8:8, 10, 12; 9:7).

(6) Do not give because of any commandment (8:8, 10; 9:7).

(7) Give beyond your ability (8:3, 11-12).

(8) Give to produce equality. This means that those who have more should give more in order to make up for the inability of those who cannot afford to give as much (8:12-14).

(9) Give joyfully (8:2).

(10) Give because you are growing spiritually (8:3-4, 7).

(11) Give because you want to continue growing spiritually (9:8, 10-11).

(12) Give because you are hearing the gospel preached (9:13)."

Preachers want us to think that all tithes were formerly taken to the Temple and should now be taken to the "church storehouse" building. Early Christians had no church. If they met in a recognized group they were killed.

Nehemiah 10:37b and Second Chronicles 31:15-19 make it clear that the people were to bring the tithes to the Levitical cities where 98% of the Levites and priests needed them for food (also Num 18:21-24). And Nehemiah 10:38 makes it clear that normally only Levites and priests had the task of bringing tithes into the Temple (also Num 18:24-28).

The "whole" tithe never went to the Temple. According to Numbers 35, Joshua 20, 21 and First Chronicles 6, Levites and priests lived on borrowed land where they farmed and raised (tithed) animals. (Also 2nd Chron. 11:13-14; Neh. 12:27-29; 13:10; Mal. 1:14.)

Malachi 3 may be one of the most abused text in the Bible. The "whole" tithe never was supposed to go to the Temple. In Malachi 3:10-11 tithes are still only food 1000 years after Leviticus 27.

Malachi's audience had willingly reaffirmed the Old Covenant (Neh.10:28-29). The blessings and curses of tithing are identical to and inseparable from those of the entire Mosaic Law. The rain in Deuteronomy 28:12, 23-24 and Leviticus 26:1-4 is only obtained by obedience to all 613 commandments in the Old Testament or Torah. Galatians 3:10 (quoting Deut. 27:26) "For as many as are of the works of the law are under the curse: for it is written, Cursed is every one that continues not in all things which are written in the book of the law to do them." Trying to earn God's blessings through tithing only brings curses for failure to keep all of the law. See also Galatians 3:19.

Beginning in 1:6 "you" in Malachi always refers to the dishonest priests and not the people (also 2:1-10; 2:13 to 3:1-5): "Even this whole nation of you --priests" (3:9). In 1:13-14 the priests had stolen tithed animals vowed to God.

Malachi 1

1 An oracle: The word of the LORD to Israel through Malachi. 2 "I have loved you," says the LORD.

"But you ask, 'How have you loved us?'

"Was not Esau Jacob's brother?" the LORD says. "Yet I have loved Jacob, 3 but Esau I have hated, and I have turned his mountains into a wasteland and left his inheritance to the desert jackals."

4 Edom may say, "Though we have been crushed, we will rebuild the ruins." But this is what the LORD Almighty says: "They may build, but I will demolish. They will be called the Wicked Land, a people always under the wrath of the LORD. 5 You will see it with your own eyes and say, 'Great is the LORD -even beyond the borders of Israel!' 6 "A son honors his father, and a servant his master. If I am a father, where is the honor

due me? If I am a master, where is the respect due me?" says the LORD Almighty. "It is you, O priests, who show contempt for my name. "But you ask, 'How have we shown contempt for your name?' 7 "You place defiled food on my altar. "But you ask, 'How have we defiled you?' "By saying that the LORD's table is contemptible. 8 When you bring blind animals for sacrifice, is that not wrong? When you sacrifice crippled or diseased animals, is that not wrong? Try offering them to your governor! Would he be pleased with you? Would he accept you?" says the LORD Almighty. 9 "Now implore God to be gracious to us. With such offerings from your hands, will he accept you?"-says the LORD Almighty.

10 "Oh, that one of you would shut the temple doors, so that you would not light useless fires on my altar! I am not pleased with you," says the LORD Almighty, "and I will accept no offering from your hands. 11 My name will be great among the nations, from the rising to the setting of the sun. In every place incense and pure offerings will be brought to my name, because my name will be great among the nations," says the LORD Almighty. 12 "But you profane it by saying of the Lord's table, 'It is defiled,' and of its food, 'It is contemptible.' 13 And you say, 'What a burden!' and you sniff at it contemptuously," says the LORD Almighty. "When you bring injured, crippled or diseased animals and offer them as sacrifices, should I accept them from your hands?" says the LORD. 14 "Cursed is the cheat who has an acceptable male in his flock and vows to give it, but then sacrifices a blemished animal to the Lord. For I am a great king," says the LORD Almighty, "and my name is to be feared among the nations."

In Nehemiah 13:5-10 priests had stolen the Levites' portion of the tithe. God's curses on the priests are in 1:14; 2:2 and 3:2-4.

Nehemiah 10:37-39 is the key to understanding Malachi 3:10, The people were commanded to bring their tithes, not to the temple, but to the nearby Levitical cities. Verse 38 says that the priests were with the Levites in the Levitical cities when they received the tithes.

According to Nehemiah 13:5, 9 the "storehouse" in the Temple was only several rooms. The real "storehouses" were in the Levitical cites per Nehemiah 10:37b. Only the Levites and priests normally brought tithes to the Temple (10:38). Two rooms in the Temple were far too small to contain the tithe from the entire nation and most of the Levites and priests lived too far away to eat from them.

Therefore, Malachi 3:10's "Bring ye all the tithes into the storehouse" only makes contextual sense if it is only commanding dishonest priests to replace the tithes they had removed from it or had failed to bring to it.

For several centuries after Calvary, Christians did not even have their own buildings (to call storehouses) because Christianity was an outlaw religion.

Although Jesus taught tithing, the New Covenant did not begin at the birth of Jesus, but at his death.

The only texts in the New Testament about tithing are set against the backdrop of Christians who were still going to the temple to tithe and keeping the law. Acts 2:42-47 and 4:32-35 are not examples of tithing to support church leaders. According to 2:46 the Jewish Christians continued to worship in the Temple. And according to 2:44 and 4:33, 34 church leaders shared what they received equally with all church members.

Finally, Acts 21:20-25 proves that Jewish Christians were still zealously observing all of the Mosaic Law 30 years later, and that must include tithing, otherwise they would not have been allowed inside the Temple to worship. Therefore, any tithes collected by the early Jewish Christians were given to the Temple system and not to support the church.

Like other ordinances of the Law, tithing was only a temporary shadow until Christ comes. (Eph. 2:14-16; Col. 2:13-17; Heb. 7:18; 10:1). The function and purpose of Old Covenant priests was replaced by the priesthood of every believer. No longer are there appointed taskmasters to judge our keeping of the law. Now, each man and woman is a priest, equal in status, responsible to the Lord. This is part of the New Covenant. (1 Pet. 2:9-10; Rev. 1:6; 5:10). Every ordinance that had previously applied to the old priesthood was blotted out at the cross. Jesus is now the only High Priest we have, but Jesus was not from the tribe of Levi. Even He was disqualified. Thus the original temporary purpose of tithing no longer exists (Heb. 7:12-19; Gal. 3:19, 24-25; 2 Cor. 3:10-18).

What then is the conclusion of this? How do we give?

The simple truth is this: We must realize that the money we give to our local church or preferred television preacher is not a tithe. It is a sum of money given to insure the continuation of the program we choose to attend or watch. It is a donation. Like a movie ticket, it pays the bills and allows profit, sometimes huge profits, to be realized by the preacher. Very little, if any of that money will go to the poor, widows, orphans, or infirm.

It does not go toward the Kingdom of God. It goes toward growing the kingdom of the preacher. If the church uses some of it for social programs that is wonderful, but it is not the same as feeding the hungry, clothing the destitute, or helping the sick. God enables those he calls by moving the hearts of believers to donate money to their cause. Just because someone's ego drives him or her to spend millions of dollars to get his or her face on TV does not mean I need to support that ego. If my pastor buys an expensive car or house, I am not obligated to support his vanity. The New Testament tells me that I am to see to the widow, orphans, sick, and those in prison. It also hints at the fact that I should not let my preacher starve by "muzzling the mouth of the ox that treads the wheat." Judging by the physique of most pastors in my area, many could use more muzzles and less wheat. Paul's template indicates that pastors should work to support themselves.

Nevertheless, we should make sure the pastors have all they need and not all they want.

The closest pattern to the true tithe is the food pantries of some churches and community shelters, where the poor come to be fed. Do not waste your money on the mega-churches and televangelists of today. Let them work in a trade, as Paul did. Instead, give directly to the poor or to those who supply the poor. That way the poor will actually get your dollar's worth and not two cents out of every dollar, as some churches and institutions actually provide after taking their cut.

Give only from the heart. The tithe is no longer an obligation. Give when the spirit moves you to give. A million people could be fed with the money it takes to support some ministries. In my little county there are several large churches. Preachers drive Mercedes and get their hair permed once a month. Their wives have plastic surgeries and wear expensive clothes. They run their churches with an iron fist, demanding their cut from all who enter. Yet, the poor walk the streets, mumbling to themselves, hungry and hopeless.

On a personal note I will say: Our hands are all He has to touch others. Our feet are all He has to find them. Our food can feed them, but at times our money can enable them to continue to drink and do drugs. Feed, clothe, and shelter those in need. Do not enable the situations that have put some in need.

Send your money to a televangelist in hopes of being blessed? Tithe and expect God, who already loves you unconditionally and gave His son as a sacrifice for you, to give you a little extra something?

Prayer and Faith

Why do we pray? Do we dare believe that we know what is better for us than God himself? Do we not believe God has our best interest at heart? If He does not want what is best for us, what good would our prayer be? Why bother a vengeful God if He does not have our best interest at heart? Does He not love us? But, if God wants what is best for us, should we not let His will be done? Does this mean keeping our opinion to ourselves? (As if He does not know it already.)

Of the most error ridden views of prayer, the most erroneous comes from a group of very wealthy preachers heading up a new movement. This new movement is a theology called by many names – Kingdom Now, Word of Faith, Dominion, Name it and Claim it, Positive Confession, and others. But the gab it and grab it theology of today is based in covetousness. This type of theology couldn't exist in socialist or communist countries. The society of sharing presented in the Book of Acts, where all people held all possessions in common, flies in the face of this thinking.

Men and women preaching this kind of prayer for pay could only survive in capitalistic or greed driven societies. The countries do not have to be especially rich. The followers simply have to be desperate or lacking contentment to a point that they can be persuaded to set aside logic and become delusional.

The concept is a simple one. If you pray for something with unwavering faith God is obliged to give it to you – no matter what.

Prosperity, health, victory, all would be never ending. But it does not take much of a leap in logic to conclude that if only one person could actually achieve this kind of faith he or she could extinguish all illness and poverty. Even death would no longer exist, since by faith the dead are raised. The universe has never worked like that, but to entertain that fact is to let one's faith waiver. Thus the theology becomes a circular trap.

This kind of theology usually comes with a price. The followers must give – give – give, because they believe God will give back to them. Who are they giving to? The preacher, of course. He, in turn, becomes wealthy and can then tell his followers to have faith like he has faith, for God has made him rich.

When the theology of preachers has become so repulsive that it brings laughter and ridicule it is time for an examination.

"Mercedes Benz" by JANIS JOPLIN

Oh Lord, won't you buy me a Mercedes Benz ?
My friends all drive Porsches, I must make amends.
Worked hard all my lifetime, no help from my friends,
So Lord, won't you buy me a Mercedes Benz ?

Oh Lord, won't you buy me a color TV ?
Dialing For Dollars is trying to find me.
I wait for delivery each day until three,
So oh Lord, won't you buy me a color TV ?

Oh Lord, won't you buy me a night on the town ?
I'm counting on you, Lord, please don't let me down.
Prove that you love me and buy the next round,
Oh Lord, won't you buy me a night on the town ?

Everybody!
Oh Lord, won't you buy me a Mercedes Benz ?
My friends all drive Porsches, I must make amends,
Worked hard all my lifetime, no help from my friends,
So oh Lord, won't you buy me a Mercedes Benz ?

That's it!

But where did this strange new theology of prayer and incantation begin?

In 1846 Ethan O. Allen was traveling the US building a reputation as America's first full-time faith-healer. By the 1950s, a hundred years later, seeds were planted that would produce a legion (I chose that word on purpose) of faith-healers. Each one attempted to distinguish themselves in some fashion by "personalizing" his approach and theology. Many emphasized prosperity, healing, material acquisition, the power of faith to compel God to do one's bidding, and the divinity of man. The age of mass communications had arrived and radio and television were easier and more financially productive than tent revivals, so the preachers took to the air. Shows spread their prosperity doctrine to hundreds of millions of people, first across the US, then across the world.

Sadly, today this "Faith" or "Word" theology is among the fastest growing segment of Christianity.

It has involved three distinct but closely related factions: Napoleon Hill "Think and Grow Rich", the Norman Vincent Peale /Robert Schuller "Positive-Possibility thinkers/Positive Mental Attitude", with their roots in "New Thought"; and the Kenneth Hagin/Kenneth Copeland "Positive Confession and Word-Faith" groups, which have their roots in E.W. Kenyon, William Branham, and the "Manifest Sons of God/Latter Rain" movement.

E.W. Kenyon (1867-1948) applied for ordination through the Southern California District of the Assemblies of God around 1925. In his application Kenyon stated that he spoke in tongues and that his teachings were in accordance with those of the Assemblies of God denomination. However, Kenyon's application was turned down due to negative references given by A.G. evangelist, May Eleanore Frey in a letter to General Chairman John William Welch, dated Jan 31, 1925. In addition to the poor personal reference, he was accused of personal contacts with the Ku Klux Klan. The letter went on to say that in spite of his testimony to the opposite he had not received Pentecostal Spirit baptism. Because of this rejection, he never thought of himself as a Pentecostal. Kenyon became an independent Baptist pastor, radio teacher, and author, developing a "metaphysical mixture" of fundamentalist, faith-cure, and transcendentalism. Ironically, Kenyon's teachings helped metaphysical religious concepts penetrate Christianity.

Many religious groups had responded to people's continued desire for the supernatural by demonstrating "miraculous" healings, but Kenyon believed he could go beyond even that. Kenyon claimed that he had found "Reality," higher than even the "Higher Life" movement from which he emerged. This movement was sweeping through England when he was there. In the Higher Life movement Christians should experience a second work of God in his life. This work of God is called "the second blessing," "the latter rain," or "being filled with the Holy Spirit." Higher Life teachers promoted the idea that Christians who had received this blessing from God could live a more holy, less sinful or even a sinless, life.

But Kenyon's "Reality was higher, better, more. This would be the solution to all of humanity's problems; in every arena of life, the believer could be absolute master by achieving and maintaining the right consciousness. This was Kenyon's pathway to the full realization of human potential.

Kenyon's promotion of his religious philosophy was a curious blend of biblical fundamentalism and metaphysical mind control. It represents one of the earliest major penetrations of the conservative American Christianity by mind-science.

Kenyon always considered himself a champion of biblical Christianity, and made clear his intention to remedy the menace of the competing metaphysical religions (like Christian Science and New Thought) by offering a superior alternative for seekers of Reality. Yet, ironically, the popular acceptance of his system, which we will show to be a "metaphysical mixture," resulted in a wide dissemination of mind-cure concepts, contrary to his intent.

His teachings on healing through "positive confession" or affirmations were posthumously popularized by American healing-revivalists, and again by independent charismatic movements.

Kenyon's views are now promoted by proponents of what has been called the "Health and Wealth" or "Faith" movement. His inspiration may have been taken in part from the Keswickean Higher Life movement. Some research has even suggested roots within Christian Science, New Thought , and Plymouth Brethren. His odd mixture of Christianity and "wish craft" are promoted today by Kenneth Hagin and Kenneth Copeland.

Napoleon Hill (October 26, 1883 – November 8, 1970) was one of the earliest producers of the modern genre of personal success books. His book, "Think and Grow Rich" is one of the best-selling books of all time. Hill's works examined the power of personal beliefs, and the role they play in personal success. "What the mind of man can conceive and believe, it can achieve," is one of Hill's hallmark expressions. Hill was greatly influenced by Andrew Carnegie. Hill discovered that Carnegie believed that the process of success could be explained in a simple formula that could be duplicated by the average person.

Carnegie commissioned Hill with letters of reference to interview over 500 successful men and women in order to discover and publish this formula for success. Hill published initially in 1928 as a study course called, The Law of Success. The Achievement formula was detailed further and, until 1941, was published in home-study courses, including the seventeen-volume "Mental Dynamite" series.

Hill later called his personal success teachings "The Philosophy of Achievement" and he considered freedom, democracy, capitalism, and harmony to be important contributing elements. For without these foundations to build upon, as Hill demonstrated throughout his writings, successful personal achievements are not possible. Negative emotions, fear and selfishness among others, had no part to play in his philosophy, and Hill considered them to be the source of failure for unsuccessful people. (Information gleaned from Wikipedia and other sources.)

Dr. Norman Vincent Peale (May 31, 1898 – December 24, 1993) was a Protestant preacher and author of The Power of Positive Thinking and a progenitor of the theory of "Positive Thinking."

Robert Schuller is the televangelist who built the Crystal Cathedral Church, from where he hosted a weekly TV show called "The Hour of Power." Schuller was strongly influenced by his mentor, Norman Peale. Schuller chose to focus on what he believes are the positive aspects of the faith. He deliberately avoids condemning people and he encourages Christians (and non-Christians) to achieve great things through Positive Thinking.

By Christianizing the concepts of Hill and Peale, Schuller took the "Think and Grow Rich" and "The Power of Positive Thinking" philosophies and produced "The Hour of Power." His ideas were forced into a rather tenuous theology that could be labeled "Pray, Pay, and someone will Grow Rich."

Well-known leaders in this new riches and wealth theology are E.W. Kenyon, Charles Capps, Kenneth Hagin, Kenneth Copeland, Frederick K.C. Price, Robert Tilton, and David Cho, to name a few.

Kenneth E. Hagin (1917 - 2004) preached and focused on the power of the spoken word. This idea came from E. W. Kenyon and W. M. Branham. In 1974 Hagin founded Rhema Bible Training Centre in an attempt to bring new preachers under his ministry by teaching the Faith or Word principles using Kenyon's Rhema doctrine. Hagin's message promised a return on investments made to God that were given to the church.

This is where many Christians go astray. A tithe, in the modern sense, is an investment in those who run the church, ministry, or religious entertainment you attend and not to God. The income of Hagin's ministries proves the point.

Kenneth Hagin, Oral Roberts, Frederick Price, Kenneth Copeland, Don Gossett, Charles Capps and other leading proponents in this movement all directly inherited their theology from Kenyon and his contemporaries. This new generation of televangelists have enjoyed the ability to propagate the Prosperity message by means of extensive and expensive media ministries, fully funded by followers giving to their organization in response to their message, thus perpetuating the influx of funds.

Cho teaches that Christians can get anything they want by calling upon the spirit world in the "fourth dimension" and envisioning (visualizing) their felt needs, no matter how crass and gross. Cho teaches that positive thinking, positive speaking, and positive visualization are the keys to success, and that anyone can literally "incubate" and give birth to physical reality by creating a vivid image in his or her mind and focusing upon it.

Oral Granville Roberts (1918 -),was considered by many to be the most prominent Pentecostal in the world in the 1980's. In 1956 Roberts was mailing his monthly magazine, Abundant Life, to over a million people. In 1969 he was reaching 64 million viewers with prime-time television programs. By 1981 he was able to open his $250 million dollar "City of Faith Medical and Research Centre," to combine the healing power of faith with medicine. Roberts' basic presuppositions were, firstly, that God is good; and, secondly, that God therefore wills to heal and prosper his people. Roberts taught that monetary giving to the church was a "seed of faith" that would return a harvest of wealth for those who had complete faith in God. This was basically the same doctrine that Hagin preached.

Charles Emmitt Capps (1934 -) is a current proponent of the Prosperity movement. After being healed under Hagin's teachings in 1969, he began teaching that words are the most powerful things in the universe. If spoken in faith, Capps taught, words carry creative power by releasing God's ability within you. He set out his message in "The Tongue, a Creative Force" (1976), and in 1980, he was ordained into the "faith ministry" by K. Copeland.

Kenneth Copeland (1937 -) is perhaps the leading proponent of the Word of Faith gospel today. In his early days, Kenneth Hagin and Oral Roberts had a life changing impact on Copeland. He enrolled in Oral Roberts University while attending Kenneth Hagin's Tulsa seminars. He also sought out the teachings of E. W. Kenyon, which had a determining influence on his theology. In 1973 Copeland began publishing "Believer's Voice of Victory." Like his spiritual fathers, Copeland emphasizes complete prosperity – spirit, soul and body – through total commitment to God's will, demonstrated by the spoken word. Like John G. Lake, M. B. Eddy and P.P. Quimby before them, Copeland's teaching raises the status of humanity to a God-like level by teaching that believers possess the ability to rescue themselves from trouble by use of their "divine right." It was Copeland who said, "You impart humanity into a child that's born of you. Because you are a human, you have imparted the nature of humanity into that born child. That child wasn't born a whale. It was born a human. Well, now, you don't have a God in you. You are one."

Although the Word of Faith movement is currently controversial and even repudiated by some sections within Pentecostalism, the key figures who were influential in creating the underlying doctrines of this movement were all Pentecostal.

Like the emphasis on Divine Healing within the Holiness movement, which naturally carried over into Pentecostalism when it emerged, the emphasis of Positive Confession theology, which pre-existed Pentecostalism, carried over into the movement from its origin because those who were key proponents of this doctrinal emphasis became Pentecostals and continued to be leaders within the movement.

Even though many Pentecostals reject some aspects of the foundational doctrines of the Word of Faith movement, general acceptance has occurred of the overall emphasis on material abundance, positivity and the power of the spoken word, and what they term, "victorious Christian living."

The leaders of this group have been successful in creating great wealth and amassing large congregations, but their movement does not yet constitute a new denomination, however it certainly represents teachings outside of orthodox Christianity.

D.R. McConnell points out that "any new religious movement [within Protestantism] must bear the scrutiny of two criteria: biblical fidelity and historical orthodoxy." Regrettably, the Positive Confession movement fails on both counts. The historical roots of this movement (which Charles Farah has called "Faith Formula Theology") lie in the occult, and most recently, in New Thought and its off-shoot, the Mind Science cults.

Its Biblical basis is found only in the peculiar interpretations of its own leaders, not in generally accepted Christian theology.

This movement teaches that faith is a matter of what we say more than whom we trust or what God you affirm in your heart. The term "positive confession" refers to the teaching that words have creative power. What you say, Word-Faith teachers claim, determines everything that happens to you. Your "confessions," that is, the things you say -- especially the favors you demand of God -- must all be stated positively and without wavering. Then God is obligated to answer. Word-Faith believers deliver their positive confessions as an incantation by which they can conjure up anything they desire: "Believe it in your heart; say it with your mouth and it will happen. That is the principle of faith. You can have what you say" (Charismatic Chaos, pp. 281, 285)? This is at the heart of the Positive Confession movement today, also known as the "name-it-and-claim-it" gospel. However, it is also the foundational message of witchcraft, as they proclaim, "As I will, so it will be!"

The Positive Confession movement is a Charismatic and sometimes Pentecostal form of Christian Science. There are great parallels in their common beliefs.

Faith is a force that both God and man can use: "Faith is a force just like electricity or gravity" (Copeland). "It is the substance out of which God creates whatever is" (Capps). "God uses faith, and so may we in exactly the same way in order to produce the same results through obedience to the same laws of faith that God applied in creation. "(Capps). "You have the same ability as God has dwelling or residing on the inside of you" (Capps). "We have all the capabilities of God. We have His faith" (Copeland).

Faith's force is released by speaking words: "Words are the most powerful thing in the universe because they are containers that "carry faith or fear and they produce after their kind" (Capps). "God had faith in His own words ... God had faith in His faith, because He spoke words of faith and they came to pass. That faith force was transported by words ... the God-kind-of-faith ... is released by the words of your mouth" (Hagin). "Creative power was in God's mouth. It is in your mouth also" (Capps).

Man is a "god": "Man was designed or created by God to be the god of this world" (Tilton, Hagin, Capps). "Adam was the god of this world ... but he sold out to Satan, and Satan became the god of this world" (Hagin). "We were created to be gods over the earth, but remember to spell it with a little 'g'." (Tilton, Hagin, Capps). Man was created in the God class ... We are a class of gods ... God himself spawned us from His innermost being ... We are in God; so that makes us part of God. Look at 2 Cor 5:17." (Copeland).

Anyone can use the faith. "Because man is a little god in God's class: very capable of operating on the same level of faith as God." (Capps) "All men are spirit beings." (Hagin) "Whether Christian or pagan, man can release this "faith force" by speaking words if he only believes in his words as God believes in His." (Hagin). "Everything you say [positive or negative] will come to pass" (Capps). "Spiritual things are created by WORDS. Even natural, physical things are created by WORDS" (Hagin).

You get what you confess: "You get what you say." (Hagin, Hunter). "Only by mouth confession can faith power be released, allowing tremendous things to happen" (Cho). "Remember, the key to receiving the desires of your heart is to make the words of your mouth agree with what you want." (Copeland). "Whatever comes out of your mouth shall be produced in your life" (Tilton).

Never make a negative confession: "The tongue can kill you, or it can release the life of God within you ... whether you believe right or wrong, it is still the law" (Capps). There is power in "the evil fourth dimension" (Cho). If you confess sickness you get it, if you confess health you get it; whatever you say you get" (Hagin). "Faith is as a seed ... you plant it by speaking it" (Capps). "The spoken word ... releases power -- power for good or power for evil" (Bashan).

So – I ask again, Why do we pray, if not for health and wealth and all of those toys we desire?

The Christian faith demands union and communion with the creator wherein He teaches us, guides us, and loves us. Through meditation, adoration, and prayer we are joined with Him and transformed from within. Such love and transformation engendered by this relationship can reunite Christians with the power, courage, and glory needed to survive in a world, which is becoming increasingly hostile to them.

With most people, and sadly, with most Christians, a crucial gap remains between God and man. What is needed is not the teaching of doctrine, law, or church tradition, nor is it any social or moral message. We need a heart-to-heart dialogue with God. We need and long for a relationship with our creator in which He loves and teaches us as a father would a child. A child knows he is loved by the kiss on his cheek, the words, the touch, and the embrace. It is in this type of communion we "know" God. He has bid us come, but the modern church has forgotten the path. It is still there, beneath the hedges of religion and pride. The hedges must be cleared away to find the path.

Prayer is not for us to change the mind of God. It is to allow Him to mold and strengthen our souls to endure His will. Prayer is not for us to beg the Almighty for favors and trinkets. Prayer is a vehicle of communion with God, in which we may sit in His presence and, in some small way, know who He is. In knowing Him, we shall know how to live closer to Him. Paul tells us to "pray without ceasing." This is not the prayer of beggary. It is the prayer of communion; it is not a discursive prayer, but one of silence and listening.

We must strive to keep our prayer life in balance between Discursive prayer and Contemplative prayer. In discursive prayer we carry on a dialogue between the Lord and ourselves. The problem in this type of prayer is we tend to do all of the talking. We bring a wish list before the throne. We repeat our requests as if He did not hear us the first time. We beg God to fill our requests, as if we could possibly know what is best in the light of eternity. We seldom listen to His answer. In contemplative prayer we stay silent and listen to the Lord. We think about Him and His glory. We learn to be still inside so we may hear His soft, beckoning voice.

Prayer is not for us to change the mind of God, but for us to be conformed to His will.

This is a state of Grace.

Anything attained here is grace. It is not dependent on our wealth or health, only our desire to know and experience Him.

In a time before his death, Mr. McLaren, minister of the Tolboth church, said, "I am gathering together all my prayers, _s,Mind_

...nons, all my good deeds, all my ill deeds; and I am
...hrow them all overboard and swim to glory on the
p.. .. Free Grace."

Thus, it is not acquisition that couples us with God,
but it is gratitude. Gratitude is the balance point between God
and man. Thankfulness is a measure of our dependence on God
and our obedience to Him. It is the path that our prayers walk
to get to God. Gratitude is how we approach Him. It is said
there are only two things that motivate us to do things: desire
and desperation. It is said, "gratitude comes from desire." This
is the idea of some philosophers, but there is a higher gratitude
not understood by the world.

There is a gratitude springing from the realization that
one has no desires, no needs, nothing lacking. Even though we
are imprisoned, if God is All then we have all. It is gratitude
from epiphany. Insight brought on by grace enables us to see
how God is providing our path and all things on it. It does not
mean we have riches or even health, but that we are where we
are supposed to be. Even in our lack or pain, we see somehow
we are exactly where God would have us to be. It is the
gratitude of knowing what we need to fulfill our purpose will
be provided on God's path for God's purpose. All things are
seen in a state of grace and balance, and we are here for a
purpose - God's purpose.

The faith we seek is not in the form of belief in our own
incantation, but it is faith in Him. We must know that it is first
by Him and through Him that we could have any measure of
faith at all. Faith is the key we turn to enter through the door of
salvation. It unlocks the door of heaven and the presence of
God. But it is not faith in words or faith in faith; it is simply the
faith in a father – God who knows what is best for his spoiled
children.

EPH 2:8 For by grace are ye saved through faith; and that not
of yourselves: it is the gift of God: Not of works, lest any man
should boast.

Faith is action based upon belief, sustained by confidence.   Dr. Gene Scott

Faith has its proper place. Faith turns the key of salvation and allows us entry into Heaven. There will be times of darkness and trouble in our journey when we will doubt we ever heard the voice of God. It is in these times that faith will triumph. However, neither faith nor knowing can come first.

God's grace must come first. God must first open our eyes to our own inadequacies and reveal to us our need for Him. God must draw us to Himself in a sovereign act of grace. He must then give us the faith by which we are saved. Faith and Grace are the two powers yoked together to pull us out of this world and into eternity.

ROM 12:3 For I say, through the grace given unto me, to every man that is among you, not to think of himself more highly than he ought to think; but to think soberly, according as God hath dealt to every man the measure of faith.

Yes, even our faith is a gift from God. Faith is manifest in the act of believing in someone we have not yet met and believing He is who He said He is, the only begotten Son of God. Faith comes to us from God by grace. We worship Him but He enables us to do so. He enables us to believe. He gives us the faith to be saved. He opens our eyes and our hearts to His word and draws us by His spirit. It is by faith we come to God and by faith we live. It is better to believe than to know, for knowing can be shaken in those times when we reach for God and cannot find Him. In those times He is silent and our souls are tested with darkness, it is only by faith we will survive. As a child whose father has left on a long journey, we no longer see Him, but we have faith He will return. We have faith He is there, still loving us. It is faith given as an act of love and grace that allows us to await His return.

HAB 2:3 For the vision is yet for an appointed time, but at the end it shall speak, and not lie: though it tarry, wait for it; because it will surely come, it will not tarry. 4 Behold, his soul which is lifted up is not upright in him: but the just shall live by his faith.

ACT 26:18 To open their eyes, and to turn them from darkness to light, and from the power of Satan unto God, that they may receive forgiveness of sins, and inheritance among them which are sanctified by faith that is in me.

ROM 1:16 For I am not ashamed of the gospel of Christ: for it is the power of God unto salvation to every one that believeth; to the Jew first, and also to the Greek. 17 For therein is the righteousness of God revealed from faith to faith: as it is written, The just shall live by faith.

ROM 3:21 But now the righteousness of God without the law is manifested, being witnessed by the law and the prophets; 22 Even the righteousness of God which is by faith of Jesus Christ unto all and upon all them that believe: for there is no difference: 23 For all have sinned, and come short of the glory of God; 24 Being justified freely by his grace through the redemption that is in Christ Jesus: ROM 3:25 Whom God hath set forth to be a propitiation through faith in his blood, to declare his righteousness for the remission of sins that are past, through the forbearance of God; 26 To declare, I say, at this time his righteousness: that he might be just, and the justifier of him which believeth in Jesus.

ROM 3:28 Therefore we conclude that a man is justified by faith without the deeds of the law.

ROM 4:16 Therefore it is of faith, that it might be by grace; to the end the promise might be sure to all the seed; not to that only which is of the law, but to that also which is of the faith of Abraham; who is the father of us all, ROM 4:23 Now it was not written for his sake alone, that it was imputed to him; 24 But for us also, to whom it shall be imputed, if we believe on him that raised up Jesus our Lord from the dead; 25 Who was delivered for our offences, and was raised again for our justification. 5:1 Therefore being justified by faith, we have peace with God through our Lord Jesus Christ: 2 By whom also we have access by faith into this grace wherein we stand, and rejoice in hope of the glory of God.

GAL 2:16 Knowing that a man is not justified by the works of the law, but by the faith of Jesus Christ, even we have believed in Jesus Christ, that we might be justified by the faith of Christ, and not by the works of the law: for by the works of the law shall no flesh be justified.

GAL 3:24 Wherefore the law was our schoolmaster to bring us unto Christ, that we might be justified by faith. 25 But after that faith is come, we are no longer under a schoolmaster. For ye are all the children of God by faith in Christ Jesus.

1TI 6:12 Fight the good fight of faith, lay hold on eternal life, whereunto thou art also called, and hast professed a good profession before many witnesses.

HEB 11:1 Now faith is the substance of things hoped for, the evidence of things not seen. 2 For by it the elders obtained a good report. 3 Through faith we understand that the worlds were framed by the word of God, so that things which are seen were not made of things which do appear. 4 By faith Abel offered unto God a more excellent sacrifice than Cain, by which he obtained witness that he was righteous, God testifying of his gifts: and by it he being dead yet speaketh. 5 By faith Enoch was translated that he should not see death; and was not found, because God had translated him: for before his translation he had this testimony, that he pleased God. 6 But without faith it is impossible to please him: for he that cometh

Joseph Lumpkin

to God must believe that he is, and that he is a rewarder of them that diligently seek him.

HEB 11:7 By faith Noah, being warned of God of things not seen as yet, moved with fear, prepared an ark to the saving of his house; by the which he condemned the world, and became heir of the righteousness which is by faith. 8 By faith Abraham, when he was called to go out into a place which he should after receive for an inheritance, obeyed; and he went out, not knowing whither he went. 9 By faith he sojourned in the land of promise, as in a strange country, dwelling in tabernacles with Isaac and Jacob, the heirs with him of the same promise: 10 For he looked for a city which hath foundations, whose builder and maker is God. HEB 11:11 Through faith also Sara herself received strength to conceive seed, and was delivered of a child when she was past age, because she judged him faithful who had promised. 12 Therefore sprang there even of one, and him as good as dead, so many as the stars of the sky in multitude, and as the sand which is by the sea shore innumerable. 13 These all died in faith, not having received the promises, but having seen them afar off, and were persuaded of them, and embraced them, and confessed that they were strangers and pilgrims on the earth.

This verse needs repeating in other forms so that it might settle in us, understood and apprehended. Those who had great faith walked through life in animal skins, tortured, persecuted, beaten, and the world was not worthy of them. Some saw miracles. Some did not. Some saw death. Some did not. But all, through faith, were looking forward to greater things, which they did not see here on this Earth.

Prosperity preaching does not work very well when one can look out their window and see men and women of faith being dipped in tar and set on fire to light the courtyard of Caesar, beaten to death or shot in a city park, or forced at threat of death to sing and pray to despot and debauched emperors of

second class countries. Spare us the selfish theologie
there are those dying for the faith.

WHAT IS FAITH? FAITH IS PUTTING IT ALL ON THE LINE.
IT IS HANGING YOUR BODY ON YOUR BELIEFS, EVEN
THOUGH YOU SEE THEM AFAR OFF AND MAY NOT
REACH THEM BEFORE YOU DIE.

Hebrews 11 (The Message)
" 32-38 I could go on and on, but I've run out of time. There are
so many more— Gideon, Barak, Samson, Jephthah, David,
Samuel, the prophets....Through acts of faith, they toppled
kingdoms, made justice work, took the promises for
themselves. They were protected from lions, fires, and sword
thrusts, turned disadvantage to advantage, won battles, routed
alien armies. Women received their loved ones back from the
dead. There were those who, under torture, refused to give in
and go free, preferring something better: resurrection. Others
braved abuse and whips, and, yes, chains and dungeons.
We have stories of those who were stoned, sawed in two,
murdered in cold blood; stories of vagrants wandering the
earth in animal skins, homeless, friendless, powerless—the
world didn't deserve them!—making their way as best they
could on the cruel edges of the world.
 39-40Not one of these people, even though their lives of faith
were exemplary, got their hands on what was promised. God
had a better plan for us: that their faith and our faith would
come together to make one completed whole, their lives of faith
not complete apart from ours."

        Even with this most holy of things, faith in God, one can
supplant the creator with the creature and fall victim to
believing in faith itself. If we place faith in our ability to have
faith it lessens our perceived dependence on God. I say
perceived dependence because we have just crossed the line
into the great lie by thinking we can fulfill our needs and do it
better than God. Faith in faith is not faith in God.

If we do not fully understand our faith comes from God, given by Him in his measure to us, we can come to believe that we have some work or contribution in this faith of ours. This belief, added to the false concept that God must respond to faith, has yielded up a doctrine that is akin to witchcraft. The doctrine of many sects of Wicca states, "As I will, so may it be." This is not so different from the "hyper-faith" concept of having enough faith to compel God to act on behalf of the one with faith. One should always stretch a truth to see if it will break. If it breaks down it is not a truth. This one does not take much stretching to come apart and not much examination to see the cracks.

What ill-thought heresy would pit Christian against Christian in a battle of faith with God as a puppet in between? This is what would happen if the concept were to be practiced by two people competing for the same job, position, raise, or possession. What right have we to expect our prayers to change the mind or path of another person? Even God allows free will, yet some expect their prayers to influence others. Worldly perspective, arrogance, pride, and greed have brought the simple concept of faith and grace into a place of wish-craft bordering on witchcraft. The "Think and Grow Rich" idea of Napoleon Hill has made its way into our churches and has destroyed our view of God's faith, replacing it with faith in faith and faith in some ability of ours to wield a wand-like power contained in our belief in ourselves. Anything that takes our spiritual eyes off of Jesus as the only source of our salvation and spiritual power is wrong. To have Him we must rely on Him. "First, you must make Him your dwelling place."
Dr. Gene Scott.

So, why do we pray? It is to come into His presence and be changed. Thus, I sit waiting for the guest. It is the longing that does the work. It is because of this that our banner and cry should always be, "It is by grace alone!"

Sources: Beyond Seduction (pp. 51-53) , Wikipedia
The Seduction of Christianity (pp. 28, 217).

MIND, MIGHT, AND MASTERY: HUMAN POTENTIAL IN
METAPHYSICAL RELIGION AND E. W. KENYON, By Kevin
Scott Smith
Dark Night Of The Soul, by Joseph Lumpkin

Magical Thinking

Magical thinking is the belief that there is a link between some action and an outcome when no connection exists. It is the belief that there is a correlation between a ritual, practice, phrase, action, or observance and an outcome. Magical thinking leads people to believe that their thoughts, actions, or words can bring about effects in the world, such as changing the outcome of an event or even the actions of thoughts of others. It is a type of causal fallacy that looks for meaningful relationships between acts and events. In other words, it is superstition.

Some actions sought as an outcome may be the winning of a game when one wears a luck shirt, or a profitable outcome of a game of craps if one performs a set of actions before casting the dice.

Out of all activities one may think of in which magical thinking may be prevalent, such as sports, or gambling, religion may top the list. Of all categories within religion, the idea of healing and miracles as related to prayer and faith is likely the most personal and the most difficult to address.

On the surface it seems obvious that mumbling words or throwing water or olive oil on a person will not repair a withered organ or severed spinal cord, but still people practice religious rituals every day with the intention of altering what they believe to be the natural or legal outcome.

Does prayer work? Data coming from psychological studies tend to conflict at times. However, we will attempt to tease out the truth from the barrage of data, by asking the right questions.

We will begin with a study on faith healers A study in Scientific America reports on faith healers.

During the past forty years, Louis Rose, a British psychiatrist, investigated hundreds of alleged faith-healing cures. As his interest became well known, he received communications from healers and patients throughout the world. He sent each correspondent a questionnaire and sought corroborating information from physicians. In Faith Healing [Penguin Books 1971], he concluded, "I have been unsuccessful. After nearly twenty years of work I have yet to find one 'miracle cure'; and without that (or, alternatively, massive statistics which others must provide) I cannot be convinced of the efficacy of what is commonly termed faith healing."

During the early 1970s, Minnesota surgeon William Nolen, M.D., attended a service conducted by Katherine Kuhlman, the leading evangelical healer of that period. After noting the names of 25 people who had been "miraculously healed," he was able to perform follow-up interviews and examinations. Among other things, he discovered that one woman who had been announced as cured of "lung cancer" actually had Hodgkin's disease—which was unaffected by the experience. Another woman with cancer of the spine had discarded her brace and followed Ms. Kuhlman's enthusiastic command to run across the stage. The following day her backbone collapsed, and four months later she died. Overall, not one person with organic disease had been helped. Dr. Nolen reported his findings, which included observations of several other healers, in Healing: A Doctor in Search of a Miracle.

C. Eugene Emery, Jr., a science writer for the Providence Journal, has looked closely at the work of Reverend Ralph DiOrio, a Roman Catholic priest whose healing services attract people by the thousands. In 1987 Emery attended one of

DiOrio's services and recorded the names of nine people who had been blessed during the service and nine others who had been proclaimed cured. DiOrio's organization provided ten more cases that supposedly provided irrefutable proof of the priest's ability to cure. During a six-month investigation, Emery found no evidence that any of these 28 individuals had been helped.

The most comprehensive examination of contemporary "healers" is James Randi's The Faith Healers. The book describes how many of the leading evangelistic healers have enriched themselves with the help of deception and fraud. Some of Randi's evidence came from former associates of the evangelists who got disgusted with what they had observed. Randi's most noteworthy experience was the unmasking of Peter Popoff, an evangelist who would call out the names of people in the audience and describe their ailments. Popoff said he received this information from God, but it was actually obtained by confederates who mingled with the audience before each performance. Pertinent data would be given to Popoff's wife, who would broadcast it from backstage to a tiny receiver in Popoff's ear. After recording one of Mrs. Popoff's radio transmissions, Randi exposed the deception on the Johnny Carson Show.

Randi also exposed the techniques used by evangelist W.V. Grant, who calls out people in the audience by name and describes their ailments. Grant obtains this information from letters people send him and by mingling with the audience before his show.

In 1999, the American Medical Association's Archives of Internal Medicine published a better-designed study of nearly a thousand consecutive patients who were newly admitted to the coronary care unit of a hospital in Kansas City. The researchers created a 35-item score sheet that was used to measure what happened to the patients during a 28-day period in which 15 groups of 5 persons ("intercessors") prayed individually for about half the patients. The intercessors were given the patients' first names and were asked to pray daily for "a speedy recovery with no complications."

The prayed-for group had a 10-11% reduction in total scores even though their average length of hospital stay was similar to that of the "usual-care" group. The researchers also noted that: (a) some patients had asked hospital clergy to pray for them; (b) many, if not most patients in both groups were probably receiving intercessory and/or direct prayer from family, friends and/or clergy, so that the study was most likely measuring the effects of "supplementary intercessory prayer"; (c) although the difference would be expected to occur by chance alone only 1 in 25 times such an experiment were conducted, chance still remains a possible explanation of the results; and (d) using the scoring method of the San Francisco study yielded no significant difference between the two groups. (End quotes from Scientific America.)

Seemingly contradictory data is presented by Scientific America in an article called, "Cure in the Mind."

A man whom his doctors referred to as "Mr. Wright" was dying from cancer of the lymph nodes. Orange-size tumors had invaded his neck, groin, chest and abdomen, and his doctors had exhausted all available treatments. Nevertheless, Mr. Wright was confident that a new anticancer drug called Krebiozen would cure him, according to a 1957 report by psychologist Bruno Klopfer of the University of California, Los Angeles, entitled "Psychological Variables in Human Cancer." Mr. Wright was bedridden and fighting for each breath when he received his first injection. But three days later he was cheerfully ambling around the unit, joking with the nurses. Mr. Wright's tumors had shrunk by half, and after 10 more days of treatment he was discharged from the hospital. And yet the other patients in the hospital who had received Krebiozen showed no improvement. (End Article).

The placebo effect takes place in the mind, not the body. It can enhance the effects of a drug, or even develop effects when no drug is involved. There is a placebo effect related to prayer and healing ministries as well as drugs.

Even though they do not act on the disease, placebos seem to affect how people feel in up to 1 out of 3 patients.

A change in a person's symptoms as a result of getting a placebo is called the placebo effect. This effect usually lasts only a short time. Sometimes the effect is positive but at times it goes the other way, and causes symptoms or worse. The unpleasant effects that happen after getting a placebo are sometimes called the nocebo effect.

Some patients can have the placebo effect without getting a pill, shot, or procedure. Some may just feel better from visiting the doctor or doing something else they believe will help. That type of placebo effect seems most related to the degree of confidence and faith the patient has in the doctor, healer, or activity.

Various articles from Scientific America report on the Placebo Effect. In the past, some researchers have questioned whether there's convincing proof that the placebo effect is a real effect. But there are studies showing that the placebo effect is real. For example, scientists have recorded brain activity in response to placebo. Since many scientific tests have shown the placebo effect, it's one way we know for sure that the mind and body are connected.

Some scientific evidence suggests that the placebo effect may be partly due to the release of endorphins in the brain. Endorphins are the body's natural pain killers. But there's probably more to it than this.

Many think the placebo effect occurs because the patient believes in the substance, the treatment, or the doctor. The patient's thoughts and feelings somehow cause short-term physical changes in the brain or body. The person may feel less anxious, so stress hormones drop. Taking a placebo may change their perception — for example, a person might re-interpret a sharp pain as uncomfortable tingling.

What's commonly called the placebo effect even plays a role in mainstream medicine. Many people feel better after they get medical treatments that they expect to work. But the opposite can also happen, and this seems to support the idea of the expectation effect even more. For example, in one study, people with Alzheimer's disease got less relief from pain medicines. These patients required higher doses — possibly because they had forgotten they were getting the drugs, or they forgot that the pain medicines had worked for them before. This suggests that past experiences also play into the placebo effect.

In one study that looked at the placebo effect in pain relief, one group got a real pain medicine and the other did not. In the following days, both groups were given a placebo that looked like the real pain medicine. Those who had gotten the real pain medicine were able to tolerate more pain than those who had not gotten pain medicines before.

Although we may not know exactly how it works, the idea that the mind can affect the body has been around for thousands of years and is well-proven in certain situations. Many ancient cultures depended on mind-body connections to treat illness.

Shamans or medicine men would not have viewed their efforts as placebos. But their healing powers may have worked partly through the patient's strong belief that the shaman's treatments would restore health. Or it could be that a sick person was going to get better anyway, but the recovery was to be because of the treatment — which might have one nothing for the illness.

Just as natural endorphins may relieve pain once they are released, some research shows the brain may respond to an imagined scene much as it would to something it actually sees. A placebo may help the brain remember a time before the symptoms and bring about a chemical change. This is a theory called remembered wellness.

Some scientists believe that the effects of many alternative therapies may simply be a placebo effect. If the patient believes in the treatment and wants it to work, it can seem to do so, at least for a while. If this effect worked on an illness that usually would not get better on its own, and it lasted, it would be considered a real cure, not a placebo effect.

Finally, there's evidence to suggest that what a patient expects about real medicines can influence how the patient feels after the medicine is taken. Even though responses from real drugs aren't typically thought of as placebo effects, some short-term effects are affected by expectations — good ones as well as bad.
(End Excerpts from Scientific America.)

One of the missing links between prayer and the placebo effect, which has remained somewhat unexamined, is "Magical Thinking." If a placebo is faith in a pill, magical thinking is faith in a action. In Christian circles this type of magical thinking has given way to the "hyper-faith", "word of faith", or "name it and claim it" movements.

Some scholars believe that magic is effective psychologically. They cite the placebo effect, psychosomatic disease, etc., as prime examples of how our mental functions exert power over our bodies.

Similarly, Robert Horton suggests that engaging in magical practices surrounding healing can relieve anxiety, which could have a significant positive physical impact. This would help to explain the persistence and popularity of such practices.

According to theories of anxiety relief and control, people turn to magical beliefs when there exists a sense of uncertainty and potential danger and little to do about it. Magic is used to restore a sense of control. In support of this theory, research indicates that superstitious behavior is invoked more often in high stress situations, especially by people with a greater desire for control. Modern religious practices of faith healing falls into the area of magical thinking, as well as the belief that relics of saints can transfer spiritual energy, or the hands or words of a person can heal. The belief that wearing your favorite lucky underwear will improve your basketball game is no more true that the belief the Bible contains teachings that only certain groups can understand or that saying certain words can heal.

These types of belief systems allow the person the illusion of control over their fate or environment. It's very appealing to believe one is able to create reality, however, with faulty logic we can easily connect cause and affect incorrectly. Doing so, we create your own evidence for the beliefs, and sustain in a circular logic and illogical belief.

In the studies mentioned we see a pattern that has not been elucidated enough. The placebo effect can be measured. Some forms of magical thinking can improve performance by increasing confidence. These are related phenomenon. They both affect our own body through our mind. They rely on a mind-body connection and interaction. The results are slight and they are transient, but they are measurable.

Whether one believes prayer, oil, speaking in tongues (glossolalia), making the sign of the cross, or self-flagellation will change the outcome of an event, it is considered magical thinking. One of the clearest examples of magical thinking in the religious, besides those already mentioned, is the underwear, called "Temple Garments," worn by Mormons.

According to the LDS Church, the temple garments, called "magical underwear" by some non-Mormons, provides protection against temptation and evil" and "strengthens the wearer to resist temptation and fend off evil influences," according to church leaders.

Virtually all wearers expressed a belief that wearing the garment provided spiritual protection and some of those interviewed asserted that the garment also provided physical protection. In Mormon folklore, tales are told of Latter-day Saints who credit their temple garments with helping them survive car wrecks, fires, natural disasters, and even the trials of war.

Marking of the garment are taking directly from the Free Masons, of which Joseph Smith was one. There is a compass stitched into the fabric on one breast area, a square on the other, and a line at the naval area. Older garments had a cut on the knee. The compass looks like a "V", the square looks like a backward "L", and the line is simply a line of stitching.

The symbols follow the basic Masonic belief of dealing with others in a square and level way. The line indicates the need for nourishment for God and the slit at the knee is a reminder that every knee shall bow to the Lord.

Below is a drawing of a garment, circa 1870s.

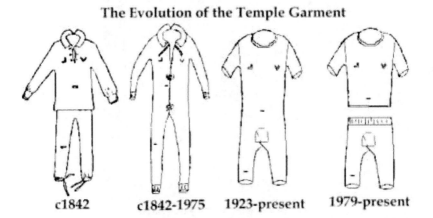

The Evolution of the Temple Garment

c1842   c1842-1975   1923-present   1979-present

Even though Joseph Smith proclaimed that its design came from God and should never be altered, it has indeed been updated and shortened compared to the picture of the modern garments. One may now select from one or two-piece garments.

In interviews with ex-wives of Mormon men, I was assured the garments were not magical enough to ward off mold, mildew, rot, or odor. This is sad because the garment is to be worn at all times. The only time it gets cleaned is when the wearer bathes in it.

Below is a picture of the modern, more chic garments.

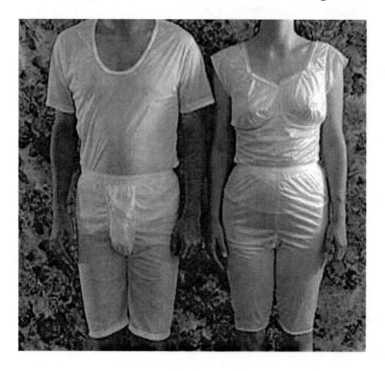

Prayer, faith, signs, symbols, words, and even underwear can be part of magical thinking. They have limited results. Many sports players, from football stars to basketball legends have been superstitious while on winning streaks, wearing the same socks or underwear for weeks at a time. The faith in a sock to help one win a game is the same faith applied to the words of a faith healer. They are limited to the easing of pain or anxiety when brain chemistry is altered slightly for a short time. Yes, I know some readers are probably declaring me a heretic at this point, but the case can be settled in one statement.

I have never seen an amputated limb restored, or missing eyes grow back. Have you?

It is a harsh reality to face, but if we are truthful with ourselves we will realize that although we may beg God for a particular outcome of an interview, or for him to heal someone of cancer, we do not often ask for the resurrection of the dead, a new arm for a thalidomide baby, or even the restoration of an extracted organ. Even in our minds "miracles" have their limits. The limits of miracles seem to be the limits of the randomness of natural chance.

The idea of magical thinking is based on a lapse of logic. Post hoc ergo propter hoc, Latin for "after this, therefore because of this", is a logical that states "Since Y event followed X event, Y event must have been caused by X event." It is often shortened to simply post hoc.

A similar fallacy, called "Cum hoc ergo propter hoc," exists when two things or events occur simultaneously or the chronological ordering is insignificant or unknown, in which the two occurrences are erroneously connected. This is also called "a false cause." It is when coincidental correlation are believed to be related. This is correlation of time, not causation. Post hoc is a particularly tempting error because temporal sequence appears to be integral to causality, but they are unrelated accept for random timing. The fallacy lies in coming to a conclusion based solely on the order of events, rather than taking into account other factors that might rule out the connection.

In other words, just because I pray for something and it happens does not mean that prayer caused the event. Praying for sunrise (or a person to beat cancer) does not mean prayer caused alterations to outcomes that would not have happened naturally on their own.

Original Sin

The term "Original Sin" did not come into existence until Augustine (c. 354-430). The idea may have been touched upon in the writings of Tertullian, but it was in Augustine's works that the idea became entrenched. Prior to this the theologians of the early church used different terminology indicating a contrasting way of thinking about Adam's fall, its effects and God's response to it. The phrase the Greek Fathers used to describe the tragedy in the Garden is "Ancestral Sin."

"Ancestral Sin" has a specific meaning. The Eastern Church, unlike its Western counterpart, never speaks of guilt being passed from Adam and Eve to their progeny, as did Augustine. Instead, it is assumed that each person bears the guilt of his or her own sin. The question becomes, "What then is the inheritance of humanity from Adam and Eve, if it is not guilt?" The Orthodox Fathers' answer is death. "Man is born with the parasitic power of death within him." Fr. Romanides Cyril of Alexandria teaches, "Our nature, became diseased...through the sin of one." It is not guilt that is passed on. It is a condition and a disease. It is death itself.

2 Chronicles 25:4 (King James Version)
4But he slew not their children, but did as it is written in the law in the book of Moses, where the LORD commanded, saying, The fathers shall not die for the children, neither shall the children die for the fathers, but every man shall die for his own sin.

Ezekiel 18:20 (King James Version)
20The soul that sinneth, it shall die. The son shall not bear the iniquity of the father, neither shall the father bear the iniquity of the son: the righteousness of the righteous shall be upon him, and the wickedness of the wicked shall be upon him.

Romans 5 (See Amplified Bible and Young's Translation.)
12Therefore, as sin came into the world through one man, and death as the result of sin, so death spread to all men, [no one

being able to stop it or to escape its power] because all men sinned. (Young reads: in which man all men sinned.)

13[To be sure] sin was in the world before ever the Law was given, but sin is not charged to men's account where there is no law [to transgress].

14Yet death held sway from Adam to Moses [the Lawgiver], even over those who did not themselves transgress [a positive command] as Adam did. Adam was a type (prefigure) of the One Who was to come [in reverse, the former destructive, the Latter saving].

15But God's free gift is not at all to be compared to the trespass [His grace is out of all proportion to the fall of man]. For if many died through one man's falling away (his lapse, his offense), much more profusely did God's grace and the free gift [that comes] through the undeserved favor of the one Man Jesus Christ abound and overflow to and for [the benefit of] many.

How can the above verses be reconciled? If the sin of the father is not visited upon the son, nor is the sin of the father counted or paid by the son, and all mankind is the descendant of Adam, how can Adam's sin be on us? It is not. It is not sin that is being addressed here. It is the result of Adam's sin and not the punishment for it that is discussed by Paul in Romans. The effect is not the same as the punishment.

We are given these clues to distinguish between sin and death:

Sin cannot be sin until there is a law to break. Yet, between Adam, the sinner and Moses, the lawgiver, there was no law, thus no sin, but all men died. God spoke directly to the individual before the law came. God's command to the person was a personal law. Adam was given a command directly by God, which he broke, having eaten from the tree forbidden by God for him to touch. Cain failed when he murdered his brother, Abel. There was no law, but when Cain lied God was not amused and cursed Cain for his actions.

It seemed that even then, if there were truth and repentance there was hope. These were personal crimes, not sins against the law. However, all men from Adam to Moses died. So, much like a man setting a wildfire, the result of Adam's sin brought death into the world because the result was the expulsion of Adam and Eve from the Garden before they could partake of the Tree of Life.

The aim of God was for Adam and Eve to be sin free and live eternally. God never restricted them from the tree of life. Their descendants would have inherited immortality. Yet, free will would have lived within each person, as it did in Adam and Eve. To live forever in sin would have indeed been a curse. The result of Adam's disobedience was mortality. God removed them from the garden before they could become immortal by eating of the tree of life. When the Young translation reads:" in which man all men sinned." The translator is attempting to point out that the punishment of death is a result of one man's sin.

Genesis 3 (The Message) 22 God said, "The Man has become like one of us, capable of knowing everything, ranging from good to evil. What if he now should reach out and take fruit from the Tree-of-Life and eat, and live forever? Never—this cannot happen!"

23-24 So God expelled them from the Garden of Eden and sent them to work the ground, the same dirt out of which they'd been made. He threw them out of the garden and stationed angel-cherubim and a revolving sword of fire east of it, guarding the path to the Tree-of-Life.

Since Adam and Eve were created with the purpose of communing with God: "They needed to mature, to grow to awareness by willing detachment and faith, a loving trust in a personal God" (Clement, 1993, p. 84). Theophilus of Antioch (2nd Century) believed that Adam and Eve were created neither immortal nor mortal. They were created with the potential to become either through obedience or disobedience (Romanides, 2002). The maturing and the choice of being mortal or immortal was given to them by the apparatus of free will. In the Garden there were two trees. One was the Tree of Life and the other the Tree of Knowledge. Only the Tree of Knowledge was forbidden. They could have eaten from the Tree of Life at any time without punishment. It was left untouched, while they chose to eat the forbidden fruit.

The freedom to obey or disobey belonged to our first parents, "For God made man free and sovereign" (Romanides, 2002, p. 32). To embrace their God-given vocation would bring life, to reject it would bring death, but not at God's hands. Theophilus continues, "…should he keep the commandment of God he would be rewarded with immortality…if, however, he should turn to things of death by disobeying God, he would be the cause of death to himself" (Romanides, 2002, p. 32)

"Sin reigned through death." (Romans 5:21) Death is the natural result of turning aside from God.

Adam and Eve were overcome with the same temptation that afflicts all humanity: to be autonomous, to go their own way, to realize the fullness of human existence without God. According to the Orthodox fathers, sin is not a violation of an impersonal law or code of behavior, but a rejection of the life offered by God (Yannaras, 1984). This is the mark, to which the word amartia - sin - (missing the mark) refers. Fallen human life is above all else the failure to realize the God-given potential of human existence, which is, as St. Peter writes, to "become partakers of the divine nature" (II Peter 1:4). St. Basil writes; "Humanity is an animal who has received the vocation to become God" (Clement, 1993, p. 76).

In Orthodox thought, God did not threaten Adam and Eve with punishment nor was He angered or offended by their sin; He was moved to compassion. The expulsion from the Garden and from the Tree of Life was an act of love and not vengeance so that humanity would not "become immortal in sin" (Romanides, 2002, p. 32). Thus began the preparation for the Incarnation of the Son of God and the solution that alone could rectify the situation: the destruction of the enemies of humanity and God, death (I Corinthians 15:26, 56), sin, corruption and the devil (Romanides, 2002).

Adam was the first man to sin. Through him, death came to mankind. No one can escape it.

This is not to say that the fall of Adam did not affect man. It did. His disobedience is mimicked in us all. As his children, we have free will and rebellion flowing in our blood. But, at any time, free will and the choice not to sin can win out. This is the most important factor. We have the choice not to sin. Adam sinned and paradise was lost. Death was introduced to man. But it is for our own sin that we are responsible. The specific act of the Original or first Sin was the sin of Adam. It is not the responsibility of all humanity.

Instead, the consequences of that act exist and plague the world. Original Sin created an environment in which God withdrew His personal communion as it was in the Garden of Eden. Now it is simply not possible without direct Divine intervention for a human being to avoid committing sin some time in his or her life. When God no longer communed with man, but withdrew, man lost his way and began to decline into "spiritual illness." Thus, the world's first sin, or the "Original Sin" is not inherited guilt. It is inherited death. People do not bear personal responsibility for the acts of Adam, no more than they are responsible for the sins of their great-grandfather, although his sins affect his offspring. In the fallen state of the world, it is impossible for anyone not to sin, but until they do… and they will… they are not sinners.

By attempting to interpret Original Sin to mean that we are all born sinners, the church has been forced, out of its own conscience, to embrace an escape clause, which is the creation of a humane yet non-biblical domain. By assuming the full results of this view of Original Sin, we have to assume all children are destined to hell. If newborns are born sinners and have not accepted Jesus as their savior, they will burn forever in hell. This is not very palatable, especially for people seeking to worship a God of love and kindness.

Protestants claim to believe in Original Sin, but do not believe in infant baptism. With no way to relieve the sinful state there is no way to remove Original Sin. In this situation it becomes blindingly obvious that through the simple logic of Original Sin, Protestants have condemned all children below the age of consent to Hell. For Protestants, Infant Baptism does not remove Original Sin; therefore, we must reconsider the meaning of Original Sin. In truth, Protestants believe in an age of accountability where the person is aware of the consequences of actions, wherein the conscience "convicts" the person of wrongdoing. This is more closely attuned to the Orthodox view of Original Sin. However, the view does lay open the problem of sociopaths and others with conditions rendering them "conscienceless."

To get around the atrocity of sending newborns to hell, the Catholic Church began to baptize small children. This is now called infant baptism and is said to remove Original Sin, allowing the child to attain heaven if he or she dies before the age of reason. Why is there an age of reason if Baptism has already removed Original Sin? Beats me... But by the age of twelve or so, the child will have gone through a series of indoctrinations or courses, and will be sprinkled, blessed and confirmed as an adult.

But infant mortality was very high and quite often the newborn died before the priest could perform baptism. The result was the creation of an entire realm, called Limbo.

The Limbo of Infants (Latin limbus infantium) is a hypothesis about the permanent status of the unbaptized who die in infancy, too young to have committed personal sins, but not having been freed from Original Sin. Since the time of Augustine, theologians considered baptism to be necessary for salvation. Some who hold this theory regard the Limbo of Infants as a state of maximum natural happiness, others as one of "mildest punishment" consisting at least of privation of the beatific vision and of any hope of obtaining it. This theory, in any of its forms, has never been dogmatically defined by the Church, but it is permissible to hold it.

905 A.D.: Pope Pius X made a definitive declaration confirming the existence of Limbo. However, this was not an infallible statement by the Pope:

"Children who die without baptism go into limbo, where they do not enjoy God, but they do not suffer either, because having Original Sin, and only that, they do not deserve paradise, but neither hell or purgatory."

Recently, within the last decade, the Catholic Church has declared Limbo non-existent and has stressed the hope that these infants may attain heaven instead of the supposed state of Limbo; however, the directly opposed theological opinion also exists, namely that there is no intermediate afterlife state between salvation and damnation, and that all the unbaptized are damned. With this, the Catholic Church has placed itself in the throws of re-examination of its own concept of inherited Original Sin and its power to send all unbaptized children to hell.

From The Times
October 4, 2006

"The Pope will cast aside centuries of Catholic belief later this week by abolishing formally the concept of limbo, in a gesture calculated to help win the souls of millions of babies in the developing world for Christ.

All the evidence suggests that Benedict XVI never believed in the idea anyway. But in the fertile evangelization zones of Africa and Asia, the Pope — an acknowledged authority on all things Islamic — is only too aware that Muslims believe the souls of stillborn babies go straight to Heaven. For the Church, looking to spread the faith in countries with a high infant mortality rate, now is a good time to make it absolutely clear that stillborn babies of Christian mothers go directly to Heaven, too.

Anyone who deludes themselves that Muslims do not know about limbo would be wrong. Dante put Jerusalem's conqueror Saladin in limbo in his Inferno, along with Ovid and Homer and other pre-Christian villains and heroes.

Even though it has never been part of the Church's doctrine formally, the existence of limbo was taught until recently to Catholics around the world. In Britain it was in the Penny Catechism, approved by the Catholic Bishops of England and Wales, that declared limbo "a place of rest where the souls of the just who died before Christ were detained." But its lack of doctrinal authority has long failed to impress the Pope, who was recorded as saying before his election: "Personally, I would let it drop, since it has always been only a theological hypothesis."

(Oct. 4, 2008) This week a 30-strong Vatican international commission of theologians, which has been examining limbo, began its final deliberations. Vatican sources said it had concluded that all children who die, do so in the expectation of "the universal salvation of God" and the "mediation of Christ", whether baptized or not.

The theologians' finding is that God wishes all souls to be saved, and that the souls of unbaptized children are entrusted to a "merciful God" whose ways of ensuring salvation cannot be known. "In effect, this means that all children who die go to Heaven," one source said.

The commission's conclusions will be approved formally by the Pope on Friday.

Christians hold that Heaven is a state of union with God, while Hell is separation from God. They have long wrestled, however, not only with the fate of unbaptized children, but also with the conundrum of what happened to those who lived a "good life" but died before the time of Jesus.

The answer since the 13th century has been limbo. What remains in an uncertain state, though, is the status of all the pre-Christian and unbaptized adult souls held by some still to be in this halfway house between Heaven and Hell.

The Pope is expected to abolish only "limbus infantium", where the souls of unbaptized infants go. The precise status of "limbus patrum", where the good people went who lived before Christ remains . . . well, in limbo.

Although it is the latter that has been subject to such dramatic representation in art and literature, no Christian mother today who miscarries, has a stillborn child or otherwise loses a baby before baptism can bear to view without a purgatorial shudder the traditional images, such as those by Giotto, of Christ freeing Old Testament figures from limbo. In propelling limbo out of its own uncertain state, the Pope is merely acknowledging the distress its half-existence causes to millions and is bringing his characteristic Teutonic sense of righteous clarity to the matter.

One of the reasons Baptists and some other Protestant denominations resist infant baptism is because they believe the souls of babies are innocent and that it is for adults to choose a life in Christ or otherwise. The early church father Tertullian opposed infant baptism on these grounds. But the teachings that took hold of the imagination and the faith of the early Christians were those of the Greek fathers such as Gregory of Nazianzus who wrote: "It will happen, I believe . . . that those last mentioned [infants dying without baptism] will neither be admitted by the just judge to the glory of Heaven nor condemned to suffer punishment, since, they are not wicked."

This seems lenient compared with St Augustine, who in 418 persuaded the Council of Carthage to condemn the British Pelagian heresy that there was an "in between" place for unbaptized babies. He persuaded the council that unbaptized babies share the general misery of the damned. The most he would concede was that their misery was not quite as bad as that of wicked dead adults. (Augustine was such an ass.)

Many of Augustine's views are losing support today. His harsh and restrictive views on sex, marriage, and innocent babies burning in hell has gripped and molded the Catholic Church for many years. Of all his doctrines, the most ill-conceived was his application of Original Sin and infant hell. But, if we hold to the belief that we all are born with Original Sin and are thus destined for hell, the fact that all stillborn and unbaptized children are hell bound is the only logical conclusion. Indeed, if one does not accept that the sprinkled water of a priest can remove such a stain, we are all destined to hell, at least until the age of understanding, after which we can apply faith to the equation for ourselves.

In this light, it is easy to see how our understanding of Original Sin may be incorrect. No sin can be inherited, neither from father to son, nor from Adam to modern man. Yet the state of the world fell and paradise was lost. God withdrew His communion with man as man sought to use his free will, refusing God's plan. As we inherit traits from our parents, so we inherit the propensity to sin. All will sin, just as all will breathe, but until we do sin, we are not sinners.

The piety and devotion of Augustine is largely unquestioned by Orthodox theologians, but his conclusions on the Atonement are not (Romanides, 2002). Augustine, by his own admission, did not properly learn to read Greek and this was a liability for him. He seems to have relied mostly on Latin translations of Greek texts.

His misinterpretation of a key scriptural reference, Romans 5:12, is a case in point (Meyendorff, 1979). In Latin the Greek idiom "eph ho" which means "because of" was translated as "in whom." Saying that all have sinned in Adam is quite different than saying that all sinned because of him. Augustine believed and taught that all humanity has sinned in Adam (Meyendorff, 1979, p. 144). The result is that guilt replaces death as the ancestral inheritance (Augustine, 1956b). Therefore the term Original Sin conveys the belief that Adam and Eve's sin is the first and universal transgression in which all humanity participates.

Admittedly, the idea of salvation as a process is not absent in the West. (One can call to mind the Western mystics and the Wesleyan movement as examples.) However, the underlying theological foundations of Eastern Church and Western Church in regard to ancestral or Original Sin are dramatically opposed. The difference is apparent when looking at the understanding of ethics itself. For the Western Church, ethics often seems to imply adherence to an external code; for the Eastern Church,

Joseph Lumpkin

ethics implies "the restoration of life to the fullness of freedom and love" (Yannaras, 1984, p. 143).

Sin is missing the mark or, put another way, it is the failure to realize the full potential of the gift of human life, and calls for a gradual approach to pastoral care. The goal is nothing less than an existential transformation from within through growth in communion with God. Daily sins are more than moral infractions; they are glimpses into the brokenness of human life and evidence of personal struggle. "Repentance means rejecting death and uniting ourselves to life" (Yannaras, 1984, 147-148).

A young monk was once asked, "What do you do all day in the monastery?" He replied, "We fall and rise, fall and rise."

Death has caused a change in the way we relate to God, to one another and to the world. Our lives are dominated by the struggle to survive. Yannaras writes that we see ourselves not as persons sharing a common nature and purpose, but as autonomous individuals who live to survive in competition with one another. Thus, set adrift by death, we are alienated from God, from others and also from our true selves (Yannaras, 1984).

Yannaras writes that the message of the Church for humanity, wounded and degraded by the 'terrorist God of juridical ethics' is precisely this: "what God really asks of man is neither individual feats nor works of merit, but a cry of trust and love from the depths." The cry comes from the depth of our need to the unfathomable depth of God's love; the Prodigal Son crying out, "I want to go home" to the Father who, seeing his advance from a distance, runs to meet him. (Luke 15:11-32)

The Apostle Paul struggled daily with his inability to be consistent in his works and deeds.

"I do not understand my own actions. For I do not do what I want, but I do the very thing I hate. Now if I do what I do not want, I agree that the law is good. So then it is no longer I that do it, but sin which dwells within me. For I know that nothing good dwells within me, that is, in my flesh. I can will what is right, but I cannot do it. For I do not do the good I

218

want, but the evil I do not want is what I do. Now if I do what I do not want, it is no longer I that do it, but sin which dwells within me. So I find it to be a law that when I want to do right, evil lies close at hand. For I delight in the law of God, in my inmost self, but I see in my members another law at war with the law of my mind and making me captive to the law of sin which dwells in my members. Wretched man that I am! Who will deliver me from this body of death?" (Romans 7:15-24)

The solution to this dilemma is stated by Paul in these terms: "For God has done what the law, weakened by the flesh, could not do: sending his own Son in the likeness of sinful flesh and for sin, he condemned sin in the flesh, in order that the just requirement of the law might be fulfilled in us, who walk not according to the flesh but according to the Spirit." (Romans 8:3-4)

What this divine/human relationship will produce, God knows, but we place ourselves in His loving hands and not without some trepidation because "God is a loving fire… for all: good or bad" (Kalomiris, 1980, p. 19). The knowledge that salvation is a process makes our failures understandable. The illness that afflicts us demands access to the grace of God often and repeatedly. We offer to Him the only things that we have, our weakened condition and will. Joined with God's love and grace it is the fuel that breathed upon by the Spirit of God, breaks the soul into flame.

In our purification the Spirit of God works within us over time in such a way that we sin less and less over great and greater periods of time. This is the work of the Spirit in us whether we are sprinkled or dunked in the Catholic Church, the Church of Christ, or just a little countryside Baptist Church.

Much of the information used in this chapter is derived from the writings of Antony Hughes, M.Div., the rector of St. Mary's Orthodox Church in Cambridge, MA, as well as Wikipedia, the BBC, Times Magazine, and other sources.

Mary: Immaculate Conception, Assumption, Co-Redeemer

Seeing as how we have been on the topic of Original Sin, it seems appropriate that we now look at the doctrine of The Immaculate Conception.

Many of my Protestant friends will affirm their belief that Jesus was conceived by the Holy Spirit and born without Original Sin, but that is not what this doctrine concludes. The doctrine of The Immaculate Conception states that Mary, the mother of Jesus, was born without sin.

To think that the Catholic Church believes that Mary was prepared as a vessel for Jesus and was born sinless may come as a surprise.

The Catholic doctrine of Immaculate Conception asserts that Mary, the mother of Jesus, was preserved by God from the stain of original sin at the time of her own conception. (That is, at the time of copulation between the parents of Mary, God interceded and stopped the transference of Original Sin to the soul that would become Mary.) According to the dogma, Mary was conceived by normal biological means, but her soul was acted upon by God (kept "immaculate") at the time of her conception.

Let us stop here and ask the obvious question. If Jesus needed an immaculate vessel, and Mary needed to be immaculate, why wouldn't Mary's mother also need to be immaculate, ad infinitum until Eve herself would have been immaculate.

The Catholic Church believes the dogma is supported by the scripture of her being greeted by Angel Gabriel as "full of Grace", as well as either directly or indirectly by the writings of many of the Church Fathers, and is often called "Mary the Blessed Virgin" (Luke 1:48). Catholic theology maintains that since Jesus became incarnate of the Virgin Mary, she needed to be completely free of sin to bear the Son of God, and that Mary is "redeemed 'by the grace of Christ' but in a more perfect manner than other human beings."

The formation of Mariology has been maturing in the Catholic and Orthodox Churches from the beginning of the church. Yet, it was not until 1854 that Pope Pius IX declared the Immaculate Conception as an official doctrine.

The Orthodox Church has rejected this doctrine since the church does not believe in Original Sin. Eastern Orthodox theologians suggest that the references among the Greek and Syrian Fathers to Mary's purity and sinlessness may refer not to an "a priori state," but to her conduct after birth.

The Conception of Mary was celebrated in England from the ninth century. Aquinas and Bonaventure, for example, believed that Mary was completely free from sin, but that she was not given this grace at the instant of her conception. The Feast of the Immaculate Conception of Mary had been established in 1476 by Pope Sixtus IV who stopped short of defining the doctrine as a dogma of the Catholic Faith.

The Feast of the Immaculate Conception, was consecrated by Pope Pius XII in 1942.

In principle this doctrine was a part of the Roman Catholic and Byzantine thinking in the Middle Ages. The apostolic constitution Munificentissimus Deus, promulgated by Pius XII on November 1, 1950, made it a doctrine necessary for salvation, stating, "The Immaculate Mother of God, the ever-Virgin Mary, having completed the course of her earthly life, was assumed body and soul into heavenly glory."

Although this is not a dogma in the Orthodox Church, there is the universal belief that there was a pre-sanctification of Mary at the time of her conception, similar to the conception of Saint John the Baptist. (Wait... What!? John flipped and jumped in the womb when Mary and Elizabeth met, and were both pregnant, but John had a special sanctification? Really?)

Another misunderstanding is that with her immaculate conception, Mary did not need a savior. On the contrary, when defining the dogma, Pope Pius IX represented Catholic tradition by affirming that Mary was redeemed in a manner more sublime. He stated that Mary, rather than being cleansed after sin, was completely prevented from contracting original sin in view of the foreseen merits of Jesus Christ, the Savior of the human race.

In a furtherance of the doctrine of Immaculate Conception, the Assumption of Mary into heaven was embraced.

In Roman Catholic doctrine, the Assumption means that Mary, the mother of Jesus, was taken (assumed) bodily into heavenly glory when she died.

Gregory of Tours in his De Gloria Martyrum of the sixth century quotes an unfounded legend about Mary's assumption. As the story became popular in both East and West it took two forms. The Coptic version describes Jesus appearing to Mary to foretell her death and bodily elevation into heaven, while the Greek, Latin, and Syriac versions picture Mary calling for the apostles, who are transported to her miraculously from their places of service. Then Jesus, after her death, conveyed her remains to heaven. The doctrine was first treated in deductive theology about 800 A.D. Benedict XIV (d. 1758) proposed it as a probable doctrine.

In the Orthodox church, the koimesis, or dormition ("falling asleep"), of the Virgin began to be commemorated on August 15 in the 6th century. The observance gradually spread to the West, where it became known as the Feast of the Assumption. By the 13th century, the belief was accepted by most Catholic theologians, and it was a popular subject with Renaissance and Baroque painters. The Assumption was declared a dogma of the Roman Catholic faith by Pope Pius XII in 1950.

Assumption of the Virgin (Latin assumere,"to take up") in the Roman Catholic church and the Orthodox church is the doctrine that after her death the body of Mary, the mother of Christ, was taken into heaven and reunited with her soul. Defined as an article of faith by Pope Pius XII in 1950, the assumption was first commemorated as the Feast of the Dormition (falling asleep) of Mary in the 6th century. This feast later developed into the Feast of the Assumption, now celebrated in the Roman Catholic Church on August 15 every year.

Feasts celebrating the death of Mary date from the fifth century. In the East the late seventh century feasts included the assumption. After the eighth century the West followed suit. Nicholas I by edict (863 A.D.) placed the Feast of the Assumption on the same level as Easter and Christmas. Cranmer omitted it from the Book of Common Prayer and it has not since been included.

The 1950 action regarding the assumption of Mary is built upon the declaration of "The Immaculate Conception" (Dec. 8, 1854), which declared Mary free from original sin. Both issue from the concept of Mary as the "Mother of God." Her special state, Pius XII felt, demanded special treatment. If Mary is indeed "full of grace" (cf. Luke 1:28, 44) the assumption is a logical outcome. Like Jesus, she is sinless, preserved from corruption, resurrected, received into heaven, and a recipient of corporeal glory. Thus Mary is crowned Queen of Heaven and assumes the roles of intercessor and mediator.

The argument in Munificentissimus Deus develops along several lines. It emphasizes Mary's unity with her divine Son, for she is "always sharing His lot." Since she shared in the past in His incarnation, death, and resurrection, now, as His mother, she is the mother of his church, which is His body. Rev. 12:1 is applied to Mary; she is the prototype of the church, for she has experienced anticipatorially corporeal glorification in her assumption. In a strange and convoluted incestuous twist, three times Mary is referred to as the "New Eve," working again the parallel of Christ as the new Adam and presenting the glorified Christ as one with the new Eve.

There is now an ongoing push within the Catholic Church to take the last step in the adoration and deification of Mary by declaring her as Co-Redeemer along side Jesus.
Pope John Paul II publicly used the term "Coredemptrix" at least six times in his pontificate, and at one point Miravalle predicted that he would proclaim the dogma before the millennial year of 2000.

By far the most significant criticism, if only on account of its source, has been that of Cardinal Joseph Ratzinger, now Pope Benedict.

Ratzinger told a German interviewer in 2000 that the "formula `Co-redemptrix' departs to too great an extent from the language of Scripture and of the (church) Fathers and therefore gives rise to misunderstandings," threatening to "obscure" the status of Christ as the source of all redemption. "I do not think there will be any compliance with this demand (for papal proclamation of the dogma) within the foreseeable future," he said at the time.

For many Christians the story of Mary holds within it, several deep lessons for the Christian mystic. Even before the great schism between the Orthodox and Roman churches, Mary held a place in the minds and hearts of the Christian church. Later, in church history, in a move to balance what was felt to be an over-emphasis on Mary and her status, the Protestant church began to diminish her status until she is now considered little more than a willing incubator for Jesus. Polarization is an all too human reaction, which leads us, in many cases, to fully reject a doctrine and even a person when we believe it, or they, are in error. The error may hold only a part of what is presented, but the rejection is full. Thus large areas of truth are thrown out with areas of error.

The Bible tells us she will be called blessed, but many do not call her anything at all. The majority of Protestant believers ignore Mary. It is the overcompensation to avoid the recurrence of the error. Throwing truth out with error, the baby that got tossed out in the bathwater of error this time happened to be the Mother of Jesus. I do not support an extreme elevation or veneration of Mary or of any creature for that matter, since such a view would cloud the vision of the preeminence of Christ. But, neither do I agree with the place to which most Protestant churches have resigned her.

Although it is true, grace shed on someone does not indicate moral or spiritual status, it is also true God had a plan for salvation from the foundations of the world and in His plan, Mary had a place. As people of faith, Mary's story has a deep and significant meaning for us. Grace is given without, and many times, in spite of spiritual condition. It was not Mary's state or condition but the willingness of her decision that drew the sovereign will of God.

In this vein the early fathers found something so fascinating and deeply spiritual about the story of Mary they elevated her to a venerated status. As we look closer into the story of Mary we will see she is the template and prototype of the true mystical experience. Her experience is the key and summation of the entire Christian process. In her we find our spiritual likeness, our history, and our story. In the story of Mary the mystical life is foretold.

LUKE 1:35 And the angel answered and said unto her, The Holy Ghost shall come upon thee, and the power of the Highest shall overshadow thee: therefore also that holy thing which shall be born of thee shall be called the Son of God. 37 For with God nothing shall be impossible. 38 And Mary said, "Behold the handmaid of the Lord; be it unto me according to thy word." And the angel departed from her. 41 And it came to pass, that, when Elisabeth heard the salutation of Mary, the babe leaped in her womb; and Elisabeth was filled with the Holy Ghost: 42 And she spake out with a loud voice, and said, Blessed art thou among women, and blessed is the fruit of thy womb. 43 And whence is this to me, that the mother of my Lord should come to me? 44 For, lo, as soon as the voice of thy salutation sounded in mine ears, the babe leaped in my womb for joy. 45 And blessed is she that believed: for there shall be a performance of those things, which were told her from the Lord. 46 And Mary said, My soul doth magnify the Lord, 47 And my spirit hath rejoiced in God my Saviour.

LUK 1:48 For he hath regarded the low estate of his handmaiden: for, behold, from henceforth all generations shall call me blessed. 49 For he that is mighty hath done to me great things; and holy is his name. 50 And his mercy is on them that fear him from generation to generation. 51 He hath shewed strength with his arm; he hath scattered the proud in the imagination of their hearts. 52 He hath put down the mighty from their seats, and exalted them of low degree.

In His grace, God chose Mary, a young woman with no obvious attributes that set her apart from hundreds of others. In her own words, she was someone who counted herself as a lowly maiden. In His power and mercy He came to her. His spirit was on her and in her and He communed with her within her heart and soul. God, being out of time and space, had a plan for creation before He created. This also includes the incarnation.

Creation was created for Jesus and through Jesus. The plan for creation was completed in the mind of God before the act of creating. Therefore, Mary was in God's plan for the birth of Jesus before creation, but because of free will she had acquiescence. It was because of her free will and the obedience that followed from it she was blessed. We cannot know why Mary was chosen and set apart. God has always used men and women who seemed common and ordinary to do great things. So it was with the mother of God. Mary, by believing the child in her was indeed sent and fathered by the Holy Spirit of God and set in her virgin body for the redemption of man, became the first Christian.

" The Holy Ghost shall come upon thee, and the power of the Highest shall overshadow thee: therefore also that holy thing which shall be born of thee shall be called the Son of God." Luke 1:35

It was not through doctrine or church that they met but through a real and powerful personal communion. This is the essence of the mystical experience. God draws us and woos us to Him and in our desire to be with Him we are allowed an intimate communion with Him. In this spiritual state of togetherness with God, the Holy Spirit of God implants Christ in our spiritual wombs. Christ forms in us, grows in us, moves in us and through us until we give birth to Him through our hearts and souls and show Him to the world in our love and actions with spontaneous acts of love and serving. It is through a heart and mind that calls out to Him and declares, "Behold the handmaid of the Lord; be it unto me according to thy word." Only in this can we contain God's Spirit. Only in this can God hold us.

By this alone comes the world's greatest experience. What we do not realize in our simplicity is each time Christ is birthed in us we are experiencing the mystical equivalent of the incarnation once again. Each time we nurture Him in us and show Him forth to others, we have become Mary and the great incarnation has come upon us.

ISA 9:6 For unto us a child is born, unto us a son is given: and the government shall be upon his shoulder: and his name shall be called Wonderful, Counsellor, The mighty God, The everlasting Father, The Prince of Peace. 7 Of the increase of his government and peace there shall be no end, upon the throne of David, and upon his kingdom, to order it, and to establish it with judgment and with justice from henceforth even for ever. The zeal of the LORD of hosts will perform this.

It is for this event that even if man had not fallen, still Christ would have come. He is the crown of mankind. He is the crowning of creation. He was destined from the foundation of creation to be the one and only avenue for the union of God and man. Such a union going far beyond any understanding communion could bring. Thus, we may commune with God but Christ lives in us, in a state that is distinct yet in union.

Sources: Cambridge Encyclopedia, Encyclopedia.StateUniversity.com, Wikipedia, EWTN Catholic Television Network, Catholic.org, mb-soft.com, Religious

Joseph Lumpkin

News, "Dark Night of the Soul" by Joseph Lumpkin, and other sources.

Baptism

Is baptism a type, shadow, and symbol, or is it actually necessary for salvation? Can one be sprinkled with water or is complete submersion needed?

Should the words of some Bible verses be taken literally, even though in other passages differing ideas may be expressed? Can some passages be viewed in a completely literal sense while others are said to be symbolic?

There are deeply disturbing problems when taking literally those passages regarding the need of baptism to be saved. A logical dissonance immediately becomes apparent between how some churches view transubstantiation and how they view baptism. With passages like the one below, it is easy to see the statement is clear and straightforward. Jesus himself is proclaiming that the bread is His body and the cup contains His blood. This is a direct statement without any equivocation on the part of the Son of God. Yet, most churches do not take this statement literally.

Matthew 26 (King James Version)
26 And as they were eating, Jesus took bread, and blessed it, and brake it, and gave it to the disciples, and said, Take, eat; this is my body. 27 And he took the cup, and gave thanks, and gave it to them, saying, Drink ye all of it; 28 For this is my blood of the new testament, which is shed for many for the remission of sins.

Some churches have doctrines, which even though dismissing the above statement, hold fast to the need to be baptized before one can see the heavenly gates. What's more, all of these denominations insist that only their preachers, pastors, or priests can perform this magic, which, by the mumbling of some words and the application of tap water, may change the soul from sinful to sanctified in a blessed instant.

The questions raised are two-fold. Can one man, in any way, change another man's soul? What is being baptized, the body or the soul? It is the soul that will see judgment. If we baptize the body, how can it affect the soul?

This colloquy is in no way an argument for transubstantiation but is instead an argument against arbitrary literalism as applied to biblical interpretation and therefore to doctrine.

First, let us look at the cornerstone verse that supports the "Baptism for Salvation" doctrine.

Mark 16 (New International Version)
15He said to them, "Go into all the world and preach the good news to all creation. 16Whoever believes and is baptized will be saved, but whoever does not believe will be condemned. 17And these signs will accompany those who believe: In my name they will drive out demons; they will speak in new tongues; 18they will pick up snakes with their hands; and when they drink deadly poison, it will not hurt them at all; they will place their hands on sick people, and they will get well."

But wait! Wasn't this chapter one of those passages we discussed earlier in the book? This is one of the chapters we can prove beyond a reasonable doubt was added later and did not occur in the older manuscripts. Let's look at exactly where the more reliable witnesses (manuscripts) end.

According to the New International Version (NIV): "The most reliable early manuscripts and other ancient witnesses do not have Mark 16:9-20."

The following is Mark 16:9-20 and is NOT included in the most reliable versions.
9 When Jesus rose early on the first day of the week, he appeared first to Mary Magdalene, out of whom he had driven seven demons. 10She went and told those who had been with

him and who were mourning and weeping. 11When they heard that Jesus was alive and that she had seen him, they did not believe it. 12 Afterward Jesus appeared in a different form to two of them while they were walking in the country. 13 These returned and reported it to the rest; but they did not believe them either. 14 Later Jesus appeared to the Eleven as they were eating; he rebuked them for their lack of faith and their stubborn refusal to believe those who had seen him after he had risen. 15 He said to them, "Go into all the world and preach the good news to all creation. 16 Whoever believes and is baptized will be saved, but whoever does not believe will be condemned. 17 And these signs will accompany those who believe: In my name they will drive out demons; they will speak in new tongues; 18 they will pick up snakes with their hands; and when they drink deadly poison, it will not hurt them at all; they will place their hands on sick people, and they will get well." 19 After the Lord Jesus had spoken to them, he was taken up into heaven and he sat at the right hand of God. 20Then the disciples went out and preached everywhere, and the Lord worked with them and confirmed his word by the signs that accompanied it.

Thus, the verse on which the "baptism for salvation" doctrine is based does not appear in reliable versions.

It is amazing and very sad that at least two major denominations have been so influenced by verses added after the apostle wrote the book. The accepted theory as to why the addition occurred concludes that the pages at the end of the book of Mark were somehow destroyed. Scribes, wishing for an ending of exhortation, devised the ending sometime in the second century. For more information on the Book of Mark and other endings found in various manuscripts see Appendix "B."

"Let my pastor baptize you or you will go to hell." Such harsh views have not disappeared over time as one might think people or denominations would mature and become more reasonable. Such gravity is placed on baptism in some denominations that churches split over such trivial matters as how long to keep the water in the baptismal pool before draining the "swamp." Is it the stagnant water that saves? If not, then is it the power of the man who dips the sinner that might be enough to save? If it is not the power of water or man that saves then we must re-assess and re-ask, "Is baptism a symbol or does the act actually save us?"

What is baptism? It is an act symbolizing our death, burial, and resurrection in Christ. In this type and symbol, complete submersion comes closest, whereas sprinkling takes on an Old Testament type of sprinkling the blood of the sacrificed animal on the people to cover their sins or to form a covenant.

Compare these verses of baptism and sprinkling.

Romans 6 (King James Version)
1What shall we say then? Shall we continue in sin, that grace may abound? 2 God forbid. How shall we, that are dead to sin, live any longer therein? 3 Know ye not, that so many of us as were baptized into Jesus Christ were baptized into his death? 4 Therefore we are buried with him by baptism into death: that like as Christ was raised up from the dead by the glory of the Father, even so we also should walk in newness of life. 5 For if we have been planted together in the likeness of his death, we shall be also in the likeness of his resurrection: 6 Knowing this, that our old man is crucified with him, that the body of sin might be destroyed, that henceforth we should not serve sin. 7 For he that is dead is freed from sin. 8 Now if we be dead with Christ, we believe that we shall also live with him: 9 Knowing that Christ being raised from the dead dieth no more; death hath no more dominion over him. 10 For in that he died, he died unto sin once: but in that he liveth, he liveth unto God. 11 Likewise reckon ye also yourselves to be dead indeed unto sin, but alive unto God through Jesus Christ our Lord.

Exodus 24 (New International Version)
The Covenant Confirmed

1 Then he said to Moses, "Come up to the LORD, you and Aaron, Nadab and Abihu, and seventy of the elders of Israel. You are to worship at a distance, 2 but Moses alone is to approach the LORD; the others must not come near. And the people may not come up with him."
3 When Moses went and told the people all the LORD's words and laws, they responded with one voice, "Everything the LORD has said we will do." 4 Moses then wrote down everything the LORD had said. He got up early the next morning and built an altar at the foot of the mountain and set up twelve stone pillars representing the twelve tribes of Israel. 5 Then he sent young Israelite men, and they offered burnt offerings and sacrificed young bulls as fellowship offerings (a) to the LORD. 6 Moses took half of the blood and put it in bowls, and the other half he sprinkled on the altar. 7 Then he took the Book of the Covenant and read it to the people. They responded, "We will do everything the LORD has said; we will obey." 8 Moses then took the blood, sprinkled it on the people and said, "This is the blood of the covenant that the LORD has made with you in accordance with all these words."

(a)-Traditionally peace offerings

Let us keep in mind that before the death of Jesus, the world was under the old covenant. Things worked differently. Under the Old Covenant types and symbols painted a picture for the practitioner of the real substance to come. In the case of Baptism, as in the entire Bible, water represents the spirit of God and the cleansing of the person.

After the death of Jesus, the spirit of God began to work in a new capacity. No longer was the spirit confined to a prophet here or a person there. The Spirit of God would be in and with all believers. No longer were types and symbols used as a picture of the true substance. Once Jesus said that no one can enter heaven unless he has been born again of water and the Holy Spirit (John 3:5). Now, after His death, the ceremony of Water baptism was placed in an inferior and obsolete role when the resurrected Jesus explained that the symbol was about to become real.

Acts 1:4-6 (New International Version)
4 On one occasion, while he was eating with them, he gave them this command: "Do not leave Jerusalem, but wait for the gift my Father promised, which you have heard me speak about. 5 For John baptized with water, but in a few days you will be baptized with the Holy Spirit."

No longer was there a need for water to be used as a picture of the Spirit, of cleansing, or of the resurrection of the soul. The Spirit was coming. From that point on, believers were given the Spirit of God and raised into life.

Baptism is a symbol of where the person is, that is saved by the spirit, not where they are going, saved after being submerged in water by a man. We are baptized to show the world the testimony of what we believe; that our old self is dead and buried and that just as rising out of the water signifies resurrection, we will "reckon" ourselves to be dead indeed unto sin, but alive unto God through Jesus Christ our Lord.

We reckon ourselves to be dead. The word "reckon" is to conclude after calculation, or to be of an opinion. In other words, nothing has changed but our opinion. This is because symbols do not change us. Only the Spirit of God does that. Baptism is not needed for salvation or church membership.

Predestination and Foreknowledge

"Hath not the potter power over the clay, of the same lump to make one vessel unto honour, and another unto dishonour?" (Romans 9:21).

The path from the mind of God to the mind of man contains a sheer precipice, which no human can ascend. Mankind is not able to apprehend the purpose or design of creation or judgment. We view the questions of predestination and foreknowledge with half-blind eyes.

How God's plan and man's free will fit together is the greatest paradox of theology. Within the enigma are the puzzle pieces of the sacrificial death of Jesus, the scope and power of that atonement, the fall of man, the grace of God, and hell itself. Yet, there are those who are so sure they understand how predestination, foreknowledge, and free will combine in God's plan that there is no place in their minds for discussion. I will tell you now I am not one of these.

Let us examine some ways men have attempted to solve the paradox. A few solutions may surprise you.

By the way – Were you destined to read this book or was it by chance you chose it? If it was predestined for you to read, for what purpose did God intend it.

There are few controversies that have divided more and burned as hot as the one between views of predestination and foreknowledge.

If God is omnipotent what He knows will happen is destined to happen. Yet, this knowledge is not the same as actively guiding an outcome. However, if God knows the outcome then the outcome cannot be altered, thus it is predestined.

If predestination is taken to its full conclusion, man has no free will at all and even those choices he believes he is making are predetermined. This flies in the face of personal responsibility. Thus if one holds fast to this argument, one must ask why we would punish anyone for an infraction of the law, say murder or rape, seeing that it was choreographed before his or her birth.

What are the rightful places for God's sovereignty and man's free will? What is man's responsibility for personal sin?

From the days of Judaism, religious men have believed that God had a plan, which He was causing to unfold. This belief in predestination was brought into Christianity from its very foundation. This is because the scripture states that Jesus was "purposed to die" from the very beginning.

Yet, Jesus asked God if the plan could be altered so that his torture and death could be avoided. Does this mean predestined plans can be changed?

Acts 2:23 (New International Version)
23This man was handed over to you by God's set purpose and foreknowledge; and you, with the help of wicked men put him to death by nailing him to the cross.

1 Peter 1 (New International Version)
17Since you call on a Father who judges each man's work impartially, live your lives as strangers here in reverent fear. 18For you know that it was not with perishable things such as silver or gold that you were redeemed from the empty way of life handed down to you from your forefathers, 19but with the precious blood of Christ, a lamb without blemish or defect. 20He was chosen before the creation of the world, but was revealed in these last times for your sake. 21Through him you believe in God, who raised him from the dead and glorified him, and so your faith and hope are in God.

So, God chose Jesus before the world was formed, and had a purpose for Him and foreknowledge of His death.

Does this mean it was set and could not be changed?

Matthew 26 (King James Version)
38 Then saith he unto them, My soul is exceeding sorrowful, even unto death: tarry ye here, and watch with me.
39 And he went a little farther, and fell on his face, and prayed, saying, O my Father, if it be possible, let this cup pass from me: nevertheless not as I will, but as thou wilt.
40 And he cometh unto the disciples, and findeth them asleep, and saith unto Peter, What, could ye not watch with me one hour?
41 Watch and pray, that ye enter not into temptation: the spirit indeed is willing, but the flesh is weak.
42 He went away again the second time, and prayed, saying, O my Father, if this cup may not pass away from me, except I drink it, thy will be done.

From this passage we see that Jesus assumed that God could change the future, even if it had been planned from the creation of the world. A predestined event may not be set in stone. Jesus was openly battling to make His free will conform to the Father's will. He wished not to be tortured and killed but submitted to God's will anyway. In some fashion, not fully understood by mankind, free will and predestination must co-exist. With this in mind let us look into the matter.

The proponents of predestination cannot agree on the exact order of events. In general it is thought that God creates us, selects from His creation who He will send to heaven and who He will not. He then allows the predestined event to unfold. The exact sequence of events gives way to differing doctrines with very long names.

Supralapsarianism
15. God calls the elect to salvation.
16. He elects some and condemns the rest.
17. God creates mankind.
18. God permits the Fall of Man.

19. God provides salvation for elect.
20. (Note that in this theory, God actively saves and actively condemns.)

Infralapsarianism
1. God creates mankind.
2. God permits the Fall of Man.
3. God elects some but passes over the rest.
4. God provides salvation for elect.
5. God calls the elect to salvation.
6. (In this theory God, actively chooses some and passively skips others.)

Amyraldism
    God creates mankind.
    God permits the Fall of Man.
    God provides salvation sufficient for all
    God elects some and passes over the rest.
    God calls the elect to salvation.
    (This is another theory that calls for active selection of some while others are passively ignored.)

Universalism
    God creates mankind.
    God permits the Fall of Man.
    God provides salvation for all.
    God calls all to salvation.
    God will either save all, no matter their wish, or He will reveal Himself to all in such a way that all of mankind will wish to be saved.
(It is not clear on the surface, but Universalism can be looked at as a type of predestination as well. This is because the doctrine states that all will be saved or chosen, even those who have chosen to oppose God in their lives.)

Arminianism is a free will doctrine. It has within its systems a single statement that sets it apart from all others. "God elects those who believe." This means the "believer" has a part in his or her destiny.

Arminianism
God creates mankind.
God permits the Fall of Man.
God provides salvation for all.
God calls all to salvation.
God elects those who believe in Him.
(In this theory, all are actively chosen by God, but their destiny depends on the believer's active choice.)

The traditional church view has always been that a person must be a Christian, must belong to their particular sect or denomination, and must follow those rules set out by the denomination and local church to be "accepted" and go to heaven. Universalism seems to have no place in the traditional church, yet there are scriptures supporting this belief. The question becomes; has God predestined humanity to be saved by sacrificing all and paying all to save all? Is it true that Jesus died to save mankind? Is it true God wishes for all men and women to be saved?

Colossians 1:15-20
15 He is the image of the invisible God, the firstborn over all creation. 16 For by Him all things were created that are in heaven and that are on earth, visible and invisible, whether thrones or dominions or principalities or powers. All things were created through Him and for Him. 17 And He is before all things, and in Him all things consist. 18 And He is the head of the body, the church, who is the beginning, the firstborn from the dead, that in all things He may have the preeminence. 19 For it pleased the Father that in Him all the fullness should dwell, 20 and by Him to reconcile (apokatallasso) all things to

Himself, by Him, whether things on earth or things in heaven, having made peace through the blood of His cross.

1 Timothy 2:3-6 (KJV)
3 For this is good and acceptable in the sight of God our Saviour; 4 Who will have (thelo) all men to be saved, and to come unto the knowledge of the truth. 5 For there is one God, and one mediator between God and men, the man Christ Jesus; 6 Who gave himself a ransom for all, to be testified in due time.

Romans 5:18-19
18 Therefore, as through one man's offense judgment came to all men, resulting in condemnation, even so through one Man's righteous act the free gift came to all men, resulting in justification of life.

John 12:32
"And I, if I am lifted up from the earth, will draw all peoples to Myself."

But what does "predestination" mean? What exactly is being guided or chosen so as to be predestined?
The Greek word translated predestine is the word from which we get our English word horizon. The Greek word horizo means to establish or set boundaries. Pre – destination is literally pre-horizon or to preset boundaries. To set the boundaries or to draw lines, or to establish the limits of something is to determine what will be. To do so ahead of time is to predestine.

Romans 8:29 (New International Version)
29 For those God foreknew he also predestined to be conformed to the likeness of his Son, that he might be the firstborn among many brothers.

The predestination of Romans 8:29 means that in eternity past, God drew some lines. He established a horizon or a set of limits around each person He had foreknown.

Here, we must decide if the limits were to restrict or to protect. Were they active and was the choice not to choose some also active or simply a passive "dismissiveness."

Remember that some doctrines of predestination have God choosing who will go to hell and some have Him choosing who will enter heaven while leaving the others to their own devices. The distinction is subtle but one is actively sending folks to hell and the other simply ignores them until they die and go there on their own.

They enter into hell on their own because they never come to know God. They do not know Him because He never called them to an awakening of their fallen state and their need for Him.

While Arminianism has all men being called by God at one time or another throughout their lives in an act called "prevenient" grace, Calvinism has only the chosen being called by "irresistible" grace.

In the fallen state, humanity is blind to the things of God, and is not aware of its spiritual needs. Before God opens their eyes, men and women are atheists, unaware they need God. They cannot love the God they do not know. They do not fear the God who they do not know exists. The state of unsaved man is summed up; "all the imaginations of the thoughts of his heart" are still "evil, only evil," continually." Scripture is clear that in our "natural state," we cannot even call out to God because we neither feel nor believe in God. Thus God must first act on the heart of man before the person can comprehend his state of depravity. "No man can come to me, except the Father which hath sent me draw him." John. 6:44.

The spirit of God awakens the person to their lost state and draws their heart to Him. The next question concerns the person's ability to resist the action of this drawing grace. Is it irresistible or not? Does the person have a say so, or are they overwhelmed by the experience? In other words, does man maintain his free will and thus have a choice to be saved or is he chosen and must obey? Calvinism is based on the "TULIP" principle outlined below.

The Synod of Dort clearly defined, in five simple points, the steps of Calvinism toward salvation.

T   Humanity is by nature Totally depraved and unable to merit salvation.

U   Some people are Unconditionally elected by God's saving grace.

L   God's atonement in Christ is Limited in its efficacy to the salvation of the Elect.

I   God's transforming grace, ministered by the Holy Spirit, is Irresistible on the part of humans.

P   The saints must Persevere in faith to the end, but none of the elect can finally be lost.

(I do not know why we must persevere if we are assured salvation. It just seems like the right thing to do.)

In the minds of those who believe in predestination, God chooses, God draws, God saves, God keeps. When it comes to salvation, man has little to say about his destiny.

In the Wesleyan way of viewing the world, the grace of God may be resisted by the will of the individual. The decision is in the hearts and minds of each person.

There is no way to prove which is the truth, for if our paths are chosen from the beginning, or if the will of God becomes our will, we would never know it. Automatons may believe they are following their own will, but it is pre-programmed into them and is therefore their natural path.

Let us assume that the question of free will is only for salvation and that we have free will in other parts of our lives. Calvinism taken to its conclusion can yield Determinism. The dictionary says Determinism is, "a doctrine that all facts and events exemplify natural laws." If Determinism is true, then we are not free but only think we are. Since we are all subject to the laws that govern the universe, we may "feel" as though we are free to do as we please, we are actually determined to act as we do based on the way the world was created, and they way we were created. That is, the way God created and thus pre-programmed us.

This means God decided before we were made who would go to heaven and who would go to hell. Determinism rules all human actions. If Determinism is true, then we have no choice to act any other way than we do, regardless of the illusion of free will.

To recap, we have various thoughts on predestination. Some have God actively or passively choosing who will go to hell. Some think God could actually set our life path before we are born. There are various flavors of the belief and they vary in how much free will we may have. Some believe our entire life is predetermined. Some believe it is only our salvation that is a fore drawn conclusion. Then there is a faction who believes that man has a say so in choosing heaven or hell. God woos us and calls us but we choose to accept the invitation or not.

But we still have not answered the first question of the limits. If predestination means to pre-set limits or boundaries, and it seems those limits or boundaries block or permit the person to know, love, and believe in God, what could this limitation be? Could it be in us and with us from our birth?

Excerpts from Times Magazine: Posted Monday, Oct. 25, 2004 –

"Ask true believers of any faith to describe the most important thing that drives their devotion, and they'll tell you it's not a thing at all but a sense--a feeling of a higher power far beyond us. Western religions can get a bit more doctrinaire: God has handed us laws and lore, and it's for us to learn and practice what they teach. For a hell-raising species like ours, however--with too much intelligence for our own good and too little discipline to know what to do with it--there have always been other, more utilitarian reasons to get religion. Chief among them is survival. Across the eons, the structure that religion provides our lives helps preserve both mind and body.

But that, in turn, has raised a provocative question, one that's increasingly debated in the worlds of science and religion: Which came first, God or the need for God? In other words, did humans create religion from cues sent from above, or did evolution instill in us a sense of the divine so that we would gather into the communities essential to keeping the species going?"

Nowhere has that idea received a more intriguing going-over than in the recently published book, "The God Gene: How Faith Is Hardwired into Our Genes" (Doubleday; 256 pages), by molecular biologist Dean Hamer. Chief of gene structure at the National Cancer Institute, Hamer not only claims that human spirituality is an adaptive trait, but he also says he has located one of the genes responsible, a gene that just happens to also code for production of the neurotransmitters that regulate our moods. Our most profound feelings of spirituality, according to a literal reading of Hamer's work, may be due to little more than an occasional shot of intoxicating brain chemicals governed by our DNA. "I'm a believer that every thought we think and every feeling we feel is the result of activity in the brain," Hamer says. "I think we follow the basic law of nature, which is that we're a bunch of chemical reactions running around in a bag."

"Hamer began looking in 1998, when he was conducting a survey on smoking and addiction for the National Cancer Institute. As part of his study, he recruited more than 1,000 men and women, who agreed to take a standardized, 240-question personality test called the Temperament and Character Inventory (TCI). Among the traits the TCI measures is one known as self-transcendence, which consists of three other traits: self-forgetfulness, or the ability to get entirely lost in an experience; transpersonal identification, or a feeling of connectedness to a larger universe; and mysticism, or an openness to things not literally provable. Put them all together, and you come as close as science can to measuring what it feels

which the very evolution of the human species turned. It's an argument that's not terribly hard to make."

"One of the best examples of religion as social organizer, according to Binghamton University's Wilson, is early Calvinism. John Calvin rose to prominence in 1536 when, as a theologian and religious reformer, he was recruited to help bring order to the fractious city of Geneva. Calvin, perhaps one of the greatest theological minds ever produced by European Christianity, was a lawyer by trade. Wilson speculates that it was Calvin's pragmatic genius to understand that while civil laws alone might not be enough to bring the city's deadbeats and other malefactors into line, divine law might be."

"Nonetheless, sticking points do remain that prevent genetic theory from going down smoothly. One that's particularly troublesome is the question of why Hamer's God gene, or any of the others that may eventually be discovered, is distributed so unevenly among us. Why are some of us spiritual virtuosos, while others can't play a note? Isn't it one of the central tenets of religion that grace is available to everybody? At least a few scientists shrug at the question. "Some get religion, and some don't," says Virginia Commonwealth University's Eaves…" --With reporting by Jeff Chu/ London, Broward Liston/ Orlando, Maggie Sieger/ Chicago and Daniel Williams/ Sydney

Some get religion and some do not. The gene is distributed unequally among people. Is this the "boundary" spoken of in the scriptures? Is this the tool of predestination? Is this God's mark for heaven or hell? We would believe we have free will. It would feel as if we do. Yet, from our birth, and maybe from the very thought of us by God in the beginning of time, we were predestined to be with or without The God Gene.

247

The Mark of Cain

Genesis 2-3 locates the garden with reference to four rivers and the regions they flow through:
"A river flowed out of Eden to water the garden, and there it divided and became four rivers. The name of the first is the Pishon. It is the one that flowed around the whole land of Havilah, where there is gold. And the gold of that land is good; bdellium and onyx stone are there. The name of the second river is the Gihon. It is the one that flowed around the whole land of Cush. And the name of the third river is the Tigris, which flows east of Assyria. And the fourth river is the Euphrates."
—Genesis 2:10-14

The Garden of Eden (Hebrew "Gan 'Edhen") is the biblical "garden of God", described most notably in the Book of Genesis (Genesis 2-3), but also mentioned, directly or indirectly, in Ezekiel, Isaiah and elsewhere in the Old Testament.

Many, especially those from the older Southern Baptist denomination think the "Mark of Cain" meant that God had cursed him by making him black. This, they believe, was the sign God placed upon him so that all men would know he was cursed by God.

Wait - what? Let's think two seconds about this...
If we take the creation story literally we would see the first couple was from the fertile crescent around the Persian gulf, near Babylon, or what is now an area from Bagdad to Kuwait.

The Bible tells us Adam and Eve were made from the dirt of the area. The book of Adam and Eve says they came from the land of black earth. They were made from earth or mud according to the text. They were from the area of the triangle described in the Bible where three rivers meet. This is Mesopotamia. Adam and Eve were likely very dark people. So – If one believes the "Mark of Cain" was meant to set Cain apart from other people and if one believes God used the color of his skin to set Cain apart and the people of the area had dark completion, the Mark of Cain may have been the fact that he was White.

We can never know with certainty what the mark was, but that did not stop the Mormon Church from excluding blacks from their priesthood. The reason given, they were cursed and this was demonstrated with the mark of Cain. It was not until 1978 that the church reversed its position. But, was the decision to ban blacks from priesthood simply a vengeful political move? On its face, yes.

During the early years of the LDS movement, black people were admitted to the church. From the beginning of the church there were at least two black men became priests, Elijah Abel and Walker Lewis. When the Mormons migrated to Missouri they encountered pro-slavery sentiments but Joseph Smith remained abolitionist in his doctrines.

Beginning in 1842, Smith made known his increasingly strong anti-slavery position. In 1842 he began studying some abolitionist literature, and stated, "It makes my blood boil within me to reflect upon the injustice, cruelty, and oppression of the rulers of the people. When will these things cease to be, and the Constitution and the laws again bear rule.

After Smith's death in 1844, Brigham Young became president of the main body of the church, and led the Mormon Pioneers to what would become the Utah territory. There, as a territorial governor, he promoted discriminatory views regarding black people.

On their way to Utah the Mormons traveled through what they referred to as "The Winter Quarters" in Nebraska.

There, William McCary, a man who was in the priesthood and who was half black began to claim to be a prophet and the possessor of other supernatural gifts. He challenged Young and was excommunicated for apostasy in March 1847 and expelled from Winter Quarters. After his excommunication, McCary began attracting Latter Day Saint followers and instituted plural marriage among his group, and he had himself sealed to several white wives.

McCary's behavior angered many of the Latter Day Saints in Winter Quarters. Researchers have stated that his marriages to his white wives "played an important role in pushing the Mormon leadership into an anti-Black position" and may have prompted Young to institute the priesthood and temple ban on black people

On January 16, 1852 Young made a pronouncement to the Utah Territorial Legislature stating that "any man having one drop of the seed of [Cain] ... in him cannot hold the priesthood and if no other Prophet ever spake it before I will say it now in the name of Jesus Christ I know it is true and others know it."

A similar statement by Young was recorded on February 13, 1849. The statement — which refers to the Curse of Cain — was given in response to a question asking about the African's chances for redemption. Young responded, "The Lord had cursed Cain's seed with blackness and prohibited them the Priesthood."

It looks like the ban in blacks in the priesthood in the Mormon Church was a knee jerk reaction leading to a spiteful judgment on all people of color.

Do I think the mark had to do with skin color? No. But if the question is entertained at least try not to be so Euro-centric as to believe Adam and Eve had to be white European people.

Judaism, and thus Christianity are Eastern religions, albeit Middle-Eastern. The first man and woman, and our religious progenitors were dark skinned people. Let us try to remember this and control our racism in our interpretation of the texts.

Job and the Petty God

Over many thousands of years God seems to have matured and mellowed. We see this in a panorama viewed from the oldest books of the Old Testament, wherein God seems petty and vicious, to the books of the New Testament, where God is presented as kind, merciful, and loving. One of the oldest books in the Bible is the book of Job. Here, we find Job, an honorable and devote man, who is blindly devoted to God. Enter Satan, the adversary and accuser. Satan could not find anything to accuse Job of doing or being, so he attacks the circumstances. Satan tells God that Job is a good man only because he has a good environment in which to live. Job had wealth, health, and the love and support of friends and family. God is happy to oblige Satan in a bet. God bets Satan that Job will remain faithful, no matter what, and he sets about to proof it by destroying Job's wealth, health, and family. The last things to go are Job's fair-weather friends who decide Job must be a sinner and deserving of all his torment.

Here, we must pause and ask ourselves a few obvious questions. Why would an omnipotent God need to prove anything? Should he not already know the outcome? In light of this question one must conclude God is either a brutal tyrant or he is not omnipotent. There is one more possibility. This exercise could be for Satan's sake. God may have tortured Job to prove to Satan, who is not omnipotent, that Job will not curse God, no matter what is done to him. The scope of this cruelty is difficult to describe, but must mimic the act of an older brother pulling the wings off a fly so the younger brother can be shown the fly will not cry out against their mutilation.

God demonstrates to Satan the steadfastness of Job's devotion by killing his children, destroying his family, allowing his animals to be stolen or killed, and making Job sick by covering him in boils so horrible that the only relief is to sit in a bed of ashes. The lack of compassion continues on a passive-aggressive level when God ceases his attack and rewards Job by restoring his possessions and family. God does not bring his children back to life, but instead allows him to have other children. This shows a lack of understanding of the human psyche that is staggering. Children and loved ones are not fungible. We, as humans, may even fall into thing trap by assuming that if our dog have a little of pups that die she will be comforted if we allow her to have another litter, as if they are interchangeable. Children are not interchangeable. If a child dies and the parent has another child it does not erase the pain of the death of the first child. God is looking at Job as we would look at an animal.

In the story of Job, God was petty, cruel, and callous. Why is this true? Possibly it is because God's lack of compassion and value of life reflects what we were at the time. The story of Job reflects our own limited value of life and understanding at the time the story was written. Our concept of God can be no higher than our highest concepts within and about ourselves. Could it be that between the time of the Old Testament and the New Testament mankind actually evolved spiritually a tiny bit?

It is possible, but the evolution is slight if at all. Mankind maintains the lack of compassion and caring showed by God in the story of Job. Moreover, looking at the story of how God felt it necessary to proof to Satan the devotion of Job by way of torture, one may say that God could claim, "The devil made me do it."

The Schizophrenic God

The vast difference in the nature and personality of the God of the Old Testament and the God of the New Testament may lead one to believe in two Gods, or at least one who is schizophrenic. Why did God change?

Stories of gods and their adventures could have been a way of expressing the mystical relationship between ancient man and the mysterious world in which he lived. If this is true, and the stories told around fires of the past were not meant to define worship, but to convey an inner feeling, our approach to religion may be incorrect in its very basis. To express awe for the creator and his or her creation did not have to become a religion, but it always did. In crystallizing into a religion, the awe and reverence was reduced to a set of rules, rituals and rites, which, because of rigidity, killed the awe. This was, and is, the pattern of religion. For now, let us look at how religions form.

No religion resonates in the human psyche without well-told mythic stories. One would hope the stories would be true, or accepted as true, in order to affect the psyche of the believer. However, whether true or not, the story must carry with it a sense of the overwhelming and supernatural power of the god and his ability to punish or deliver his people. One man's myth is another man's religion.

In time, stories became religion. The great god in the sky ceased being a story conveying a mystical or emotional message, and became a religion controlled by a distant and uninvolved god. As this happened, the people could not relate to such a god, even though they had constructed the religious structure over time themselves. God became inaccessible and had to be replaced by other gods.

These gods may have been more accessible, but because they were closer to human and had a division of power, talent, or dominion, they were, by necessity, inferior to the original father-god. Because of this, there needed to be more of them. Each time the template for the original God was somehow divided, by sex, geography, or power, another lesser god came into existence.

Religions holding to monotheism fought against the division of god. Judaism and later Islam built their foundations on this one unalterable statement; "God is one."

Indeed, this is why many Muslims and Jews view the idea of the trinity within the Christian faith as blasphemous. Jesus is the Christian expression of the love and accessibility of the one true God toward humanity, but the apparent division of oneness expressed by the trinity is, in itself, an affront to those who hold to the idea that God is One. However, even Jews and Muslims have made this mistake in their past.

From the time of the ancient Jews, man has struggled with the inability to understand and balance the manifold attributes of God. In an attempt to make god more integral with their society, their idea of god tended to change in order to fit better and more understandably within the society at the time.

If the society is focused on family and procreation, then god must be also. If the people were focused on war, their god would be a mighty man of war. As a society, we create the image of god according to what we are familiar with and what we need. In the case of modern Christianity, even though Jesus was likely a very dark man with thick, coarse, black hair, most pictures render him as a man with a lighter complexion, with straight, flowing, brown hair. In the west, we have done a wonderful job of creating God in our own image.

Religions do not usually spring into existence and remain stable or stagnant. Religions evolve and morph, changing with the social pressures, absorbing various beliefs, customs, and practices from converts and those around whom the practitioners live. So it was with Judaism.

Scholars have long wondered why the God of the Old Testament had two names, El, usually translated as God, and

Yahweh (Jehovah), usually translated as Lord. Moreover, the two deities seem to have different personalities.

The Canaanites, Eli, Il, or El was the supreme god, and the creator of all. El, or 'il-'ib was a general name for a deity, which may have been a god of the ancestors. As such, he was depicted as a gray or white haired, wise old man who guided his people. In the beginning, he was probably a desert god who, according to the older myths, had two wives and built a sanctuary with them and his new children in the desert. The idea of El having two wives shows up again in the Old Testament in a metaphorical story of El marrying Judah and Israel.

The close connection in the religions of the Canaanites and the Hebrews are notable. There are indications that the Hebrew people are a break off of the Canaanites. During the Egyptian rule of Canaan, it re-organized the territory. As a result, many peasants were left homeless and had to live in their caravans. Egyptians began calling them "caravan people." The ancient Egyptian word for caravan people was similar to the word Hebrew. This is one of several theories but seems to be probable. Remember that the titles of Jews or Israelites came from the name of the men Judah and Israel. Genesis 32:28 explains that God changed Jacob's name to Israel, which is why the Hebrews were also called Jacobites by some.

Three pantheon lists found at Ugarit begin with the four gods, El, Dagnu (the Dagon), and Ba'l'sapan, who was also called Hadad. Hadad was a storm god, whose other name was Ba'al.

Since El is a name for god in general, there would be names encountered such as Tôru El, or the Bull God. ("Bull El" or "the bull god"). Other names for El are bitnyu binwuti "Creator of creatures," 'aba ban 'ili "father of the gods," and 'aba 'adami "father of man." He is also called 'El 'ôlam "God Eternal."

In one of the early myths, El lies with his two wives, who give birth to Shachar ("Dawn") and Shalim ("Dusk"). Again, his wives become pregnant and give birth to "the gracious gods," "cleavers of the sea," "children of the sea." The names of his wives were Athirat, also known as Asherah, and Rahmay ("Merciful"). Asherah was El's chief wife. Later, El would morph into a god of war, as the Jews would need such a deity in their conquests. Still, the compassionate face of the wise father god remained in the minds of the people and would be resurrected later in the New Testament.

According to the book, "Canaanite Myth and Hebrew Epic; Essays in the History of the Religion of Israel," written by Frank Moore, published by Cambridge, Mass., Harvard University Press, 1973, and his book, "From Epic to Canon: History and Literature in Ancient Israel", published by Johns Hopkins University press, c1998, Dr. Moore states in part:

"Religion, as a phenomenon of set rules and doctrine, was unknown and would be incomprehensible to the Canaanites and Israelites. Events transpired because the gods either willed it or did not oppose it. Plans and battles failed when the god opposed the plans or the planners, or if the gods were more inclined to the plan or persons of the enemies. Such beliefs saw the gods as fickle, arbitrary, and quixotic."

"In Syria-Palestine survival depended on the annual rains and rainfall varied widely from year to year. It was clear to Canaanites and Israelites that rainfall and thus crops were provided by the god whose powers included storms, rain, and fertility. This alone may be the answer to why the deity known as Ba'al remained in the Hebrew houses and temples for so long. Ba'al was the god of storms, and thus rain and crops."

"Unlike the people, who valued the rains and crops above all, for a king it was important to have a god of power and war. El was such a god."

"El was a strong ruler and the divine warrior. We see El as the figure of the divine father. The one image of El that seems to run through all of his myths is that of the patriarch. Unlike the gods who represent the powers of nature (such as storms, rain, or procreation), El is the first social or family god. In the Akkadian, Amorite, and Canaanite religion, El frequently plays the role of "god of the father," who is fair, stern, and wise."

Joseph Lumpkin

(End citation)

We can see this quite clearly in the distinct change between the God of the Pentateuch and the God of the Gospels. Notice, I pointed to the God of the Gospels and not the New Testament, since in the beginning of these books Jesus had not been born and had not died, forming the new covenant of the New Testament. This keeps both faces of God in the same Old Testament covenant. Thus, the change cannot be blamed on the sacrifice of Christ. Up until the sacrifice, we can still view everything through the eyes and laws of the Old Testament.

Even though we are taught that Judaism was always a monotheistic religion, this was not always the case. The evolution of Judaism into its current form gives us insight into the first steps away from monotheism and the balance between male and female energies and attributes contained within one God. Oddly, or maybe not so strangely, this path was followed by many belief systems, so we will use Judaism as a general example of what stages religions may go through.

For those who may doubt that the ancient Jews were polytheists, I offer the following:

Exodus 20:2-17 NKJV
"I am the Lord your God, who brought you out of the land of Egypt, out of the house of bondage. You shall have no other gods before Me."

The passage is an acknowledgment that there were other gods. In our western society, which is so different from the polytheistic societies of the time, we have learned to equate this passage as a warning against having any item or desire, such as money or success, come before God, but this interpretation is a modern one and does not fit the time or society of the text.

Another example of the implication of the acknowledgment of multiple gods is Exodus 15:

Exodus 15

Amplified Bible (AMP)

1) Then Moses and the Israelites sang this song to the Lord, saying, I will sing to the Lord, for He has triumphed gloriously; the horse and his rider or its chariot has He thrown into the sea.

2) The Lord is my Strength and my Song, and He has become my Salvation; this is my God, and I will praise Him, my father's God, and I will exalt Him.

3) The Lord is a Man of War; the Lord is His name.

4) Pharaoh's chariots and his host has He cast into the sea; his chosen captains also are sunk in the Red Sea.

5) The floods cover them; they sank in the depths [clad in mail] like a stone.

6) Your right hand, O Lord, is glorious in power; Your right hand, O Lord, shatters the enemy.

7) In the greatness of Your majesty, You overthrow those rising against You. You send forth Your fury; it consumes them like stubble.

8) With the blast of Your nostrils the waters piled up, the floods stood fixed in a heap, the deeps congealed in the heart of the sea.

9) The enemy said, I will pursue, I will overtake, I will divide the spoil; my desire shall be satisfied upon them; I will draw my sword, my hand shall destroy them.

10) You [Lord] blew with Your wind, the sea covered them; [clad in mail] they sank as lead in the mighty waters.

11) Who is like You, O Lord, among the gods? Who is like You, glorious in holiness, awesome in splendor, doing wonders?

The question, "Who is like You, O Lord, among the gods?" assumes there are other gods and Yahweh is mightier.

In the book of Jeremiah, we see one of these gods called out by name. It is the title given to the wife of God. The number and significance of the objects of veneration to her confirms the suggestion that the people held this goddess in high regard. So many pillar figurines have been excavated in Judah, that they are now regarded as "a characteristic expression of piety" for those who worship El and his consort.

Judaism was formed in part by the pressures of the mingling of peoples and customs around Canaan, also called the Ugarit region. The ancient Canaanite city-state of Ugarit is of utmost importance to those who study the Old Testament. Writings found there have greatly aided in our understanding of the meaning of various Biblical passages, as well as in deciphering difficult Hebrew words. Ugarit was at its height around the 12th century BCE. This was the period corresponding with the entry of Israel into Canaan.

The evolution of the people we now call Jews was formed under the pressures of the polytheistic Canaanites culture. In the time of the formation of the religion of El, the city of Ugarit was a major hub that society.

It was from tablets found in archeological excavations of this area that we find the names of deities such as El, the God in the Jewish and Christian scriptures, and then, Ba'al, the god of storms, who was his sworn enemy. Later, we shall see that Ba'al came to be represented by a bull as well.

According to the Journal of Semitic Studies, the general recognition of the "Great God, El" was recorded as far back as the first half of the second millennium B.C. E. That is around 1800 B.C.E.

During this time-period, gods were local to certain areas. Cities would have a patron deity, and individuals may have a household deity they worshiped also. The Hebrews venerated El beginning in the period before Moses, while, the Canaanites and Phoenicians were mingling and mixing religious traditions. El was a god of war and considered the father of other deities such as Ba'al.

"There has been much misunderstanding of the nature of Canaanite-Phoenician culture. It must be emphasized this was a relatively homogeneous civilization from the Middle Bronze Age down to the beginning of the Achaemenian period, after which it was swallowed up in large part by much more extensive cultures. Chronologically speaking, it is certain that

"Phoenician" is simply the Iron-Age equivalent of Bronze Age "Canaanite".... Phoenician culture did not finally expire until the triumph of Christianity in the fourth century."

"From the geographical standpoint, there was a homogeneous civilization, which extended in the Bronze Age from Mount Casius, north of Ugarit, to the Negeb of Palestine, and in the Iron Age from north of Arvad (at least) to the extreme south of Palestine. This civilization shared a common material culture (including architecture, pottery, etc.) through the entire period, and we now know that language, literature, art, and religion were substantially the same in the Bronze Age.

From the twelfth century on, we find increasing divergence in higher culture, but material culture remained practically the same in all parts of the area. The differences (except in the case of Israelite religion) were no greater than they were in different parts of the Mesopotamian area of culture, which was geographically much more extensive. The situation in Canaan is in a number of ways comparable to that in Egypt, but the civilization of Egypt was more homogeneous as compared to Canaanite culture."

"Since Israel emerged from the same Northwest-Semitic background as the Phoenicians and other Canaanite groups, which continued to exist down into the Iron Age, one would expect to find extremely close relationships in both material and higher culture. It is true that Israelite ties with Egypt were very strong, both historically and geographically, but it is doubtful whether Canaanite and Phoenician bonds with Egypt were any less close. Quite aside from the close ties of reciprocal trade, remember that Palestine, Phoenicia, and Egypt were, as a rule, part of the same political organization, in which Egypt generally played the controlling part. So far as we know, the only exceptions, during the period, which interests us particularly, were during the 18th century B.C., again at the end of the 13th, and from the middle of the 12th to the late tenth. After the early ninth century B.C., Egyptian political influence in Asia decreased greatly, but was compensated by the steady development of reciprocal trade relations."

(W. F. Albright, Some Canaanite-Phoenician Sources of Hebrew Wisdom in "Wisdom in Israel and in the Ancient Near East," edited by M. Noth and D. Winton Thomas, published by Brill, 1969)

The Sumerians, around 3,000 BC, living around the modern-day Syria and Iraq were the first civilization to leave carvings and reliefs depicting a prototype angel. To their complex religion and the pantheon of gods, they added messengers of the gods. These messengers of the gods ran errands and delivered communications between gods and humans.

As Samaria declined and Babylon and Assyria rose in power, the idea of "angels" spread into the two rising powers. Carvings of angels around this time bear this out. By 2,500 BC, angles, or messenger gods, had started to appear in the Egyptian culture as well.

Around 1900 B.C.E., Semitic tribes, who also had multiple gods, conquered Samaria. The Semitic tribes added the Samarian messengers or angles to their own pantheon of gods. Then, they made this more complex by ranking the forces of the angels, creating a blend, which found its way into Zoroastrianism, monotheistic Judaism and beyond.

What need does an omnipresent and all-powerful god have for ethereal messengers, servants, and soldiers? If god can be anywhere and do anything at any time, why does he need any other creature to do his bidding? The answer is found in the difficulty of simply doing away with the gods of old. The idea of polytheism within Judaism was kept alive in the concept of angels. Could angels be a polytheistic escape clause for a religion that was becoming monotheistic? Could we be viewing the evolution of a religion over a period of three millennia?

When we look at the history of gods and their servants, we see remnants from a time when man could only conceive of a god similar to himself. The all-powerful and all knowing god had been replaced with gods of war, and gods of weather, and gods of procreation, etc. There were male gods and female gods. Were we attempting to balance the male and female parts of our society through God?

In a society built upon war and survival, the world and our view of God must have taken on a harsh tone. It is easy to assume that a male-driven theology would have only male attributes, and certainly, this monocular approach had its effect, but that is only part of the story. There is also the love prose of Solomon, and the passionate and flowing poetry of King David.

Around 1500 BC, the next major worship to appear was that of Mithras, Mithras was a light-bringer god, whose cult flourished between 1500 BC and the time of Christ. The religion based itself in what was then known as the Persian angels and the god, Mithras. Mithras was often depicted as more of an Angel in the broad horizontal bands of sculpted and painted decorations on the walls and ceilings of buildings, called friezes, which were created around this time.

The Phoenician era saw a shift in Canaanite religion. The larger pantheon was pushed to the side in favor of previously, less important, singular deities who became or, in the case of Baalat, already was, the patron city-gods, affirmed by ruling priest-kings. Baal or Ba'al is the root of Baatat.

Early scholars and demonologists, unaware of Hadad, or that "Ba`al" in the Bible referred to any number of local spirits, came to regard the term as referring to but one personage. Until archaeological digs at Ras Shamra and Ebla uncovered texts explaining the Syrian pantheon, the Ba'al Zebûb (or Beelzebub) was frequently confused with various Semitic gods. Ba'al and Beelzebub, in some Christian writings, might refer to Satan, himself. The Biblical and historical evidence shows that the Moabites worshiped Ba'al. Pre-Islamic and Muslim sources reveal that the Meccans took over the idol, Hubal, from the Moabites.

It is likely that Ba'al was the idol of the golden calf that the Israelites worshiped while Moses was upon the Mountain receiving the Ten Commandments. The vision of the people and the idol drove Moses to break the original tablets. What is more difficult to follow is that the symbol of El was, at one time, the bull or calf, and could have been associated with an old and idolatrous way of worshiping El or Ba'al.

Several deities bore the title "Baal" (Lord) and more than one goddess bore the title "Baalat" (Lady). Biblical references to baals associated with various places include Baal Hazor, Baal Hermon, Baal Heon, Baal Peor, Baal Perazim, Baal Shalisha, Baal Tamar, Baal Zephon and others. However, as early as the period of the Book of Judges, we find references to a more generalized sense of the term — Baal Berith — Lord of the Covenant. Thus, the conception of Baal was clearly in universal as well as place-specific terms. (Similarly, the Israelites conceived their God as the God of the whole earth, the God of Issac, the God of Jacob, the God of the Hebrews, and the God of one specific mountain: Sinai.)

The deity opposed by the biblical prophets as "Baal" was usually a version of Baal-Hadad, the major deity of the Hittites, Syrians, and Assyrians. Baal-worship extended from the Canaanites to the Phoenicians. Both Baal and his consort Astarte were Phoenician fertility symbols. The "Baal" worshipped by Queen Jezebel is referred to as Baal-Melqart. Both Hadad and Melqart are found in lists of Phoenician deities, but it is difficult to know whether Jezebel's form of Baal-worship differed much from the worship of Baal-Hadad. The King of Aram was named after this deity.

1 King 20
ASB
1 Now Ben-hadad king of Aram gathered all his army, and there were thirty-two kings with him, and horses and chariots. And he went up and besieged Samaria and fought against it. 2 Then he sent messengers to the city to Ahab king of Israel and said to him, "Thus says Ben-hadad, 3 'Your silver and your gold are mine; your most beautiful wives and children are also mine.'" 4 The king of Israel replied, "It is according to your word, my lord, O king; I am yours, and all that I have." 5 Then

the messengers returned and said, "Thus says Ben-hadad, 'Surely, I sent to you saying, "You shall give me your silver and your gold and your wives and your children," 6 but about this time tomorrow I will send my servants to you, and they will search your house and the houses of your servants; and whatever is desirable in your eyes, they will take in their hand and carry away.'"

Baal Hammon, generally identified by modern scholars either with the northwest Semitic god El or Dagon, was the supreme god of the Carthaginians.

One of the most important points to understand is in the early periods, the minds of the people "cross-connected" the gods El, Yahweh, and Baal. In one mythology, El is the father of gods and sits in court judging and directing other gods, one of whom is his son, Baal. These early cross-connections and mutual identifications become confusing. To simplify the contorted flow of this period in our religious history, remember that Baal, El, and Yahweh were all gods and all were worshiped together at one time or another. We see that in time, El and Yahweh became identified as the same god, due in part to one mythology that has the father, El, and the son, Baal, at odds and in conflict.

Part of the confusion comes from the fact that the names and biblical renderings of the names overlap. For example, the name "Baal" means lord. However, in the English bible the name Yahweh is usually rendered as "Lord". The name El is translated as God, but the people of the time considered all of these deities to be a god. These various issues have led to a tangled and confusing history.

Since the name "Baal" means lord, the name has been attached to many deities. One famous name is Baal Zebub. Scholars continue to be unsure of the meaning of the name. Many believe that zebub may substitute for an original "zbl" which seems to mean "prince," and is a title frequently attributed to Baal in mythological texts. However, some believe the word means "flies" and is connected to an Ugaritic text in which Baal affects the expulsion of the flies, which were thought to be the cause of a person's sickness.

Other versions of the deity Baal are Beelzebub and Beelzeboul. The names are clumsy transliterations and the name is more accurately "Baal Zebûb." He was a deity worshiped in the Philistine city of Ekron (2 Kings 1:2). Scholars have also suggested that the term was originally Baal Zebu, which means "Lord Prince." However, the Jews seized on the fact that zebûb was a Hebrew noun meaning 'fly', so they berated the deity by calling him Baal Zebub or "Lord of Flies," pointing to the fact that flies were always found on dung.

Baals were often worshiped in "high places where a priest or prophet of the local "baal" would offer animal, vegetable, or wine offerings. The Book of Kings describes the prophets of Baal engaged in shaman-like ecstatic dances. The prophets of Baal are also described as engaging in self-mutilation. In mythology, Baal died. During the mourning of Anat, between Baal's death and resurrection, she cut herself:

She cuts cheek and chin.
She lacerates Her forearms.
She plows like a garden Her chest,
Like a vale, She lacerates Her back.
"Baal is dead!"

Temples of Baal existed in or near larger towns. Worship involved ritual sex between a king or priest and a female priestly counterpart, symbolizing the union of heaven and earth, which brings on the blessing of rain and crops. Later this ritual would spread into the use of Temple Prostitutes, who would be used by the followers in exchange for donations and ritual practice. It was this practice that so provoked prophetic objections to Baal-worship.

The first religion involving ritual sacred prostitution associated with the goddess Ishtar began in Babylon. Possibly, the Canaanite worship of Astarte, the consort of Baal was linked to the worship of Istar.

Israelites allegedly participated in such rituals also. This is illustrated by the story of Judah when he fathered twin boys through his daughter-in-law Tamar, who had disguised herself as a sacred prostitute in the town of Timnah (Gen. 38:15-38). The practice was widespread, and is hard to say at what point the Israelite tribes began to think of the practice as something condemned by God.

Child sacrifice is another issue. The prophet Jeremiah indicates that infant sacrifice was offered to Baal as well as to other gods (Jer. 19:5). However, it seems to be more prevalent with other deities such as Moloch.

Up to this point, the gods of El and Baal were closely connected. El was a god of war and Baal was a thundering storm god. Both were powerful and were related in some of the early stories. They were part of the same mythos, pantheon and family of gods.

The people of the region worshiped a god called, "El." The wife of El was Ashtoreth, whose title was, "The Queen of Heaven." Ugaritic polytheism consists of a divine council or assembly. The divine family, made up of the chief god, his wife, and their offspring, populates this assembly. The chief god, El, and his wife, Ashtoreth, are said to have produced seventy divine children, some of whose names may be familiar, as they include Baal, Astarte, Anat, Resheph, the sun-goddess Shapshu, and the moon-god Yerak.

Some sources also list the name, Yah, or Yahweh. These children came to be called, "the stars of El." Below the divine counsel are the helpers of the divine household. Kothar wa-Hasis was the head of these helpers. Some scholars believe that the servants or helpers of the divine household came to be known as the entities the Bible calls "angels." The word for angel means messenger, and these helpers were in fact, messenger-gods. Ashtoreth would become Asherah in the Israelite's worship.

In the earliest stages of this religion, Yahweh appears to be simply one of these seventy children, each of whom was the patron deity of the seventy nations. We see this idea of city-state having patron gods brought into the ancient Greek religions as well. The idea also appears in the Dead Sea Scrolls reading and the Septuagint translation of Deuteronomy 32:8.

Deuteronomy 32:8-9
Douay-Rheims 1899 American Edition (DRA)
8) When the Most High divided the nations: when he separated the sons of Adam, he appointed the bounds of people according to the number of the children of Israel
9) And his people Jacob became the portion of the Lord, Israel was the line of his inheritance.

Some sources, including the Masoretic Text; Dead Sea Scrolls (see also Septuagint) renders "children of Israel" as "sons of God."

As the patriarch, El, had divided the land, each member of the divine family received a nation of his own: Israel is the portion of Yahweh. The statement, "according to the number of the children of Israel" is thought to include the seventy children.

Psalm 82 also presents the god, El, presiding over a divine assembly at which Yahweh stands up and makes his accusation against the other gods.

Psalm 82
Amplified Bible (AMP)
A Psalm of Asaph.
1) GOD stands in the assembly [of the representatives] of God; in the midst of the magistrates or judges He gives judgment [as] among the gods.
2) How long will you [magistrates or judges] judge unjustly and show partiality to the wicked? Selah [pause, and calmly think of that]!
3) Do justice to the weak (poor) and fatherless; maintain the rights of the afflicted and needy.

4) Deliver the poor and needy; rescue them out of the hand of the wicked.

5) [The magistrates and judges] know not, neither will they understand; they walk on in the darkness [of complacent satisfaction]; all the foundations of the earth [the fundamental principles upon which rests the administration of justice] are shaking.

6) I said, You are gods [since you judge on My behalf, as My representatives]; indeed, all of you are children of the Most High.

7) But you shall die as men and fall as one of the princes.

8) Arise, O God, judge the earth! For to You belong all the nations.

Why did Baal split away to become the archenemy of El? The answer may be as simple as assimilation versus annihilation. As it is with kingdoms, so it is with religions. If there is a close enough fit and the opponent is weaker, there can be assimilation, but if the opponent is stronger or there is strong opposition between the factions, there can be little assimilation. Destruction is the only recourse. El was the head or father of the gods. In the mythos of the people, El divided the lands into sections and gave each of his sons a separate region to rule. This made Yahweh the patron god of Israel.

There would be an obvious fit and a way to integrate the belief in the father god and the son, who protects Israel. However, the tension between Baal and El was different in the eyes of those serving Yahweh. Baal was not their patron deity. Baal and El were often at odds in the stories and lore of that mythology. Baal could not be assimilated easily. There was no way to bring in an opposing force when Yahweh, a parallel force, was already becoming associated with El. The natural response was to oppose the spread of Baalish beliefs and combine the gods of Yahweh and El, thus identifying them as one, that one being the high God, God the father, the Lord, God all mighty. However, the worship of Baal had ritual sex and both male and female sacred prostitutes. The people did not wish to leave their god or their sex.

Modern scholars suggest that the Lord of the Hebrews, Yahweh, the Canaanite deity, Baal, were possibly not so distinct.

Psalm 82:1 states: "God presides in the great assembly; he gives judgment among the gods."

Many commentators believe this verse harkens back to a time when the Hebrew religion was not yet monotheistic. Some suggest that Yahweh and Baal were originally considered sons of El. Since they were "brothers" and both "Sons of El", the worship of Yahweh and Baal could have been nearly indistinguishable.

The later prophets and temple priests condemned worshiping Yahweh in the "high places," declaring that only Jerusalem's altar was authorized. Yet earlier prophets, and even Elijah himself, offered sacrifices at these very high places. Similarly, the establishment of sacred pillars was condemned as related to the worship of Baal and Ashera. Both Baal and Ashera (or Asherah were considered fertility gods, and the sacred pillars were phallic symbols of stone.

The goddess, Ashera, came to be identified as the wife of god. The Jews lost or did not establish the idea of the all-powerful and complete god having a male and female side or force. To account for the feminine force with humankind, they substituted a pagan goddess. To understand the muting of the original feminine force within Judaism and later within Christianity, one must delve back into a history that, until recently, was hidden, if not occluded. We will cover the wife of god later.

The worship of El was firmly established within the Old Testament. The patriarch Jacob erected a stone pillar in honor of El at Bethel (Gen. 28:18-19); Moses set up twelve pillars at Mount Sinai where he offered sacrifices. (Exodus 24) and Joshua established a sacred pillar at Shechem (Josh. 24:26). Even the name, Beth-El, tells the story that this was the house of El. With El as the main and more powerful god, and the prohibition of the worship of Yahweh and Baal in the high places, the worship of Baal and Yahweh resembles each other closely in the early days of Israel's history. However, we shall see that El and Yahweh began to merge into a single deity, and the worship of Baal would be more distinct later. This is clearly reflected through the teachings of both prophet and priest.

Whether Yahweh was the son of El in the beginning of the mythos or not, at some time in the 8th century BCE, the names and deities begin to merge and be identified as one. Where El was a patriarchal and punitive God, Yahweh tended to interact with mankind. We see this merging in the story of Abraham, as he rejects his father's god and is called into communion with the "one true God." In Genesis 14, Abraham interacts with Melchizedek, a priest of El Elyon, and Abraham verbally equates Yahweh with El Elyon. Remember, as a rule, in our Bible "El" is translated as "God" (Elyon means the highest or the most high), and "Yahweh" is translated as "Lord."

Genesis 14
Amplified Bible (AMP)
17) After his [Abram's] return from the defeat and slaying of Chedorlaomer and the kings who were with him, the king of Sodom went out to meet him at the Valley of Shaveh, that is, the King's Valley.

18) Melchizedek, king of Salem [later called Jerusalem] brought out bread and wine [for their nourishment]; he was the priest of God Most High,

19) And he blessed him and said, Blessed (favored with blessings, made blissful, joyful) be Abram by God Most High, Possessor and Maker of heaven and earth,

20) And blessed, praised, and glorified be God Most High, Who has given your foes into your hand! And [Abram] gave him a tenth of all [he had taken].

21) And the king of Sodom said to Abram, "Give me the persons and keep the goods for yourself."

22) But Abram said to the king of Sodom, "I have lifted up my hand and sworn to the Lord, God Most High, the Possessor, and Maker of heaven and earth,

23) That I would not take a thread or a shoelace or anything that is yours, lest you should say, I have made Abram rich."

Because the two identities were merging into one, the deity now known as Yahweh-El (Lord God) was the husband of the goddess, Asherah, also known as the "Queen of Heaven."

According to the Old Testament book of Genesis in the Hebrew text, there was a balance of male and female forces within God from the beginning. Neither male nor female, both male and female, God showed the male energy of forming and shaping, as well as the female energy of nurturing and brooding. Although one may have a difficult time in distinguishing God the Spirit from the Spirit of God, the word for "spirit" is "ruach" and is a female word.

Genesis 1
Amplified Bible
1) In the beginning God (prepared, formed, fashioned, and) created the heavens and the earth.

2) The earth was without form and an empty waste, and darkness was upon the face of the very great deep. The Spirit of God was moving (hovering, brooding) over the face of the waters.

The Holy Spirit is the designated representation of the feminine principle. This idea is supported by the Hebrew word for "spirit." Jerome, the author of the Latin Vulgate, knew this when he rendered the passage into Latin. He is quoted as saying:

"In the Gospel of the Hebrews that the Nazarenes read it says, 'Just now my mother, the Holy Spirit, took me.' Now, this should offend no one, because "spirit" in Hebrew is feminine, while in our language [Latin], it is masculine, and in Greek, it is neuter. In divinity, however, there is no gender."

In Jerome's Commentary on Isaiah 11, the explanation contains a pointed observation. There was a tradition among a sect of Early Christians, which believed that the Holy Spirit was our Lord's spiritual mother. Jerome comments that the Hebrew word for "spirit" (ruach or ruak) is feminine, meaning, that for the 1st Century Christians in the Aramaic world, the Holy Spirit was a feminine figure. This was likely because in the beginning, the converts to this new cult of Judaism, called Christianity, were mostly Jews. The gender was lost in the translation from the Hebrew into the Greek, rendering it neuter, and then it was changed to a masculine gender when it was translated from the Greek into the Latin.

The Bible, in the book of Genesis, describes a male/female God with the male creating and the female brooding. Except, man could not hold onto that unfamiliar concept, and the primitive Jews chose to take up the Canaanite deities of the God, El, and his wife, Asherah. But, she was simply a fertility goddess. Although scholars argue that she was not a god because she had no headdress, the fact that she was the wife of God makes her a goddess.

Although the balance of male and female energies was presented in Genesis from the outset, primitive man was not ready to accept or understand the spiritual truth of balance. Instead, they made themselves a goddess to balance out the nature of their god, and embraced her fully and completely.

The most dramatic indication of this is the many figurines from the biblical period (the Iron Age) that have been discovered in Israel. These are figurines of females; male figurines are practically nonexistent. They are not "Canaanite" figurines: images of upright female figures with divine symbols that were very common in the late Bronze Age (Canaanite occupation), but disappeared in Israelite times. Even the earliest Israelite figurines, which date from the time of the Judges (the Early Iron Age), are markedly different from those of Canaan. These Israelite figurines are plaques that represent women lying on beds. The style shows considerable continuity with Late Bronze Age styles. However, the Israelite difference is obvious. The females in the Israelite figurines have no divine headdress or any other symbols of divinity. Even in this early period, the time of the settlement of Canaan, Israel was modifying earlier traditions to eliminate rival deities.

The plaque figurines disappeared from Judah by the time of the monarchy. A new type of figurine became quite prominent in the eighth century; a solid figure in the round, with a "pillar" base, breasts, and molded head, sometimes with no arms, sometimes with arms holding breasts, and sometimes with arms raised. These figurines are found in areas, which appear cultic in some respect; neither have a sacrificial or incense altar; and both show evidence that food preparation, eating, and drinking took place there. This activity was clearly not part of the official sacrificial cult, but may have been a tolerated, nonconformist worship. These pillar figurines are also found in domestic settings, interestingly, from the last years of settlement.

These pillars hold no divine insignia, wear no crowns, and carry no symbols of their power. The pillars arise; moreover, long after the Canaanite plaques have disappeared. They are not Canaanite goddess figurines. There is also no reason to suspect that these figurines represent the development of an Israelite goddess. They may not be personalized goddesses at all. Instead, they are a visual metaphor, which show in see able and touchable form that which is most desired. In other words, they are a kind of tangible prayer for fertility and nourishment.

Could it be possible that the figurine is a kind of tree with breasts? Such a tree of nourishment is known from an Egyptian painting. Here the tree is identified with Isis; elsewhere such a tree is an attribute of Hathor. There is an inscribed cult stand discovered in Ta'anach, dated from the late tenth century B.C.E. that has a naked goddess flanked by two lions and, on another register, a tree flanked by two lions.

It is significant that there are no trappings of divinity on these figurines. Moreover, the same people who had these figurines in their houses did not name their children with a name that called for Asherah's blessings or protections. Just as the asherah associated with the stele and altars at the local shrines was not seen by the people to be in conflict with the worship of YHWH, so too it would seem that these figurines were not idolatrous in their eyes. There is no evidence at all to suppose that the people imagined the figurines to represent God's consort. They have no pubic triangle, nothing to suggest attachment, and they appear alone, not as part of a male-female couple. The figurines and the altar asherah to which they may be analogous, may represent a divine power, not fully articulated, or personified, and not "worshiped" as some sort of a goddess that could rival YHWH.

The dating of these figurines is significant, for they come into being in the eighth century, precisely the period in which the official royal cult has removed the asherah from Samaria. The asherah with its tree associations had brought the divine and natural worlds closer together. These tree-based breast-figurines may do the same. The breasts, and possibly the tree trunk, address a desire for and anxiety about fertility. Through these figurines, the people could be reminded that the divine blessings of fertility are in their midst, that the divine is indeed a beneficent bestower of abundance.

A religion that states that fertility depends entirely upon people's behavior creates enormous strain: it places a great responsibility on the people to behave well and, at the same time, requires them to understand the difficult abstract idea that fertility is indeed automatically attendant upon such good behavior. The asherah-tree at the altars and the tree-based figurines at cult sites and in houses are a way of ensuring and demonstrating the fact that there really is a power of fertility that can be seen and touched, which guarantees the rewards of right relationship with God.

In Israel, where YHWH is the one who grants "the blessings of breast and womb," the force for fertility, represented by the figurines, may not have been seen as a separate deity. Quite possibly, it was not consciously personalized at all. In this way, the people were able to add a reminder of divinity to their homes, and a visualization of abundance (the lactating tree) while they continued to maintain devotion to the one invisible transcendent God.

Frymer-Kensky, Tikva, In the Wake of the Goddesses: Women, Culture, and the Biblical Transformation of Pagan Myth, The Free Press, MacMillan 1992

In the Hebrew Bible, there is a very strong association of Asherah with trees. For example, she is found under trees (1K14:23; 2K 17:10)), is made of wood by human beings (1K 14:15, 2K16:3-4) and is erected by human beings (2K17:1). The Asherah often occurs in conjunction with shrines on high places, which may also be to other gods such as Baal, and is frequently mentioned in association with the host of heaven.

Richard Pettey (1990:153-4) has cataloged each reference and produced tables showing all combinations of Asherah with images, pillars, high places and altars. Using these, he argued that Asherah, always associated with the worship of a deity whether YHWH or Baal, is a cultic object used along with the altars, high places, and pillars in the service of such deities, which included Yahweh [this is also the position of widely quoted biblical exegete, Saul Olyan. 1988].

It is rather surprising, considering the numerous references to trees in connection with Asherah, that Pettey does not include them in his formula. To the question, was Asherah a goddess of the Israelites? He answers both no and yes. "Certainly no," he says, "the biblical authors were unanimous in their abhorrence of Asherah worship, but, yes, she was, without doubt, popularly accepted as the goddess of Israel. One thing is certain: the Asherah with attendant asherim has many forms, but is never far from trees or the wood of trees...."(Pettey 1990: 210)

The Mishnah's definition of an Asherah is: "any tree worshiped by a heathen, or any tree, which is worshiped..."

The great rabbi Akibah said, "wherever thou findest a high mountain or a lofty hill and a green tree know that an idol is there." (Danby: 1933:441). "Trees described by the rabbis as being an asherah, or part of an asherah, include grapevines, pomegranates, walnuts, myrtles and willows." (Danby: 1933: 90,176). From this, we see that these early lawmakers denied Asherah as part of the Hebrew religion, but recognized her as a divinity worshiped by the "heathen," and treated her as a living tree or living part of a tree.

John Day's third category has Asherah as both a sacred object and a goddess. This reading he believes is now most accepted and most consistent with the evidence (1983: 398). Ruth Hestrin, of the Israel Museum in Jerusalem, goes further, and built this into an extremely satisfactory solution to the conundrum. (Hestrin 1991:50-59) She maintains that the goddess Asherah is represented in the Bible by three of her manifestations - as an image representing the goddess herself, as a green tree, and as the asherim, tree trunks. She points out that this interpretation fits well with that of the rabbi's statement in the Mishnah. (Interestingly, the question, "Is She One or Many?" is one of the most pressing questions now being addressed by the present-day goddess movement (see Long: Feminist Theology, May 1997), and although it cannot be pursued here, it seems as if a study of biblical Asherah may provide some clues to answers.)

We see traces in the Bible of Asherah worship when King Solomon brought the practice to Jerusalem. Solomon "loved YHVH," but "also burned incense in high places." This refers to the practice of burning incense to Asherah whose statues were always placed in high areas, on hilltops, etc. Solomon married the daughter of Pharaoh, a Sidonian Princess, and a Hittite Princess, and daughters of the ruling elite of Moab, Ammonites, and Edomites. Many of these women came from the old pagan religions that worshiped Asharah, also known by some as Ishtar. To appease his wives, Solomon allowed the idols to be placed in the Holy of Holies next to the Ark of the Covenant.

The worship of Asharah ended in the Kingdom of Israel, at least, when the Assyrians sacked it in 721 BCE. There was a remnant of the Israelites who still remained behind in Samaria and tried to continue the Asherah worship along with the worship of YHVH.

Excepts from an article by Christopher B. Siren – May 25th, 1998 based on John C. Gibson's Canaanite Mythology and S. H. Hooke's Middle Eastern Mythology

Little is known of the history of the God, El, and his family. Most information came from an excavation of the city of Ugarit in 1928 and the digs there in the late 1930's. The Canaanite myth stories recovered from the city of Ugarit, in what is now Ras Sharma, Syria dates back to at least 1400 B.C.E., in its written form, while the deity lists and statues from other cities, particularly Gubla date back as far as the third millennium B.C.E. Gubla, during that time, maintained a thriving trade with Egypt and was described as the capital during the third millennium B.C.E. Despite this title, like Siduna (Sidon), and Zaaru (Tyre), the Egyptians colonized the city and lorded over the whole region.

Between 2300 and 1900 B.C.E., many of the coastal Canaanite cities were abandoned, sacked by the Amorites, with the inland cities of Allepo and Mari lost to them completely. The second millennium B.C.E. saw a resurgence of Canaanite activity and trade, particularly noticeable in Gubla and Ugarit.

By the 14th century B.C.E., their trade extended from Egypt, to Mesopotamia, and Crete. All of this was under the patronage and dominance of the 18th dynasty of Egypt. Zaaru managed to maintain an independent kingdom, but the rest of the Canaanite cities soon fell into unrest, while Egypt lost power and interest. In 1230 B.C.E., the Israelites began their invasion and, during this time, the Achaean "Sea Peoples" raided much of the Eastern Mediterranean, working their way from Anatolia to Egypt. This led to the abandonment of Ugarit in 1200 B.C.E., and in 1180 B.C.E., a group of them established the country of Philistia, i.e. Palestine, along Canaan's southern coast.

The practice of the day was that whenever a people were conquered, they would take up the religion of the victors, believing the gods of those who conquered them must be more powerful than their god. This was not the case when Israel was sacked. Instead, the Israelites held fast to their belief that they alone were the chosen people of God. The question then became, "Why is our God angry with us that he would allow us to be destroyed?" For the answer, they turned back to the Ten Commandments and the Law. This was the turning point when the Jewish people became monotheistic. A ground swell arose against the worship of the consort of God, and she was banished from the nation, leaving a void of the Sacred Feminine in the psyche of the people. After all, the total of all female attributes and energy was tied up in the fertility and mother goddess, the queen of heaven, who was no longer welcome.

Jeremiah 7
Amplified Bible (AMP)

15) And I will cast you out of My sight, as I have cast out all your brethren, even the whole posterity of Ephraim.

16) Therefore do not pray for this people [of Judah] or lift up a cry or entreaty for them or make intercession to Me, for I will not listen to or hear you.

17) Do you not see what they are doing in the cities of Judah and in the streets of Jerusalem?

18) The children gather wood, the fathers kindle the fire, and the women knead the dough, to make cakes for the queen of heaven; and they pour out drink offerings to other gods, that they may provoke Me to anger!

Jeremiah 44
Amplified Bible (AMP)

15) Then all the men who knew that their wives were burning incense to other gods, and all the women who stood by

a great assembly, even all the people who dwelt in Pathros in the land of Egypt, answered Jeremiah:

16) "As for the word that you have spoken to us in the name of the Lord, we will not listen to or obey you.

17) But we will certainly perform every word of the vows we have made: to burn incense to the queen of heaven and to pour out drink offerings to her as we have done, we and our fathers, our kings and our princes - in the cities of Judah and in the streets of Jerusalem; for then we had plenty of food and were well off and prosperous and saw no evil.

18) But since we stopped burning incense to the queen of heaven and pouring out drink offerings to her, we have lacked everything and have been consumed by the sword and by famine."

19) [And the wives said] "When we burned incense to the queen of heaven and poured out drink offerings to her, did we make cakes [in the shape of a star] to represent and honor her and pour out drink offerings to her without [the knowledge and approval of] our husbands?"

20) Then Jeremiah said to all the people to the men and to the women and to all the people who had given him that answer.

21) "The incense that you burned in the cities of Judah and in the streets of Jerusalem, you and your fathers, your kings and your princes, and the people of the land, did not the Lord [earnestly] remember [your idolatrous wickedness] and did it not come into His mind?

22) The Lord could no longer endure the evil of your doings and the abominations, which you have committed; because of them therefore has your land become a desolation and an [astonishing] waste and a curse, without inhabitants, as it is this day.

23) Because you have burned incense [to idols] and because you have sinned against the Lord and have not obeyed the voice of the Lord or walked in His law and in His statutes and in His testimonies, therefore this evil has fallen upon you, as it is this day."

It is difficult to know why the void of the feminine was not filled with the principles the people once understood, just as it is difficult to know why the people could not fully conceive of such an abstract form of God as a spirit containing both male and female energies. Perhaps Genesis, being written around the 5th or 6th centuries B.C.E., articulated an understanding of what the Hebrews worked out after hundreds of years of polytheism. Many parts of the Old Testament were written after the decision to adopt monotheism, but before the transition was completed.

With biblical condemnations of her cult and the eradication of symbols and inscriptions in the Jerusalem temple, eventually the wife of god disappeared from view. The idea of a divine family, with a god and his wife, was established again in the teachings of the Church of Jesus Christ of Latter Day Saints.

As the religion of Yahweh developed, God El, was cast in the role of the Divine King ruling over all the other deities. This religious outlook appears, for example, in Psalm 29:2, where the "sons of God," or divine sons or children, are called upon to worship Yahweh, the Divine King.

Psalm 29
Amplified Bible (AMP)
A Psalm of David.

1) ASCRIBE to the Lord, O sons of the mighty, ascribe to the Lord glory and strength.

2) Give to the Lord the glory due to His name; worship the Lord in the beauty of holiness or in holy array.

3) The voice of the Lord is upon the waters; the God of glory thunders; the Lord is upon many (great) waters.

4) The voice of the Lord is powerful; the voice of the Lord is full of majesty.

5) The voice of the Lord breaks the cedars; yes, the Lord breaks in pieces the cedars of Lebanon.

6) He makes them also to skip like a calf; Lebanon and Sirion (Mount Hermon) like a young, wild ox.

7) The voice of the Lord splits and flashes forth forked lightning.

8) The voice of the Lord makes the wilderness tremble; the Lord shakes the Wilderness of Kadesh.

9) The voice of the Lord makes the hinds bring forth their young, and His voice strips bare the forests, while in His temple everyone is saying, Glory!

10) The Lord sat as King over the deluge; the Lord [still] sits as King [and] forever!

11) The Lord will give [unyielding and impenetrable] strength to His people; the Lord will bless His people with peace.

The temple revealed various expressions of polytheism, such as images of lesser gods in the forms of cherubim and seraphim and thus demonstrated that this place was Yahweh's palace, and was populated by those under his power. The other gods became mere expressions of Yahweh's power, and the divine messengers were understood as little more than minor divine beings expressive of Yahweh's divine nature. The idea of angels and demons began to emerge as lesser beings that were controlled by the One True God. This head god became the godhead of today.

Since Baal simply means 'Lord', Yahweh could be called "Lord". Also, there is no reason why the term could not be applied to Yahweh as well as other gods. The Israelites did not always consider Baal and Yahweh worship incompatible.

Several prominent Israelites bore "ba'al" names. The judge, Gideon, was also called Jeruba'al, meaning "Ba'al strives." A descendant of Jacob's firstborn son was named Ba'al (I Chron. 5:5). An uncle of King Saul was also named Ba'al (I Chron. 9:35-39). One of Saul's sons was Eshba'al, Saul's grandson was Meriba'al, and Be'eliada was a son of David. 1 Chronicles 12:5 mentions the name Bealiah, meaning either Ba'al-Yahweh, or "Yahweh is Ba'al", that is to say, "Yahweh is Lord."

After Gideon's death, according to Judges 8:33, the Israelites started to worship a Ba'al Berith ("Lord of the Covenant"). Was this the god the Jews came to call "Lord", which is Yahweh? Shechem supported Abimelech's attempt to become king by giving him 70 shekels from the temple of Ba'al Berith (Judges 9:4). This "Lord of the Covenant" appears similar to the one described in Joshua 24:25 as involving a covenant with Yahweh.

Judges 9:46 goes on to say that these supporters of Abimelech entered "the House of El Berith," which was apparently the same temple earlier referred to as belonging to Ba'al. Thus, all three names of Ba'al, mean "lord." El, usually rendered as "God" in our Bible, and Yahweh, normally rendered as "Lord" (with a capital "L"), all refer to a Covenant Deity at Shechem. If the terms and names merged or somehow were interchangeable in this period, the three names could refer to one deity.

The fact that altars devoted to Yahweh, even in the Temple of Jerusalem itself, were characterized by horned altars that also indicates a carryover from more primitive days with El and Baal (both of whom were sometimes portrayed as bulls), and were not worshiped on common hilltop altars with Yahweh.

It is also possible that some hymns, which originally described Baal, may later have been ascribed to the worship of Yahweh. Psalm 29 is thought to be an adaptation of a Canaanite hymn originally devoted to Baal.

The voice of the Lord is over the waters;
The God of glory thunders,
The Lord thunders over the mighty waters...
The voice of the Lord strikes with flashes of lightning.
The voice of the Lord shakes the desert;
The Lord shakes the Desert of Kadesh.
The voice of the Lord twists the oaks and strips the forests bare.
And in his temple all cry, "Glory!"

Psalm 18 also describes the Hebrew God in terms that could easily apply to storm god Baal, the "Rider of Clouds."

The earth trembled and quaked
and the foundations of the mountains shook;
They trembled because he was angry.
Smoke rose from his nostrils;
consuming fire came from his mouth
burning coals blazed out of it.
He parted the heavens and came down;
dark clouds were under his feet.
He mounted the cherubim and flew;
he soared on the wings of the wind.
He made darkness his covering
his canopy around him — the dark rain clouds of the sky.
Out of the brightness of his presence clouds advanced
with hailstones and bolts of lightning.
YHWH thundered from heaven
the voice of the Most High resounded.

It is quite plausible that in the minds of many Israelites, the Lord Baal and the Lord Yahweh were two names for the same deity, an awesome God who thundered from on high and yet lovingly blessed them with rain to bring fertility and prosperity.

The prophet Jeremiah reminded his followers that various evil practices were something that God never commanded, nor would allow (Jer. 7:31; 19:5; 32;35). Since scripture and doctrine, like laws, are written to correct an error, we can assume that the Jews believed these practices were what God wanted and the prophet was setting them straight. However, not before some offered up their children. In fact, the victorious judge, Jephthah, is recorded as offering his own daughter as a burnt sacrifice, not to Ba'al or some pagan deity, but to Yahweh himself (Judges 11). Jeremiah later condemned this practice. Worship such as this was condemned as the wrongful practice in the worship of God.

As the rites and rituals of Yahweh became established, the prophets condemned the false worship of Yahweh, that is, the worship emulating the manner of the worship of Baal, further separating worshipers of Ba'al from the worship of Yahweh.

Lines of style and persona were drawn between Yahweh and Baal. Prophets etched it more and more clearly. The Book of Kings records the words of Elijah to those assembled on Mount Carmel: "How long will you waver between two opinions? If the Lord is God, follow him; but if Baal is God, follow him" (1 Kings 18:21).

This is the story of the battle of miracles between the prophets of Ba'al and the prophet of God. Elijah gives the prophets of Ba'al a chance to call down the power of their god to bring fire down to the alter to consume a sacrifice. After dancing, chanting, and cutting themselves for hours, they fail. Elijah's God sends fire from heaven, consuming the sacrifice, even after Elijah demand water to be poured on it. The people respond by killing the prophets of Ba'al.

The prophet Hosea put the issue more subtly when he declared:
I will seduce Israel and bring her into the wilderness, and I will speak tenderly and to her heart…. And it shall be in that day, says the Lord (Yahweh), that you will call Me 'Ishi' (Husband), and you shall no more call Me 'Baali' (your Lord). For I will take away the names of the baalim (other lords) out of her mouth, and they shall no more be mentioned or seriously remembered by their name (Hosea 2:14-17). When a Hebrew word has a suffix of "im" it is a plural word. Ba'alim would refer to more than one Ba'al or lord.

Israelite Opposition to Baal
In the beginning, the Israelites shared many religious beliefs with the Canaanites, but as the people established regional differences, and the gods of El and Yahweh began to meld, monotheism began to develop. As the worship of Yahweh and Ba'al became further separated, and Yahweh and El were being identified as the same deity, Ba'al became the rival to El and the advisory of god and the Israelite people.

Remember, that in Canaanite mythology, El and Ba'al are at odds. This amplified as lines were drawn between the worship styles of the various gods and the proper way to worship El-Yahweh. Ba'al finally devolves into the satanic archetype in the Bible during the time of Moses.

Numbers 25
The Message Bible
The Orgy at Shittim
1-3 While Israel was camped at Shittim (Acacia Grove), the men began to have sex with the Moabite women. It started when the women invited the men to their sex-and-religion worship. They ate together and then worshiped their gods. Israel ended up joining in the worship of the Baal of Peor. GOD was furious, his anger blazing out against Israel.
4 GOD said to Moses, "Take all the leaders of Israel and kill them by hanging, leaving them publicly exposed in order to turn GOD's anger away from Israel."
5 Moses issued orders to the judges of Israel: "Each of you must execute the men under your jurisdiction who joined in the worship of Baal Peor."
6-9 Just then, while everyone was weeping in penitence at the entrance of the Tent of Meeting, an Israelite man, flaunting his behavior in front of Moses and the whole assembly, paraded a Midianite woman into his family tent. Phinehas son of Eleazar, the son of Aaron the priest, saw what he was doing, grabbed his spear, and followed them into the tent. With one thrust he drove the spear through the two of them, the man of Israel and the woman, right through their private parts. That stopped the plague from continuing among the People of Israel. But 24,000 had already died.
10-13 GOD spoke to Moses: "Phinehas son of Eleazar, son of Aaron the priest, has stopped my anger against the People of Israel. Because he was as zealous for my honor as I myself am, I didn't kill all the People of Israel in my zeal. So tell him that I am making a Covenant-of-Peace with him. He and his

descendants are joined in a covenant of eternal priesthood, because he was zealous for his God and made atonement for the People of Israel."

14-15 The name of the man of Israel who was killed with the Midianite woman was Zimri son of Salu, the head of the Simeonite family. And the name of the Midianite woman who was killed was Cozbi daughter of Zur, a tribal chief of a Midianite family.

16-18 GOD spoke to Moses: "From here on make the Midianites your enemies. Fight them tooth and nail. They turned out to be your enemies when they seduced you in the business of Peor and that woman Cozbi, daughter of a Midianite leader, the woman who was killed at the time of the plague in the matter of Peor."

The sin was so great that even Phinehas, the son of Aaron, was sent to run through an Israelite man and his forbidden Midiante wife with his spear. The Midianites, as well as the Moabites, now became mortal enemies of Israel.

Over and over, the lure of the sex and fertility cults took the Israelites back to Ba'al and Asherah worship. Over and over God punished, corrected, and saved the Israelites. (Below you will see the name "Othniel". He was the first judge of Israel.)

Judges 3
The Message Bible
1-4These are the nations that GOD left there, using them to test the Israelites who had no experience in the Canaanite wars. He did it to train the descendants of Israel, the ones who had no battle experience, in the art of war. He left the five Philistine tyrants, all the Canaanites, the Sidonians, and the Hivites living on Mount Lebanon from Mount Baal Hermon to Hamath's Pass. They were there to test Israel and see whether they would obey GOD's commands that were given to their parents through Moses.

5-6 But the People of Israel made themselves at home among the Canaanites, Hittites, Amorites, Perizzites, Hivites, and

Jebusites. They married their daughters and gave their own daughters to their sons in marriage. And they worshiped their gods.

Othniel

7-8 The People of Israel did evil in GOD's sight. They forgot their GOD and worshiped the Baal gods and Asherah goddesses. GOD's hot anger blazed against Israel. He sold them off to Cushan-Rishathaim king of Aram Naharaim. The People of Israel were in servitude to Cushan-Rishathaim for eight years.

9-10 The People of Israel cried out to GOD and GOD raised up a savior who rescued them: Caleb's nephew Othniel, son of his younger brother Kenaz. The Spirit of GOD came on him and he rallied Israel. He went out to war and GOD gave him Cushan-Rishathaim king of Aram Naharaim. Othniel made short work of him.

11 The land was quiet for forty years. Then Othniel son of Kenaz died.

Ehud

12-14 But the People of Israel went back to doing evil in GOD's sight. So GOD made Eglon king of Moab a power against Israel because they did evil in GOD's sight. He recruited the Ammonites and Amalekites and went out and struck Israel. They took the City of Palms. The People of Israel were in servitude to Eglon fourteen years.

15-19 The People of Israel cried out to GOD and GOD raised up for them a savior, Ehud son of Gera, a Benjaminite. He was left-handed. The People of Israel sent tribute by him to Eglon king of Moab. Ehud made himself a short two-edged sword and strapped it on his right thigh under his clothes. He presented the tribute to Eglon king of Moab. Eglon was grossly fat. After Ehud finished presenting the tribute, he went a little way with the men who had carried it. But when he got as far as the stone images near Gilgal, he went back and said, "I have a private message for you, O King." The king told his servants, "Leave." They all left.

20-24 Ehud approached him — the king was now quite alone in his cool rooftop room — and said, "I have a word of God for you." Eglon stood up from his throne. Ehud reached with his left hand and took his sword from his right thigh and plunged it into the king's big belly. Not only the blade but the hilt went in. The fat closed in over it so he couldn't pull it out. Ehud slipped out by way of the porch and shut and locked the doors of the rooftop room behind him. Then he was gone.

When the servants came, they saw with surprise that the doors to the rooftop room were locked. They said, "He's probably relieving himself in the restroom."

25 They waited. And then they worried — no one was coming out of those locked doors. Finally, they got a key and unlocked them. There was their master, fallen on the floor, dead!

It was after this event that King Ahab and his Phoenician wife, Jezebel, introduced the worship of her god, Ba'al, once again to the courts. When the prophets of Yahweh protested, she attempted to rid the court of all influences of Yahweh. Once again, enter Elijah onto the scene to conduct the famous test between Ba'al and Yahweh. Elijah and the prophets of Ba'al fought for control of the high place at Mount Carmel. The contest came down to who could produce an irrefutable sign from their god. Baal's prophets fail to produce a sign that Ba'al has accepted their sacrifice, while Yahweh consumes Elijah's sacrifice with fire from heaven. The crowd rewards the failure of Baal's prophet by massacring all 450 of them (I Kings 18).

Later, the massacre continued when King Jehu took Ahab's throne and killed everyone in Jezreel who was related to Ahab, as well as all his servants, generals, priests, and close friends. (2 Kings 10:11). Jehu finished the purging by pretending to throw a party in honor of Ba'al," stating: "Ahab served Ba'al a little, but Jesus will serve him much." After gathering together anyone who wished to worship or celebrate in Baal's temple,

Jehu and 80 of his soldiers killed all those in attendance and burned the temple to the ground.

(2 Kings 10:27 - 29)
The Message Bible
And the bloody slaughter began. The officers and guards threw the corpses outside and cleared the way to enter the inner shrine of Baal. They hauled out the sacred phallic stone from the temple of Baal and pulverized it. They smashed the Baal altars and tore down the Baal temple. It's been a public toilet ever since.
28 And that's the story of Jehu's' wasting of Baal in Israel.
29 But for all that, Jehu's didn't turn back from the sins of Jeroboam son of Neat, the sins that had dragged Israel into a life of sin—the golden calves in Bethel and Dan stayed.

However, as verse 29 indicates, Jehu's did not go far enough. He failed to stop the unauthorized manner of worship on the unsanctioned altars to Yahweh/El at Dan and Bethel. The golden calf, which was a left over relic of the Canaanite worship of El as a pagan deity, remained. The god, El, evolved from an idol into the name used to identify the one true god. The idolatry of the past with its dead, lifeless statues had to be destroyed to make way for the new idea of a god that needed no representation and no restrictions. It was not. Not only did the incorrect manner of Yahweh worship continue, but also Ba'al worship remained and would later spread.

Based on the continued worship of El/Yahweh using idols of a calf, we should raise an eyebrow and ask an obvious question. Was this the same problem with the Golden Calf the people of Israel worshiped while Moses was on the mountain receiving the Ten Commandments? Was the golden calf an idol to the correct god who was being worshiped in an incorrect way? Yes. Look closely at Young's Literal Translation:

Exodus 32:1-6

Young's Literal Translation (YLT)
Exodus 32
1)And the people see that Moses is delaying to come down
from the mount, and the people assemble against Aaron, and
say unto him, `Rise, make for us gods who go before us, for this
Moses -- the man who brought us up out of the land of Egypt --
we have not known what hath happened to him.'
2) And Aaron smith unto them, `Break off the rings of gold
which [are] in the ears of your wives, your sons, and your
daughters, and bring in unto me;'
3) and all the people themselves break off the rings of gold
which [are] in their ears, and bring in unto Aaron,
4) and he received from their hand, and doth fashion it with a
graving tool, and doth make it a molten calf, and they say,
`These thy gods, O Israel, who brought thee up out of the land
of Egypt.'
5) And Aaron seethe, and bidet an altar before it, and Aaron
called, and smith, `A festival to Jehovah -- to-morrow;'
6) and they rise early on the morrow, and cause burnt offerings
to ascend, and bring nigh peace-offerings; and the people sit
down to eat and to drink, and rise up to play.

"A festival to Jehovah (Yahweh) tomorrow." The golden
calf was the idol made to the god Yahweh/El, taking the form
of the old El worship of the Canaanite war god, whose image
was a calf or a bull.

It seemed that the kings of Israel, along with the priesthood
of Yahweh, which had been now firmly established, kept a
policy of zero tolerance against Ba'al worship for a short while.
However, the people were difficult to control, and there were
always kings that were more permissive.

Let's face facts, if a religion advocated sex and parties in the
name of worship, it would be difficult for many to refuse. We
shall look deeper into this in a moment when we discuss the
existence of Temple Prostitutes in the house of God.

Ba'al worship remained in practice, always causing the
prophets of Yahweh to complain. Hosea grumbled, "The more

I called Israel, the further they went from me. They sacrificed to the Ba'al and they burned incense to images. " (Hosea 11:2)

Even the occasional king relapsed. Manasseh, the son of King Hezekiah (c. 687 B.C.E.) allowed altars to Ba'al to be rebuilt. It seemed that, even then, politics won out, and kings gave into the people for the sake of pleasing the people and strengthening their following.

As the common folk continued to worship the fertility and storm gods, the evidence of that worship built up and was left behind. Some survived the passage of time. Archaeologists found evidence that the worship of Ba'al and Asherah was practiced consistently alongside that of the Yahweh and at times, it was not only condoned, but also sanctioned by the temple priesthood. Most of the evidence was found outside of Jerusalem. By the time King Josiah (640–609 B.C.E.) took the throne, even the Temple of Jerusalem sported temple prostitutes. These "sacred vessels" were involved in the fertility cult associated with Ba'al and Ashera.

2 Kings 23
The Message Bible
1-3) The king acted immediately, assembling all the elders of Judah and Jerusalem. Then the king proceeded to The Temple of God, bringing everyone in his train—priests and prophets and people ranging from the famous to the unknown. Then he read out publicly everything written in the Book of the Covenant that was found in The Temple of God. The king stood by the pillar and before God solemnly committed them all to the covenant: to follow God believingly and obediently; to follow his instructions, heart and soul, on what to believe and do; to put into practice the entire covenant, all that was written in the book. The people stood in affirmation; their commitment was unanimous.
4-9) Then the king ordered Hilkiah the high priest, his associate priest, and The Temple sentries to clean house—to get rid of everything in The Temple of God that had been made for worshiping Baal and Asherah and the cosmic powers. He had

them burned outside Jerusalem in the fields of Kidron and then disposed of the ashes in Bethel. He fired the pagan priests whom the kings of Judah had hired to supervise the local sex-and-religion shrines in the towns of Judah and neighborhoods of Jerusalem. In a stroke he swept the country clean of the polluting stench of the round-the-clock worship of Baal, sun and moon, stars — all the so-called cosmic powers. He took the obscene phallic Asherah pole from The Temple of God to the Valley of Kidron outside Jerusalem, burned it up, then ground up the ashes and scattered them in the cemetery. He tore out the rooms of the male sacred prostitutes that had been set up in The Temple of God; women also used these rooms for weavings for Asherah. He swept the outlying towns of Judah clean of priests and smashed the sex-and-religion shrines where they worked their trade from one end of the country to the other — all the way from Geba to Beersheba. He smashed the sex-and-religion shrine that had been set up just to the left of the city gate for the private use of Joshua, the city mayor. Even though these sex-and-religion priests did not defile the Altar in The Temple itself, they were part of the general priestly corruption and had to go.

10-11) Then Josiah demolished the Topheth, the iron furnace griddle set up in the Valley of Ben Hammon for sacrificing children in the fire. No longer could anyone burn son or daughter to the god Molech. He hauled off the horse statues honoring the sun god that the kings of Judah had set up near the entrance to The Temple. They were in the courtyard next to the office of Nathan-Melech, the warden. He burned up the sun-chariots as so much rubbish.

12-15) The king smashed all the altars to smithereens — the altar on the roof shrine of Ahaz, the various altars the kings of Judah had made, the altars of Manasseh that littered the courtyard of The Temple — he smashed them all, pulverized the fragments, and scattered their dust in the Valley of Kidron. The king proceeded to make a clean sweep of all the sex-and-religion shrines that had proliferated east of Jerusalem on the south slope of Abomination Hill, the ones Solomon king of

Israel had built to the obscene Sidonian sex goddess Ashtoreth, to Chemosh the dirty-old-god of the Moabites, and to Milcom the depraved god of the Ammonites. He tore apart the altars, chopped down the phallic Asherah-poles, and scattered old bones over the sites. Next, he took care of the altar at the shrine in Bethel that Jeroboam son of Neat had built—the same Jeroboam who had led Israel into a life of sin. He tore apart the altar, burned down the shrine leaving it in ashes, and then lit fire to the phallic Asherah-pole.

After the exile, Ba'al is not mentioned again. However, "Bel and the Dragon," a book in the apocrypha which was part of the Book of Daniel in some versions of the Bible, tells the story of the prophet Daniel as he de-bunks the trickery of the priests and their deceptive practices by which they attempted to make the people believe that Bel (which is likely Ba'al) was alive and eating the sacrifices offered. The story takes place in Babylonia where the worship was that of Bel/Marduk.

Bel.1
[1] And king Astyages was gathered to his fathers, and Cyrus of Persia received his kingdom.
[2] And Daniel conversed with the king, and was honoured above all his friends.
[3] Now the Babylons had an idol, called Bel, and there were spent upon him every day twelve great measures of fine flour, and forty sheep, and six vessels of wine.
[4] And the king worshiped it and went daily to adore it: but Daniel worshiped his own God. And the king said unto him, Why dost not thou worship Bel?
[5] Who answered and said, Because I may not worship idols made with hands, but the living God, who hath created the heaven and the earth, and hath sovereignty over all flesh.
[6] Then said the king unto him, Thinkest thou not that Bel is a living God? seest thou not how much he eateth and drinketh every day?

[7] Then Daniel smiled, and said, O king, be not deceived: for this is but clay within, and brass without, and did never eat or drink any thing.

[8] So the king was wroth, and called for his priests, and said unto them, If ye tell me not who this is that devoureth these expenses, ye shall die.

[9] But if ye can certify me that Bel devoureth them, then Daniel shall die: for he hath spoken blasphemy against Bel. And Daniel said unto the king, Let it be according to thy word.

[10] Now the priests of Bel were threescore and ten, beside their wives and children. And the king went with Daniel into the temple of Bel.

[11] So Bel's priests said, Lo, we go out: but thou, O king, set on the meat, and make ready the wine, and shut the door fast and seal it with thine own signet;

[12] And to morrow when thou comest in, if thou findest not that Bel hath eaten up all, we will suffer death: or else Daniel, that speaketh falsely against us.

[13] And they little regarded it: for under the table they had made a privy entrance, whereby they entered in continually, and consumed those things.

[14] So when they were gone forth, the king set meats before Bel. Now Daniel had commanded his servants to bring ashes, and those they strewed throughout all the temple in the presence of the king alone: then went they out, and shut the door, and sealed it with the king's signet, and so departed.

[15] Now in the night came the priests with their wives and children, as they were wont to do, and did eat and drink up all.

[16] In the morning betime the king arose, and Daniel with him.

[17] And the king said, Daniel, are the seals whole? And he said, Yea, O king, they be whole.

[18] And as soon as he had opened the dour, the king looked upon the table, and cried with a loud voice, Great art thou, O Bel, and with thee is no deceit at all.

[19] Then laughed Daniel, and held the king that he should not go in, and said, Behold now the pavement, and mark well whose footsteps are these.

[20] And the king said, I see the footsteps of men, women, and children. And then the king was angry,

[21] And took the priests with their wives and children, who shewed him the privy doors, where they came in, and consumed such things as were upon the table.

[22] Therefore the king slew them, and delivered Bel into Daniel's power, who destroyed him and his temple.

By 400 B.C.E., monotheism and the worship of Yahweh was so well established that it pushed out Israel's pagan past. However, owing to the sordid and violent opposition to the Baal cult by the Yahweh priests, kings, and followers, Ba'al was typecast as the main enemy of El/Yahweh and became a demon. Later, Ba'al was reputed to be a great demon, and has been named by many Rabbis as the "Prince over Persia."

Daniel 10
NIV
10) A hand touched me and set me trembling on my hands and knees. 11) He said, "Daniel, you who are highly esteemed, consider carefully the words I am about to speak to you, and stand up, for I have now been sent to you." And when he said this to me, I stood up trembling.
12) Then he continued, "Do not be afraid, Daniel. Since the first day that you set your mind to gain understanding and to humble yourself before your God, your words were heard, and I have come in response to them. 13) But the prince of the Persian kingdom resisted me twenty-one days. Then Michael, one of the chief princes, came to help me, because I was detained there with the king of Persia. 14) Now I have come to explain to you what will happen to your people in the future, for the vision concerns a time yet to come." 15) While he was saying this to me, I bowed with my face toward the ground and was speechless. 16) Then one who looked like a man touched my lips, and I opened my mouth and began to speak. I said to the one standing before me, "I am overcome with anguish because of the vision, my lord, and I feel very weak. 17) How

can I, your servant, talk with you, my lord? My strength is gone and I can hardly breathe."

18) Again the one who looked like a man touched me and gave me strength. 19) "Do not be afraid, you who are highly esteemed," he said. "Peace! Be strong now; be strong."

When he spoke to me, I was strengthened and said, "Speak, my lord, since you have given me strength."

20) So he said, "Do you know why I have come to you? Soon I will return to fight against the prince of Persia, and when I go, the prince of Greece will come; 21) but first I will tell you what is written in the Book of Truth. (No one supports me against them except Michael, your prince.

Puritan Christians preached that Ba'al was Satan, or the demon we now know as Metastophilis, Satan's helper.

The Development of Satan

In the beginning, in the days of the birth of religion, where primitive man worshiped a supreme, all-powerful deity, whether it was a Sun god, or some idea represented by an idol, there was no duality. That is to say, there was no anti-god, no opposite force, no Satan, no Devil, no spiritual advisory. God was the only force in the universe. Although it is now common to find Christians speaking of the universe as a place divided between the good and evil forces of God and Satan respectively, this was not how primitive man, nor even the Jewish writers of the Old Testament, viewed the world.

As far as the writers of the Old Testament were concerned, everything that happened was an act of God. God was the only real power in the universe. When bad things happened to people, they did not blame a devil or Satan, since he was still a "bit player" or "an extra" in the cosmic drama, and was only a creation and tool of God. When bad things happened, people assumed that they had offended God in some way. If crops failed or disease invaded the land, it was because God was unhappy and needed to be appeased. This was commonly done through rituals and sacrifice.

The peaceful meadows will be laid waste because of the fierce anger of the Lord. Like a lion he will leave his lair, and their land will become desolate because of the sword of the oppressor and because of the Lord's fierce anger. (Jeremiah 25:37-38)

When good things happened, people believed that they had pleased God in some way. Deuteronomy 28:1-68 sums this up by saying that blessings and curses are set out for obeying and disobeying God.

The LORD will send on you curses, confusion and rebuke in everything you put your hand to, until you are destroyed and come to sudden ruin because of the evil you have done in forsaking him. The LORD will plague you with diseases until he has destroyed you from the land you are entering to possess. The LORD will strike you with wasting disease, with fever and inflammation, with scorching heat and drought, with blight and mildew, which will plague you until you perish. (Deuteronomy 28:20-23)

The ancient notion of God's blessing or punishment was assumed to be in play in all aspects of human life. Something as ubiquitous as infertility was considered to be a sign of God's curse. (Genesis 30:1-2). Crop failure was traced back to God's punishment for failing in the Garden of Eden. In Genesis 3:17-19, the ground is cursed by God to produce thorns. God, and only God, was the source of both good and evil in the world. When the Jewish nation was taken into exile by the Babylonians in 586 BCE, and the temple in Jerusalem was destroyed, the prophets believed this catastrophe was the result of God's judgment against the people for becoming too lax in following the law and worshiping God.

As time went on, there were lesser gods, sons of god, or other types of entities, which could ultimately be controlled by the supreme god but who, from time to time, may do the "dirty work" of god. This was the beginning of a growing feeling that God was good and thus would not bring harm to his children. The idea of the gray haired fatherly God was bumping up against the idea of evil in the world. How to solve this problem? The religious belief of "Dualism", the absolute evil enemy of God, was born in the minds of the people.

Job 1
The Message Bible
6-7 One day when the angels came to report to God, Satan, who was the Designated Accuser, came along with them. God singled out Satan and said, "What have you been up to?"

299

Satan answered God, "Going here and there, checking things out on earth."

8 God said to Satan, "Have you noticed my friend Job? There's no one quite like him—honest and true to his word, totally devoted to God and hating evil."

9-10 Satan retorted, "So do you think Job does all that out of the sheer goodness of his heart? Why, no one ever had it so good! You pamper him like a pet, make sure nothing bad ever happens to him or his family or his possessions, bless everything he does—he can't lose!

11 "But what do you think would happen if you reached down and took away everything that is his? He'd curse you right to your face, that's what."

12 God replied, "We'll see. Go ahead—do what you want with all that is his. Just don't hurt him." Then Satan left the presence of God.

In the text, the word "Satan" is "accuser" and the word "angels" is actually, "Sons of God."

The founder of Persian dualism was Zarathustra, or, as the Greeks called him, "Zoroaster"--a name which in its literal translation means "golden splendor." Zoroaster was the prophet of Mazdaism. In Persia, Mazda was a god, the Omniscient One. In an essay titled, "On the Date of Zoroaster," Prof. A. V. Williams Jackson places the life of the prophet between the latter half of the seventh and the middle of the sixth century. Dr. E. W. West points out that the calendar reform introduced in the year 505 B. C., the names of the months were supplanted by Zoroastrian names.

There were two religious parties in the days of Zoroaster: the worshipers of the daêvas or nature-gods, and the worshipers of Ahura, the Lord. Zoroaster appears in the Gathas as a priest of the highest rank who became the leader of the Ahura party. Zoroaster not only degraded the old nature-gods, the daêvas, into demons, but also regarded them as representatives of a fiendish power which he called Angrô

Mainyush, or Ahriman, which means "the evil spirit," and Druj, meaning "falsehood."

The Scythians in the plains of Northern Asia who worshiped their highest deity under the symbol of a serpent were a fierce enemy of Persia. As it is human nature to demonize one's enemy, it was natural that their snake god, Afrasiâb, became identified with the archfiend Ahriman, or the evil one who was in opposition to Mazda.

According to Zoroaster, as the sun received divine worship, so the flame, which is lit in praise of Ahura Mazda, is a symbol only of him who is the light of the soul and the principle of all goodness.

Zoroaster taught that Ahura did not create Ahriman, but that he was possessed of independent existence. The evil spirit was not equal to the Ahura Mazda in dignity or power, but both were original beings that were creative, although one was good and the other evil. Neither could die in the conventional sense, because they were, by our standards, uncreated. They were the representatives of opposing and contradictory principles. This doctrine, in a nutshell, is the doctrine of dualism and seems to have first originated in Persia, where it found its way into Judaism, and then into Christianity and Islam. The idea of dualism in expressed in the words of the thirtieth Yasna, or saying.

"Well known are the two primeval spirits correlated but independent; one is the better and the other is the worse as to thought, as to word, as to deed, and between these two let the wise choose aright."

Since dualism expresses itself in couplets of opposites, Ahura Mazda, the Omniscient Lord, reveals himself through "the excellent, the pure and stirring word." On the rock inscription of Elvend, which had been made by the order of king Darius, we read these lines:
"There is one God, omnipotent Ahura Mazda,
It is He who has created the earth here;

301

It is He who has created the heaven there;
It is He who has created mortal man."

Their worship continues:
"May Ahura be rejoiced! May Angrô be destroyed by those
who do truly what is God's all-important will.
"I praise well-considered thoughts, well-spoken words, and
well-done deeds. I embrace all good thoughts, good words, and
good deeds; I reject all evil thoughts, evil words, and evil
deeds.
"I give sacrifice and prayer unto you, O Ameshâ-Spentâ! even
with the fullness of my thoughts, of my words, of my deeds,
and of my heart: I give unto you even my own life.
"I recite the, 'Praise of Holiness,' the Ashem Vohu:
"'Holiness is the best of all good. Well is it for it, well is it for
that holiness which is perfection of holiness!
"'I confess myself a worshiper of Mazda, a follower of
Zarathustra, one who hates the daêvas (devils) and obeys the
laws of Ahura.'"

Lenormant characterizes the God of Zoroaster as follows:
"Ahura Mazda has created asha, purity, or rather the
cosmic order; he has created both the moral and material world
constitution; he has made the universe; he has made the law; he
is, in a word, creator (datar), sovereign (ahura), omniscient
(mazdâo), the god of order (ashavan). He corresponds exactly
to Varuna, the highest god of Vedism."
"This spiritual conception of the Supreme Being is
absolutely pure in the Avesta, and the expressions that
Ormuzd has the sun for his eye, the heaven for his garment, the
lightning for his sons, the waters for his spouses, are
unequivocally allegorical. Creator of all things, Ormuzd is
himself uncreated and eternal. He had no beginning and will
have no end. He has accomplished his creation work by
pronouncing the Word,' the 'Ahuna-Vairyo. The Word existed
before everything else,' reminding us of the eternal Word, the
Divine Logos of the Gospel."

Histoire Ancienne de l'Orient, V., p. 388.

Concerning Ahriman, Lenormant says:
"The creation came forth from the hands of Ormuzd, pure
and perfect like himself. It was Ahriman who perverted it by
his infamous influence, and labored continually to destroy and
overthrow it, for he is the destroyer (paurou marka) as well as
the spirit of evil. The struggle between these two principles, of
good and of evil, constitutes the world's history. In Ahriman
we find again the old wrathful serpent of the Indo-Iranian
period, which is the personification of evil and who in Vedism,
under the name of Ahi, is regarded as an individual being.

The myth of the serpent and the legends of the Avesta are
mingled in Ahriman under the name of Aji Dahâka, who is said
to have attacked Atar, Traêtaona, and Yima, but is himself
dethroned. It is the source of the Greek myth that Apollo slays
the dragon Python. The Indo-Iranian religion knows only the
struggle that was carried on in the atmosphere between the
fire-god and the serpent-demon Afrasiâb. And it was,
according to Professor Darmesteter, the doctrine of this
struggle, which, when generalized and applied to all things in
the world, finally led to the establishment of dualism."

"There were two general ideas at the bottom of the Indo-
Iranian religion; first, that there is a law in nature, and
secondly, that there is a war in nature." (Sacred Books of the
East, IV., p. lvii),
The law in nature proves the wisdom of Ahura, who is
therefore called Mazda, the Wise. The war in nature is due to
the intrusion of Ahriman into the creation of Ahura.

The fire sacrifice was accompanied by partaking of the
haoma drink, a ceremony which reminds us on the one hand of
the soma sacrifice of the Vedic age in India and on the other
hand, of the Lord's Supper of the Christians.

We know through the sacred scriptures of the Persians that
little cakes (the draona) covered with small pieces of holy meat
(the myazda) were consecrated in the name of a spiritual being,

303

a god or angel, or of some great deceased personality, and then distributed among all the worshipers that were present. But more sacred still than the draona with the myazda is the haoma drink which was prepared from the white haoma plant, also called gaokerena. Says Professor Darmesteter: "It is by the drinking of gaokerena that men, on the day of the resurrection, will become immortal." The sacrament of drinking the gaokerena was celebrated in the times of early Christianity, and was very similar to the Christian communion."

According to the Zoroastrian doctrine, after death, the soul passes the bridge or accounting, where it is judged. This bridge stretches over hell, from the peak of Judgment to the divine Mount Alborz, and becomes, according to the most common statements of the doctrine, broad to the good, and narrow to the wicked. The good person walks a broad path while the wicked walk a path no wider than a razor's edge. Evil people fall into the power of Ahriman and are doomed to hell. The good person enters the life of bliss. In an odd parallel to purgatory, those divided in their nature between good and evil remain in an intermediate state until the great judgment-day they called âka.

The preaching of Zoroaster consisted of a teaching regarding a great crisis at hand, which will lead to the destruction and remaking or renovation of the world. Into this new world Saviors will come. They will be born from the lineage born or seed of Zoroaster. One Savior would be great in power and deed. He will resurrect the dead. He will be the "son of a virgin" and the All-conquering." His name shall be the Victorious, Righteousness made flesh, the Savior. Then the living shall become immortal, yet their bodies will be transfigured so that they will cast no shadows, and the dead shall rise, "within their lifeless bodies incorporate life shall be restored." The great battle between absolute good and absolute evil, end of the world, the newly cleansed and remade earth, the resurrection of the dead by the messiah, and life eternal, all bring the book of Revelation firmly to mind. We cannot doubt the influence of Zoroaster's religion upon Judaism and early Christianity.

But there are many Jewish ceremonies preserved to the present day, which bear a close resemblance to the ritual of ancient Mazdaism. There is, for instance, an Assyrian cylinder, which represents a worshiper standing before the idol of a god. Behind him are the tree of life and a priest carrying in his left hand a rosary, while the deity hovers above them in a similar shape to the Ahura-Mazda pictures of the Persians.

The Primitive Stages of Hebrew civilization are not sufficiently known to describe the changes and phases which the Israelites' idea of the Godhead had to undergo before it reached the purity of the Yahweh conception.

Jewish religion was evolving. It was leaving behind the worship of the warlike god, El, along with idol worship and human sacrifice, and embracing the protector, Yahweh. There was a feeling that Yahweh must be pure and good, since now there was a contract in force consisting of protection and guidance from Yahweh in exchange for the fidelity of the Jewish people.

The Israelites must have a demon (not unlike the Egyptian Typhon), to blame for their misfortune. This gave birth to the custom of sacrificing a goat to Azazel, the demon of the desert. The idea strongly suggests that the Israelites had absorbed the idea of dualism in which both deities were regarded as somewhat equal. If they were not equal, but god was still fully in control, sacrifice to any other deity would make no sense. One would sacrifice to God in order to persuade him to control or destroy the evil one.

Leviticus 16:
"And Aaron shall cast lots upon the two goats; one for the Lord, and the other for Azazel. And Aaron shall bring the goat upon which the Lord's lot fell, and offer him for a sin-offering. But the goat on which the lot fell for Azazel, shall be presented alive before the Lord, to make atonement with him and to let him go to Azazel in the desert."

305

The name Azazel is derived from aziz, which means strength, and El, God. Azazel is "The Strength of God." Yahweh was worshiped by the sacrifice of a goat by killing it, while the sacrifice to Azazel was to lay one's hands on a goat, called the scapegoat, and impart the sins onto the animal. Some believed the animal was released into the desert to carry the curse of the people's sin away and then die. However, it appears the animal was actually thrown over a cliff and killed, insuring the life of the animal would be payment for the sins of the people. We can see this idea in the translation of the verse: The New English Bible: "one to be for the Lord and the other for the Precipice." Lev 16:8

Azazel makes an appearance in the Book of Enoch, as one of the leaders of the Fallen Angels or Sons of God. He is considered to be the one who taught men many evil arts and traditions, and was doomed to the abyss. The Book of Enoch is later quoted and referenced by Jude and Peter in their New Testament books, and became part of Christian views and beliefs about angels and demons today.

As the scapegoat sacrifice was distanced from the demon, Azazel, and became symbolic of a "commuting of Sin," Satan became more prominent in the lore of the Jewish faith.

The belief in a God of both Good and Evil was replaced by the belief in a powerful demon. Satan, the author and originator of evil, must have been the serpent of Genesis 3:1. However, Satan was still a puppet and not equal to God. He was a tempter and troublemaker, and still a minor player in the universe.

Satan, or the Devil, is rarely mentioned in the Old Testament. The word Satan, which means "enemy" is used as a proper name, signifying the Devil, and appears only five times. One of the five events is recorded in two parallel passages. Oddly, one of the passages actually attributes the action to Yahweh in the older passage, and to Satan in the one written after it.

2 Samuel 24. 1:
"The anger of the Lord was kindled against Israel, and he moved David against them to say, Go, number Israel and Judah."

1 Chron. 21. 1:
"Satan stood up against Israel and provoked David to number Israel."

In all the Pentateuch, Satan is not mentioned at all. Acts of punishment, revenge, and temptation are performed by Yahweh himself, or by an angel at his direction. Satan was one of these malicious servants of God, who enjoys performing the functions of a tempter and avenger. The prophet Zechariah speaks of Satan as an angel whose office it is to accuse and to demand the punishment of the wicked. In the Book of Job, where the most poetical and grandest picture of the Evil One is found, he accuses God's people unjustly.

Abraham's attempted sacrifice of his son, the slaughter of the first-born in Egypt, the razing of Sodom and Gomorrah, even the evil spirit, which came upon Saul, as well as the punishments of David, the perverse spirit which made the Egyptians err (Isaiah 19. 14), the lying spirit working in the prophets of Ahab (1 Kings 22. 23; see also 2 Chron. 18. 20-22), are all the acts of God and God alone.

Satan, in the canonical books of the Old Testament, is an adversary of man, but not of God. Satan is a subject and servant of God. In the non-canonical books, his place and station are somewhat different.

As we have discussed, nations, tribes, and cultures, especially of adjacent territories borrow and mix gods and their attributes. Add to this the fact that when nations are at odds, it is common to make demons of the opponent's gods. This helps demonize the people as well. In war, whether in actual battle or in the decline of personal relationships, there are stages: Dehumanize, Demonize, Destroy without guilt.

Joseph Lumpkin

Through this process, Beelzebub, the Phoenician god, became another name for Satan. Gehenna, the place where Moloch was worshiped in the valley of Tophet, was replaced by Sheol, the Hebrew name for hell. The idol of Moloch was made of brass, and its stomach was a furnace. According to the prophets (Is. 62: 5; Ez. 16: 20; Jer. 19: 5), children were placed in the monster's arms to be consumed by the heat of the idol. The foreign gods became the symbol of abomination among the Israelites.

When, in 586 B.C.E., the Babylonians took the nation of Israel into exile, the Israelites came into contact with new religions and cosmologies, that challenged their ideas of God and the known universe. Because the Axial Age was under way and the idea of God expanded into the hearts of man, the Israelite God was no longer confined to the temple in Jerusalem. God was everywhere and within those who followed Him. As if to balance new ideas of the purity and omnipresence of God, the idea of Satan also changed.

In the writings known as the Apocrypha and those called the Midrash writings, which cover 400 B.C.E. to 200 A.D. of Jewish history, Satan takes on an expanding role of independence and autonomy. Evil separated from God, who was seen more and more as pure, holy, good, and just. No evil can survive His presence. God could no longer have anything to do with evil. Anything seen as bad, wrong, destructive, or evil was the work of Satan. Moreover, it was a very small step from viewing Satan as the purveyor of God's wrath to the origin of evil. Now, he was no longer passively tempting God's people, but actively targeting them for destruction. As Zoroastrianism was absorbed into the Jewish religion, Jews began to understand the cosmos as a divided realm of good and evil.

Nations that opposed the Jews were considered evil and were led by Satan. However, if any party or group within Israel opposed the party in power, they too were labeled evil.

At the time of Jesus, the Roman Empire occupied Jerusalem. In the Jewish community there were three groups vying for space on the religious stage: the Sadducee, the Pharisee, and the Essenes. The smallest and most radically fundamental of these were the Essenes, who believed Satan had taken control of the world through the occupying Roman forces. The Sadducees were more liberal and did not openly oppose the Romans.

The Essences broke away from the Jewish community at large and withdrew from the areas where Romans actively lived and ruled. Their withdrawal was literally, a withdrawal from Satan's kingdom. It was also during this time that the story of Satan's fall from heaven developed, and began to be accepted as the true understanding of Satan.

The book of Enoch, written during this time, was an expansion of the story told in Genesis of the fallen angels and how they left heaven to have sex with the women on earth. Their union produced giants, monsters, nephilim, and "men of renown". They taught and produced evil and wickedness on the earth. The Book of Enoch has formed our "angelology", "demonology", and even our view of sex within the modern church, since the fall of the watchers was blamed on sex and lust.

Satan in the New Testament

Old Testament contained five passages or so directly referring to Satan. The New Testament is full of metaphors and descriptions. From Peter's description of a lion seeking to devour believers to the beast of Revelations, the New Testament is rife with passages warning the reader to beware.

Before beginning his ministry, Jesus was tempted by the devil after he had fasted for forty days in the wilderness. (Matthew 4:1-11, Luke 4:1-13).

As well as believing Satan to be an independent entity opposed to God and the establishment of God's kingdom on earth (Matthew 16:23), Jesus also referred to the Jewish religious leaders, or those who opposed his teaching, as "children of the devil".

"You belong to your father, the devil, and you want to carry out your father's desire. He was a murderer from the beginning, not holding to the truth, for there is no truth in him. When he lies he speaks his native language, for he is a liar and the father of lies." (John 8:44)

The Apostle Paul also spoke of Satan's ability to deceive us when he described him as an angel of light in 2 Corinthians 11:14. Christians were taught to resist and fight Satan in Ephesians 6:10-18, James 4:7. But the personalizing and externalizing of Satan may have been the worst movement to come out of the Axial Age and the years that followed.

For 50,000 years, our ideas of god were externalized and worked out in bloody rituals and sacrifices. We blamed everything good and bad on god. We worked to appease and placate this fickle, quixotic, rash, and unpleasant deity. Then, mankind grew up and began seeing a new vision of god. We began seeking him within. We expressed our new mysticism in compassion and insight. We began to understand the inter-connected world by treating others as we wished to be treated. It was the beginning of individual responsibility.

Maybe, by breaking evil away from good, we were attempting to purify our god as well as ourselves. Maybe we were attempting to answer the question of how bad events can issue forth from perfect good. Now, by externalizing Satan as we had once externalized god, we began devolution back to blaming forces outside ourselves and thus once again sink back into lack of personal responsibility, a condition which has grown to an endemic in Christianity. Having an enemy who is invisible, powerful and evil, and whose sole purpose is to obstruct, tempt, and destroy us is the perfect foil to blame for our own weaknesses, shortcomings, failures and bad judgment.

As much as the revelations within the Axial Age allowed us to grow, the modern view of Satan has done much to delay our spiritual growth. "The devil made me do it" and "it is the work of Satan" has become the battle cry of a dysfunctional religion and spiritually sick society, even within our modern religious systems of Judaism and Christianity.

Satan is not omnipresent, nor omniscient. Therefore, he cannot attack in more than one place at a time, or know where to be in order to successfully attack. So, our errors are not caused by some unseen adversary, but by simple fate and human weakness. We cannot control fate, however, we can control our actions and decisions, and must take responsibility for them both. The search for both good and evil leads us to look within ourselves. Our thoughts come from our own frailties and desires.

It is unspeakable arrogance to think that a malevolent power from heaven would take such personal interest in you or me to spend time targeting us for some scheme to mess up our day, such as breaking our washers, dryers, or cars in order to torment us, or place sinful thoughts within our minds.

The Axial Age
Explaining the Unexplainable

"In religion and politics, people's beliefs and convictions are in almost every case second-hand, and without examination, from authorities who have not themselves examined the questions at issue but have taken them at second-hand from another."

Mark Twain

In 1949, Karl Jaspers, the German psychologist and philosopher, published "The Origin and Goal of History," and coined the term, "The Axial Age", to describe the period from 800 BCE to 200 BCE. During this span of time, which in relation to the age of humanity, was a blink of an eye, revolutionary religious and spiritual awakenings appeared in synchronicity around the world, with major hubs in China, India, and throughout the Middle East.

Anatomically modern humans arose in Africa approximately 200,000 years ago. Modern behavior was established only 50,000 years ago. Spiritually, humans may have come into their present stage only 3000 years ago. This is a single grain of sand in the archeological hourglass.

Jaspers saw in the recent shift of religious and philosophical thought, similarities that could not be accounted for without direct transmission of ideas between regions, and there was no evidence of "cross-pollination" of ideas or concepts to be found.

Jaspers argued that during the Axial Age "the spiritual foundations of humanity were laid simultaneously and independently."

In Karen Armstrong's book, "The Great Transformation," Armstrong expands on Japers' thesis, stating that the insights

312

representing liberal religion occurred almost simultaneously and independently about 2500 years ago in four different areas of the world: China, India, Greece, and the Middle East.

Religion can be broadly understood as a system of beliefs and practices concerned with sacred things and/or symbols uniting individuals into a single moral community. The religious laws, rituals, and beliefs form a cohesive moral structure. If "religions" did specifically relate to the sacred, one could use the same definition for governments. Moreover, religions can become governments unto themselves. Therefore, a "religion" does not require a supernatural being as the object of worship, but it does have to represent a commitment to a particular moral or ethical code.

In the pre-Axial Age, religion always revolved around a deity. After the Axial Age, some religions, such as Buddhism, did not revolve around a god, but involved an inward journey toward deeper self-awareness.

Armstrong further suggests that the history of the last two and a half millennia is seen as a continuous struggle between those who acknowledge and value the newly evolved spiritual insights and those who may have a much older and more restrictive concept of the nature of religion. There is no way to know the number of mystics or progressive religious thinkers that influenced any changes in the ancient world's religions, but archeology shows us that changes were molded mostly, if not totally, by migrations to and from adjacent regions, mixing cultures and gods.

This does not answer the nagging questions of why we persist in "structured" religions, and why all major religions carry the same moral or ethical imperatives. Jesus, among others, so beautifully summed up these imperatives: "Love God and treat others as you want to be treated." The rest is commentary.

Immanuel Kant (1724–1804) was a German philosopher. Kant sought to find and identify the foundational principle of the metaphysics of morals. He attempted to analyze and articulate commonsense ideas about morality. Kant looked for the principles on which we base all of our ordinary moral judgments. He took the position that all rational people are born with an innate sense of morality. Thus, normal, sane, adult human beings will usually make the same judgment calls based on an inborn sense of right and wrong.

This is a wonderful idea, but seems rather naive considering the amount of crime and abuse we see today. Neither does it answer certain questions such as, "If man is intrinsically good, why did we insist on human sacrifice in our past?" Today, crime runs rampant and Kant's theory does not seem to hold water. Possibly Kant's arguments only come to light when there are few negative social pressures involved. Studies have shown that the number of human sacrifices in primitive cultures rises rapidly under pressures of famine and pestilence. Under extreme circumstances, they sometimes turned to cannibalism.

There are at least two "wired in" processes going on here. The highest and oldest is self-preservation. The secondary impulse, which Kant describes, is based on following a social norm in order to enable the group, family, or tribe to survive. In other words, we are inclined to work as a team. This may explain our ability to stand by and see humans killed or sacrificed as long as the group acts in accord. We can call this a "mob mentality."

However, maybe there is something to this idea of humans drawing on some very widely shared moral viewpoint that contains some general judgments. Outside of the religious ceremony for punishing someone who has broken a moral imperative, such as – do not murder, do not steal – most societies do have the same basic moral structure.

Kant sought to discover a rational basis for one's sense of duty, and from this devise a principle by which one can distinguish between right and wrong. Right and wrong hinge on the intent. The intention or motive for the action determines whether it is right and wrong. It opposes the view that the end justifies the means and does not account for the outcome of an action. The morality of an action has no regard for its current situation. It is universal and does not take into account the action regardless of circumstance.

Kant's starting point was his observation that we all experience an innate moral duty. Conscience triggers feelings of shame and guilt when we violate our internal moral compass. In this way, morality stands an empirical test. Since we seek to avoid the negative feelings of a disturbed conscience, we first attempt to do good. The highest form of good is good will. To have good will, one must perform one's duty for the sake of duty and for no other reason.

From this, Kant concluded that moral duty is objectively revealed through reason. Morality can be known by using reason and can be verified or falsified.

To quote Kant:

"To act morally is to perform one's duty, and one's duty is to obey the innate moral laws."

"A good will is not good because of what it affects or accomplishes… it is good through its willing – that is good in itself."

If only a small seed of Kant's ideas are correct, it could answer the question of why religions in every corner of the globe have the same basic moral laws. Moral laws, however, are separate from religion. Religion is simply a vehicle for a moral code, since both religion and its commandments developed around the need to solidify and guide a society. Primitive man did not have courts. They had priests acting as judges.

So, why did this moral compass develop in humans? Possibly, it was due to a consequence of evolutionary pressures. Humans were weak, slow, hairless creatures in a world of beasts and natural elements. The only way to survive was to ban together. If a person went against the family, tribe, or group, he or she would be ostracized and would have to face the world alone. Loners did not survive well. Over time, those with the highest social quotient or teamwork flourished in the hostile environment.

The good of the many won out over the good of the individual. This could be the beginning of our internal moral code. This code is at odds with the older code of individual survival. The greater imperative is personal survival at all cost. This impulse must be consciously overridden by communal cooperation. Herein is the difference between what Kant describes and what we see in society. Some people are balanced one way and some another.

This code is wired in to our developing brains on a subconscious level. Meaning, the code could not be subjective since we had no way to "think" about it. However, it was made objective through the development of codified laws. Later, we grew and developed enough to intensely consider our laws, our conscience, and the internal battles.

Until the Axial Age, the focus of religion was external, particularly on rituals and ceremony intended to influence or control a god or gods to protect the family or tribe, bring rain, guarantee success in battle, and so on.

During the Axial Age, this changed and an internal search for god began. There may have been several influences driving this evolution. The world became smaller with migrations and the advent of transportation via horseback. Cities grew and developed, continuous warfare mixed gods as the conquered tribe adopted the beliefs of the victor, considering their gods as more powerful. The amalgam of tribes and formation of armies began the demise of tribalism and the splitting of families through death and conscription into military service. The shattering of tribes and families brought about the rise of individual focus. Previously, consequences or punishment from actions of one individual or tribal member affected the entire family or tribe. With individuals separated from families and tribes, the perpetrator carried the consequences alone.

Continual hardships of war, disease, and changes in societies caused people to question the efficacy of their traditional god and religious practices prompting them to look for alternatives.

In China, India, Greece, and Israel, the spirit of humankind awakened in a flash. Wise men, shamans, sages, prophets, philosophers, and scholars independently articulated their insights. The religious traditions they created or influenced are alive in the major religions of today. Confucianism, Taoism, Hinduism, Buddhism, philosophical rationalism, and monotheism arose as though they were orchestrated and coordinated by a single hand.

The insights common to all religious enlightenment of the Axial Age include the ideas of reciprocity, compassion, love, altruism, and the individual's mandate to end the suffering of others. The ideas of compassion and reciprocity are summed up in the actions of treating other justly and as you wished to be treated. Judaism would go on to embody these values in their laws. In turn, the newly awakened Judaism translated that ideal, which has evolved into a monotheistic religion in which members seek communion with God.

In the years centering around 500 BCE, great advances in religion, philosophy, science, democracy, and many forms of art occurred independently and almost simultaneously in China, India, the Middle East, and Greece.

Today, humanity still uses the spiritual foundations laid in that ancient time. In those times of social upheaval and political turmoil, spiritual and religious pioneers became the standard-bearers of a new religious, cultural, and social order. Great religious leaders rose up in various areas of the world attracting many followers, thereby changing many sociological, cultural, economic and spiritual beliefs.

In China, many individual thinkers, such as Confucius, Lao-Tse, and Mo Tzu, began to reflect on the ethical and spiritual implications of human existence. In time, their teachings became known throughout the world. Confucianism, Taoism, and Jainism are only a few religions to be founded or affected by them.

In India, the authors of the Upanishads expanded the scope of their explorations to include metaphysical thinking in the search for the ultimate truth and the meaning of life and death.

317

India experienced a dramatic social and intellectual transformation, and produced the teachings of the Buddha and Mahavira. Like China, new teachings ran the whole gamut of philosophical schools of thought, including skepticism, materialism, and nihilism.

In Palestine, the prophets Elijah, Isaiah, and Jeremiah made their appearance. Although the law and moral code of the Israelites dates back before this age, and may have been influenced by the code of Hammurabi of 1750 BCE, the prophets reached beyond the law and called believers into a relationship with Yahweh.

In Mesopotamia, cultural and art developmented but the concept of an omnipotent and omniscient creator God did not exist.

In Greece, developments were more philosophical than spiritual. Greece witnessed the appearance of Thales, Xenophanes, and Heraclitus who regarded all existence to be in a state of flux, exemplifying his concept by stating, "one cannot step in the same river twice." Parmenides commented on the nature of permanent "being" as opposed to the impermanent phase of "becoming". Democritus devised the first atomic theory of nature, which later gave way to the scientific nature of matter and atoms.

These philosophers influenced the minds of Socrates, Plato, and Aristotle. They examined the very nature of existence, life, and thought, itself.

Each philosopher and thinker forced his or her culture to question and reinterpret previously devised cosmologies. Until that point in time, every cosmology was a cosmology put forth by a religious myth and none were based in reason or science, even though the scientific method was lacking.

Even as philosophers were dividing science from religion, mystics were emerging from crystallized religions of old to seek the real internal world that lay beyond the senses.

Buddhism propagated the preaching of the eight-fold path. Right View and Right Intention are the wisdom factors of the Noble Eightfold Path. Right Speech, Right Action, and Right

Livelihood address ethical conduct. Right Effort, Right Meditation, Right Concentration address mental cultivation. The wisdom factors continually affect ethical conduct and mental cultivation.

This leap became the source of major and lasting cultural traditions enduring to the present time, giving way to a secondary stage or influence of spiritual transformation in which religions such as Judaism spawned the world's two major religions of Christianity and Islam.

The almost simultaneous changes in China, India, Palestine, and Greece seem too remarkable to be accidental; especially considering the lack of influence one movement could have had on another, seeing the countries are widely separated from each other. The only example of intellectual communication among these countries appears to be the conjecture that in the 6th century BCE the Greek poet Alcaeus may have known the prophecies of Isaiah.

Religions began to influence and build on each other within different countries. Some religions became opposed to killing, while others value all life. Ideas and beliefs of Jainism influenced a newly developing Hinduism and the new religion of Buddhism. The dualistic idea of good and evil contained within Zoroastrianism would influence the Jewish ideas of good and evil and the notion of Satan. The new face of Judaism would give way to Christianity and Islam.

The idea of an "Axial Age" has no specific time line. It is a general idea based around a broad period of time wherein a global awakening occurred. Figures such as Jesus and Muhammad came after the Axial Age. However, Jesus and Muhammad both reaped the rewards of the spiritual awakening. This spiritual awakening within Judaism was the foundation that took the religion into a search for communion with Yahweh, El, God, or Allah. Jaspers' concept of the Axial Age is an observation and not a law of history. Yet, there were mighty spiritual changes taking place within the "Axial Age."

Possibly, Zarathustra, the founder of Zoroastrianism, lived before the Axial Age. The history of Zoroastrianism varies widely. Some sources say the founder appeared around 1200 BCE in what is now Iran. Perhaps Zoroastrianism emerged from a prior religion in a common prehistoric Indo-Iranian belief system dating back to the early second millennium BCE. According to Zoroastrian tradition, Zoroaster was a reformer who exalted the deity of Wisdom, Ahura Mazda, to the status of Supreme Being and Creator, while demoting various other deities and rejecting certain rituals.

Zoroastrianism only enters recorded history in the mid-5th century BCE. It was within this period that the religion came into its own.

In the Middle East, Judaism was undergoing a tremendous upheaval. Recent studies and archeological excavations reveal that the Jews were not only polytheistic, but may have been in the midst of changing deities, from the war god El, to the god Yahweh, who invited them into communion and protection. Although the Jews vacillated between the two differing deities with differing personalities, the change began. In the late 18th century, Bible scholars refined their abilities to follow the wording and phrasing within the Old Testament and determine that it was the result of several writers and an editing process that took place in successive layers over centuries. Each writer's contribution brought current events and their individual spiritual or religious viewpoints which drove the evolution of Judaism.

Scholars in Germany noted that in most of the duplicated stories, one set described God using the Hebrew word El or Elohim (usually translated "God"), while the other set used God's name of Yahweh (written as the tetragrammaton of Y-H-W-H with the Hebrew letters of yodh, he, waw, he.) Evidently, there were at least two different authors. The main authors used the label "E" for Elohim and the other called "J" (German for Y), for Yahweh. YHWH is also seen as YHVH. This because W and V is reversed when pronouncing the name or letters in German. Thus, YHWH becomes YHVH and yields the name, Jehovah.

Later, closer and more precise analysis of grammar, vocabulary, and writing style within the Old Testament revealed evidence of at least four authors. There was a writer obsessed with laws and genealogy called "P" for the Priestly author. His hand is seen most clearly in Leviticus. The other is called "D" for the Deuteronomist, since the book of Deuteronomy is grammatically and politically different from the earlier books. Writer "J" focused on humanity and "E" pontificates about religious and moral concerns. The multiple-author view is now called the "Documentary theory."

Later, an editor, called the Redactor, combined the four different books. Sometimes, the Redactor put different authors' stories of the same events in succession, for example, the creation stories. Some he interwove, such as the two stories of Noah's Flood and of Joseph's mistreatment by his brothers. Evidence of varying stories of the flood has been uncovered, but the story in the Bible seems to weave many of them into a single narrative. The Redactor also added transitional phrases such as, "and it came to pass," "and it was so," and "in the fullness of time" between sections to tie them together.

Armstrong indicates, at this point, the shift from legalism to compassionate equality as evidence of Axial Age spirituality.

Leviticus 19:33-34
33 When an alien lives with you in your land, do not mistreat him. 34 The alien living with you must be treated as one of your native-born. Love him as yourself, for you were aliens in Egypt. I am the LORD your God.

Leviticus 19:18
"Thou shalt not avenge, nor bear any grudge against the children of thy people, but thou shalt love thy neighbour as thyself: I am the LORD."

Although it is held as one of the main principles of the entire Bible and the statement sounds universally fair, the term "neighbor" meant roughly "kinsman," and could be interpreted as applicable only to fellow Jews.

Tobit 4:14-15
"Take heed to thyself, my child, in all thy works; and be discreet in all thy behavior. And what thou thyself hatest, do to no man."

Armstrong points out that the Axial insight moment did not last long after the return of the Jews from captivity. The wrathful god was back with a vengeance. This tenuous hold on spiritual evolution is somewhat childlike, and is seen in our everyday lives. When the Jews were in captivity or under military or political oppression, it was easier for them to see how all men should be treated with equal compassion. Once they were free and had a superior hand, it became easier for them to be the despot. Following this, their god again reflected his warlike and oppressive attitude.

The sixth century BCE, in particular, was a period of radical changes in basic religious concepts and the sudden emergence of new ideas. A radical change in humanity's spiritual development occurred and became a major source of most of our present-day faith traditions.

Any acceptable theory of causation cannot satisfactorily explain the rapid transformation. Eventually, most of the new doctrines became organized as religious systems, concerned with world-views and world-values. Although we may trace many of the old traditions, rituals, beliefs, and ceremonies back to pre-Axial Age religions, they were incorporated into new religions and were remade and redefined afresh.

Princeton University psychologist, Julian Jaynes, postulated one theory of the rapid and global change in his book, The Origin of Consciousness in the Breakdown of the Bicameral Mind, published by Houghton Mifflin/Mariner Books (1976, 2000)

At the heart of this book is a revolutionary idea that human consciousness did not begin in our "animal" stage of evolution, but was a learned process. Jaynes presents a theory of the bicameral mind which speculates that ancient peoples could not "think" as we do today and were, therefore "unconscious," a result of the domination of the right hemisphere. Only catastrophe and cataclysm forced humankind to "learn" consciousness, and birthed our modern state of consciousness out of an earlier mentality only 3,000 years ago. We are still developing along these lines. Before 1,000 BCE, human history and culture issued forth from the brain's left hemisphere. The implications of this new paradigm extend into virtually every aspect of human psychology, history, culture, and religion.

In general, the left and right hemispheres of your brain process information in different ways. We know that the cerebral cortex is the part of the brain that houses rational functions. It is divided into two hemispheres connected by a thick band of nerve fibers (the corpus callosum), which sends messages back and forth between the hemispheres. In addition, brain research confirms that, in nearly every human activity, the brain involves both hemispheres. We know that the left side of the brain is the seat of language and processes thought in a logical and sequential order. The right side operates more visually and processes thought intuitively, holistically, and randomly. The right side of the brain produces intuition and "gut feelings."

Nobel Prize Winner (1981), Roger Sperry, conducted what are sometimes called the "split-brain" experiments. A patient suffering from uncontrolled seizures had an area of his brain surgically removed in an attempt to control his illness. The area was the corpus callosum, the wiring between the left and right hemispheres, suspected of having lesions.

Following his surgery, he conducted a series of tests wherein he isolated each "half" of the patient from the other. The left and right eye sight and hands had a divider coming up to the face and chest. He then presented different visual and tactile information to the patient's left or right side, without the other side knowing. The results were astounding.

With their communications link severed, each side of the patient's brain functioned independently. Although this did not prevent normal daily functions, he encountered some unexpected findings when each side was examined independently of the other.

With the left side of the body isolated, the right hand and eye could name an object, but the patient could not explain the use of the object. When shown to the left hand and eye, the patient could explain and demonstrate the object's use, but could not name it. Further studies indicated that various functions of thought are physically separate and localized to a specific area on either the left or right side of the human brain. This functional map is consistent for an estimated 70 to 95 percent of us.

However, the disconnection between the left and right sides of the brain did not cause the patient to revert to a "pre-Axial-Age" condition of being emotionally, intuitively, or spontaneously driven, nor was the patient rendered incapable of thinking about future events as related to present decisions.

Whether the patient functioned from a dominant left or right side of the brain, no "spiritual de-evolution" occurred. This observation alone could engender skepticism regarding the Bicameral Mind theory as being the driving force behind our spiritual leap into internalization of God and our ability to see ourselves in others and others within ourselves. Moreover, the theory does not speculate about the interconnectivity between the hemispheres specifically, but rather it speaks of an odd unilateralism within the brain. Humans, if healthy, are bi-lateral creatures with a balanced left and right side. Bicameral Mind theory asks us to assume that one side of the brain is so dominant that the other side of the brain is overwhelmed or silenced.

Sperry determined the function of each side of the brain and labeled the modes of each.

"The main theme to emerge... is that there appear to be two modes of thinking, verbal and nonverbal, represented rather separately in left and right hemispheres respectively and that our education system, as well as science in general, tends to neglect the nonverbal form of intellect. What it comes down to is that modern society discriminates against the right hemisphere."
-Roger Sperry (1973)

The basic breakdown of left and right brain functions are as follows:

LEFT	RIGHT
Logical	Emotional
Detail oriented	Big Picture oriented
Facts	Imagination
Science	Religion
Order	Spatial Perception
Form	Images
Functionality	Symbols
Reality	Fantasy
Facts	Philosophy and Faith

Ideally, both sides of the brain work together in people with optimum mental ability. This coordinating ability may be the key to superior intellectual abilities. In most people, however, the left-brain takes control, choosing logic, reasoning, and details over imagination, holistic thinking, and artistic talent, due to the present demands of society. This was not the case a few thousand years ago.

Now, this is where the concept of a dominant right-brain human may get confusing. If the right brain is in charge of our intuitive and philosophical side, why did its dominance not allow us to plunge into our mystical, altruistic, compassionate, spiritual inward journey? The answer seems to be that the right brain cannot clearly conceive of future events, cause and effect, or our relationship to the cosmos. Although the right brain thrives on the big picture, it does not see the full picture in a logical way. In other words, it seems to take both the left and right sides of our brain working together to keep a correct perspective of where we are and where we are going in an internal search.

In human history preceding the Axial Age, man believed he needed to make sacrifices, of both human and animal, to the gods. In order to appease and influence the gods, man carried out particular rituals and ceremonies, placing their priests and religious leaders in high esteem. Today, modern society has not only eclipsed, but also suppressed these right brain activities.

Our personality, and to a certain degree, our abilities are a result of the degree to which these left and right brains interact, or, in some cases, do not interact. "Left brain" types are analytical and orderly, while "right brain" types are artistic, unpredictable, and creative.

Experiments show that most children are classified as "highly creative" (right brain) before entering school. Because our educational system places a higher value on "left brain" skills such as mathematics, logic, and language than it does on drawing or using our imagination, only ten percent of these same children will classify as highly creative by age 7. By the time we are adults, high creativity remains in only 2 percent of the population.

These experiments discount the idea of pure evolution in brain size as a springboard into the Axial Age. Although there is a general correlation between brain size and intellectual ability, the form and function of the brain is as important. Homo erectus, our distant ancestor, had a brain size of about 1200 cc. Modern Homo Sapiens have an average brain of about 1400 cc. However, the Neanderthal people who failed to evolve into humans had a brain size of 1500 cc, which is larger than modern man has today. There are "genius" brains measuring as small as 1000 cc. and as large as 2000 cc and is further evidence that brain size alone does not yield intelligence.

At this point, the size of the human brain at birth may be maxed out due to the natural size of a typical woman's pelvic opening. In addition, larger brain size requires a highly stable temperature and a larger supply of high protein and energy. We use one quarter of our caloric intake for brain energy consumption. Yet, if our development thus far is due to changes in the "interconnectivity" of the brain and the balancing of the left and right sides, there is hope that we can finally move forward and leave the ritual and ceremony of religion behind and embrace the compassionate and humanitarian side of our spiritual journey.

At the present, we are sitting on a razor's edge attempting to decide on which side to fall. We still see the horrors of what vengeful religions and vengeful gods can do. The Christian church mounted the bloody crusades well into the 1600's, although it reached a fervor around 1290 when the Catholic Church ordered the murder of an entire region containing the Cathar Christians in what is now France. The pre-Axial-Age frenzy is being carried out today in the forms of fundamentalism within Islam, the Zionist movement of the Jews, and the judgmental and hateful aspects of the Christian church.

Even today we see three forms of human awareness, the bicameral or god-run man; the modern or problem-solving man; and contemporary forms of pre-bicamerality man where religious frenzy, with externalized and stern concepts of god rule the day.

We have spoken so far of two different and separate ideas. We have raised the issue of the inability of ancient man to look within and find the connection between himself, his fellow man, and his god. Ancient man did not have the ability to think beyond the immediate. We have also spoken of the imbalance in either strength or communication of the left side of the brain.

According to Jaynes, the right hemisphere of the brain dominated ancient man. However, after the Axial Age, there arose true mystics - men and women who departed this conventional external world and began an inward journey.

"O, what a world of unseen visions and heard silences, this insubstantial country of the mind! What ineffable essences, these touchless rememberings, and unshowable reveries! And the privacy of it all! A secret theater of speechless monologue and prevenient counsel, an invisible mansion of all moods, musings, and mysteries, an infinite resort of disappointments and discoveries. A whole kingdom where each of us reigns reclusively alone, questioning what we will, commanding what we can. A hidden hermitage where we may study out the troubled book of what we have done and yet may do. An introcosm that is more myself than anything I can find in a mirror. This consciousness that is myself of selves, that is everything, and yet is nothing at all - what is it? And where did it come from? And why?"
Julian Jaynes

This is a beautifully articulated description of the mystical experience, but it does not make the theory correct. Certain questions beg to be answered.

If the left side of the brain was quiescent and the left side controlled logic, reason, planning, form, function, and science, how then did ancient man build the pyramids?

The Great Pyramid of Giza is the most substantial ancient structure in the world. According to prevailing archaeological theory, three kings of the fourth dynasty built the three pyramids on the Giza plateau between 2575 and 2465 BC. The Great Pyramid was originally 481 feet, five inches tall and measured 755 feet along its sides, covering an area of 13 acres, or 53,000 square meters. It is large enough to contain the European cathedrals of Florence, Milan, St. Peters, Westminster Abbey, and St. Paul's. Approximately 2.5 million limestone blocks weighing on average 2.6 tons each comprise the pyramid's construction.

The total mass is more than 6.3 million tons, which is a greater amount of building material found in all the churches and cathedrals built in England since the time of Christ. If Julian Jaynes' theory is correct, how could such a feat be accomplished by men driven almost exclusively by the right side of his brain? Possibly, we need to re-visit this theory.

What drove mankind to awaken spiritually between the years of 800 BCE and 200 BCE? Alternatively, is the question itself erroneous? When two contradictory statements appear, check the premise.

Recent experiments have shown real-time patterns and differences between the wakeful and sleeping brain. One of the most interesting and marked differences is the response to non-sensory input. While visually monitoring the brain with magnetic imaging, scientists generated a magnetic pulse and directed it into the sleeping brain. The brain responded by "lighting up" the area effected by the pulse. The response looked liked the brain simply echoed the pulse by a rapid "blip" of activity, which quickly died.

When the same magnetic pulse was introduced into the wakeful brain, the brain resonated like a bell being struck. The echo seen in the wakeful brain did not stop with the simple response. Instead, the response activated adjoining areas, passed from one area of the brain to another, around, and through the brain as each area processed the occurrence. It is the interconnectivity of the brain that brings about consciousness. Could it be that Jaynes was actually on to something, but simply went too far in his assumptions? Maybe it was not simply a matter of balancing hemispheric dominance that caused the great shift of the Axial Age, but instead a subtle evolutionary change in the connections between the areas of the brain.

This is not to insinuate that ancient man was not as conscious or wakeful as modern man is today, or any more or less intelligent. Simply, through the connections within and between areas of the brain, we may find the sense of who or what we are, and where we reside in god and in the universe. It is possible that we are over-analyzing the entire concept and what was happening spiritually was exactly what happens in all other areas of human progress. Great men have great ideas that are built upon present concepts, which push humanity forward into the next stage.

We may never know the reason the Axial Age graced us. The brain and nervous system are made of soft tissue, which disintegrates. They do not withstand the ravages of time. Thus, any theory concerning the brain can only be inferred and never proven, at least not with our current science. Whether the Axial Age was brought about by the social changes driving individualism, migration, or the modes of travel on horseback occurring in certain regions, or whether it was by a change in brain connections or chemistry, we do not know. We do know, however, there was a pattern; and within a certain epoch of time, man became a spiritual creature, leaving his primitive gods behind.

How and why did this happen globally and simultaneously? We do not know, but it begs the question, Will it happen again, and if so, when? When will the second Axial Age come and what new spiritual insights will it bring?

Possibly it will bring the death of religion and the rise of a truly spiritual race.

There was a time we burned people alive as a sacrifice to God. There was a time, not so long ago we burned people alive if they acted oddly. We claimed they were witches. Then it was discovered they were probably under the influence of a mold called Ergot, which grows on Rye, from which their breads were made. Rye grain is occasionally infected with the ergot fungus. Ergot contains several psychoactive chemicals such as ergotamine, a compound used in the synthesis of LSD.

Now we burn people alive with our speech and actions, destroying them in the eyes of society. Maybe one day we will work as hard to help and love others.

The Pinnacle of the Axial Age

Jesus represents the pinnacle of the Axial Age. No matter what one may think about his nature or divinity, his teachings convey everything positive resulting from the Axial Age. He addresses the heart and mind of man and asserts that it is the mental, subjective, inner world of mankind that brings either peace or violence – heaven or hell.

Recently, scholars, academics, and theologians have argued and speculated on how Christians of the first century viewed Jesus. Was he divine or not? Did the first Christians believe he was god or just a teacher? I believe the question itself is incorrect, leading to a false premise from which false conclusions arise. Jesus was not yet taken off the cross before differences as to who or what he was appeared between followers. Christianity in the first century was even more diverse than it is today. Different factions viewed Jesus through the lens of their prior religious backgrounds and beliefs, exactly as we do today.

The first Christians were converted Jews. They were expecting a messiah sent from God, not God himself. The job of this savior was to bridge the gap between God and man, and bring harmony and communion back between Yahweh and his people. This is quite clear, if one were simply to read the way God and the readers are addressed within the New Testament.
21. Romans 1:7 To all that be in Rome, beloved of God, called to be saints: Grace to you and peace from God our Father, and the Lord Jesus Christ...
22.
23. Romans 4:24 But for us also, to whom it shall be imputed, if we believe on him that raised up Jesus our Lord from the dead...

24. Romans 5:1 Therefore being justified by faith, we have peace with God through our Lord Jesus Christ...

25. Romans 5:11 And not only so, but we also joy in God through our Lord Jesus Christ, by whom we have now received the atonement...

26. Hebrews 13:20 Now the God of peace, that brought again from the dead our Lord Jesus, that great shepherd of the sheep, through the blood of the everlasting covenant...

27. 1 Peter 1:2 Elect according to the foreknowledge of God the Father, through sanctification of the Spirit, unto obedience and sprinkling of the blood of Jesus Christ: Grace unto you, and peace, be multiplied...

28. 2 Peter 1:2 Grace and peace be multiplied unto you through the knowledge of God, and of Jesus our Lord...

There are many other such passages, but we shall not belabor the point. The salutations of these epistles acknowledge God as God and Jesus as Lord. The salutations also imply that Jesus is the Christ, the messiah, and the mediator, but not God or even a God. Let me put this in perspective. Lord was a formal way of addressing a superior.
In the Spanish translations of the Bible the word is correctly rendered, "señor." The definition is, "Title used as a courtesy title before the surname, full name, or professional title of a man in a Spanish-speaking area. Used as a form of polite address for a man in a Spanish-speaking area." This word, translated, "lord" is:
κυ ριος , kurios , *koo'-ree-os* From κυ ρος kuros (*supremacy*); *supreme* in authority, that is, (as noun) *controller*; by implication *Mr.* (as a respectful title).
It is not the "Lord" rendered from the name, Yahweh.
Since we no longer used the word, it takes on a greater meaning than was intended. This is an example of the American Christian filtering ideas through his or her background. Early Christians had these filters also. Some came from a background influenced by Plato, who believed the

world was the creation of an insane angel, thus all matter was corrupt. It was impossible for the holy God even to contact earthly matter, as it would be contrary to his nature of holiness and purity. For these people, the idea of divinity inhabiting human flesh was unthinkable. Jesus could not have been God in human form.

Historically speaking, the fate of the Jews who followed Jesus is one of the puzzles of the history. Centuries of Christian anti-Semitism, and Jewish resentment of Christianity have obscured the history of Jewish Christians. Pieces of history have been removed, distorted, or simply left unreported. There was an argument between James and Paul about how much, if any, of the Jewish law and custom such converts to Christianity should keep. Some Jewish converts wondered how the self-sacrifice of Jesus related to the animal sacrifices in the law, and believed that the law and customs should be continued, while others believed that Jesus was the sacrifice, once and for all, encouraging followers to give up the law and Jewish religious customs. Both sides were previously taught by Jewish custom to hate the Gentiles and now did not know what to do with the Gentile believers.

Proto-orthodox authors clearly agree that the Ebionites were Jewish followers of Jesus. They were not the only group of Jewish-Christians known to have existed at the time, but they were the group that generated some of the greatest opposition. The Ebionite Christians, about whom we are most informed, believed that Jesus was the Jewish Messiah sent from the Jewish God to the Jewish people in fulfillment of the Jewish Scriptures. They also believed that in order to belong to the people of God, one needed to be Jewish. They observed the Sabbath, kept the kosher, and circumcised their male children. These were the people that opposed Paul in Galatia. The Ebionite Christians were their spiritual descendants.

Bart Ehrman points out, the Ebionites had a foundation, even during the time of Paul. In the book of Galatians, we see Paul arguing and writing against people who held similar to beliefs to the Ebionites. Therefore, the Ebionites may not have been established as late as modern day Christians purport. Rather, Ebionites could very well be the very same descended, first century followers mentioned in the book of Galatians,and not only a first century group but a group appearing 30-50 years after Jesus' death!

Their insistence on staying (or becoming) Jewish should not seem especially peculiar from a historical perspective, since Jesus and his disciples were Jewish. But the Ebionites' "Jewishness" did not endear them to most other Christians who believed that Jesus allowed them to bypass the requirements of the Law for salvation. The Ebionites, however, maintained that the original disciples authorized their views, especially Peter and Jesus' own brother, James, head of the Jerusalem church after the resurrection.
(Bart, Ehrman, Lost Christianities. Oxford University Press, 2003. PP. 100)

Another aspect of the Ebionites' Christianity that set it apart from most other Christian groups was their understanding of who Jesus was. The Ebionites did not subscribe to the notion of Jesus' pre-existence or his virgin birth. These ideas were originally distinct from each other. The two New Testament Gospels that speak of Jesus being conceived of a virgin (Matthew and Luke) do not indicate that he existed prior to his birth. For them, Jesus was the Son of God, not because of his divine nature or virgin birth, but because of his adoption by God to be his son. Although the New Testament was not around at this time, we can now see this view expressed in the scene when Jesus was Baptized, and the voice of God was heard saying, "This is My Son -- the Beloved; hear ye him;" Luke 9:35. This kind of Christology is, consequently, called "adoptionist." To express the matter more fully, the Ebionites believed that Jesus was a real flesh-and-blood human like the rest of us, born as the eldest son of the sexual union of his parents, Joseph and Mary. What set Jesus apart from all other people was that he kept God's law perfectly, and therefore was the most righteous man on earth.

Keeping in mind that the New Testament was a long way from existing as we know it, and keeping in mind that Paul was simply a Jewish Rabbi insisting that a person is made right with God apart from keeping the Law, in the minds of the Ebonites, Paul was a heretic, a religious snob and an intellectual bully, who led people astray.

So according to the Ebionites, Jesus was not divine, he was a man like everyone else, yet what made him special and set him apart was that he was the Jewish Messiah, and that he perfectly followed the law. The Ebionites summarily dismissed Paul, his ideas, and his writings. They considered him an apostate of the Law.

The doctrines of this sect are said by Irenaeus to be like those of Cerinthus and Carpocrates. They denied the Divinity and the virginal birth of Christ; they clung to the observance of the Jewish Law; they regarded St. Paul as an apostate, and used only a Gospel according to St. Matthew (Adv. Haer., I, xxvi, 2; III, xxi, 2; IV, xxxiii, 4; V, i, 3).

Besides the Ebionites, there existed a later Gnostic development of the same heresy. These Ebionite Gnostics differed widely from the main schools of Gnosticism, in that they absolutely rejected any distinction between Jehovah the Demiurge (maker of the physical world) and the Supreme Good God. They believed the universe was divided into two realms; good and evil. The Son of God rules over the realm of the good, and to him is given the world to come, but the Prince of Evil is the prince of this world (cf. John 14:30; Ephesians 1:21; 6:12). This Son of God is the Christ, a middle-being between God and creation, not a creature, yet not equal to, nor even to be compared with, the Father.

Their belief in salvation is different than what became orthodox. Man is saved by knowledge (gnosis), by believing in the supreme God, the Teacher, and by being baptized unto remission of sins. At this point, the initiated person receives knowledge and strength to observe all the precepts of the law.

Another divergence from orthodox belief is Marcionism. The sect originated from the teachings of a man named

Marcion, a Christian theologian, and son of a Christian Bishop. Marcion began to formulate his theology around the year 144. This was well before an official Bible and most of what the latter church power dictated as doctrine.

Marcion could not reconcile the God of the Jewish Bible with the God of the New Testament. The Old Testament God commanded genocide, and mass murder, as well as the slaughter of thousands of animals at a time. He regarded the God of the Old Testament as an evil "lesser god," much like the Gnostic regarded the god who made the physical world. Subsequently, Marcion rejected the Jewish Bible and its god.

Zephaniah 2:12
You Ethiopians will also be slaughtered by my sword," says the LORD. And the LORD will strike the lands of the north with his fist. He will destroy Assyria and make its great capital, Nineveh, a desolate wasteland, parched like a desert. The city that once was so proud will become a pasture for sheep and cattle. …

Ezekiel 9:5
Then I heard the LORD say to the other men, "Follow him through the city and kill everyone whose forehead is not marked. Show no mercy; have no pity! Kill them all - old and young, girls and women and little children…

Deuteronomy 3:6
6 And we utterly destroyed them, as we did unto Sihon king of Heshbon, utterly destroying the men, women, and children, of every city…

Marcion saw a different God, in the New Testament. It was a God of love, mercy, grace, and forgiveness.

Barth Erhman, a major New Testament scholar, writes about the Marcionites in Lost Christianities:

"Living at the same time and also enjoying the unwanted attention of the proto-orthodox opponents, though standing at just the opposite end of the theological spectrum, were a group of Christians known as the Marcionites. In this instance, there is no question concerning the origin of the name. These were followers of the second century evangelist/theologian Marcian, known to later Christianity as one of the arch heretics of his day, but by all accounts one of the most significant Christian thinkers and writers of the early centuries. The Marcionites on the other hand, had a highly attractive religion to many pagan converts, as it was avowedly Christian with nothing Jewish about it. In fact, everything Jewish was taken out of it. Jews, recognized around the world for customs that struck many pagans as bizarre at best, would have difficulty recognizing the Marcionite religion as an offshoot of their own. Not only were Jewish customs rejected, so, too, were the Jewish scriptures and the Jewish God. From a historical perspective, it is intriguing that any such religion could claim direct historical continuity with Jesus."

"I should say a word about the theology Marcion developed, which was seen as distinctive, revolutionary, compelling, and therefore dangerous. Among all Christian texts and authors at his disposal, Marcion was especially struck by the writings of the apostle Paul, and in particular the distinction Paul drew in Galatians and elsewhere between the Law of the Jews and the gospel of Christ.

As we have seen, Paul claimed that a person is made right with God by faith in Christ, not by doing the works of the Law. This distinction became fundamental to Marcion, and he made it absolute. The Gospel is good news of deliverance; it involves love, mercy, grace, forgiveness, reconciliation, redemption, and life. The Law, however, is the bad news that makes the gospel necessary in the first place; it involves harsh commandments, guilt, judgment, enmity, punishment, and death. The Law is given to the Jews. Christ gives the gospel."

Marcion concluded that there must in fact be two Gods; the God of the Jews, as found in the Old Testament, and the God of Jesus, as found in the writings of Paul.

Once Marcion arrived at this understanding, everything else naturally fell into place. The God of the Old Testament was the God who created this world and everything in it, as described in Genesis. The God of Jesus, therefore, had never been involved with this world but came into it only when Jesus appeared from heaven. The God of the Old Testament was the God who called the Jews to be his people and gave them his law. The God of Jesus did not consider the Jews to be his people (for him; they were the chosen of the other God), and he was not a God who gave laws.

The God of Jesus came into this world in order to save people from the vengeful God of the Jews. He was previously unknown to this world and had never had any previous dealings with it. Hence Marcion sometimes referred to him as God the stranger. Not even the prophecies of the future Messiah come from this God, for these refer not to Jesus but to a coming Messiah of Israel, to be sent by the God of the Jews, the creator of this world and the God of the Old Testament. Jesus came completely unexpectedly and did what no one could possibly have hoped for: He paid the penalty for other people's sins, to save them from the wrath of the Old Testament God.

Marcion's New Testament consisted of eleven books. Most of these were the letters of his beloved Paul, the one predecessor whom Marcion could trust to understand the radical claims of the gospel. Why, Marcion asked, did Jesus return to earth to convert Paul by means of a vision? Why did he not simply allow his own disciples to proclaim his message faithfully throughout the world?

According to Marcion, it was because Jesus' disciples were followers of the Jewish God and readers of the Jewish Scriptures and never did correctly understand their master. Confused by what Jesus taught them, wrongly thinking he was the Jewish Messiah, even after his death and resurrection they continued not to understand, interpreting Jesus' words, deeds, and death in light of their understanding of Judaism. Jesus then had to start afresh, and he called Paul to reveal to him 'the truth of the gospel.' That is why Paul had to confront Jesus' disciple Peter and his earthly brother James, as seen in the letter to the Galatians. Jesus had revealed the truth to Paul, and these others simply never understood.

Marcion returned to Asia Minor to propagate his version of faith, and he was fantastically successful in doing so. We cannot be sure exactly why, but Marcion experienced an almost unparalleled success on the mission field, establishing churches wherever he went, so that within a few years, one of his proto-orthodox opponents, the apologist and theologian in Rome, Justin, could say that he was teaching his heretical views to many people of every nation." (Apology 1.26). (Bart, Ehrman. Lost Christianities. Oxford University press, 2003. PP. 103-109)

Then, there are the Gnostics. They flourished in the second and third century, but their root can be traced back the oldest Christian sects from 30 to 120 C.E., such as the Simonians, Ophites, Naassenes, Cerinthians, and others. The Gnostics, as a group, were so diverse in their beliefs, it is difficult to label one belief Gnostic and one not.

Many believed that the world was not compatible with the divine nature of God, thus if Jesus was from God, he could not have a mortal body. He was a spirit tricking us in to believing he was a man. He did not die on the cross. It was part of the illusion.

Some believed that Jesus had a divine nature trapped within his body. He came to show us this fact so that we could find our divine nature and escape the corrupt world. In the Gospel of Judas (available from Fifth Estate Publishing), we see this play out as Jesus appoints Judas to the special task of making sure Jesus is killed and can be released from his body, thereby again becoming one with the supreme God.

The common thread of all Gnostics seems to be the belief that there was knowledge that passed to the believer, which allowed him or her to be saved. This knowledge ignites the Christ spirit, which was in each of us from the beginning, but has been lost or forgotten. Jesus came to show us this by letting us see the seed of God within him that we all have within us.

They believed that sin was the lack of knowledge about yourself and your divine spark. When you became one with God within yourself, you became one with all that is. This is salvation. There was no original sin, only ignorance of our own purpose and divine nature.

However, this doctrine had no place for institutional control. If salvation is left to the individual to follow the template laid down by Jesus himself, where and how could the emerging church gain control? It could not, so the idea of man's divine spirit was deemed heresy by the church, and all but stamped out, surviving only among a few sects and teachers throughout the subsequent centuries, and ending, for the most part, in the great slaughter of the Cathers (the last great Gnostic sect) by the Roman church in 1290 A.D.

If Jesus came to show us the way to become messiahs ourselves, saying to us, "Greater things than me will you do...", there would be no place for organized religion, so the church tried to kill the idea, and when they could not do that, they killed the people.

The diverse views of God and his Messiah, Jesus, are most astounding. Was Jesus a man or a spirit? Was he God, a god, the God, a servant, a man...? Christianity was not united on these fronts. We were not in harmony even in our basic doctrines.

If one were to rule a people, the people must be in harmony. The church wished to rule, and the King wished to rule. These desires would come to a head in Nicaea

In A.D. 312, Constantine won control of the Roman Empire in the battle of Milvian Bridge. Attributing his victory to the intervention of Jesus Christ. He had seen a vision of a cross and heard a voice telling him to conquer. Because of his vision he made Christianity the religion of the empire. "One God, one Lord, one faith, one church, one empire, one emperor" became his motto.

The new emperor soon discovered that there was no "one faith and one church." Instead there were factions split by theological disputes, especially the differing understandings of the nature of Christ. Arius, a priest of the church in Alexandria, asserted that God created Christ before the beginning of time. Therefore, the divinity of Christ was similar to the divinity of God, but not of the same essence.

Bishop Alexander and his successor, Athanasius affirmed that the divinity of Christ, the Son, is of the same substance as God, the Father. Otherwise Christians would be guilty of polytheism. It would imply that knowledge of God in Christ was not final knowledge of God. They must have forgotten that when Jesus was asked about the end of the world, he replied that he did not know. Only God knew.

Constantine convened a council in Nicaea in A.D. 325 and demanded the rift be settled. There were threats and commands until a creed reflecting some compromise was produced and signed by a majority of the bishops. There were actually more than just these two sides, but the others were removed from the church, excommunicated, or done away with. The remaining parties continued to battle each other until A.D. 381, when a second council met in Constantinople. It adopted a revised and expanded form of the A.D. 325 creed, now known as the Nicene Creed.

The evolution of God is now firmly in the hands of man. We shall qualify and quantify what is and is not God. We shall do so with measuring sticks of our own making. Two of these rods are canon and doctrine. With these measuring rules in hand those in power will make the world conform to their standards. Belief or doctrine limits the accepted canon. In turn, canon will support doctrine as we turn to the scriptures to prove our point. We will now discuss canon, doctrine, and how man shaped God.

Addicted to Religion

In a list of addictions; drugs, alcohol, sex, and gambling, one does not expect to see "religion" listed, yet it is one of the most insidious. It tears families apart and binds people to abusive leaders. It manipulates victims with shame and guilt.

The reasons for the addiction can be placed in just a few categories. There are those who hold tightly to the illusion that if they are righteous enough, do all the right things, say all the right words, pray enough, and can be religious enough God will not let anything happen to them. This concept forms a straightjacket of conduct and thought processes, which are imposed with tyrannical zeal on those around them.

There are those who use their religion as a way to manipulate and crush the expression of others. These are easily recognized if one watches dispassionately their actions when they are challenged. They may have treated someone badly, gossiped, or berated someone. When called on their actions they will declare their righteousness. If the conversation becomes heated they will always declare the language or attitude with which they are being confronted is inappropriate. Thus they attempt to shift the argument from their offending actions to the fact they are being offended by the manner of the confrontation. Sadly, many times this works and the religious person attempts to seize the moral high ground in spite of the enormity of their prior offense. No one can be better than them or good enough for them. It is arrogance at its most destructive.

For the religious tyrant, the ability to control, manipulate, and cause shame, doubt, and guilt in others causes spikes in the pleasure chemicals in the brain the same way a sadist finds pleasure in their ability to control, oppress, harm, and cause pain in others. These people are usually miserable except when passing judgment on others.

Power corrupts, but power also enable those who are already corrupted by pride and narcissism. Power and control are tools to express the personal preferences of sociopaths. There is a reason that the more accomplished sociopaths flock to politics and religion. Power and control are addictive. From Charles Manson to Swaggart, Bakker, Copeland, Crouch and Jim Jones; from abusive priests to corrupt popes, religion has afforded many hucksters and confidence men (and women) pathways to manipulate, control, threaten, cajole, and fleece the flock.

Religious addictions are driven by the need to feel like one has control over an uncontrollable world. It is also driven by the need to feel special, superior, and to control others. To sway the outcome of situations and those around them if the addictive urge of millions of addicts. They attempt to manipulate God and man, and some wish to take the wealth of both.

Addictions are strengthened when brain chemicals, which make us experience pleasure, are increased. Gambling, sex, risk taking, drinking, and drugs can do this. So can religion. Those raucous church services with music, singing, chanting, messages that motivate, and repetitive rhythms cause the pleasure centers of our brains to produce a chemical soup of excitement. An energetic orator can top off the cocktail.

Support groups of people experiencing the same pleasure can help maintain the high by continuing to remind the practitioner of the experience. In a short time the person is looking forward to the next service. Then they cannot wait for the next service. Then they try to create the feelings of the service on their own by listening to the same type of music, and using the same words and languages of the group.

It is at this point the cycle of this type of religious addiction is complete. When they cannot read the Bible, pray, or attend church enough they experience moodiness caused by withdrawal of chemicals. They begin to associate with only church members and they withdraw from family and friends who do not share their fixations. Their actions now mimic the actions of an alcoholic as they do the same things: Moody behavior, befriending other addicts, retreating from non-addicts, and planning the next time they can indulge.

The language of the religion addict may change. Use of religious phrases and expressions begin to appear in normal conversations and become inappropriate. "Praise God, Praise the Lord, Halleluiah, Thank you Jesus, and a number of other expressions will begin to pepper normal secular conversations.

Their thoughts are not on the problems at hand but on church and religion. They become to "heavenly minded to be of any worldly good." Like a person always smoking pot, their mood and mind have become altered and less useful. People who try to force them to re-engage the world will be labeled as sinners, heretics, and unworthy of their time.

Conclusion

After seeing the history and development of religion, as man made doctrine is stacked upon politically motivated dogma, we must ask where God may abide in all of this. We see the systems and balances inherent in nature. Is there intelligence behind the balance and systems within biology and nature or are they simply the result of random acts, which hit upon a balance, like a coin tossed a million times finally comes to rest standing in its rim? Do we still choose to believe that there is a God? If so, do we choose to seek him or her out?

If we choose not to seek God it will not change the fact that God does or does not exist. The reality will be whatever it may be. Doing nothing may seem the easier path. Certainly, it will lead to fewer questions and quandaries, such as which path to take toward to goal of knowing God. Indeed, even in our knowing there will be no proof others will accept.

We know that religion is not the road to God. Doctrine is like glass. You can see some of the truth through it, although it is distorted, but it will always separate us from experiencing the truth on a personal basis. Since religion is nothing more than a set of rules expressed as line upon line of doctrine and dogma it is a natural wedge between man and any God there may be.

Religion is toxic, oppressive, and mean spirited. It controls and lords over its people. It is ripe with superstition. It is exclusive and divisive, separating people as it divides one religion from another, then separating one denomination within a religion from another. Finally, religion gives narcissists, the petty, and the power hungry a stage to lord over and control others.

Religion cannot teach the simple principles of love and compassion. Treating others as we wish to be treated demands empathy. Religion is about rules. Spirituality is about feelings, compassion, empathy, and love. Yet, spirituality is an uncharted path on which everyone walks alone and in different directions.

345

The rules of spirituality are simple – There are no rules. You are on your own. It is just you and God. Be quiet, be still, and you will feel the source of all.

It takes maturity to discard rules and guideline and trust ones self and the outcome to fate – or even trust the god one is unsure even exists.

Can we grow up? Can we escape our superstitious and regulated thinking and come to a deep and abiding knowledge of ourselves and our spiritual source?

Will there be a second Axial Age? Is there hope that we can unbind ourselves from religions, sects, and denominations to find acceptance, compassion, and the love of God?

Can we open our minds and hearts to accept other concepts of "God" as our source of life and spirit, and simply seek our source without ascribing gender or personality traits, which we cannot possibly comprehend?

In espousing the following point I know I will incur the wrath of many. However, if we think about it carefully we will find it to be true. Church attendance, obedience to the law, knowledge of the Scriptures, prayer if empty repetition, even worship if it is empty of spirit, will not change the heart of man. Only by being in God's presence can we hope to get to know Him intimately and be changed by exposure to Him; as a child is changed and molded by the parent.

In this little book we have caused some to doubt their faith. We may have rendered doctrine in shambles, but hopefully we have taken steps to throw away all of those things we have held so dear that worshiped them more than their supposed source. In the minds of many, religion has eclipsed its own source, and the source of our souls.

Most of our accepted doctrine is based on political maneuverings, man made opinions, and Bible verses chosen by a few, and taken out of context by others, or added to the original material far beyond the time of the apostles. All of these we must count as useless in our journey to enlightenment.

If scripture and doctrine were enough, we could have kept the law and we would have obtained happiness, if simply doing the right thing would have made anyone happy.

Doctrine and law were not enough. We must turn back to the first cause. It is not Bible nor doctrine, but God, whatever you believe god to be. Break away from religion and seek the source of life and happiness. Can we do something so simple and difficult as to sit quietly, listen to and absorb this source? After all, one reason religion exists is the security of following rules and not having to think or journey for ourselves.

If we wish to know this source, we can do so, if we choose to extend our relationship to a state of intimacy. The act of knowing by experience is quite different from knowing by reading what others claim to be the truth. Words cannot carry spiritual truth. Only experience can communicate it. This is because internal and mystical landscapes have no signposts, no markers, and no language.

Where to start and what to do are the first and most important questions. Yet, the answers could be the simplest. There has never been a true religion that has not expressed the two basic directives espoused by Jesus. Each time they have been spoken with conviction the speaker has suffered by the hands of some and worshiped by others. From Siddhartha Buddha to Jesus, the message has been the same. Be kind. Have compassion. Seek inside your self for the truth and the source that keeps it alive.

To begin our journey let us turn back to those few things Jesus himself instructed us to do.
Matthew 22:36-40

Master, which is the great commandment in the law? Jesus said to him, You shall love the Lord your God with all your heart, and with all your soul, and with all your mind. This is the first and great commandment. And the second is like unto it, You shall love your neighbor as yourself. On these two commandments hang all the law and the prophets.

You shall love the Lord your God with all your heart, and with all your soul, and with all your mind is the sum and fulfillment of the first 4 of the 10 commandments which define our responsibility to God.

You shall love your neighbor as yourself is the sum and fulfillment of the last 6 commandments which define our responsibility to each other.

On these two commandments hang all the law and the prophets. Jesus Christ hung on the cross to fulfill the law and the prophets and to teach us how to live. The rest of the Bible is commentary. To add one word to this would cause division and exclusion.

The love of God means unity and love.

How do we measure our progress toward our communion with God and love of our neighbor? It is not by any self-imposed rule or by self-indulgent pharisaic standards. It is only this:

James 1:27 (New International Version)

27 Religion that God our Father accepts as pure and faultless is this: to look after orphans and widows in their distress and to keep oneself from being polluted by the world.

Do you seek to know and love God?

Do you seek to help and care for others?

Do you take care not to get caught up in the world system of greed and power? (This includes the politics of nations and denominations.)

If it is in our hearts to love and to do just these little things, we will do well.

Appendix "A"

Appendix "A" contains a partial list of predictions, starting with the earliest known apocalyptic utterance. It was written in a terse, informational style using many sentence fragments; so if you are an O.C.D. English teacher, turn back now. They rest of us will enjoy the laugh. This list is taken from several Internet sources, which, in turn, document their sources. For more information please see: www.lifepositive.com, www.2think.org, www.abhota.info, www.religioustolerance.org, and other sites.

2800 BC - According to Isaac Asimov's Book of Facts (1979), an Assyrian clay tablet dating to approximately 2800 BC was unearthed bearing the words "Our earth is degenerate in these latter days. There are signs that the world is quickly coming to an end. Bribery and corruption are common." This is one of the earliest examples of moral decay in society being interpreted as a sign of the soon-coming end of days.

634 BC - Apocalyptic thinking gripped Romans, who feared the city would be destroyed in the 120th year of its founding. There was a myth that 12 eagles had revealed to Romulus a mystical number representing the lifetime of Rome, and some early Romans hypothesized that each eagle represented 10 years. The Roman calendar was counted from the founding of Rome, 1 AUC (ab urbe condita) being 753 BC. Thus 120 AUC is 634 BC. (Thompson p.19)

389 BC – The first prophecy of Rome's destruction came and went. This caused some to figure that the mystical number revealed to Romulus represented the number of days in a year (the Great Year concept), so they expected Rome to be destroyed around 365 AUC (389 BC). (Thompson p.19)

Joseph Lumpkin

1st Century - Jesus said, "Verily I say unto you, there be some standing here, which shall not taste of death, till they see the Son of Man coming in his kingdom." (Matthew 16:28) Apostles waited for His return until their death. Paul preached about the soon return of Jesus.

70 A.D. - The Essenes, a sect of Jewish ascetics with apocalyptic beliefs, may have seen the Jewish revolt against the Romans in 66-70 as the final end-time battle. (Source: PBS Frontline special Apocalypse!)

2nd Century - The Montanists believed that Christ would come again within their lifetimes and establish a new Jerusalem at Pepuza, in the land of Phrygia. Montanism was perhaps the first bona fide Christian doomsday cult. It was founded around 156 A.D. by the prophet Montanus and two followers, Priscilla and Maximilla. Even though Jesus did not return, the cult lasted for several centuries. Tertullian was the most famous follower of this sect. He is quoted as saying, "I believe it just because it is unbelievable." (Gould p.43-44)

247 A.D. - Rome celebrated its thousandth anniversary this year. At the same time, the Roman government dramatically increased its persecution of Christians. Christians came to believe that this was the End Of Days. (Source: PBS Frontline special Apocalypse!)

365 A.D. - Hilary of Poitiers predicted the world would end in 365. (Source: Ontario Consultants on Religious Tolerance)

380 A.D. - The Donatists, a North African Christian sect headed by Tyconius, looked forward to the world ending in 380. (Source: American Atheists)

Late 4th Century - St. Martin of Tours (316-397) wrote, "There is no doubt that the Antichrist has already been born. Firmly established already in his early years, he will, after reaching maturity, achieve supreme power." (Abanes p.119)

500 A.D. - Roman theologian Sextus Julius Africanus (160-240) claimed that the End would occur 6000 years after the Creation. He assumed that there were 5531 years between the Creation and the Resurrection, and thus expected the Second Coming to take place no later than 500 A.D. (Kyle p.37, McIver #21)

500 A.D. - Hippolytus (died ca. 236), believing that Christ would return 6000 years after the Creation, anticipated the Parousia in 500 A.D. (Abanes p.283) Parousia is the return of Jesus to the earth.

500- A.D. The theologian Irenaeus, influenced by Hippolytus' writings, also saw 500 as the year of the Second Coming. (Abanes p.283, McIver #15)

793 A.D. - Apr 6, 793 - Spanish monk Beatus of Liébana prophesied the end of the world in the presence of a crowd of people, who became frightened, panicked, and fasted through the night until dawn. Hordonius, one of the fasters, was quoted as having remarked, "Let's eat and drink, so that if we die at least we'll be fed." This was described by Elipandus, bishop of Toledo. (Abanes p. 168-169, Weber p.50)

800 A.D. - Sextus Julius Africanus revised the date of Doomsday to 800 A.D. (Kyle p.37)

800 A.D. - Beatus of Liébana wrote in his Commentary on the Apocalypse, which he finished in 786, that there were only 14 years left until the end of the world. (Abanes p.168)

806 A.D. - Bishop Gregory of Tours calculated the End occurring between 799 and 806. (Weber p.48)

848 A.D. - The prophetess Thiota prophesied that the world would end this year. (Abanes p.337)

All dates shown here forward are A.D. unless otherwise noted.

970 - Mar 25, 970 – In Lotharingia, (a portion of the lands assigned to Emperor of the West, Lothair I,) theologians foresaw the end of the world on Friday, March 25, 970, when the Annunciation and Good Friday fell on the same day. They believed that it was on this day that Adam was created, Isaac was sacrificed, the Red Sea was parted, Jesus was conceived, and Jesus was crucified. Therefore, it followed that the end must occur on this day! (Source: Center for Millennial Studies)

992 - Bernard of Thuringia thought the end would come in 992. (Randi p.236)

995 – After the prophecy failed, seeing The Feast of the Annunciation and Good Friday also coincided in 992, some mystics conclude that the world would end within 3 years of that date, repeating the 970 prophecies. (Weber p.50-51)

1000 – Whenever a couple of zeros appear at the end of the date there will be apocalyptic thoughts. There are many stories of paranoia around the year 1000. There are tales describing terror gripping Europe in the months before the date. There is disagreement about which stories are genuine since scholars claim ordinary people may not have even aware of what year it was. (See articles at "Center for Millennial Studies.") (Gould, Schwartz, Randi)

1033 - Jesus disappointed the Y-1-K crowd, so some irrepressible mystics re-thought the date, claiming there was a simple mistake. The return would occur at the thousandth anniversary of the Crucifixion, bringing the date to 1033. Burgundian monk Radulfus Glaber described a rash of millennial paranoia during the period from 1000-1033. (Kyle p.39, Abanes p.337, McIver #50)

1184 - Various Christian prophets foresaw the Antichrist coming in 1184. I do not know why. (Abanes p.338)

1186 – (Sep 23, 1186) - After calculating that a planetary alignment would occur in Libra on September 23, 1186 (Julian calendar), John of Toledo circulated a letter, known as the "Letter of Toledo", warning that the world was to going to be destroyed on this date, and that only a few people would survive. (Randi p.236)

1260 - Italian mystic Joachim of Fiore (1135-1202) determined that the Millennium would begin between 1200 and 1260. Where do these guys get their dates? (Kyle p.48)

1284 - Pope Innocent III expected the Second Coming to take place in 1284, 666 years after the rise of Islam. (Schwartz p.181)

1290 - The Joachites, who were followers of Joachim of Fiore, rescheduled the End of Time to 1290 when his 1260 prophecy failed. If at first you don't succeed, try, try again. (McIver #58)

1306 - In 1147 Gerard of Poehlde, believing that Christ's Millennium began when the emperor Constantine came to power, figured that Satan would become unbound at the end of the thousand-year period and destroy the Church. Since Constantine rose to power in 306, the end of the Millennium would be in 1306. (Source: Christian author Richard J. Foster)

1335 – The Joachites were still around, trying to figure things out. Their third prophecy of doomsday was 1335. Again, I have no idea why. (McIver #58) Joachites were very much preoccupied with the role of the Jews in prophecy and believed they had discovered the keys to understanding the timing of Bible prophecy.

1367 - Czech archdeacon, Militz of Kromeriz, claimed the Antichrist was alive and ready to march onto the stage of time. He would reveal himself between 1363 and 1367. The End would come between 1365 and 1367. Anti-psychotics were not invented yet. (McIver #67)

1370 - There is a thin line between visions and delusions. The proof is in the truth. Jean de Roquetaillade, a French ascetic foresaw the Millennium beginning in 1368 or 1370. The Antichrist was to come in the year 1366. (Weber p.55)

1378 - Arnold of Vilanova, a Joachite, wrote in his work "De Tempore Adventu Antichristi" that the Antichrist was to come in 1378. (McIver #62)

1420 - Feb 14, 1420 - Martinek Hausha, a Czech prophet, also known as Martin Huska was a member of the Taborite movement. He warned that the world would end in February 1420, February 14 at the latest. The Taborites rejected the corrupted church and insisted on biblical authority, not Papal authority. Even though Taborite theologians were versed in scholastic theology, they were among the first intellectuals to break free from centuries-old scholastic methods. (McIver #71, Shaw p.43)

1496 - The beginning of the Millennium, according to some 15th Century mystics. (Mann p. ix)

1504 - Italian artist Sandro Botticelli, a follower of Girolamo Savonarola, wrote a caption in Greek on his painting The Mystical Nativity: "I Sandro painted this picture at the end of the year 1500 in the troubles of Italy in the half time after the time according to the eleventh chapter of St. John in the second woe of the Apocalypse in the loosing of the devil for three and a half years. Then he will be chained in the 12th chapter and we shall see him trodden down as in this picture." He thought the

Millennium would begin in three and a half years.. (Weber p.60)

1524 - Feb 1, 1524 - According to calculations of London astrologers made in the previous June, the end of the world would occur by a flood, (I thought God told us that would never happen again.), starting in London on February 1 (Julian). Around 20,000 people abandoned their homes, and a clergyman stockpiled food and water in a fortress he built. (Randi p.236-237)

1524 - Feb 20, 1524 - Astrologer Johannes Stoeffler saw the conjunction on a different day. The planetary alignment in Pisces, a water sign, was seen as the end of the Millennium, and the coming of the end by world flood. (Randi p.236-237)

1525 - Anabaptist Thomas Müntzer believed this date was the beginning of a new Millennium, and the "end of all ages." He led an unsuccessful peasants' revolt. The government disagreed with his prediction. He was arrested, tortured, and executed. (If he really thought it was the end of everything one wonders why a revolt would matter.) (Gould p.48)

1528 - Stoeffler's first attempt to predict the end of the world in 1524 failed. He then recalculated Doomsday to 1528. (Randi p.238) (Actually, up until today, all predictions have failed. The proof is that you are reading this.)

1528 - May 27, 1528 - Reformer Hans Hut predicted the end would occur on Pentecost (May 27, Julian calendar). (Weber p.67, Shaw p.44)

1532 - Frederick Nausea, a Viennese bishop, was certain that the world would end in 1532. He had heard reports of strange occurrences, including bloody crosses appearing in the sky alongside a comet. (I wonder if Mr. Nausea was sick when he got it wrong.) (Randi p. 238)

1533 - Anabaptist prophet Melchior Hoffman's prediction for the year of Christ's Second Coming, to take place in Strasbourg. He claimed that 144,000 people would be saved, while the rest of the world would be consumed by fire. (Kyle p.59) (We should note that usually wherever the prophet resides would be where the end begins. If a prophet predicts the end of time, normally only his followers are destined to make it out alive.)

1533 - Oct 19, 1533 - Mathematician Michael Stifel calculated that the Day of Judgement would begin at 8:00am on this day. (McIver #88)

1534 - Apr 5, 1534 - Jan Matthys predicted that the Apocalypse would take place on Easter Day (April 5, Julian calendar.) He went on to say only the city of Münster would be spared. (Shaw p.45, Abanes p.338) (He must have lived near the city.)

1537 - French astrologer Pierre Turrel announced four different possible dates for the end of the world, using four different calculation methods. The dates were 1537, 1544, 1801 and 1814. (Randi p. 239) He was playing the odds.

1544 - Pierre Turrel's doomsday calculation #2. (Randi p. 239)

1555 - Around the year 1400, the French theologian Pierre d'Ailly wrote that 6845 years of human history had already passed. Using the "day as a thousand years" calculation. The "week of years theory places the 7th day or 7000 years at 1555. (McIver #72)

1556 - Jul 22, 1556 - A Swiss medical student, Felix Platter, writes about a rumor that on Magdalene's Day the world would end. (Weber p.68, p.249)

1583 - Apr 28, 1583 - Astrologer Richard Harvey predicts The Second Coming of Christ would take place at noon, on this day.

A conjunction of Jupiter and Saturn would occur. Numerous astrologers in London had predicted the end. (Skinner p.27, Weber p.93) (A conjunction is when two planets align, according to how they appear in the sky. They must appear within a few degrees of one another.)

1584 - Cyprian Leowitz, an astrologer, predicted the end would occur in 1584. (Randi p.239, McIver #105)

1588 - The end of the world according to the sage Johann Müller (Also known as Regiomontanus – Latin for King's Mountain). He was a mathematician and astrologer. (Randi p. 239)

1600 - Martin Luther believed that the End would occur no later than 1600. (Weber p.66)

1603 - Dominican monk Tomasso Campanella believed that the sun would collide with the Earth. (Weber p.83)

1623 - Eustachius Poyssel, a numerologist used his occult art to calculate 1623 as the year of the end of the world. (McIver #125)

1624 - Feb 1, 1624 - The same astrologers who predicted the deluge of February 1, 1524 recalculated the date to February 1, 1624 after their first prophecy failed. (Randi p.236-237) This way they would not have to be alive to endure another embarrassment.

1648 - Using the Kabbalah, a type of Hebrew numerology, Sabbatai Zevi, a rabbi from Smyrna, Turkey, predicted the Messiah's coming would be in 1648. There would be signs and miracles. People may have been excited, that is until he revealed that the Messiah would be Zevi himself. (Randi p.239, Festinger)

Joseph Lumpkin

1654 – The sighting of a nova in 1572 brought physician Helisaeus Roeslin of Alsace, to claim the world would end in 1654 in a firestorm. (Randi p.240)

1657 - A group calling themselves "The Fifth Monarchy Men," predicted the apocalyptic battle and the overthrow of the Antichrist would take place between 1655 and 1657. They were what we would call a fundamentalist group who attempted to take over Parliament. They wanted to make the country a theocracy. The problem with theocracy is that the ruling party gets to determine what God's laws are. (Kyle p.67)

1658 - In his writings called, "The Book of Prophecies," Christopher Columbus claimed that the world was created in 5343BC, and would last 7000 years. Assuming no year zero, that means the end would come in 1658. Columbus was influenced by Pierre d'Ailly. (McIver #77)

1660 - Joseph Mede claimed that the Antichrist appeared way back in 456, and the end would come in 1660. This meant there was a 1204-year spread from start to finish. (McIver #147)

1666 – Many times there are no reasonable explanation of the dates reached by the prophets. In this case we can see the reasoning, although it is somewhat dubious. The date is 1000 (millennium) + 666 (number of the Beast). The date seems right because it followed a period of war in England. Londoners feared that 1666 would be the end of the world. Their fears were heightened by The Great Fire of London in 1666. (Schwartz p.87, Kyle p.67-68)

1666 - Rabi Sabbatai Zevi recalculated the coming of the Messiah to 1666. He was arrested for inciting public fear, and given the choice of converting to Islam or execution. He wisely elected to convert. (Festinger)

1673 - The prophecy of the group having failed the first time, Deacon William Aspinwall, a leader of the Fifth Monarchy movement, claimed the Millennium would begin by this year. (Abanes p.209, McIver #174)

1688 - John Napier, the mathematician who discovered logarithms, calculated this as the year of doom. (Weber p.92)

1689 - Pierre Jurieu, a Camisard prophet, predicted that Judgement Day would occur in 1689. The Camisards were Huguenots of the Languedoc region of southern France. (Kyle p.70)

1694 - Anglican rector John Mason calculated this year as the beginning of the Millennium. (Kyle p.72)

1694 - Drawing from theology and astrology, German prophet Johann Jacob Zimmerman determined that the world would end in the fall of 1694. Zimmerman gathered a group of pilgrims and made plans to go to America to welcome Jesus back to Earth. However, he died in February of that year, on the very day of departure. Johannes Kelpius took over leadership of the cult, which was known as Woman in the Wilderness. These were truly ladies in waiting. (Cohen p.19-20) (Kyle p.66)

1697 - The beginning of the Millennium, according to Anglican rector Thomas Beverly. (Kyle p.72, McIver #224)

1697 - The notorious witch hunter Cotton Mather of New England claimed the end of the world would be in 1697. After the prediction failed, he revised the date two more times. (Abanes p.338) (Does this mean he was "witchy – washy?")

1700 - John Napier was a physicist, astronomer, astrologer, mathematician, and the inventor of logarithms. This date is his second doomsday calculation, based on the Book of Daniel. (Weber p.92)

1700 - In his 1642 book, "The Personal Reign of Christ Upon Earth," a Fifth Monarchy Man, Henry Archer, set this as the date of the Second Coming. (McIver #158)

1705 - The Camisard group got busy predicting, and could not stop. 1705 was just the first of many predictions for the end of the world. (Kyle p.70)

1706 - The end, according to some Camisard prophets. Strike two!(Kyle p.70)

1708 - The end, according to some Camisard prophets. Strike three! (Kyle p.70)

1716 - Cotton Mather's end-of-the-world prediction #2. (Abanes p.338)

1719 - Apr 5, 1719 - The calculated return of a comet was to wipe out the Earth, according to Jacques Bernoulli, of the famous mathematical Bernoulli family. (Randi p.240-241)

1734 - Cardinal Nicolas of Cusa claimed doomsday was to come between 1700 and 1734. This was predicted in the 15th century. (Weber p.82, McIver #73)

1736 - Cotton Mather's end-of-the-world prediction #3. This guy never stops. He is the energizer bunny of doomsday prophets. (Abanes p.338) (Remember – this guy was the witch burner. If anyone else had missed like this he would have torched them.)

1736 - Oct 13, 1736 - William Whitson predicted that London would meet its doom by flood on this day, prompting many Londoners to gather in boats on the Thames. (Randi)

(Remember the rainbow, guys... God's promise not to drown the world...?)

1757 - In a vision, angels supposedly informed mystic Emanuel Swedenborg that the world would end in 1757. Few took him seriously. (Randi p.241, Weber p.104) Must have been those Swedish meatballs.

1761 - Apr 5, 1761 - William Bell claimed the world would be destroyed by earthquake on this day. There had been an earthquake on February 8 and another on March 8. He figured those were warnings. Kind of the one-two-three of earthquakes. The paranoia of Londoners gave way to anger and he was tossed into Bedlam, the London insane asylum that gave us that wonderful word. However, being that it was London, they did the deed in a very civilized manner. (Randi p.241)

1763 - Feb 28, 1763 - Methodist George Bell foresaw the end of the world on this date. (Weber p.102)

1780 - May 19, 1780 Smoke from large-scale forest fires to the west darkened New England skies for several hours. Being the nervous group that they were, the New Englanders believed that Judgment Day had arrived. (Abanes p.217)

1789 - Antichrist will reveal himself, according to 14th century Cardinal Pierre d'Ailly. (Weber p.59)

1790 - The Second Coming of Christ, according to Irishman Francis Dobbs. (Schwartz p.181)

1792 - The end of the world according to the Shakers. (Abanes p.338) The Shakers were originally located in England in 1747, in the home of Mother Ann Lee. The parent group was called the Quakers, which originated in the 17th century. Both groups believed that everybody could find God within him or herself, rather than through the organized church. Shakers tended to be more emotional in their worship. They are strict believers in celibacy, hence, their small numbers.

1794 - Charles Wesley, brother of Methodist Church founder John Wesley, predicted Doomsday would be in 1794. (Source: Ontario Consultants on Religious Tolerance)

1795 - English sailor Richard Brothers, calling himself "God's Almighty Nephew," predicted the Millennium would begin between 1793 and 1795. He expected the ten lost tribes of Israel would return. He also said God told him he would become king of England. He was shown the front door of the local insane asylum. (Kyle p.73, McIver #301)

1801 - Pierre Turrel's doomsday calculation - Strike three! The first one targeted 1537. (Randi p. 239)

1805 - Earthquake would wipe out the world in 1805, followed by an age of everlasting peace when God will be known by all. Presbyterian minister Christopher Love, was beheaded later. (Schwartz p.101)

1814 - Pierre Turrel's doomsday calculation. Fourth attempt... Please stop... just stop! The third attempt was in 1801. (Randi p. 239)

1814 - Dec 25, 1814 - This one is truly strange. A 64-year-old virgin prophet named Joanna Southcott claimed she would give birth to Jesus on Christmas Day. Witnesses claimed that she did appear pregnant. She died on Christmas Day. An autopsy proved that she was not pregnant. (Skinner p.109)

1820 - Oct 14, 1820 – Following on the heels of Southcott's death, a follower, John Turner, claimed the world would end. The prophecy failed and John Wroe took over leadership of the cult. (Randi p.241-242)

1836 - John Wesley, the founder of the Methodist, foresaw the Millennium beginning in 1836. He said the sign would be that the Beast of Revelation would rise from the sea. (McIver #269)

1843 - Harriet Livermore predicted Christ would return to the earth on this date. (McIver #699)

1843 - Apr 28, 1843 - Belief among William Miller's followers spawned gossip that the Second Coming would take place on this day. (Festinger p.16)

1843 - Dec 31, 1843 - Millerites expected Jesus to return at the end of 1843. (Festinger p.16)

1844 - Mar 21, 1844 - William Miller, leader of the Millerites, predicted Christ would return sometime between March 21, 1843 and March 21, 1844. He gathered a following of thousands of devotees. After the failed prophecy the cult experienced a crisis. They re-grouped and began reinterpreting the prophecy. This is more revisionist history of the church. (Gould p.49, Festinger p.16-17)

1844 - Oct 22, 1844 - Rev. Samuel S. Snow, an influential Millerite, predicted the Second Coming on this day. The date was soon accepted by Miller himself. On that day, the Millerites gathered on a hilltop to await the coming of Jesus. After the inevitable no-show, the event became known as the "Great Disappointment." It is said that Snow sold "ascension garments" to the waiting host and made a lot of cash on the deal. (Gould p.49, Festinger p.17)

1845 - The remaining members of Miller's cult, now called the Second Adventists, and the forerunners of the Seventh Day Adventists, claimed this would be the Second Coming. (Kyle p.91)

1846 – Obviously, the first time failed, so this is another Second Coming according to the Second Adventists. (Kyle p.91)

1847 - Harriet Livermore's Parousia prediction #2. (McIver #699)

1847 - Aug 7, 1847   "Father" George Rapp, founder of a sect known as the Harmonists (aka the Rappites,) established a commune in Economy, Pennsylvania. He was convinced that Jesus would return before his death. His speech on his deathbed was moving - "If I did not know that the dear Lord meant I should present you all to him, I should think my last moment's come." Rapp died before making the introduction. (Cohen p.23, Thompson p.283, Encyclopedia Britannica) (Thus, the first Rapp group began and ended.

1849 - Yet another Second Coming according to the Second Adventists. (Kyle p.91)

1851 - AND, another Second Coming according to the Second Adventists. (Kyle p.91)

1856 - The Book of Revelation speaks of the King of the North invading Israel. The Crimean War in 1853-56 was seen by some as the Battle of Armageddon. Russia had planned to take control of Palestine from the Ottoman Empire. (McIver #437)

1862 - John Cumming of the Scottish National Church proclaimed the end of 6000 years since Creation. The world would end and the 1000 year reign of Jesus would begin. (Abanes p.283)

1863 - In 1823 Southcott, follower John Wroe, attempted and failed to walk on water. He then underwent a public circumcision. Many men may have been embarrassed. He then calculated that the Millennium would begin in 1863. (Skinner p.109)

1867 - The Anglican minister Michael Paget Baxter was an obsessive - compulsive date setter. Writer and philosopher, Charles Taylor, of the 19th century documented Baxter's follies as he predicted the End of the world. (McIver #348)

1868 - Michael Baxter claimed the Battle of Armageddon would take place this year. (Abanes p.338, McIver #349)

1869 – Baxter is back predicting another end. (McIver #350)

1870 - Jun 28, 1870 - France would fall, Jerusalem would be the center of the world, followed by Christ's millennial reign on Earth. This according to Irvin Moore's book "The Final Destiny of Man." (McIver #746)

1872 – Remember Baxter? He predicted another Armageddon in 1871-72 or thereabouts. (McIver #351)

1874 - The end of the world according to the Jehovah's Witnesses. This is the first in a long, long, long list of failed doomsday prophecies by this group. (Gould p.50, Kyle p.93)

1876 - The Parousia according to the newly formed Seventh Day Adventists, a group founded by former Millerites. (Abanes p.339)

1878 - You will lose count if you aren't careful. The end of the world according to the Jehovah's Witnesses. (Kyle p.93)

1880 - Thomas Rawson Birks in his book First Elements of Sacred Prophecy determined that the end of the world would be in 1880 by employing the time-honored Great Week theory. (McIver #371)

1881 – Redundant! The end of the world according to the Jehovah's Witnesses. (Kyle p.93)

1881 - The end of the world according to some pyramidologists, using the inch per year method. (Randi p.242)

1881 - 16th century prophetess Mother Shipton is said to have written the couplet:

The world to an end shall come
In eighteen hundred and eighty one.

In 1873, it was revealed that the couplet was a forgery by Charles Hindley, who published Mother Shipton's prophecies in 1862. People continued to buy and buy off on the book. (Schwartz p.122, Randi p.242-243)

1890 - Northern Paiute leader Wovoka predicted the Millennium. The prediction came from a trance he experienced during a solar eclipse in 1889. Wovoka was a practitioner of the Ghost Dance cult, a hybrid of apocalyptic Christianity and American Indian mysticism. (Gould p.56-57, p.69) As a note: Many spiritualists claim we all have American Indian guides in the spirit world. If one does the math it is immediately clear there aren't enough dead American Indians to go around.

1891 - In 1835 Joseph Smith, founder of Mormonism, foresaw the Second Coming taking place in 56 years' time, or about 1891. (Source: exmormon.org) As a side note, Smith also looked into a magic bag with stones in it to make his predictions. One such prediction was that the people of the moon were nice, conservative folk, who dressed in the Quaker fashion. (If someone these days were to stick his head into a bag and say things like this, he would be arrested for "huffing" glue.)

1895 - Reverend Robert Reid of Erie, Pennsylvania predicted and waited for The Millennium... and waited, and waited. (Weber p.176)

1896 – Baxter's back! Michael Baxter wrote a book entitled, "The End of This Age," in which he predicted the Rapture in 1896. According to Rev. Baxter, only 144,000 true Christians were to take the trip. (Thompson p.121) Recall that the rapture was not written about until the 1790's.

1899 - Charles A.L. Totten predicted that 1899 was a possible date for the end of the world. (McIver #924) Every day is a possible date.

1900 - Father Pierre Lachèze foresaw Doomsday occurring in 1900, eight years after the Temple in Jerusalem was to be rebuilt. (Weber p.136)

1900 - Followers of Brazilian ascetic Antonio Conselheiro expected the end to come by the year 1900. (Thompson p.125-126)

1900 - Nov 13, 1900 Over 100 members of the Russian cult Brothers and Sisters of the Red Death committed suicide, expecting the world to end on this day. (Sources: Portuguese article)

1901 – The sect of Catholic Apostolic Church claimed that Jesus would return by the time the last of its 12 founding members died. The last member died in 1901. (Boyer p.87)

1901 – Baxter's back. Rev. Michael Baxter foresaw the end of the world in 1901 in his book "The End of This Age: About the End of This Century." (Thompson p.121)

1908 – March 12, 1908 - Once again, it's Michael Baxter. In his book, "Future Wonders of Prophecy," he wrote that the Rapture was to take place on March 12, 1903 between 2pm and 3pm, and Armageddon was to take place on this day, which is after the Tribulation. One could argue the need to catch away the church after leaving it through the tribulations. (McIver #353)

1908 - Oct 1908 - Pennsylvanian grocery store owner Lee T. Spangler claimed that the world would meet a fiery end during this month. Possibly he planned to smoke some ribs. (Abanes p.339)

1910 - One of the many manic times for the J.W.'s. The end of the world according to the Jehovah's Witnesses. (Kyle p.93) This, of course, was followed by a period of depression and a dose of Prozac.

1910 - May 18, 1910 - The arrival of Halley's Comet would have many believing that cyanide gas from the comet's tail would poison the Earth's atmosphere. Con artists took advantage of people's fears by selling "comet pills" to make people immune to the toxins. There is a sucker born every minute. (Weber p.196-198, Abanes p.339)

1911 - 19th century Scottish astronomer and pyramidologist Charles Piazzi Smyth measured the Great Pyramid of Giza and converted inches to years, concluding that the Second Coming would occur between 1892 and 1911. (Cohen p.94)

1914 - Oct 1, 1914 – Yet another amazing prediction by The Jehovah's Witnesses. They viewed World War I as the Battle of Armageddon. (Skinner p.102)

1915 - The beginning of the Millennium according to John Chilembwe, fundamentalist leader of a rebellion in Nyasaland (present-day Malawi). (Gould p.54-55, p.69) When the world didn't end he chose to force change.

1918 - The end of the world according to the Jehovah's Witnesses. For the sake of your herbivorous lions, please stop! (Kyle p.93)

1918 - Dec 17, 1919 - According to meteorologist Albert Porta, a conjunction of six planets on this date would cause a magnetic current to "pierce the sun, cause great explosions of flaming gas, and eventually engulf the Earth." Panic erupted in many countries around the world because of this prediction, and some even committed suicide. A similar prediction surfaced again in the 1970's regarding a planetary alignment in 1982. This was known as the Jupiter effect. (Abanes p.60-61)

1925 - The end of the world according to the Jehovah's Witnesses. You must be kidding! (Kyle p.93)

1925 - Feb 13, 1925 Margaret Rowan claimed the angel Gabriel appeared to her in a vision and told her that the world would end at midnight on this date, which was Friday the 13th. (Abanes p.45)

1928 - Spring 1928 - J.B. Dimbleby calculated that the Millennium would begin in the spring of 1928. The true end of the world, he claimed, wouldn't take pace until around the year 3000. (McIver #495)

1934 – The final battle was to begin in 1934 according to Chicago preacher Nathan Cohen Beskin, as he stated in 1931. (Abanes p.280)

1935 - Sep 1935 - In 1931, Wilbur Glen Voliva announced, "the world is going to go 'puff' and disappear in September, 1935." (Abanes p.287) Well… ok then.

1936 - Herbert W. Armstrong, founder of the Worldwide Church of God, told members of his church that the Rapture would take place in 1936. Only his true followers would be saved. After the prophecy failed, he changed the date three more times. I suppose this was one of the things that would later lead his son, Ted, to separate from the church and start his own cult. Later, Ted would love his secretary more than the church or his wife. (Shaw p.99)

1938 - Gus McKey wrote a pamphlet claiming the 6000th year since Creation would come between 1931 and 1938, signifying the end of the world. (Abanes p.283)

1941 - The end of the world according to the Jehovah's Witnesses. It just makes you angry after a while. (Shaw p.72)

1943 - Herbert W. Armstrong's second Rapture prediction. (Shaw p.99)

1945 - Sep 21, 1945 - In 1938 a minister named Long had a vision of a mysterious hand writing the number 1945 and a voice saying the world would be destroyed at 5:33pm on September 21. His prophecy failed, and he never had his eyesight or hearing checked. (Source: Portuguese article)

1947 - In 1889, John Ballou Newbrough (Known to himself as "America's Greatest Prophet") foresaw the destruction of all nations and the beginning of post-apocalyptic anarchy in 1947. I guess he wasn't such a great prophet after all. Newbrough was the founder of the Oahspe cult. (Randi p.243)

1952 - Billy Graham was speaking in 1950 when he announced, "We may have another year, maybe two years. Then I believe it is going to be over." (Source: Article by Hugo McCord)

1953 - Jan 9, 1953 – The end of the world, according to Agnes Carlson, the founder of a Canadian cult called the Sons of Light. (Source: Portuguese article)

1953 - Aug 1953 – In his book "The Great Pyramid, Its Divine Message," Pyramidologist, David Davidson, wrote that the Millennium would begin sometime during this month. (Source: article by John Baskette)

1954 - Dec 21, 1954 - Dorothy Martin (a.k.a. Marian Keech, aka Sister Thedra), leader of a cult called Brotherhood of the Seven Rays, also known as The Seekers claimed the world was to be destroyed by terrible flooding on this date. Martin claimed to channel an extra-terrestrial, who gave her knowledge of impending natural disasters. Her group was small, consisting of only a few firm believers. What made this case special was that the group allowed psychologists in to observe the group's reaction to the outcome. This case became the subject of Leon Festinger's book When Prophecy Fails, the classic, ground-breaking case study of cognitive dissonance and the effect that failed prophecy has on "true believers." (Festinger, Heard p.46-48, McIver #1949)

1957 - Apr 23, 1957 According to Jehovah Witness leader, Mihran Ask, a pastor from California, "Sometime between April 16 and 23, 1957, Armageddon will sweep the world! Millions of persons will perish in its flames and the land will be scorched." (Watchtower, Oct 15, 1958, p.613) Should we count this as a J.W. prophecy?

1958 - David A. Latimer, in his book "Opening of the Seven Seals and the Half Hour of Silence," predicted that the Second Coming would take place in 1956 or 1958, right after the Battle of Armageddon. (McIver #1501)

1959 - Apr 22, 1959 Victor Houteff, founder of the Davidians -- an offshoot of the Seventh Day Adventists -- prophesied that the End would be coming soon, but he never set a date. After his death, however, his widow Florence prophesied that the Rapture would take place on April 22, 1959. Hundreds of faithful gathered at Mount Carmel outside Waco to await the big moment, but it was not to be. (Thompson p.289) The cult continued fairly intact until 1981 when Vernon Howell joined the Branch Davidians. Howell heard from God and began to take over the cult. His authority and influence grew. Twenty-four-year-old Howell wedded fourteen-year-old Rachel Jones. Soon afterward Howell was forced out of Mt. Carmel with his wife. They moved to Waco, Texas. The group split and members of the group begin to live under Howell's leadership. Howell married thirteen-year-old Karen Doyle and twelve-year-old Michelle Jones (Rachel's little sister) as his third "wife." In spring of 1990 Vernon Howell changed his name to David Koresh. Koresh's temperament became increasingly volatile and irrational. He began preaching about a great war and the end of days. He claimed the government would attack. He had begun stockpiling weapons and provisions. In May-June 1992 the Bureau of Alcohol, Tobacco, and Firearms (ATF) launched its investigation of Koresh and the Davidians. Raids followed. Six Davidians died and four ATF agents were killed. Numerous individuals on both sides were injured. Raid turned to siege and between seventy-five and eighty-five Davidians died in the flames, including approximately twenty-five children. Nine members survived.

1960 - Pyramidologist Charles Piazzi Smyth (see the 1911 entry) claimed that the Millennium would begin no later than 1960. (Source: article by John Baskette)

1962 - Feb 4, 1962 - Psychic and astrologer, Jeanne Dixon, calculated a planetary alignment on this day. It was going to destroy the world. The Antichrist was to be born the following day. (Abanes p.340) Jeanne always had an eye toward the theatrical. That's ok, until you start believing your own press.

1966 – Second miss by The Nation of Islam. They claimed that between 1965 and 1966, an apocalyptic battle would occur, resulting in the fall of the United States. (Kyle p.162) All of the "white devils" would be killed.

1967 - The establishment of the Kingdom of Heaven, according to Rev. Sun Myung Moon. (Kyle p.148) Moon claimed to be the messiah.

1967 - Jim Jones, of the People's Temple, had visions that a nuclear holocaust was to take place in 1967. (Weber p.214) "Can you say kool aid?"

1967 - Aug 20, 1967 - George Van Tassel, who claimed to have channeled an alien named Ashtar, proclaimed this time would be the beginning of the third woe of the Apocalypse, during which the southeastern US would be destroyed by a Soviet nuclear attack. (Alnor p.145) (And I thought that Ashtar was the other name for Chemosh, the Moabite god who demanded child sacrifice.)

1967 - Dec 25, 1967 - Danish cult leader Knud Weiking claimed that a being named Orthon was speaking to him, saying that there would be a nuclear war by Christmas 1967 that would disturb the Earth's orbit. His followers built a survival bunker in preparation for this catastrophe. Just as a note, if the earth's orbit is changed by only .5%, life as we know it would cease since temperatures would not support life. Bunkers would not work very well.

1969 - Aug 9, 1969 - Second Coming of Christ, according to George Williams, leader of the Morrisites, a 19th century branch of Mormonism. (Robbins p.77)

1969 - Nov 22, 1969 - The Day of Judgment, according to Robin McPherson, who supposedly channeled an alien named Ox-Ho. (Shaw p.154)

The 1960's must have brought out the lunatics. Everyone was channeling someone or some thing. Ever notice that no one channels Mr. Nobody?

1972 - Herbert W. Armstrong's Rapture prediction. (Shaw p.99) Armstrong pumped up his followers, telling them that only they know the truth and will go to heaven. Then he predicts the end so the flock would gather closer, be more devoted, and give more.

1973 - David Berg, also known as Moses David, leader of the Children of God, also known as the Family of Love, or just "The Family", predicted in his publication "The End time News" that the United States would be destroyed by the Comet Kohoutek in 1973. (McIver #2095)

1975 - The end of the world according to the Jehovah's Witnesses. (Kyle p.93) In this period of time I saw several J.W.'s that I knew run up huge credit card debt. When I asked about their reasoning I was informed they were not worried about paying it back since they would not be here. I also pointed out that in the event they would be correct, the debts they left would force those left to pay higher rates. That seemed to be our problem, not theirs. Bankruptcies followed for many J.W.s.

1975 - Herbert W. Armstrong's Rapture prediction number 4. (Shaw p.99) It is amazing that these guys have followers, barring those with memory problems.

1975 - The Rapture, so said preacher Charles Taylor. This begins a compulsive streak of predictions for Mr. Taylor. (Abanes p.99)

1976 - Charles Taylor's Rapture prediction number 2. (Abanes p.99)

1977 - John Wroe (the Southcottian who had himself publicly circumcised in 1823) set 1977 as the date of Armageddon. (Randi p.243)

1977 - William Branham predicted that the Rapture would take place no later than 1977. Just before this, Los Angeles was to fall into the sea after an earthquake, the Vatican would achieve dictatorial powers over the world, and all of Christianity would become unified. (Babinski p.277) All those buying surfside homes in Arizona were disappointed.

1977 - Pyramidologist Adam Rutherford expected that the Millennium would begin in 1977. (Source: article by John Baskette)

1978 - In his book, "The Doomsday Globe," John Strong drew on scriptures, pyramidology, pole shift theory, young-earth creationism and other mysticism to conclude that Doomsday would come in 1978. (McIver #3237)

1980 - In his book, "Armageddon 198?", author, Stephen D. Swihart, predicted the End would occur sometime in the 1980s.

1980 - Charles Taylor's Rapture prediction number 3. (Abanes p.99)

1980 - Apr 1, 1980 - Radio preacher, Willie Day Smith, of Irving, Texas, claimed this would be the Second Coming. (Source: What About the Second Coming of Christ?)

1980 - Apr 29, 1980 -Leland Jensen, founder of the Bahá'ís "Under the Provisions of the Covenant", which is a small sect that mixes Bahá'í teachings with pyramidology and Bible prophecy, predicted that a nuclear holocaust would occur on this day, killing a third of the world's population. After the prophecy failed, Jensen rationalized that this date was merely the beginning of the Tribulation. (Robbins p.73)

1981 – Rev. Sun Myung Moon again announces the establishment of the Kingdom of Heaven. (Kyle p.148) I guess God didn't hear him the first time.

1981 - Charles Taylor's Rapture prediction number 4. (Abanes p.99)

1981 - Pastor Chuck Smith, founder of Calvary Chapel, wrote in his book "Future Survival," "I'm convinced that the Lord is coming for His Church before the end of 1981." Smith arrived at his calculation by adding 40 (one "Biblical generation") to 1948 (the year of Israel's statehood) and subtracting 7 for the Tribulation. (Abanes p.326) Way to go, Chuck!

1981 - June 28, 1981 - Rev. Bill Maupin, leader of a small Tuscon, AZ, sect named Lighthouse Gospel Tract Foundation, preached to his congregation, "rapture day was coming." Those who were saved would be "spirited aloft like helium balloons." Some 50 people gathered in a Millerite-like fashion. August 7, 1981. When his June 28 prediction failed, Bill Maupin claimed that doomsday would take place 40 days later. Maupin said that just as Noah's ark was gradually raised to safety over a period of 40 days, the same would happen to the world. (Source: Philosophy and the Scientific Method by Ronald C. Pine and Interviews with former members.) Have you ever noticed that the more words in a church's title the more whacked they can be?

1982 - Charles Taylor's Rapture prediction number 5. (Abanes p.99) Number five? Number five! GEEEZ!

1982 - Using the Jupiter Effect to support his thesis, Canadian prophet Doug Clark, claimed there would be earthquakes and fires that would kill millions. First, Jesus was to return and rapture Christians away from the Tribulation (Abanes p.91)

1982 - Emil Gaverluk of the Southwest Radio Church suggested that the Jupiter Effect would pull Mars out of orbit and send it careening into the Earth. (Abanes p.100-101)

1982 - Mar 10, 1982 – The book, "The Jupiter Effect," by John Gribbin and Stephen Plagemann, stated that when the planets lined up, their combined gravitational forces were supposed to bring the end of the world. The book sold well and the theory inspired several apocalyptic prophecies. (Abanes p.62)

1982 - Jun 25, 1982 – One of the most persistent and greatest hoaxes of the twentieth century is that of Maitreya and his prophet, Benjamin Crème. Crème is a British artist and founder of Tara Center. Over the years he predicted Maitreya's arrival on the world scene several times. He finally set a date of April 25, 1982. Of course once a date is set humiliation is not far behind. Supposedly Maitreya rung him up to tell him it just wasn't time yet.

Some history will help here. The Prophecy of Maitreya, stating that gods, men, and other beings will worship him implies that he is a teacher and a type of messiah. A quote from a Buddhist text reads,

" (all) will lose their doubts, and the torrents of their cravings will be cut off: free from all misery they will manage to cross the ocean of becoming; and, as a result of Maitreya's teachings, they will lead a holy life. No longer will they regard anything as their own, they will have no possession, no gold or silver, no home, no relatives! But they will lead the holy life of chastity under Maitreya's guidance. They will have torn the net of the passions, they will manage to enter into trances, and theirs will be an abundance of joy and happiness, for they will lead a holy life under Maitreya's guidance." (Trans. in Conze 1959:241)

Maitreya's coming is characterized by a number of physical events. The oceans are predicted to decrease in size, allowing Maitreya to cross them freely. Apparently this Messiah can't teleport or fly.

The event will also allow the unveiling of the "true" path of how to live. A new world will be built on these precepts. The coming ends a low point of human existence between the Gautama Buddha and Maitreya.

Crème's propaganda web page reads, "He has been expected for generations by all of the major religions. Christians know him as the Christ, and expect his imminent return. Jews await him as the Messiah; Hindus look for the coming of Krishna; Buddhists expect him as Maitreya Buddha; and Muslims anticipate the Imam Mahdi or Messiah."

Crème also took out an ad in the Los Angeles Times proclaiming "THE CHRIST IS NOW HERE", referring to the coming of Maitreya within 2 months. Crème supposedly received the messages from Maitreya through "channeling." (Grosso p.7, Oropeza p.155)

1982 - Fall 1982 - In the late '70s, Pat Robertson predicted the end of the world on a May, 1980 broadcast of the 700 Club. "I guarantee you by the end of 1982 there is going to be a judgment on the world," he said. (Boyer p.138)

1983 - Apocalyptic war between the U.S. and the Soviet Union, according to "The End Times News Digest." (Shaw p.182)

1983 - Charles Taylor's Rapture prediction number 6. (Abanes p.99)

1984 - Oct 2, 1984 - The end of the world according to the Jehovah's Witnesses. (Shermer p.203, Kyle p.91) You have got to love the unashamed, amazing chutzpah of these guys. The reasons they arrive at their dates show an amount of pure arrogance that is frightening. Since they believe that only 144,000 people will occupy heaven and since only members of their sect will make the cut, then when their membership reached 144,000 the rapture must occur. When that did not work, they reasoned that some were members but not true believers. Since money talks maybe the 144,000 will be made up of those who follow the rules and tithe. How ridiculous.

1985 - The end of the world according to Lester Sumrall in his book, "I Predict 1985." (Abanes p.99, 341)

1985 - Charles Taylor's Rapture prediction number 7. (Abanes p.99) It is time for a recap on Taylor. 1980 - Prophecy promoter Charles Taylor predicted the millennial reign of Christ to begin in 1995. He predicted the rapture would be in 1975, then in 1976, 1980, 1982, 1983, 1985, 1986, 1987, and, of course, 1989.

1985 - The Socialist National Aryan People's Party was convinced that Jesus would return in 1985. (Weber p.209) That's right, people. If you are white you can take the flight.

1985 - Mar 25, 1985 - The beginning of World War III, as prophesied by Vern Grimsley of the doomsday cult Family of God Foundation. This cult was a small offshoot of the Urantia Foundation, a loosely organized religious group that uses as its scripture a tedious 2000 page tome called the Urantia Book.

According to the on-line source, the Sceptic's Dictionary, "In short, the UB is over 2,000 pages of "revelations" from superhuman beings which "correct" the errors and omissions of the Bible. "Urantia" is the name these alleged super humans gave to our planet. According to these super mortal beings, Earth is the 606th planet in Satania which is in Norlatiadek which is in Nebadon which is in Orvonton which revolves around Havona, all of which revolves around the center of infinity where God dwells. Others aren't so sure of the celestial origin of these writings. Matthew Block, for example, has identified hundreds of passages in the UB that are clearly based on human sources, but which are not given specific attribution. William Sadler, (the main author), admits on page 1343 that he used many human sources.

1987 - Charles Taylor's Rapture prediction number 8. (Abanes p.99) I thought about simply listing the prophecies from this guy in one line, but thought it better to place them in the time line simply for the humor.

1987 - Apr 29, 1987 Leland Jensen of the Bahá'ís "Under the Provisions of the Covenant" predicted that Halley's Comet would be pulled into Earth's orbit on April 29, 1986, and chunks of the comet would pelt the Earth for a year. The gravitational force of the comet would cause great earthquakes, and on April 29, 1987, the comet itself would crash into the

Earth wreaking widespread destruction. When the prophecies failed, Jensen rationalized the failure as follows: "A spiritual stone hit the earth." (Robbins p.73, 78) What?

1987   Charles Taylor's Rapture prediction number 9. (Abanes p.99) One must wonder what Taylor thinks when he reads lists like this one and sees his name over and over, and over, and over, and....

1987 - Aug 17, 1987 - Everyone must visualize whirled peas. This is the year of the "Harmonic Convergence," bringing world peace. New Age author José Argüelles claimed that Armageddon would take place unless 144,000 people gathered in certain places in the world in order to "resonate in harmony" on this day. (McIver #2023, Kyle p.156, Wojcik p.207)

1988 – The reports of our death have been greatly exaggerated. Hal Lindsey's bestseller, "The Late, Great Planet Earth," calls for the Rapture in 1988, reasoning that it was 40 years (one Biblical generation) after Israel gained statehood. (Abanes p.85)

1988 - Charles Taylor's Rapture prediction number ten. (Abanes p.99)

1988 - Canadian prophet Doug Clark suggested 1988 as the date of the Rapture, in his book "Final Shockwaves to Armageddon." (Abanes p.91)

1988 - David Webber and Noah Hutchings of the Southwest Radio Church suggested that the Rapture would take place "possibly in 1987 or 1988." (Abanes p.101)

1988 - TV prophet J.R. Church (got to love this name for a preacher) in his book, "Hidden Prophecies in the Psalms," used a theory that each of the Psalms referred to a year in the 20th century. This would mean that Psalm 1 represents the events in 1901, and so on. Why the twentieth century was so special can only be due to the fact Mr. Church was living in it. The Battle of Armageddon would take place in 1994. (Abanes p. 103)

1988 - Colin Deal wrote a book entitled, "Christ Returns by 1988: 101 Reasons Why." (Oropeza p.175) There is one reason why not. It is because no one knows the day.

1988 - Sep 13, 1988 - Edgar C. Whisenant lightened the wallets of many a believer with his best-selling book, "88 Reasons Why The Rapture Will Be In 1988." He predicted the Rapture between September 11 and 13 (Rosh Hashanah). After Whisenant's prediction failed, he insisted that the Rapture would take place at 10:55 am on September 15.
After that prediction failed, he released another book: "The Final Shout: Rapture Report 1989." When that prediction failed, Whisenant pushed the date of the Rapture forward to October 3. (Kyle p.121, Abanes p.93, 94) I think they were written around the same time.

1989 - Charles Taylor's Rapture prediction number 11. (Abanes p.99) Are you keeping track of these, because, if this guy lives long enough, sooner or later he will get it right. The problem with apocalyptic prophecies is if you do get it right, there will be no one left to know it.

1989 - In his 1968 book, "Guide to Survival," Salem Kirban used Bishop Ussher's calculations to predict that 1989 would be the year of the Rapture. (Abanes p.283)

1989 - In 1978, Oklahoma City's Southwest Radio Church published a pamphlet entitled God's Timetable for the 1980s in which were listed prophecies for each year of the 1980s, culminating with Christ's return and the establishment of his kingdom on Earth in 1989. With the exception of a couple of predictable astronomical events, none of the predictions came true.

1990 - Baptist preacher Peter Ruckman predicted that the Rapture would come round about the year 1990. (Source: article by Thomas Williamson)

1990 - The Jupiter Effect strikes again. Writer Kai Lok Chan, a Singaporean prophet, foresaw Jesus Christ returning sometime between 1986 and 1990. Armageddon (a war between the US and USSR) would take place between 1984 and 1988. He argued that the Jupiter Effect corroborated his claims. (McIver #2195)

1990 - Apr 23, 1990 - Elizabeth Clare Prophet, leader of the Church Universal and Triumphant, foresaw nuclear devastation and the end of most of the human race on this day, and convinced her followers to sell their property and move with her to a ranch in Montana. (Kyle p.156, Grosso p.7) In doing research, I have never heard such dribble as when I was instructed in her doctrine. According to E.C.P. Jesus is now a non-player. Michael has taken his place and is, of course, talking to her.

1991 - The Rapture, according to fundamentalist author Reginald Dunlop. (Shaw p.180)

1991 - Louis Farrakhan declared that the Gulf War would be the "War of Armageddon which is the final war." (Abanes p.307)

1991 - Mar 31, 1991 - An Australian cult looked forward to the Second Coming at 9:00 am on this day. They believed that Jesus would return through Sydney Harbor! (Source: Knowing the Day and the Hour)

1992 - Charles Taylor's Rapture prediction number 12. (Abanes p.99) Did I mention that he is the energizer bunny of Armageddon predictions?

1992 - Apr 26, 1992 - It was on April 26, 1989, Doug Clark announced on Trinity Broadcasting Network's show, " Praise the Lord," that World War III would begin within 3 years. (Abanes p.92) It was around this period of time I was employed at one of the TBN down link transmitters as assistant engineer. Many times I received mail from little old ladies saying that they were giving their last few pennies on Earth to further the Kingdom of God. Pink hair dye, gaudy clothing, and jet fuel took most of it.

1992 - Apr 29, 1992 - When the LA riots broke out in response to the verdict of the Rodney King trial, members of the white-supremacist group Aryan Nations thought it was the final apocalyptic race war they had been waiting for. (20/20, NBC, Dec 12, 1999)

1992 - Sep 28, 1992 - Christian author Dorothy A. Miller in her book, "Watch & Be Ready! " predicted the "last trumpet" would sound on Rosh Hashanah, heralding the Second Coming. (McIver #2923)

1992 - "Rockin'" Rollen Stewart, a born-again Christian who made himself famous by holding up "John 3:16" signs at sporting events, thought the Rapture would take place on this day. Stewart went insane, setting off stink bombs in churches and bookstores and writing apocalyptic letters in a mission to make people get right with God. He is now serving a life sentence for kidnapping. (Adams p.18-20)

1992 - Oct 28, 1992 – The Hyoo-Go or Rapture movement was spreading through South Korea like a plague. Lee Jang Rim, leader of the Korean doomsday cult Mission for the Coming Days (also known as the Tami Church), predicted that the Rapture would occur on this date. Lee was convicted of fraud after the prophecy failed. (Thompson p.227-228, McIver #2747)

1993 - David Berg of the Children of God claimed in "The Endtime News!" that the Second Coming would take place in 1993. The Tribulation was to start in 1989. (McIver #2095, Kyle p.145)

1993 - Nov 14, 1993 - This was Judgment Day, according to self-proclaimed messiah Maria Devi Khrystos (A.K.A. Marina Tsvigun), leader of the cult Great White Brotherhood. (Alnor p.93)

1993 - Dec 9, 1993 - The United nations recognized Israel on May 15, 1949. James T. Harmon added 51.57 years to the date and subtracted 7 to arrive at the date of the Rapture, approximately December 9, 1993. He also suggested 1996, 2012 and 2022 as alternative rapture dates. So, we still have a chance at this one. (Oropeza p.89)

1994 - R.M. Riley, in his book "1994: The Year of Destiny," wrote that 1994 would be the year of the Rapture. (McIver #3098)

1994 - Charles Taylor's Rapture prediction number 13. (Abanes p.99) YAWN!

1994 - Om Saleem, an Arab Christian, prophesied that the Rapture would take place in 1994, after this the Antichrist was to reveal himself. (Oropeza p.148)

1994 - Dutch authors Aad Verbeek, Jan Westein and Pier Westein predicted the Second Coming in 1994 in their book, "Time for His Coming." (McIver #3348)

1994 - May 2, 1994 - Neal Chase of the Bahá'ís, "Under the Provisions of the Covenant," predicted that New York would be destroyed by a nuclear bomb on March 23, 1994, and the Battle of Armageddon would take place 40 days later. (Robbins p.79) It looks like everyone in the cult takes turns rolling dice to predict the end of time.

1994 - June 9, 1994 - Pastor John Hinkle claimed that God told him the Apocalypse would take place on this day. In a cataclysmic event, God was supposed to "rip the evil out of this world." When the prophecy failed, he claimed that it's only the beginning and it's taking place invisibly. (Oropeza p.167-168) I love invisible prophecies. I am wearing invisible pants right now.

1994 - Jul 25, 1994 - On July 19, 1993, Sister Marie Gabriel Paprocski announced to the world her prophecy that a comet would hit Jupiter on or before July 25, 1994, causing the "biggest cosmic explosion in the history of mankind" and bringing on the end of the world. Indeed, a comet did hit Jupiter on July 16, 1994. However, it is important to note that her announcement was made nearly two months after astronomer Brian Marsden discovered that Comet Shoemaker-Levy 9 would hit Jupiter. (Skinner p.116, Levy p.207)

1994 - Sep 23, 1994 - Reginald Dunlop claimed this was the last date encoded in the Great Pyramid of Giza, meaning that the world would not last beyond this date. (Oropeza p.128)

1994 - Sep 27, 1994   Harold Camping, head of Oakland's Family Radio and host of the station's Biblical discussion talk show, "Open Forum," predicted the end in his book, "1994?" (Camping p.526-7, p.531) I am assuming the question mark on the title begs an answer. No! No! He gave another prediction of Sep 29, 1994. And another for Oct 2, 1994. No, Harold. No! Sit... stay... (Abanes p.95)

1995 - Armageddon, according to Henry Kresyler, head of the doomsday group "Watchers in the Wilderness." (Shaw p.181)

1995 - Mar 31, 1995 - Harold Camping's doomsday prediction #4. He gave up setting dates afterwards. (Abanes p.95)

1996 - James T. Harmon's Rapture prediction number 2. (Oropeza p.89)

1996 - Nov 1996 - The Second Coming of Christ, as foreseen in doomsday author Salty Dok's book "Blessed Hope, 1996." (Oropeza p.48) Why is the blessed hope the destruction or escape from the world and seldom relates to our contribution to it?

1996 - Dec 13, 1996 - David Koresh predicted his own resurrection, according to the surviving Branch Davidian cult members. Koresh was a no-show. (Jordan p.113)

1996 - Dec 17, 1996- Psychic Sheldan Nidle predicted that the world would end on this date, with the arrival of millions of space ships. (Abanes p.341) According to Nidle's website, "Sheldan Nidle was born in New York City on Nov. 11, 1946, and grew up in Buffalo, New York. His first extraterrestrial and UFO experiences began shortly after his birth and were highlighted all through his childhood by various modes of contact phenomena, as well as accompanying manifestations - light-form communications, extraterrestrial visitations, and teaching/learning sessions on board spacecraft. During most of his life, he has enjoyed ongoing telepathic communications and direct 'core knowledge' inserts (etheric and physical implants). Sheldan has visually observed and physically experienced spacecraft throughout the years."

1997 - Mary Stewart Relfe claiming that God communicated with her in her dreams. She predicted the Second Coming in 1997, right after the battle of Armageddon. She continued, "America will burn" and be totally destroyed in 1993 or 1994. (Kyle p.120, Oropeza p.104)

1997 - Mar 23, 1997 - Richard Michael Schiller predicted that an asteroid trailing behind Comet Hale-Bopp would bring destruction to the Earth on this date. As the date drew near he claimed the world would be destroyed 9 months later when the Earth supposedly would pass through the comet's tail.

1997 - Mar 26, 1997 - The infamous Heaven's Gate suicides occurred between March 24 and March 26, during a window of time predicted, a UFO trailing behind Comet Hale-Bopp would pick up their souls. Similarity between their prophecy and Schiller's one above are striking. The rumor of something following the comet started when amateur astronomer Chuck Shramek mistook a star for what he thought was a "Saturn-like object" following the comet. (Alnor p.13, 38)

1997 - Oct 1997 - The Rapture, according to Brother Kenneth Hagin.

1997 - Oct 23, 1997 - 6000th anniversary of Creation according to the calculations of 17th Century Irish Archbishop James Ussher. This date was a popular candidate for the end of the world. (Gould p.98)

1997 - Nov 27, 1997 - According to the Sacerdotal Knights of National Security, "A space alien captured at a UFO landing site in eastern Missouri cracked under interrogation by the CIA and admitted that an extraterrestrial army will attack Earth on November 27 with the express purpose of stripping our planet of every natural resource they can find a use for -- and making slaves of every man, woman and child in the world!" (Source: Ontario Consultants on Religious Tolerance)

1998 – According to Larry Wilson of "Wake Up America Seminars," the Second Coming would be around 1998. The Tribulation was supposed to start in 1994 or 1995, and during this period an asteroid was to hit the Earth. (Robbins p.220)

1998 - Centro, a religious cult in the Philippines, predicted that the end of the world would come in 1998. (Source: Ontario Consultants on Religious Tolerance)

1998 - The year of the Rapture, claimed Donald B. Orsden in his book, "The Holy Bible - The Final Testament": What is the Significance of 666?. "Take your super computers, you scientists, and feed the number 666 into them. The output will be the proof God gives that 1998 is the year Jesus will take the faithful with him...." (McIver #2986) During a period from 1999 and 2008 I worked as a system analyst on one of the fastest supercomputers in the U.S. The project was named, "Hypersonic Missile Technology." Out of the dozen or so rocket scientists there, none had the slightest idea of what he could possibly mean.

1998 - Henry R. Hall, author and nut case, predicts that the world will end in 1998 because, among other reasons, 666 + 666 + 666 = 1998. (McIver #2488)

1998 - Jan 8, 1998 – Thirty-one members of a splinter group of the Solar Temple cult headed by German psychologist Heide Fittkau-Garthe were convinced that the world would end at 8:00 pm on this day, but that the cult members' bodies would be picked up by a space ship. They were arrested by police on the Island of Tenerife, in the Canary Islands. The cultists were planning a mass suicide. (Hanna p.226 and FACTNet)

1998 - Mar 8, 1998 - All religions have their doomsday cults. One such cult is from Karnataka in southern India. They claimed that much of the world would be destroyed by earthquakes on this day, and the Indian subcontinent would break off and sink into the ocean. After the destruction, Lord Vishnu would appear on Earth. The leaders of the cult claimed that El Nino and the chaotic weather that accompanied it was a sign of the coming destruction.

1998 - Mar 31, 1998 - Hon-Ming Chen, leader of the Taiwanese cult God's Salvation Church, or Chen Tao - "The True Way" - claimed that God would come to Earth in a flying saucer at 10:00 am on this date. Moreover, God would have the same physical appearance as Chen himself. On March 25, God was to appear on Channel 18 on every TV set in the US. Chen chose to base his cult in Garland, Texas, because he thought it sounded like "God's Land." (Shermer p.204, McIver #2199)

1998 - May 31, 1998 - Author Marilyn J. Agee used convoluted Biblical calculations to predict the date of two separate Raptures. In her book "The End of the Age," she boldly proclaimed, "I expect Rapture I on Pentecost [May 31] in 1998 and Rapture II on the Feast of Trumpets [September 13] in 2007." (Agee)
When this failed she moved the date to Jun 7, 1998, then to Jun 14, 1998, then to Jun 21, 1998, and again on Sep 20, 1998, and May 22, 1999, and May 30, 1999, and June 20, 1999, and June 10, 2000, and Aug. 20, 2000 and May 28, 2001, and Nov 3, 2001, and Dec 19, 2001, and Jul 19, 2002, and Sep 13, 2007 (Oropeza p.89)

1998 - The Rapture, as per Tom Stewart's book 1998: Year of the Apocalypse. (McIver #3226)

1998 - Jun 6, 1998 - Eli Eshoh uses some numerical slight of hand to show that the Rapture was to take place in 1998. When nothing happened he claimed that it did indeed occur, but the number raptured was small enough not to be noticed. So... Eli was left behind?

1998 - Jul 5, 1998 - The Church of the SubGenius called themselves the only "One True Faith", (Don't they all?) designated this day X-Day. They expected the Xists from Planet X would arrive in flying saucers and destroy humanity on this day. Only ordained clergy who have paid their dues to the Church would be "ruptured" to safety! When that didn't come to pass, XX-Day was proclaimed to be July 5, 1999 and was declared the true end of the world. I can't wait until XXX-Day to see if they show up naked.

1998 - Sep 30, 1998 - Using Edgar Cayce's prophecies, Kirk Nelson predicted the return of Jesus on this date in his book "The Second Coming 1998."

1998 - Oct 10, 1998 - Monte Kim Miller, leader of the Denver charismatic cult "Concerned Christians", was convinced that the Apocalypse would occur on this date, with Denver the first city to be destroyed. The cult members mysteriously disappeared afterwards; but later resurfaced in Israel, where they were deported on suspicion of planning a terrorist attack at the end of 1999. Miller had also claimed he will die in the streets of Jerusalem in December 1999, to be resurrected three days later. (Sources: Watchman Fellowship, Ontario Consultants on Religious Tolerance)

1999 - Nov 1998 - The Second Coming and the beginning of the Tribulation, according to Ron Reese. He wrote that he had "overwhelming evidence" that this was true. (McIver #3081) He never showed anyone the evidence.

1999 - End of the world according to some Seventh Day Adventist literature. (Skinner p.105, Mann p.xiii) These mainline religions attempt to hide their mistakes from their followers. Most of their prophecies are never discussed with their believers.

1999 - End of the world according to the Jehovah's Witnesses. (Skinner p.102, Mann p.xiii) Speaking of hiding huge errors, the J.W.'s neglect to tell their followers that the church fathers were apocalyptic idiots.

1999 – It is astrologer Jeanne Dixon again. She claimed the height of the Antichrist's power would be in 1999 when a terrible holocaust will occur, according to her book, "The Call to Glory." Dixon also claimed the Antichrist was born on Feb. 5, 1962. (Kyle p.153, Dixon p.168)

1999 - Edgar Cayce, The Sleeping Prophet, claimed a pole shift would cause natural disasters and World War III would begin. (Skinner p.127)

1999 - Linguist Charles Berlitz predicted the end of the world in his book, "Doomsday: 1999 A.D." (Kyle p.194)

1999 - Mar 25, 1999 - On September 25, 1997, Hal Lindsey predicted on his TV show, "International Intelligence Briefing," that Russia would invade Israel within 18 months. (Abanes p.286)

1999 - Apr 3, 1999 - The Rapture, according to H.J. Hoekstra. He believed we live on the inside of a hollow Earth. He used numerology to calculate the date of the Rapture.

1999 - May 8, 1999 - According to an astrological pamphlet circulating in India, the world was to meet its doom by a series of severe natural disasters on this date. This prediction caused many Indians to panic. (Source: BBC News)

1999 - Jun 30, 1999 - "Father" Charles L. Moore appeared on the Art Bell show November 26-27, 1998, claiming he knew the Third Secret of Fatima. According to Moore, the prophecy said that an asteroid would strike the Earth on June 30, bringing the End.

1999 - July 1999 - The month made famous by 16th century soothsayer Nostradamus, the month that people have wondered about for over four centuries, is now at long last a part of history. (Source: The Mask of Nostradamus by James Randi): The Quatrain reads,
"L'an mil neuf cens nonante neuf sept mois

Du ciel viendra un grand Roy deffraieur
Resusciter le grand Roy d'Angolmois
Avant apres Mars regner par bon heur."

The year 1999, seven months,
From the sky will come a great King of Terror:
To bring back to life the great King of the Mongols,
Before and after Mars to reign by good luck. (Quatrain X.72)

Between the time of Nostradamus and now the calendar
changed. His seventh month, 13th day equates to August 13 of
1999. Both dates yielded nothing. According to Escape666.com,
Nostradamus' King of Terror was to descend on Earth in
September, heralding the beginning of the Tribulation and the
Rapture. Escape666 said, regarding Nostradamus' infamous
quatrain X.72: "now we know EXACTLY when he meant:
SEPTEMBER 1999." However, as the end of September
approached, they changed their date to October 12. They were
embarrassed to try again.

1999 - Members of the Stella Maris Gnostic Church, a
Colombian doomsday cult, went into Colombia's Sierra
Nevada mountains over the weekend of July 3-4, 1999,
weekend to be picked up by a UFO that would save them from
the end of the world, which is to take place at the turn of the
millennium. The cult members have disappeared. (Source: BBC
News.)

1999 - Jul 5, 1999 – Remember X-day? Well, this is XX-day,
according to the Church of the SubGenius. The Xists from
Planet X and their saucers never came. Now all eyes are on
XXX-day: July 5, 2000. Since it is XXX-day we assumed they
will show up naked and have orgies.

1999 - Jul 7, 1999 - The Earth's axis was to shift a full 90 degrees
at 7:00am GMT, resulting in a "water baptism" of the world,

according to Eileen Lakes. (Get it? Baptism predicted by Lakes?) The site read,"

7:00 a.m., on Wednesday, July 7, 1999

at the World Greenwich Mean Time

The earth will turn right by 90 degrees very instantly." Very instantly seems a little redundant, so we reported her writing to the Department of Redundancy Department.

1999 - Jul 28, 1999 - A lunar eclipse would signify the end of the Church Age and the beginning of the Tribulation, according to Gerald Vano. (Source: The Doomsday List.)

1999 - Aug 1999 - A cult calling itself Universal and Human Energy, also known as SHY (Spirituality, Humanity, Yoga), predicted the end of the world in August. (Source: FACTNet)

1999 - Aug 6, 1999 - The Branch Davidians believed that David Koresh would return to Earth on this day, 2300 days (Daniel 8:14) after his death. (Source: Ontario Consultants on Religious Tolerance)

1999 - Aug 11, 1999 - During the week between August 11 and August 18 a series of astronomical events took place: the last total solar eclipse of the millennium (Aug 11), the Grand Cross planetary formation (Aug 18), the Perseid meteor shower (Aug 12), the returning path of NASA's plutonium-bearing Cassini space probe's orbit (Aug 17-18), and Comet Lee's visit to the inner solar system. Add to this the fact that some of these events are taking place before the end of July according to the Julian calendar (See Nostradamus' prediction), and you have a recipe for rampant apocalyptic paranoia. Many alarmists were convinced that the Cassini space probe would crash into the Earth on August 18. The nuclear fuel it carried would poison a third of the world's population with its plutonium, fulfilling the prophecy of Revelation 8:11 concerning a star named Wormwood -- supposedly a metaphor for radiation poisoning

("Chernobylnik" is the Ukrainian word for a purple-stemmed subspecies of the wormwood plant). But as expected, Cassini passed by the Earth without a hitch.

1999 - Aug 14, 1999 - Escape666.com originally proclaimed on their website that a doomsday comet would hit Earth between August 11-14. (McIver #3362).

1999 - Aug 18, 1999 - The end of the world, as foreseen by Charles Criswell King, also known as "The Amazing Criswell." In his 1968 bestseller "Criswell Predicts:" "The world as we know it will cease to exist...on August 18, 1999.... And if you and I meet each other on the street that fateful day...and we chat about what we will do on the morrow, we will open our mouths to speak and no words will come out, for we have no future." August 18 happens to be Criswell's birthday. (Abanes p.43)

1999 - Aug 24, 1999 - In 1996, Valerie James wrote in The European Magazine, "The configuration of planets which predicted the coming of Christ will once again appear on Aug 24, 1999." (Ontario Consultants on Religious Tolerance)

1999 - Sep 1999 - The End, according to televangelist Jack Van Impe. (Shaw p.131)

1999 - Sep 3, 1999 - Judgment Day was to be on September 2 or 3, according to the notorious Japanese doomsday cult Aum Shinrikyo. Only members of Aum were to survive. These were the same people who gassed public transportation with sarin gas.

1999 - Sep 9, 1999 - 9/9/99 was to be the date when all older computers were to reset or crash due to their clocks running out of bits. Y2K would bring modern civilization to its knees. (Source: SF Gate)

1999 - Sep 11, 1999 - Bonnie Gaunt used the Bible Codes to prove that Rosh Hashanah 5760 (September 11, 1999) is the date of the Rapture.

1999 - Michael Rood also jumped on the Rosh Hashanah bandwagon. He claimed that this day is the first day of the Hebrew calendar year 6001, and after it failed, he changed the date to April 5, 2000. In reality, this day was the first day of 5760, but Michael claimed that there was a mistake in the calendar.

1999 - Sep 23, 1999 - Author Stefan Paulus combines Nostradamus, the Bible and astrology to arrive at September 23 as the date that a doomsday comet will impact the Earth. (Paulus p.57)

1999 - The Korean "Hyoo-go" movement spawned the Tami Sect. Proponents predict the demise of this earth in October 1999. (Source: Korea Times)

1999 - Jack Van Impe, your typical televangelist, having missed his last prediction just one month ago, predicted the Rapture and the Second Coming for October 1999. (Wojcik p.212)

1999 - Nov 7, 1999 - Internet doomsday prophet, Richard Hoagland, claimed that an "inside source" called him anonymously and warned of three objects that will strike the earth on this day. The objects were supposedly seen during the August 11 eclipse.

1999 - Nov 29, 1999 - According to a vision he received in 1996, Dumitru Duduman claims that the destruction of America (i.e. Babylon) will occur around November 29, 1999.

1999 - Dec 21, 1999 - Sometime between November 23 and December 21, 1999, the War of Wars was to begin, claimed

Joseph Lumpkin

Nostradamus buff Henry C. Roberts. (Skeptical Inquirer, May/June 2000, p.6)

1999 - Dec 25, 1999 - The Second Coming of Christ, according to doomsday prophet Martin Hunter. (Oropeza p.57)

1999 - Dec 31, 1999 - Hon-Ming Chen's cult God's Salvation Church, now relocated to upstate New York, preached that a nuclear holocaust would destroy Europe and Asia sometime between October 1 and December 31, 1999. (Source: the Religious Movements Page)

2000 – It is true that each time the century mark rolls around people get edgy and make a lot of predictions. When it comes to those millennium markers people go a little crazy. The years 1000 and 2000 were favorites among prophets. Here as just a few of those predictions.

2000 - When his 1988 prediction failed, Hal Lindsey suggested the end might be in 2000, according to his recently published book, entitled "Planet Earth - 2000 A.D." (Lindsey p.306)

2000 - This is "The beginning of Christ's Millennium" according to some Mormon literature, such as the publication, "Watch and Be Ready: Preparing for the Second Coming of the Lord." The New Jerusalem will descend from the heavens in 2000, landing in Independence, Missouri. (McIver #3377, Skinner p.100) Like I said, the deed is always done where the prophet resides, because it is all about them.

2000 - 19th century mystic Madame Helena Petrova Blavatsky, the founder of Theosophy, foresaw the end of the world in 2000. (Shaw p.83)

2000 - In his book, "Observations upon the Prophecies of Daniel, and the Apocalypse of St. John", Sir Isaac Newton predicted that Christ's Millennium would begin in the year 2000 (Schwartz p.96)

2000 – Pop psychic, Ruth Montgomery predicted Earth's axis will shift and the Antichrist will reveal himself in 2000. (Kyle p.156, 195)

2000 - The establishment of the Kingdom of Heaven, according to Rev. Sun Myung Moon. (Kyle p.148)

2000 - The Second Coming, followed by a New Age, according to Edgar Cayce. (Hanna p.219)

2000 - The Second Coming, was forecasted in Ed Dobson's book, " The End: Why Jesus Could Return by A.D. 2000."

2000 - The end of the world according to Lester Sumrall in his book, "I Predict 2000." (Abanes p.99, 341)

2000 - The tribulation is to occur before the year 2000, said Gordon Lindsay, founder of the Christ for the Nations Ministry. (Abanes p.280)

2000 - According to a series of lectures given by Shoko Asahara, founder of Aum Shinrikyo (the group that set off poison gas in a subway), in 1992, 90% of the world's population would be annihilated by nuclear, biological and chemical weapons by the year 2000. (Thompson p.262)

2000 - One of the earliest predictions for the year 2000 was made by Petrus Olivi in 1297. He wrote that the Antichrist would come to power between 1300 and 1340, and the Last Judgment would take place around 2000. (Weber p.54)

2000 - According to American Indian spiritual leader Sun Bear, the end of the world would come in the year 2000 if the human race didn't shape up. (Abanes p.307)

2000 - 18th century fire-and-brimstone preacher Jonathan Edwards concluded that Christ's thousand-year reign would begin in 2000. (Weber p.171)

2000 - The world will be devastated by AIDS in the year 2000, according to Indian guru Bhagwan Shree Rajneesh. Afterwards, the world will be rebuilt by a peaceful matriarchal society. (Robbins p.164)

2000 - Religious fundamentalist and conspiracy theorist, Texe Marrs, stated that the last days could "wrap up by the year 2000." (Abanes p.311)

2000 – The Convulsionaries was one of the radical apocalyptic sects that emerged in early 18th century France. One of the members, Jacques-Joseph Duguet, anticipated the Parousia in 2000. (Kyle p.192)

2000 - Timothy Dwight (1752-1817), President of Yale University, foresaw the Millennium starting by 2000. (Kyle p.81)

2000 - Martin Luther looked at 2000 as a possible end-time date, before finally settling on 1600. (Kyle p.192) Both were one of those "zero years."

2000 - Sukyo Mahikari, a Japanese cult, preaches that the world might be destroyed in a "baptism of fire" by 2000. (Source: ABC News)

2000 - A Vietnamese cult headed by Ca Van Lieng predicted an apocalyptic flood for 2000. But doomsday came much earlier for the cult members: he and his followers committed mass suicide in October 1993. (Source: Cult Observer archives)

2000 - End of Days will take place, say members of a Mormon-based cult near the Utah-Arizona border. Hundreds of members of the Fundamentalist Church of Jesus Christ of Latter-day Saints pulled their kids out of school in preparation for the Big Day. (Sep. 12, 2000 CNN article)

2000 - The Christian apocalyptic cult House of Prayer, headed by Brother David, expected Christ to descend onto the Mount of Olives in Jerusalem on this day. The Israeli government recently kicked them out of the country in a preemptive strike against their potential attempt to bring about the Apocalypse through terrorist acts such as blowing up the Dome of the Rock.

2000 - Bobby Bible, a 60-year-old fundamentalist, believed that Jesus would descend from Heaven at the stroke of midnight in Jerusalem and rapture his church.

2000 - A Philippine cult called Tunnels of Salvation taught that the world would end on January 1. The cult's guru, Cerferino Quinte, claimed that the world would be destroyed in an "all consuming rain of fire" on January 1. In order to survive the world's destruction, the cult members built an elaborate series of tunnels where he had stockpiled a year's worth of supplies for 700 people. (CESNUR)

2000 - UK native Ann Willem spent the New Year in Israel, expecting to be raptured by Jesus on New Year's Day. "It didn't happen the way it was supposed to," she said of the failure of the Rapture to take place. (USA Today p.5A, 1/3/00)

2000 - Jerry Falwell, a televangelist that some might mistake for a stand up comic is always a ray of sunshine and hope, which reminds me of Eeyore, foresaw God pouring out his judgment on the world on New Year's Day. According to Falwell, God "may be preparing to confound our language, to jam our communications, scatter our efforts, and judge us for our sin and rebellion against his lordship. We are hearing from many sources that January 1, 2000, will be a fateful day in the history of the world." (Christianity Today, Jan. 11, 1999)

2000 - Timothy LaHaye and Jerry Jenkins, authors of the bestselling Left Behind series of apocalyptic fiction, expected the Y2K bug to trigger global economic chaos, which the Antichrist would use to rise to power. (Source: Washington Post)

2000 - Jan 16, 2000 - Religious scholar Dr. Marion Derlette claimed the world is to end on January 16, according to an article in Weekly World News. This event is to occur after a series of natural and man made catastrophes starting in 1997, and will be followed by an era of paradise on Earth. (This date is shown as January 6, 2000 in Richard Abanes' book "End-Time Visions." (Abanes p.43)

2000 - Feb 11, 2000 - On his broadcast on the morning of Feburary 7, 2000, televangelist Kenneth Copeland claimed that a group of scientists and scholars (he gave no specifics) studied the Bible in great detail and determined that Feb 11 would be the last day of the 6000th year since Creation, a date when the Apocalypse would presumably happen. Copeland did not imply he believed this to be accurate, though, but he went on to say that the Rapture will come soon. (Has anyone ever seen Copeland smile? So much for the joy of the Lord being our strength.)

2000 - Mar 2000 - The Rapture is to take place in March 2000, 3 1/2 years after Christ's Second Coming, according to Marvin Byers. (Oropeza p.29)

2000 - Apr 6, 2000 - The Second Coming of Christ according to James Harmston of the Mormon sect, "True and Living Church of Jesus Christ of Saints of The Last Days." (As opposed to the false death church?) (McIver #2496)

2000 - Apr 2000 - The Whites, a family of ascetic doomsday cultists living near Jerusalem, expected the End to take place in March or April after the Ark of the Covenant was to reappear in a cave in the Old City in Jerusalem. They claimed that there was a mistake in the chronology of the Hebrew calendar and that the year 6001 will begin this Spring. In reality, Sep. 11, 1999 to Sep. 30, 2000 is the Hebrew year 5760. This means that the Hebrew year 6000 is 2240 A.D.

2000 - May 5, 2000 - According to archaeologist Richard W. Noone in his book, "5/5/2000 Ice: The Ultimate Disaster", a buildup of excess ice in Antarctica is causing the earth to become precariously unbalanced. All that's needed to upset this supposed imbalance and cause the pole shift, which would cause billions of tons of ice to go cascading across the continents. Where did this fool get his degree.

2000 - The Nuwaubians, also known as the Holy Tabernacle Ministries or Ancient Mystical Order of Melchizedek, claimed that the planetary lineup would cause a "star holocaust," pulling the planets toward the sun. (Alnor p.121)

2000 - May 9, 2000 - Toshio Hiji, having analyzed the quatrains of Nostradamus, announced that the Giant Deluge of Noah would inundate the Earth on May 9, 2000, and "all humans will be perished." (OK, that was a quote and his English stank.) Prior to this, a third of the world's population was to be destroyed during an alien attack on October 3, 1999. But, what happens if the 1999 thing doesn't occur.

2000 - May 17, 2000 - "Dr." Rebecca S. Harrison claimed that Jesus would reappear on "EArth" (her capitalization) on May 17, to be followed by "A Mighty Battle" in June 2003.

2000 - Lakhota prophetess White Buffalo Calf Woman predicted that Jesus would return in a UFO this year.

2000 - Jun 2000 - A Ugandan cult calling itself the World Message Last Warning Church claims the End will come in June. Previously they had claimed the world would end in 1999. (Source: ABC News)

2000 - Jul 5, 2000 - XXX-day, according to the Church of the SubGenius. "THIS time the saucers will be XXX naked"!

2000 - Aug 20, 2000 - A man claiming the title of prophet and calling himself Ephraim claimed the 7-month Battle of Armageddon would begin on this day and the Rapture should have been March 20-22, 2000.

2000 - Sep 2000 - Jerry Grenough foresaw the end of the present age, and perhaps the Rapture, in September of 2000, using various passages from the Bible to divine this date. His prediction, of course, has been removed from his website, but it remains listed at the Doomsday List

2000 - Sep 17, 2000 - According to the measurements within the Great Pyramid of Giza, the Second Coming will occur on this date. (Abanes p.71)

2000 - Sep 19, 2000 - Somewhere between September 16 and 19, Phil Stone expects something he had dubbed the "Coastlands Disaster" to occur. He has derived his chronology from the Bible.

2000 - Sep 29, 2000 - According to the Jewish-based cult, "Love the Jew", whose website has disappeared without a trace, claimed the world would end on Rosh Hashanah, 2000. According to the cult, "America will be destroyed in one hour after the Rapture by an all out nuclear attack by Russia. Russia may also decide to destroy other countries as well at this time, such as South America, Mexico, Canada; notably the entire

Western hemisphere will be a wasteland." A reference to the cult is available at The Doomsday List.

2000 - Oct 2000 - Elizabeth Joyce predicted nuclear war in October 2000 as a result of conflict in the Middle East. Her other failed prophecies, included one of the sun splitting in two. (Source: Doomsday has been canceled!)

2000 - Oct 9, 2000 - Christian prophet Grant R. Jeffrey suggested this date as the "probable termination point for the last days. (Abanes p.341, McIver #2608)

2000 - Oct 14, 2000 - According to the House of Yahweh, the seven-year Tribulation began on September 13, 1993, when Yitzhak Rabin shook hands with Yasser Arafat at the White House. This means the end of the world is due on October 14, 2000. (Source: religioustolerance.org)

2000 - Nov 17, 2000 - The famous handshake between Arafat and Rabin on Sep 13, 1993 started the seven-year peace process, claims David Zavitz, and Armageddon will take place seven years later. David shows on this page why he thinks the Last Day will be on November 17, 2000.

2000 - Dec 31, 2000 - Joseph Kibweteere's doomsday prediction number two. On March 17, 2000, over 600 members of a Ugandan cult calling itself the "Movement for the Restoration of the Ten Commandments of God" sealed themselves into a church and were burned to death. It remains to be seen if it was a mass suicide, or a murder by their leader. Cult leader Joseph Kibweteere, who had previously claimed that the world would end on December 31, 1999, re-set his doomsday prediction to December 31, 2000 when his first prediction failed. (Source: CESNUR) I am convinced that the longer the name of the church or sect, the more insane the leader.

2001 - Mar 2001 - Dale Sumberèru claimed in his book "The Greatest Deception: An Impending Alien Invasion," claimed that March 22, 1997 was the beginning of the Tribulation, and the Second Coming will take place between July 2000 and March 2001. It seemed his book, "The Greatest Deception," was correctly named. (McIver #3239)

2001 - May 5, 2001 - Gabriel of Sedona, leader of the New Age doomsday cult "Aquarian Concepts Community", located in Sedona, Arizona, predicted the destruction of humanity between May 5, 2000 and May 5, 2001. Only people faithful to the cult will be saved from this destruction by UFOs. Beware of those UFO types.

2001 - Jul 2001 - Jamaican cult leader Brother Solomon and his Seventh-Day Adventist followers had staked out some space on the Mount of Olives in anticipation of witnessing the Second Coming, which he was convinced would occur sometime between mid-April 2000 and July 2001. Ganja will rot your brain.

2001 -Sep 11, 2001 - Not a single prophet, soothsayer, or fortuneteller saw what was coming. The World Trade Center was destroyed and the Pentagon attacked by madmen, causing thousands of deaths. This should prove beyond a doubt that the future is God's alone.

2001 - Sep 18, 2001   Charles Taylor, the daddy of all false doomsday prophets, takes another swipe at it. The rapture will be on Rosh Hashanah. (Oropeza p.57)

2001 - Dec 8, 2001 - The author of "The Ninth Wave" web site was convinced that the Church would be raptured on this date, and people will explain the disappearance as alien abductions.

2001 - Pyramidologist Georges Barbarin, subscribing to the concept of the Great Week, predicted that Christ's Millennium would begin in 2001. (Mann p.118)

2001 - According to the Unarius Academy of Science, aliens they called "space brothers" were to land near El Cajon, California, ushering in a new age. When it did not occur their explanation was, "The Space Brothers have not landed because we, the people of Earth, are not ready to accept advanced peoples from another planet." (Heard p.26-27) Well duh! Some people can't even deal with advanced people in their own neighborhood.

2001 - Gordon-Michael Scallion predicted major earth changes taking place between 1998 and 2001, culminating in a pole shift. (Heard p.26-27)

2001 - Nation of Islam numerologist Tynetta Muhammad figured that 2001 would be the year of the End. (Weber p.213) Every religion has its fools.

2002 - The end of the world, according to Church Universal and Triumphant leader Elizabeth Clare Prophet, following a 12-year period of devastation and nuclear war. (Kyle p.156) Clare never missed a beat. People are still buying her books and listening to her dribble.

2002 – According to the doomsday list, "Charles R. Weagle's now-defunct website, warning2002ad.com predicted a "nuclear judgment" on the world's industrialized nations in 2002.

2003 - May 5, 2003 - A UFO will pick up true believers on this date, according to the Nuwaubians, a Georgia cult headed by Dr. Malachi Z. York, who claims to be the incarnation of God and a native of the planet Rizq. (Like in, "believing this guy is taking a risk.) (Time Magazine, July 12, 1999)

2003 - May 13, 2003 - Nancy Lieder of ZetaTalk believes that the "end time" will take place on this day with the approach of a giant planet known as the "12th Planet." This planet supposedly orbits the sun once every 3600 years. The planet will cause...you guessed it! A pole shift!! Ms. Lieder gives some information about this on her Troubled Times site.

2003 - May 15, 2003 - A Japanese cult called Pana Wave, whose members dress in white, claimed that a mysterious 10th Planet would pass by Earth, causing its axis to tip. (Source: WWRN)

2003 - Nov 29, 2003 - The human race would all but wiped out by nuclear war between Oct 30 and Nov 29, 2003, according to Aum Shinrikyo. (Alnor p.98) These guys are like the crabby uncle you never liked, who always talked about killing people in the war. (Call a friend to see if they were right.)

2004   Major world events beginning in August 1999 will lead to full-scale war in the year 2000, followed by a rebirth from the ashes in 2004, according to Taoist prophet Ping Wu.

2005 - Oct 4, 2005 - The end of the world, according to John Zachary in his 1994 book "Mysterious Numbers of the Sealed Revelation." The Tribulation was to begin on August 28, 1998. I'm sorry. You got the wrong number. (McIver #3477)

2004 - Oct 17, 2004   Clay Cantrell took the dimensions of Noah's Ark and through some of his own unique mathematics arrived at this day as the date of the Rapture.

2005 – This actually marks the beginning of the end, since we are now waiting for the death of Pope Benedict for the prophecy to take place. In 1143, St. Malachy prophesied that there would only be 112 more popes left before the end of the world. Pope Benedict is the 111th, which means that the antichrist will be here in the early 21st century. According to

Malachy, the last pope will be named Peter of Rome. (Skinner p.74-75)

2005 - Oct 18, 2005 - The beginning of Christ's Millennium, according to Tom Stewart in his book 1998: "Year of the Apocalypse." The Rapture was to take place on May 31, 1998, and the return of Jesus on October 13, 2005. (McIver #3226)

2006 - An atomic holocaust started by Syria was to take place between the years 2000 and 2006, according to Michael Drosnin's book, " The Bible Codes" (O'Shea p.178). Here's an excerpt from Drosnin's discredited book: "I checked 'World War' and 'atomic holocaust' against all three ways to write each Hebrew year for the next 120 years. Out of 360 possible matches for each of the two expressions, only two years matched both - 5760 and 5766, in the modern calendar the years 2000 and 2006. Rips, a supposed expert on Bible Code, later checked the statistics for the matches of 'World War' and 'atomic holocaust' with those two years and agreed that the results were 'exceptional.'"

2006 - The British cult, The Family, believed the end will come in 2006.

2007 - Apr 29, 2007 - In his 1990 book, "The New Millennium", Pat Robertson suggests this date as the day of Earth's destruction. (Abanes p.138)

2007 - Aug 2007 - Thomas Chase uses an incredible mishmash of Bible prophecy, numerology, Y2K, Bible codes, astrology, Cassini paranoia, Antichrist speculation, news events, New Age mysticism, the shapes of countries, Hale-Bopp comet timing, and more to show that Armageddon will happen around the year 2007, perhaps in August of that year.

2008 - Apr 6, 2008 - The beginning of Christ's millennial reign, according to Philip B. Brown.

2009 - According prophetess Lori Adaile Toye of the "I AM America Foundation," a series of Earth changes beginning in 1992 and ending in 2009 will cause much of the world to be submerged, and only 1/3 of America's population will survive. You can even order a map of the flooded USA from her website!

2010 - The final year according to the Hermetic Order of the Golden Dawn. (Shaw p.223)

2011 - Another possible date for Earth's entry into the Photon Belt. (See the May 5, 1997 entry)

2011 - Dec 31, 2011 - In an interesting parallel to the Harmonic Convergence concept, Solara Antara Amaa-ra, leader of the "11:11 Doorway" movement, claims that there's a "doorway of opportunity" lasting from January 11, 1992 to December 31, 2011 in which humanity is given the final chance to rid itself of evil and attain a higher level of consciousness, or doom will strike. (Wojcik p.206)

2012   James T. Harmon's Rapture prediction #3. (Oropeza p.89)

2012- Dec 21, 2012 - Terence McKenna combines Mayan chronology with a New Age pseudoscience called "Novelty Theory" to conclude that the collision of an asteroid or some "trans-dimensional object" with the Earth, or alien contact, or a solar explosion, or the transformation of the Milky Way into a quasar, or some other "ultra novel" event will occur on this day.

Dec 23, 2012 The world to end, according to the ancient Mayan calendar. (Abanes p.342)

2012 - NASA recently published a report detailing new magnetism on the Sun that will probably result in Major Solar

Changes and destruction of satellite communications, GPS, Air Traffic, and Power Grids.

The report clearly states that a new Solar Cycle is possible resulting from a knot of magnetism that popped over the sun's eastern limb on Dec. 11th. 2007.

The report goes on to mention specific years which major Earthly impact will be seen. The exact quote which mentions these years states;

"Many forecasters believe Solar Cycle 24 will be big and intense. Peaking in 2011 or 2012, the cycle to come could have significant impacts on telecommunications, air traffic, power grids and GPS systems. (And don't forget the Northern Lights!) In this age of satellites and cell phones, the next solar cycle could make itself felt as never before."

Appendix "B"

Information on the Ending of the Book of Mark

Mark 16:9-20 has been called a later addition to the Gospel of Mark by most New Testament scholars in the past century. The main reason for doubting the authenticity of the ending is that it does not appear in some of the oldest existing witnesses. The writing styles suggest that it came from another hand. The Gospel is obviously incomplete without these verses, and so most scholars believe that the final leaf of the original manuscript was lost, and that the ending, which appears in English versions today (verses 9-20) was supplied during the second century. More than one scribe saw the book as incomplete and so supplied their versions of the ending.

Scholars have pointed out that the witnesses which bring the verses into question are few, and that the verses are quoted by church Fathers very early, even in the second century. To represent this point of view we give below a long excerpt from F.H.A. Scrivener, together with its footnotes.

Scrivener was the undisputed expert in the 19th century of the existing Greek New Testament manuscripts, and on the KJV in its various editions. He did a thorough study of these ancient texts and published many of his findings. For example it was his opinion that some parts of the KJV follow only loosely the Greek text but very closely the Latin Vulgate. "In some places the Authorised Version corresponds but loosely with any form of the Greek original, while it exactly follows the Latin Vulgate,"The Westminster Study Edition of the Holy Bible (Philadelphia: Westminster Press, 1948). vv. 9-20. This section is a later addition; the original ending of Mark appears to have been lost. The best and oldest manuscripts of Mark end with ch. 16:8. Two endings were added very early. The shorter reads: "But they reported briefly to those with Peter all that had been commanded them. And afterward Jesus himself sent out through them from the East even to the West the sacred and incorruptible message of eternal salvation." The longer addition appears in English Bibles; its origin is uncertain; a medieval source ascribes it to an elder Ariston (Aristion), perhaps the man whom Papias (c. A.D. 135) calls a disciple of the Lord. It is drawn for the most part from Luke, chapter 24, and from John, chapter 20; there is a possibility that verse 15 may come from Matthew 28:18-20. It is believed that the original ending must have contained an account of the risen Christ's meeting with the disciples in Galilee (chs. 14:28; 16:7).

A Commentary on the Holy Bible, edited by J.R. Dummelow (New York: MacMillan, 1927), pages 732-33. 9-20. Conclusion of the Gospel. One uncial manuscript gives a second termination to the Gospel as follows: 'And they reported all the things that had been commanded them briefly (or immediately) to the companions of Peter. And after this Jesus himself also sent forth by them from the East even unto the West the holy and incorruptible preaching of eternal salvation.'

Internal evidence points definitely to the conclusion that the last twelve verses are not by St. Mark. For, (1) the true conclusion certainly contained a Galilean appearance (Mark 16:7, cp. 14:28), and this does not. (2) The style is that of a bare catalogue of facts, and quite unlike St. Mark's usual wealth of graphic detail. (3) The section contains numerous words and expressions never used by St. Mark. (4) Mark 16:9 makes an abrupt fresh start, and is not continuous with the preceding narrative. (5) Mary Magdalene is spoken of (16:9) as if she had not been mentioned before, although she has just been eluded to twice (15:47, 16:1). (6) The section seems to represent a secondary tradition, which is dependent upon the conclusion of St. Matthew, and upon Luke 24:23f.

On the other hand, the section is no casual or unauthorised addition to the Gospel. From the second century onwards, in

411

nearly all manuscripts, versions, and other authorities, it forms an integral part of the Gospel, and it can be shown to have existed, if not in the apostolic, at least in the sub-apostolic age. There is a certain amount of evidence against it (though very little can be shown to be independent of Eusebius the Church historian, 265-340 A.D.), but certainly not enough to justify its rejection, were it not that internal evidence clearly demonstrates that it cannot have proceeded from the hand of St. Mark. Bruce Metzger, A Textual Commentary on the Greek New Testament (Stuttgart, 1971), pages 122-126.16:9-20 The Ending(s) of Mark.

Four endings of the Gospel according to Mark are current in the manuscripts. (1) The last twelve verses of the commonly received text of Mark are absent from the two oldest Greek manuscripts, from the Old Latin codex Bobiensis, the Sinaitic Syriac manuscript, about one hundred Armenian manuscripts, and the two oldest Georgian manuscripts (written A.D. 897 and A.D. 913). Clement of Alexandria and Origen show no knowledge of the existence of these verses; furthermore Eusebius and Jerome attest that the passage was absent from almost all Greek copies of Mark known to them. The original form of the Eusebian sections (drawn up by Ammonius) makes no provision for numbering sections of the text after 16:8. Not a few manuscripts which contain the passage have scribal notes stating that older Greek copies lack it, and in other witnesses the passage is marked with asterisks or obeli, the conventional signs used by copyists to indicate a spurious addition to a document.

Several witnesses, including four uncial Greek manuscripts of the seventh, eighth, and ninth centuries as well as Old Latin, the margin of the Harelean Syriac, several Sahidic and Bohairic manuscripts, and not a few Ethiopic manuscripts, continue after verse 8 as follows (with trifling variations):

"But they reported briefly to Peter and those with him all that they had been told. And after this Jesus himself sent out by means of them, from east to west, the sacred and imperishable proclamation of eternal salvation."

All of these witnesses except this one also continue with verses 9-20.
The traditional ending of Mark, so familiar through the AV and other translations of the Textus Receptus, is present in the vast number of witnesses. The earliest patristic witnesses to part or all of the long ending are Irenaeus and the Diatessaron. It is not certain whether Justin Martyr was acquainted with the passage; in his Apology (i.45) he includes five words that occur, in a different sequence, in ver. 20.

In the fourth century the traditional ending also circulated, according to testimony preserved by Jerome, in an expanded form, preserved today in one Greek manuscript. Codex Washingtonianus includes the following after ver. 14:

"And they excused themselves, saying, 'This age of lawlessness and unbelief is under Satan, who does not allow the truth and power of God to prevail over the unclean things of the spirits [or, does not allow what lies under the unclean spirits to understand the truth and power of God]. Therefore reveal thy righteousness now — thus they spoke to Christ. And Christ replied to them, 'The term of years of Satan's power has been fulfilled, but other terrible things draw near. And for those who have sinned I was delivered over to death, that they may return to the truth and sin no more, in order that they may inherit the spiritual and incorruptible glory of righteousness which is in heaven.' "

How should the evidence of each of these endings be evaluated? It is obvious that the expanded form of the long ending has no claim to be original. Not only is the external evidence extremely limited, but the expansion contains several non-Markan words and as well as several that occur nowhere else in the New Testament. The whole expansion has about it an unmistakable apocryphal flavor. It probably is the work of a second or third century scribe who wished to soften the severe condemnation of the Eleven in 16.14.

The connection between ver. 8 and verses 9-20 is so awkward that it is difficult to believe that the evangelist intended the section to be a continuation of the Gospel. Thus, the subject of verse 8 is the women, whereas Jesus is the presumed subject in verse 9; in verse 9 Mary Magdalene is identified even though she has been mentioned only a few lines before (15.47 and 16.1); the other women of verses 1-8 are now forgotten.

In short, all these features indicate that the section was added by someone who knew a form of Mark that ended abruptly with ver. 8 and who wished to supply a more appropriate conclusion. In view of the inconsistencies between verses 1-8 and 9-20, it is unlikely that the long ending was composed ad hoc to fill up an obvious gap; it is more likely that the section was excerpted from another document, dating perhaps from the first half of the second century.

The internal evidence for the shorter ending is decidedly against its being genuine. Besides containing a high percentage of non-Markan words, its rhetorical tone differs totally from the simple style of Mark's Gospel.

Finally it should be observed that the external evidence for the shorter ending resolves itself into additional testimony supporting the omission of verses 9-20. No one who had available as the conclusion of the Second Gospel the twelve verses 9-20, so rich in interesting material, would have deliberately replaced them with four lines of a colorless and generalized summary. Therefore, the documentary evidence supporting (2) should be added to that supporting. Thus, on the basis of good external evidence and strong internal considerations it appears that the earliest ascertainable form of the Gospel of Mark ended with 16.8. At the same time, however out of deference to the evident antiquity of the longer ending and its importance in the textual tradition of the Gospel, the Committee decided to include verses 9-20 as part of the text, but to enclose them within double square brackets to indicate that they are the work of an author other than the evangelist.

Bruce Metzger, The Canon of the New Testament: its Origin, Development, and Significance (Oxford: Clarendon Press, 1987), pp. 269-270.

Today we know that the last twelve verses of the Gospel according to Mark (xvi. 9-20) are absent from the oldest Greek, Latin, Syriac, Coptic, and Armenian manuscripts, and that in other manuscripts asterisks or obeli mark the verses as doubtful or spurious. Eusebius and Jerome, well aware of such variation in the witnesses, discussed which form of text was to be preferred. It is noteworthy, however, that neither Father suggested that one form was canonical and the other was not. Furthermore, the perception that the canon was basically closed did not lead to a slavish fixing of the text of the canonical books. Thus, the category of 'canonical' appears to have been broad enough to include all variant readings (as well as variant renderings in early versions) that emerged during the course of the transmission of the New Testament documents while apostolic tradition was still a living entity, with an intermingling of written and oral forms of that tradition.

Already in the second century, for example, the so-called long ending of Mark was known to Justin Martyr and to Tatian, who incorporated it into his Diatesseron. There seems to be good reason, therefore, to conclude that, though external and internal evidence is conclusive against the authenticity of the last twelve verses as coming from the same pen as the rest of the Gospel, the passage ought to be accepted as part of the canonical text of Mark."

This ends the quotes from Scrivener.

So, what is being said here? Bluntly stated, there is a mountain of evidence that points to the fact that none of the various endings to Mark is authentic. Yet, there is one ending that seems to have been accepted and that one we should keep, simply because it has been included for so long. I vehemently disagree. No error should be propagated simply because we are accustomed to it.

Let us re-examine the truth at every turn, and conform to the truth instead of twisting the truth around our preconceived ideas. Adding error in scripture to errors in reason only brings us back to where we have been, and where many still are.

CPSIA information can be obtained at www.ICGtesting.com
Printed in the USA
LVOW13s2003110214

373266LV00034B/1802/P